AFRICA'S SILK ROAD

AFRICA'S SILK ROAD

China and India's New Economic Frontier

Harry G. Broadman

with contributions from
Gozde Isik
Sonia Plaza
Xiao Ye
and
Yutaka Yoshino

 THE WORLD BANK

b 2243062
0 1254315
7011017

ISBN-10: 0-8213-6835-4
ISBN-13: 978-0-8213-6835-0
e-ISBN: 0-8213-6836-2
e-ISBN-13: 978-0-8213-6836-7
DOI: 10.1596/978-0-8213-6835-0

Cover credit: Harry G. Broadman

Library of Congress Cataloging-in-Publication Data
Boardman, Harry G.
  Africa's silk road : China and India's new economic frontier / Harry G. Broadman, with contributions from Godze Isik . . . [et al.].
    p. cm.
    ISBN-13: 978-0-8213-6835-0
    ISBN-10: 0-8213-6835-4
    ISBN-10: 0-8213-6836-2 (electronic)
  1. Africa—Commerce—China. 2. China—Commerce—Africa. 3. Africa—Commerce—India. 4. India—Commerce—Africa. 5. Africa—Foreign economic relations—China. 6. China—Foreign economic relations—Africa. 7. Africa—Foreign economic relations—India. 8. India—Foreign economic relations—Africa. I. Broadman, Harry G. II. Title.
HF1611.Z4C62 2006
382.096051—dc22

                                                                        2006029062

Contents

Figures

Tables

Foreword

The dramatic new trend in South-South economic relations is transforming traditional patterns of economic development, and this is nowhere more evident than in African-Asian trade and investment flows. Indeed, while China and India emerge as economic giants in Asia, Africa is coming into its own, finding a vital role in this transformation.

As illustrated in *Africa's Silk Road: China and India's New Economic Frontier*, these new South-South economic relations present real opportunities—as well as challenges—to African countries. They also highlight the need for complementary reforms by China and India to support more vigorous African development.

In analyzing Africa's intensifying relationships with China and India, *Africa's Silk Road* examines the trends to date and considers the implications of these developments for the economic future of the African continent. The diagnosis cautions that the opportunities engendered by China and India's trade and investment with Africa will not necessarily be converted into growth and poverty reduction in the region. A critical finding of the study is that it is not just the quantity of these trade and investment flows that matters—it is also the quality of the overall commercial relationships underlying as well as shaping these flows.

Both African and Asian policy makers need to devise appropriate policy responses to make the quality of these relationships even better. For China and India, the study points to the need for reform of policies that inhibit the potential export of Africa's products. This includes, among other things, elimination of the escalating tariffs that make high valued-added exports from Africa commercially unviable in Chinese and Indian markets.

On the African side, the main challenge is how to make best use of the positive spillover effects that Asian investments are having on the continent. Clearly, improving the competitiveness of African domestic markets is a priority. So, too, is the creation of sound institutions, so that when commercial opportunities do arise they can be effectively exploited, taking advantage of knowledge and technology transfers and paving the way for job creation. Furthermore, while there is scope for African countries to apply certain aspects of the industrial policy measures utilized in Asia, the lessons from those experiences suggest that a cautious approach be adopted. In all of these cases the opportunity-challenge nexus is very much a factor. In general, policies should help tilt the outcomes in favor of the opportunity side. Most important, reforms need to be country-specific.

We in the international development community also need to play a proactive role in supporting African countries to help strengthen their institutional capacities, improve governance and transparency—particularly in the extractive and natural resources industries—and facilitate domestic economic adjustments to rising Chinese and Indian competition.

Africa's Silk Road is the first of a new series of studies from the Africa Region of the World Bank Group. Forthcoming studies will focus on facing the continent's growth challenge, developing African financial markets, and filling Africa's "infrastructure gap."

Gobind T. Nankani
Regional Vice President for Africa

Acknowledgments

This study was prepared by Harry Broadman, with key contributions from Gozde Isik, Sonia Plaza, Xiao Ye, and Yutaka Yoshino. Additional contributions came from Magdi Amin, Joseph Battat, Melissa Bennett, William Butterfield, Stephan Dreyhaupt, Vivien Foster, Chung Hoon Hwang, Beata Smarzynska Javorcik, Annemarie Meisling, Maiko Miyake, Cecilia Sager, Uma Subramanian, Lesley Wentworth, Robert Whyte, Wenhe Zhang, and Xin Zhuo.

The peer reviewers were Alan Gelb, Richard Newfarmer, and Simeon Djankov. The team thanks them for their very helpful comments and suggestions.

The study benefited from other useful comments, suggestions and information provided at various stages by Demba Ba, Deepak Bhattasali, Paul Brenton, David Bridgman, Shantayanan Devarajan, Philip English, Ejaz Ghani, Bernard Hoekman, Giuseppe Iarossi, Elke Kreuzwieser, Daniel Lederman, Muthukumara Mani, Will Martin, Jacques Morriset, Gobind Nankani, Benno Ndulu, Marcelo Olarreaga, John Page, John Panzer, Lucy Payton, Sanjivi Rajasingham, Dilip Ratha, Onno Rühl, Ritva Reinikka, Jorge Saba Arbache, Sudhir Shetty, Jee-Peng Tan, Anthony Thompson, Dileep Wagle, and Kangbin Zheng.

Preliminary results from the research underlying this study were presented at ABCDE 2006, held in Tokyo (May 29–30, 2006). The comments and insights given were helpful in sharpening the analysis.

Centre de Recherches Economiques Appliquées (CREA) (Senegal), Emerging Market Focus (Pty) Ltd. (South Africa), Economic and Social Research Foundation (Tanzania), and Institute of Statistical, Social and Economic Research (ISSER) (Ghana) implemented the firm-level survey for this study in their respective countries using the instrument developed by the World Bank team.

The team is most grateful for the time devoted by the CEOs of the various companies that participated in the business case studies carried out in May 2006 in Accra, Dakar, Johannesburg, and Dar es Salaam.

Administrative support was provided by Yanick Brierre, Ann Karasanyi, and Kenneth Omondi. Thanks are due to Delfin Sia Go, Gozde Isik, and Ann Karasanyi, and other colleagues in the respective World Bank country offices for efficiently and enthusiastically supporting the business case study mission. In conducting the survey and the business case studies in Ghana, Senegal, South Africa, and Tanzania, the team also received valuable assistance from the World Bank staff based in those countries, including Fatim Diop Bathily, Kofi Boateng Agyen, Jemima Harlley, Anna Jacob, Evelyne Kapya, and Paula M. Lamptey.

A team at Grammarians, Inc., composed of Mellen Candage, Kate Sullivan, Joanne Endres, Carol Levie, Sherri Brown, and Winfield Swanson conducted editing, typesetting, and indexing of the book. The cover design was done by Debra Naylor and her team at Naylor Design, Inc. The World Bank Office of Publisher coordinated final quality control and printing.

Acronyms and Abbreviations

ACP	Africa, the Caribbean, and the Pacific
AGOA	African Growth and Opportunity Act
ATI	Africa Trade Insurance Agency
AVE	ad valorem equivalent
BCSs	Business Case Studies
BIT	bilateral investment treaty
CBU	complete-build-up
CEMAC	Economic and Monetary Community of Central Africa
CII	Confederation of Indian Industry
CIS	Commonwealth of Independent States
CKD	complete-knock-down
COMESA	Common Market for Eastern and Southern Africa
DFID	United Kingdom Department for International Development
DFIZ	Dakar Free Industrial Zone
DOT	Direction of Trade Statistics
DTC	Diamond Trading Company
DTIS	Diagnostic Trade Integration Study
DTT	double taxation treaty
EAC	East African Community
EBA	Everything But Arms
EBID	ECOWAS Bank for Investment and Development

EBP	Enterprise Benchmarking Program
ECCAS	Economic Community of Central African States
ECOWAS	Economic Community of West African States
EFE	Free Export Enterprises
EOU	Export Oriented Units
EPA	Economic Partnership Agreement
EPA	export promotion agency
EPCG	Export Promotion Capital Goods
EPZ	export processing zone
EU	European Union
ExIm	Export-Import
FDI	foreign direct investment
FFE	Foreign Funded Enterprise
FIAS	Foreign Investor Advisory Service
FTA	free trade agreement
G-8	Group of Eight
GATS	General Agreement on Trade in Services
GATT	General Agreement on Tariffs and Trade
GDI	gross domestic income
GDP	gross domestic product
GIPA	Global Investment Prospects Assessment
GSP	Generalized System of Preferences
HACCP	Hazard and Critical Control Point
ICA	Investment Climate Assessment
ICF	Investment Climate Facility
ICT	information and communications technologies
IF	Integrated Framework for Trade-Related Technical Assistance to Least Developed Countries
ILO	International Labor Organization
IMF	International Monetary Fund
IPA	investment promotion agency
ISO	International Organization for Standardization
IT	information technology
LAC	Latin America and the Caribbean
LDB	Live Database
LDC	least developed country
LOC	line of credit
MENA	Middle East and North Africa

MFA	Multifibre Arrangement
MFN	most favored nation
MIDP	Motor Industry Development Program
MIGA	Multilateral Investment Guarantee Agency
MNC	multinational corporation
NEPAD	New Economic Partnership for Africa's Development
NTB	nontariff barrier
ODA	Official Development Assistance
OECD	Organisation for Economic Co-operation and Development
OEM	original equipment manufacturer
OFDI	outward foreign direct investment
OLS	ordinary least squares
R&D	research and development
RIA	regional integration agreement
RTA	regional trade agreement
SACU	Southern Africa Customs Union
SADC	Southern African Development Community
SEZ	Special Economic Zone
SITC	Standard International Trade Classification
SME	small and medium enterprise
SOE	state-owned enterprise
sqkm	square kilometer
SSA	Sub-Saharan Africa
TA	technical assistance
TACT	Air Cargo Tariff
TCMCS	Coding System of Trade Control Measures
TEST	Textile Support Team
TRAINS	Trade Analysis and Information System
TRI	Trade Restrictiveness Index
TRIMs	trade-related investment measures
UEPB	Uganda Export Promotion Board
UN	United Nations
UNCTAD	United Nations Conference on Trade and Development
UNIDO	United Nations Industrial Development Organization
US	United States
VAT	value added tax
WAEMU	West African Economic and Monetary Union
WBAATI	World Bank Africa-Asia Trade and Investment

WDI	World Development Indicators
WEO	World Economic Outlook
WTO	World Trade Organization

Note: All dollar amounts are U.S. dollars ($) unless otherwise indicated.

Overview

Connecting Two Continents

China and India's newfound interest in trade and investment with Africa—home to 300 million of the globe's poorest people and the world's most formidable development challenge—presents a significant opportunity for growth and integration of the Sub-Saharan continent into the global economy. These two emerging economic "giants" of Asia are at the center of the explosion of African-Asian trade and investment, a striking hallmark of the new trend in South-South commercial relations. Both nations have centuries-long histories of international commerce, dating back to at least the days of the Silk Road, where merchants plied goods traversing continents, reaching the most challenging and relatively untouched markets of the day. In contemporary times, Chinese trade and investment with Africa actually dates back several decades, with most of the early investments made in infrastructure sectors, such as railways, at the start of Africa's post-colonial era. India, too, has a long history of trade and investment with modern-day Africa, particularly in East Africa, where there are significant expatriate Indian communities. Today's scale and pace of China and India's trade and investment flows with Africa, however, are wholly unprecedented.

The acceleration of South-South trade and investment is one of the most significant features of recent developments in the global economy.

For decades, world trade has been dominated by commerce both among developed countries—the North—and between the North and the developing countries of the South.[1] Since 2000 there has been a massive increase in trade and investment flows between Africa[2] and Asia. Today, Asia receives about 27 percent of Africa's exports, in contrast to only about 14 percent in 2000. This volume of trade is now almost on par with Africa's exports to the United States and the European Union (EU)—Africa's traditional trading partners; in fact, the EU's share of African exports has halved over the period 2000–05.[3] Asia's exports to Africa also are growing very rapidly—about 18 percent per year—which is higher than to any other region.[4] At the same time, although the volume of foreign direct investment (FDI) between Africa and Asia is more modest than that of trade—and Sub-Saharan Africa accounts for only 1.8 percent of global FDI inflows[5]—African-Asian FDI is growing at a tremendous rate. This is especially true of Asian FDI in Africa.[6]

China and India each have rapidly modernizing industries and burgeoning middle classes with rising incomes and purchasing power. The result is growing demand not only for natural resource–extractive commodities, agricultural goods such as cotton, and other traditional African exports, but also more diversified, nontraditional exports such as processed commodities, light manufactured products, household consumer goods, food, and tourism. By virtue of its labor-intensive capacity, Africa has the potential to export these nontraditional goods and services competitively to the average Chinese and Indian consumer and firm.

With regard to investment, much of the accumulated stock of Chinese and Indian FDI in Africa is concentrated in extractive sectors, such as oil and mining. While this has been grabbing most of the media headlines, greater diversification of these countries' FDI flows to Africa has in fact been occurring more recently. Significant Chinese and Indian investments on the African continent have been made in apparel, food processing, retail ventures, fisheries and seafood farming, commercial real estate and transport construction, tourism, power plants, and telecommunications, among other sectors. Moreover, some of these investments are propelling African trade into cutting-edge multinational corporate networks, which are increasingly altering the "international division of labor." China and India are pursuing commercial strategies with Africa that are about far more than resources.

Despite the immense growth in trade and investment between the two regions, there are significant asymmetries. While Asia accounts for one-quarter of Africa's global exports, this trade represents only about 1.6 percent of the exports shipped to Asia from all sources worldwide. By the same token, FDI in Asia by African firms is extremely small, both in absolute and relative terms. At the same time, the rise of internationally competitive Chinese and Indian businesses has displaced domestic sales as well as exports by African producers, such as textile and apparel firms, whether through investments by Chinese and Indian entrepreneurs on the Sub-Saharan continent or through exports from their home markets. This competition spurs African firms to become more efficient, but it also creates unemployment and other social costs during the transition. Not surprisingly, some African governments are responding with policies that protect domestic businesses.

As the global marketplace continues to be increasingly integrated, with rapidly changing notions of comparative advantage, much is at stake for the economic welfare of hundreds of millions of people in Sub-Saharan Africa. With this newest phase in the evolution of world trade and investment flows taking root—the increasing emergence of South-South international commerce, with China and India poised to take the lead—Africans cannot afford to be left behind, especially if growth-enhancing opportunities for trade and investment with the North continue to be as limited as they have been. Nor can the rest of the world, including Africa's international development partners, afford to allow Africans to be unable to genuinely participate in—and most important, benefit from—the new patterns of international commerce.

Objectives of the Study

Against this backdrop, there is intense interest by policy makers and businesses in both Africa and Asia, as well as by international development partners, to better understand the evolution and the developmental, commercial, and policy implications of African-Asian trade and investment relations. This interest is reflected, perhaps most notably, in the South-South discussions held during the African-Asian summit in Jakarta in April 2005 celebrating the fiftieth anniversary of the Bandung Declaration, where the dramatic rise in international commerce between the two regions figured prominently, as well as at the July 2005 G-8 summit in Gleneagles, where the leaders of the North underscored the growing importance of South-South trade and investment flows, especially as they pertain to the prospects for fostering growth and poverty reduction in Africa.

Yet despite the sizeable—and rapidly escalating—attention devoted to this topic, especially by some of the world's most senior officials, there is, surprisingly, a paucity of systematic data available on these issues to carry out rigorous analysis, and from which inferences of a similar caliber could be drawn to meet the interest and provide the desired understanding. The vast majority of accessible information is based on anecdotes or piecemeal datasets, which make a well-informed assessment difficult to generate.

This study utilizes new firm-level data from a large World Bank quantitative survey and from originally developed business case studies, both carried out by the World Bank in the field in mid-2006 in four countries—Ghana, Senegal, South Africa, and Tanzania. The survey and business case studies focused on the African operations of Chinese and Indian businesses, as well as the operations of domestic (African-owned) and other internationally owned firms located in Africa.[7] Based on these data, official government statistics, and existing data compiled by the World Bank and other donors, the study seeks to answer:

- *What* has been the recent evolution of the pattern and performance of trade and investment flows between Africa and Asia, especially China and India, and *which* factors are likely to significantly condition these flows in the future?

- *What* have been the most important impacts on Africa of its trade and investment relations with China and India, and *what* actions can be taken to help shape these impacts to enhance Africa's economic development prospects?

In focusing on these questions the study examines four key factors that are significantly affecting trade and investment between Africa and Asia:

- *"At-the-border" trade and investment policies*, including policies affecting market access (tariffs and nontariff barriers (NTBs)); FDI policy regimes; and bilateral, regional, and multilateral trade agreements;

- *"Behind-the-border" (domestic) market conditions*, including the nature of the business environment; competitiveness of market structures; quality of market institutions; and supply constraints, such as poor infrastructure and underdeveloped human capital and skills;

- *"Between-the-border" factors*, including the development of cross-border trade-facilitating logistical and transport regimes; quantity and quality of information about overseas market opportunities, including through expatriates and the ethnic diasporas; impacts of technical standards; and the role of migration;

- *Complementarities between investment and trade*, including the extent to which investment and trade flows leverage one another; the effects of such complementarities on scale of production and ability of firms to integrate across markets; participation in global production networks and value chains; and spillover effects of transfers of technology.

The first set of factors is typically presumed by most observers to be dominant in affecting trade and investment relations between Africa and Asia. This study finds, however, that the effects of formal trade and investment policies are likely to be of equal, if not secondary, importance compared to the latter three sets of factors. The analysis finds that behind-the-border and between-the-border conditions, as well as the interactions between investment and trade flows, are the major elements that influence the extent, nature, and effects of Africa's international commerce with China and India, and therefore these are the areas on which the priority for policy reforms likely should be placed.

The assessment undertaken in this study is largely economic in nature. In this regard, the analysis focuses on political economy, governance, and institutional issues insofar as they directly have economic implications. Important as these issues are, however, the intention here is not to focus on them per se; they are topics deserving of separate, dedicated study.

Moreover, the study's prism is largely on the impacts on Africa of China and India's trade and investment flows to that continent, rather than the reverse. To be sure, the analysis does cover lessons that can be drawn from Asia's economic success stories that might be applicable for Africa. But a focus on the implications of African-Asian trade for China and India is beyond the scope of the study.

Finally, Sub-Saharan Africa is not a country: it is a very heterogeneous continent comprising 47 nations with great variations in physical, economic, political, and social dimensions. The bulk of the analysis focuses on those African countries for which new data have been collected specifically for this study, or for which there are systematic data from which economically meaningful analysis, including cross-country comparisons, can be made. The countries that are the subject of the analysis were chosen to be somewhat representative of the continent, but there is no pretense that the study's findings are necessarily applicable to all African countries.

The following sections summarize the study's main findings.

Africa in the Global Economy

Economic development patterns in Africa have become increasingly diverse over the last decade, with more and more success stories; see figure 1. Since the mid-1990s, 19 Sub-Saharan countries have had annual GDP growth of 4.5 percent or higher. The rise in the world price of oil is certainly a major factor at play for some of these countries. One-third of the world's resource-dependent economies are in Africa. Yet even excluding the oil-rich countries, the fastest growing group of African countries (total 15 countries) has had an average growth rate of at least 4.5 percent. These countries host 34 percent of the region's people. By contrast, the 13 slowest-growing economies in Africa have seen less than 3 percent growth on average, with some having near zero or negative growth. These countries, many either engaged in conflict or having recently emerged from conflict, account for 20 percent of the region's people.

Africa is quite diverse in other aspects. Geography has played a major role in shaping its economic fortunes. The continent has the largest number of countries per square area in comparison with other developing regions, with each on average sharing borders with four neighbors. Africa is also highly geographically segmented. A large proportion of its population lives in countries with an unfavorable geographic and economic basis for development. Forty percent of Africans live in landlocked countries, compared with 23 percent of the population in East and Central Asia. Moreover, Africa's low population density is accentuated by high internal transport costs, estimated at nearly twice the levels of other developing regions. The result is that, except for South Africa and Nigeria—the two dominant economies in Africa—the continent is comprised of countries that have small and shallow markets.

All told, these conditions—compounded by underdeveloped market institutions, constraints on business competition, and weak governance—make international trade and investment in Africa costly. World trade and investment flows have dramatically expanded in the last 15 years, but the African continent's overall trade performance in the global marketplace

FIGURE 1
Africa's Development Pattern is Increasingly Diverse, with More and More Success Stories

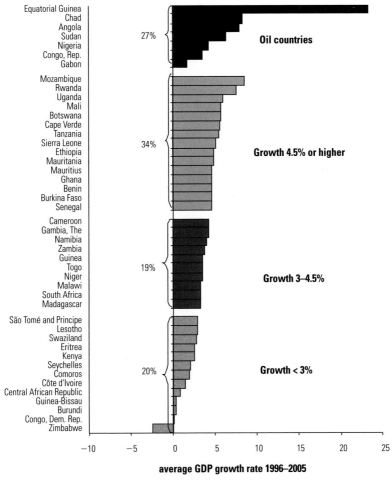

average GDP growth rate 1996–2005

Source: World Bank World Development Indicators.

has been very disappointing. In fact, Africa's overall export market share has continuously fallen over the last six decades; see figure 2. Unless reversed, this pattern does not bode well for sustained growth on the continent. In spite of Africa's recent rapid growth of FDI inflows, the continent accounts for 1.8 percent of global net FDI flows; see figure 3.

Africa's merchandise exports are dominated by oil. In fact, Sub-Saharan Africa is the only region of the world that has not exhibited an increasing

FIGURE 2
Africa's Share of World Exports Has Been Declining

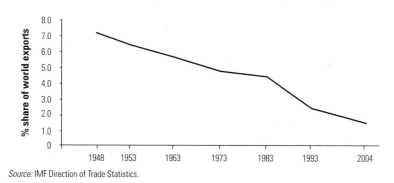

Source: IMF Direction of Trade Statistics.

share of non-oil exports over the last two decades; see figure 4. This disappointing performance means that Africa has not taken full advantage of international trade to leverage growth.

The countries in Africa experiencing strong growth outside the oil-producing nations have been buoyed, in part, by global price increases in other primary export commodities. As illustrated in figure 5, with the exception of raw materials, whose prices have been relatively stagnant, other commodities, including metals and non-oil minerals, have experienced noticeable increases in their price levels. This worldwide rise of com-

FIGURE 3
Africa Accounts for 1.8 Percent of Global FDI Flows

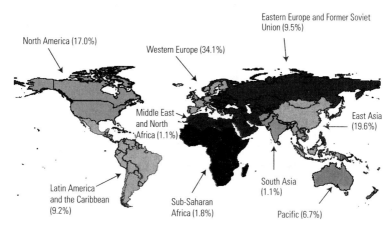

Source: World Bank World Development Indicators.

FIGURE 4
Africa Is Virtually the Only Region that Has Not Increased its Share of Non-Oil Exports

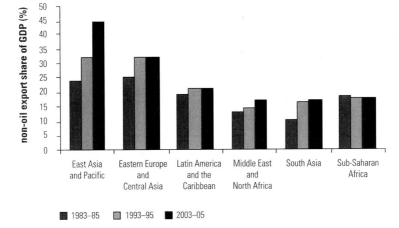

■ 1983–85   ▨ 1993–95   ■ 2003–05

Source: IMF Direction of Trade Statistics.

modity prices has been engendered in large part by the rapid growth of Asian developing countries, especially China and India. They contributed close to 40 percent of global import growth for precious stones, 30 percent for crude oil, and 20 percent for metallic ores; see figure 6. Their demand for these commodities is likely to grow, or at least not change from current levels, in the foreseeable future.

FIGURE 5
Prices Have Risen for Many of Africa's Major Export Commodities, Not Just Oil

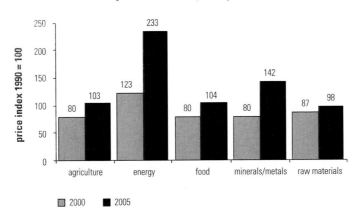

☐ 2000   ■ 2005

Source: World Bank staff estimates.

FIGURE 6

China and India's Contribution to Global Commodity Demand, 2000–04

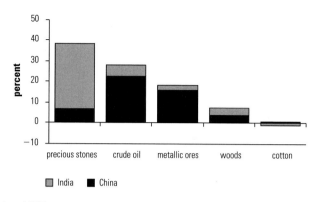

Source: Goldstein et al. 2006.

Still, a number of countries in Africa are diversifying their exports, no longer relying solely on the export of a few raw commodities. Exports are increasingly composed of light manufactured goods, processed foods, horticulture, and services such as tourism. Some countries—such as Nigeria and South Africa—have been increasing their shares of exports in technology-based products. In fact, they are moving up the technology ladder and exporting low- to medium-technology products in sectors where Asian countries are increasingly putting less emphasis.

Country-Level Patterns and Performance of African-Asian Trade and Investment Flows

There has been a dramatic increase in trade flows between Africa and Asia, and this trend is a major bright spot in Africa's trade performance. These trade flows are largely driven by economic complementarities between the two regions. Africa has growing demand for Asia's manufactured goods and machinery, and demand in Asia's developing economies is growing for Africa's natural resources, and increasingly for labor-intensive goods. Factor endowments and other economic resources will likely continue to yield these strong country-level African-Asian complementarities, indicating the likely sustainability of the current African-Asian trade boom.

The volume of African exports to Asia is growing at an accelerated rate: while exports from Africa to Asia grew annually by 15 percent between

1990 and 1995, they have grown by 20 percent during the last five years (2000–05). Asia is now a major trading partner of African countries. Asia accounts for 27 percent of Africa's exports, an amount that is almost equivalent to the EU and US share of Africa's exports, 32 percent and 29 percent, respectively. Despite this growth, Africa's exports still remain relatively small from the Asian perspective: Africa's exports to Asia account for only 1.6 percent of Asian global imports.

The recent growth of African exports to Asia largely reflects a sharp upturn in its exports to China and India. African exports to these two countries have been rising dramatically; see figures 7a and 7b. Though China and India still account for only 13 percent of all of Africa's exports, Africa's exports to China and India have grown 1.7 times the growth rate of the continent's total exports worldwide. Between India and China, it is China that is the more dynamic destination market for Africa's exports. Exports to China grew by 48 percent annually between 1999 and 2004, compared to 14 percent for India. Ten percent of Sub-Saharan exports are now to China and some 3 percent are to India. China has overtaken Japan as the leading importer of African products in Asia.

The growth in African exports to China and India in the last few years is largely driven by large unmet domestic demand for natural resources in those countries, reflecting growing industries as well as increasing consumption by households. Petroleum is the leading commodity, followed by

FIGURE 7
A Steady, Dramatic Rise of China and India as Destinations for African Exports

| a. Average annual merchandise export growth rate, Africa to Asia | b. Africa's merchandise imports from China and India |

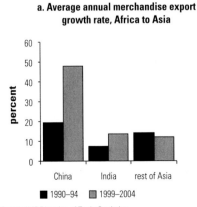 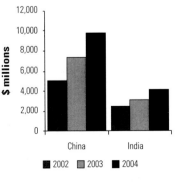

Source: IMF Direction of Trade Statistics.

ores and metals. That oil dominates Africa's exports to China and India is part of the larger profile of Africa's global export pattern.

Africa's rapidly growing exports to China and India are not limited to fuels and other mineral and metal products. Labor-intensive raw or semi-processed agricultural commodities that are used for further processing either for industrial use (timber, cotton) or for consumer use (food products) are also increasingly imported by China and India. Still, taken together, petroleum, metals, and agricultural raw materials account for 85 percent of Africa's exports to China and India.

The current geographic distribution of Africa's origin markets for the continent's exports to China and India is concentrated. Five oil- and mineral-exporting countries account for 85 percent of Africa's exports to China. South Africa alone accounts for 68 percent of Sub-Saharan exports to India.

Asian exports to Africa are also increasing. Over the last five years, they have grown at an 18 percent annual rate, higher than that of any other region, including the EU. These exports are largely manufactured goods, which have surged into African markets. Some of them are intermediate inputs for products assembled in Africa and shipped out to third markets, such as the EU and United States, or capital goods (machinery and equipment) for African manufacturing sectors themselves. At the same time, there is also a sizable amount of African imports of consumer nondurables from Asia, which compete against Africa's domestically produced products.

African-Asian FDI flows are also growing rapidly, but the volume of such flows is more modest than that of trade. While there is some African FDI in China and India, this investment is dominated by the flows of Chinese and Indian FDI in Africa. As of mid-2006, the stock of China's FDI to Africa is estimated to be $1.18 billion.

The vast majority of Chinese and Indian FDI inflows to Africa over the past decade have been largely concentrated in the extractive industries. Because such investments are typically capital intensive, they have engendered limited domestic employment creation. However, in the last few years, Chinese and Indian FDI in Africa has begun to diversify into many other sectors, including apparel, agroprocessing, power generation, road construction, tourism, and telecommunications, among others. Chinese and Indian FDI in Africa has also become more diversified geographically; figure 8 shows the current country distribution of Chinese FDI flows to Africa.

FIGURE 8
Current Chinese FDI Outflows to Africa are Largely, But Not Exclusively, Resource-Oriented

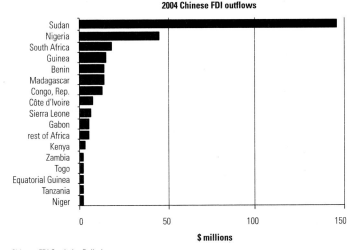

2004 Chinese FDI outflows

$ millions

Source: Chinese FDI Statistics Bulletin.

Examining the Determinants of the Patterns of African-Asian Trade Flows

What are the principal factors that account for the differences observed in the patterns of African-Asian trade flows? At-the-border formal trade policies are often at the forefront of negotiations and discussions on international commerce. Obviously, tariff and nontariff barriers (NTBs) are the primary targets of trade liberalization. It is thus important to investigate the impact of such factors on the patterns of Africa's trade flows with Asia. More liberal import policies (for example, low tariff rates) taken by individual countries should facilitate more trade flows among such countries. Preferential market access measures or free trade agreements also should stimulate more trade flows.

However, changes in formal trade policies are only a necessary and not a sufficient condition for engendering cross-border trade. For trade to take place, tradable, internationally competitive goods and services need to be produced. Most African nations, like other developing countries, possess a rather thin base of internationally competitive private sector enterprises and the related institutions and infrastructure needed for them to be able to engage in sustainable and commercially attractive international transactions. Under these conditions, arguably there would be limited or perhaps no supply response to any beneficial reforms in trade and investment policies that might materialize. Simply put, without such reforms, new trade and investment opportunities will likely go unexploited by Africa. At the same time, for the goods and services produced to be traded efficiently, sufficient capacity is needed for trade-facilitating infrastructure, institutions, and services to lower "between-the-border" trade-related transactions costs.

A large number of *qualitative* studies have been conducted to analyze how "at-the-border," "behind-the-border," and "between-the-border" factors influence the trade performance of developing countries. Prominent among them are the Diagnostic Trade Integration Studies (DTISs) carried out under the Integrated Framework for Trade-Related Technical Assistance to Least Developed Countries (IF) program. DTISs have been developed for 26 countries in Africa to identify country-specific bottlenecks for promoting trade in those countries. These studies find that these three factors are indeed major parameters affecting African trade performance. But due to their country-specific, qualitative nature, these instruments have little capacity to systematically gauge how these various factors impact African countries across the board. Nor do they give a sense of the relative importance of such impacts. To do so requires a *quantitative* cross-country approach.

"Gravity models" of bilateral trade flows provide useful information as to how significant are the various policy factors in influencing the pattern of overall trade flows between Africa and Asia on a cross-county basis. An estimated multivariate gravity model is applied to bilateral trade flows of African countries to and from various countries in the world, including Asian countries as well as African countries themselves. In addition to standard economic and geographic factors such as GDP, GDP per capita, physical distance, and common language, among others, the model incorporates variables depicting the stance of formal trade policies (at-the-border factors), intensity of domestic business constraints (behind-the-border factors), and extent of development of institutions and infrastructure that facilitate trade and lower transactions costs (between-the-border factors). (The model also incorporates variables that permit an assessment of the extent to which African-Asian investment and trade flows complement (or leverage) rather than substitute for one another; see below.)

Table 1 summarizes the direction of statistically significant impacts from various factors based on the signs of coefficients estimated by Ordinary Least Squares (OLS) regressions. (Although not reported in the table, most of the economic, geographical, historical, and cultural factors have the predicted signs and their coefficients are statistically significant.) All of the statistically significant coefficients display the expected sign. Moreover, the results from the estimation procedures show that the same factors are equally important when examining Africa's trade performance on a global basis or its trade performance vis-a-vis Asia in particular. This indicates the robustness of the estimated model.

The empirical analysis shows that, on a cross-country basis, in addition to trade policy variables, both behind-the-border and between-the-border factors significantly influence the trade performance of African countries. In fact, the analysis suggests that the impacts of behind-the-border and between-the-border factors on the export propensity and orientation of international commerce between African and Asian countries are at least

TABLE 1
What Determines Bilateral African-Asian Trade Flows? Relative Roles of "At-the-Border," "Behind-the-Border," and "Between-the-Border" Factors

Indicator	All merchandise trade		Manufactured trade	
	Exports from Africa	Imports to Africa	Exports from Africa	Imports to Africa
At-the-border factors				
Importer trade testrictiveness	n.s.	n.s.	−	n.s.
Regional trade agreement	+	+	+	n.s.
Preferential market access	n.s.	n.s.	+	n.s.
Between-the-border factors				
Customs procedure—exporter	−	n.s.	−	n.s.
Customs procedure—importer	+	n.s.	n.s.	n.s.
Internet access—exporter	+	+	+	+
Internet access—importer	n.s.	n.s.	n.s.	n.s.
Port quality—exporter	−	+	−	+
Port quality—importer	+	+	+	+
Behind-the-border factors				
Domestic business procedure—exporter	−	n.s.	−	n.s.
Power infrastructure quality—exporter	n.s.	n.s.	+	n.s.

Source: Authors' calculations based on 2002–04 average figures. See chapter 2 for details.

Note: Only the signs of significant coefficients are shown (level of significance above 10 percent). "n.s." represents a coefficient not statistically significant.

equal to or even greater than those of formal at-the-border policies. For example, it is estimated that a 10 percent reduction in domestic barriers to new business start-ups or a 10 percent improvement in domestic electric power service would increase Africa's manufactured exports by about 28 percent or 15 percent respectively.

We now turn to examine in detail the overall impacts of these various factors on African-Asian trade and investment.

Role of At-the-Border Policies

Tariff structures of African countries as well as China and India still have some unfavorable elements that constrain mutual trade. Because China, India, and most African countries are members of the World Trade Organization (WTO), as a rule, their tariffs are generally set on a nondiscriminatory, Most-Favored-Nation (MFN) basis. One of the objectives of the WTO Doha Round, which at present is suspended, is to seek a global agreement to lower countries' various MFN tariffs.

With some important exceptions, the import tariff rates African exporters face in Asia are higher than those they face in the United States and the EU. Among Asian countries, the tariff levels of China and India on African products remain high. Tariff rates on agricultural products are high in both countries. The prevalence of high tariff rates in India is broadly based. China is a relatively liberalized market. It has zero tariffs for its most highly demanded raw materials, including crude petroleum and ores, but has moderate-to-high tariffs on other imports, especially on inedible crude materials from the South. China has announced plans to further lower its tariffs and bring about lower dispersion in the structure of tariffs by the end of 2007.

Particularly problematic is the fact that in certain cases, tariff escalation in Asian markets has been discouraging the export of higher value-added processed products from Africa. This is especially true for some of Africa's leading exports to China and India, including coffee, cocoa beans, and cashews, to pick but three examples; see table 2.

Like Asian countries, Africa also has many tariff peaks against Asian imports. Textiles, yarn, apparel, footwear, and light manufactured goods are among Africa's largest imports from Asia; they also carry some of the highest tariffs in Africa. However, other significant imports from China and India, including electronics, machinery, and transportation equip-

TABLE 2
Africa's Leading Exports Face Escalating Tariffs in China and India

SITC	Product	African imports			
		China	India	Japan	Asia average
211	Raw hides	6.5	0.1	0	0.8
611	Leather	8.8	14.7	0.7	4.6
612	Manufactures leather	14.6	15.0	1.9	7.9
222	Oil seeds	5.0	30.0	0.4	2.0
423	Vegetable oils	10.0	45.0	—	27.7
07111	Coffee, not roasted	8.0	100.0	0	2.3
07112	Coffee, roasted	15.0	30.0	9.1	9.1
0721	Cocoa beans, raw	8.0	30.0	0	2.8
0722	Cocoa powder	15.0	—	—	0.2
333	Petroleum oils, crude	0	—	—	0.2
334	Petroleum products, refined	7.4	15.0	2.1	0.3
66722	Diamonds, sorted	3.0	—	0	2.2
66729	Diamonds, cut	8.0	15.0	0	6.0
6673	Other precious/semi-precious stones	7.3	15.0	0	9.0
897	Jewelry	26.8	15.0	0.9	15.7
263	Cotton	27.0	10.0	0	14.8
6513	Cotton yarn	5.0	15.0	—	5.0
652	Cotton fabrics, woven	10.0	15.0	1.0	5.6
84512	Jerseys, etc. of cotton	14.0	—	5.7	6.8
8462	Under garments, knitted	14.1	15.0	6.9	5.2

Source: UNCTAD TRAINS.

Note: Darker shades represent higher levels of processing; — = data not available.

ment, generally have relatively low tariffs. Although African tariff barriers have been lowered significantly, some high tariffs on intermediate inputs into African countries constrain African manufacturing exports. This bias against exports is an obvious target for reform by African policy makers.

Non-tariff barriers (NTBs), such as technical standards, pose special challenges to African exports to Asia (as well as elsewhere). Most countries in Africa lack the institutional capacity and resources to fully implement or effectively enforce these standards. This diminishes the ability of domestic producers to penetrate certain export markets in Asia, including China and India.

As in other areas of the world, there has been a proliferation of regional and bilateral trade and investment agreements on the African continent in recent years, including reciprocal agreements among other countries in the South, including China and India. No bilateral free trade agreements

(FTAs) are currently in effect between Asian and African countries, but several are either under negotiation or have been proposed; these include a China–South Africa FTA, an India-Mauritius economic cooperation and partnership agreement, and an India-SACU (Southern Africa Customs Union) FTA.

The fashioning of the emerging "spaghetti bowl" of regional trade agreements among African countries, while perhaps being done with good intentions, in practice is not having demonstrable salutary effects; see figure 9. Many Chinese and Indian investors—not to mention African and other foreign investors—find them at best, ineffective, or at worst, confusing, and not conducive to attracting international commerce.

FIGURE 9
The Spaghetti Bowl of African Regional Trade Agreements is Not Investor Friendly

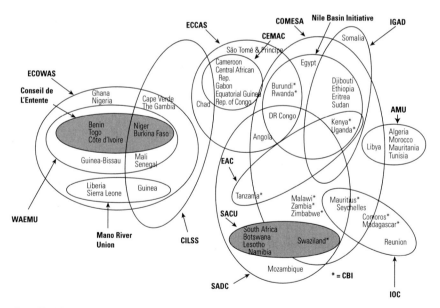

Source: World Bank.

Note: AMU: Arab Maghreb Union; CBI: Cross Border Initiative; CEMAC: Economic and Monetary Community of Central Africa; CILSS: Permanent Interstate Committee on Drought Control in the Sahel; COMESA: Common Market for Eastern and Southern Africa; EAC: East African Cooperation; ECOWAS: Economic Community of Western African States; IGAD: Inter-Governmental Authority on Development; IOC: Indian Ocean Commission; SACU: Southern African Customs Union; SADC: Southern African Development Community; WAEMU: West African Economic and Monetary Union.

There are also a few African-Asian preferential arrangements. Of significance in this regard is the unilateral liberalization by China in early 2006 of certain African imports: tariffs were eliminated on 190 commodities from 25 African countries. There are also preferential arrangements provided by developed countries in the North, such as the U.S. African Growth and Opportunity Act (AGOA) and the EU Everything But Arms (EBA) programs, which also facilitate market access for exports from Africa produced by Chinese and Indian firms operating in Africa. Among other effects, these have encouraged Asian investment in manufacturing sectors such as the apparel industry in Lesotho and automobile assembling in South Africa. The size of the benefits derived from preferential arrangements diminishes significantly when market barriers for other competitors are lowered, challenging the sustainability of such regimes.

In addition to formal international agreements, African-Asian trade and investment are also influenced—in varying degrees—by other instruments. Investment promotion agencies (IPAs) and public-private investors' councils in African and Asian countries have been playing an increasing and critical role in facilitating international commerce between the two regions. China and India have also established various other mechanisms in the hopes of stimulating trade and investment with Africa. A recent—and perhaps most notable—initiative is the January 2006 release in Beijing of "China's Africa Policy."[8] The white paper identifies a large set of economic issues over which China proposes to cooperate with Africa, including trade, investment, debt relief, economic assistance, finance, agriculture, and infrastructure.

While some export and investment incentives, such as export processing zones (EPZ), have been successful in China and India, in Africa, with only a few exceptions, their potential to stimulate exports has not effectively materialized. Export incentives in African countries have also had mixed results in creating backward production linkages and enhancing value-added in processed exports. The general ineffectiveness of such incentives on the African continent is due, in part, to significant implementation and enforcement challenges in the face of generally weak institutional capacities. Without strong governance discipline and incentives in place, opportunities for discretionary behavior and corruption have arisen. The ineffectiveness of export and investment incentives is also due to the lack of the requisite infrastructure and labor skills.

"Behind-the-Border" Factors

Competition is a potent force in affecting Africa's integration with Asia, particularly with businesses from China and India, and the influence occurs through a variety of channels. Domestic competition matters significantly in explaining the performance of firms operating in Africa—regardless of nationality—both in terms of productivity and international integration through exports. Intense competition on the sales side enhances both productivity and export performance. Tougher import competition, lower barriers to entry and exit, and less reliance on sales to government through public procurement, for example, tend to result in a higher propensity to export, again, across firms of all nationalities. The more competitive are African input markets, the more competitive are product markets, and both productivity and export performance are enhanced.

Scale strongly influences the performance of firms operating in Africa. This is true regardless of the nationality of the business. Larger firms outperform surveyed smaller firms both in terms of productivity and exports. Smaller firms in Africa face tougher competition overall than do larger firms, resulting in higher firm turnover among smaller businesses. However, in the case of competition from imports, larger firms are more affected, in part because they have a higher propensity to import and a greater tendency to populate import-sensitive sectors than do their smaller counterparts.

The sectors in Africa that exhibit more competition are not only able to attract more FDI, but also are more effective in penetrating foreign markets through exports. In this way, domestic competition and international integration are mutually reinforcing. The lesson for African firms is clear: "success at home breeds success abroad," a finding consistent with recent experience in other regions of the world, including firms in the "transition" countries in the former Soviet Union.[9]

There is a clear role played by the entry of Chinese and Indian investors in fostering domestic competition in African markets; see figure 10. In fact, a mutually reinforcing effect is found: African firms that face more competitive markets at home have greater involvement with Chinese and Indian capital, while the African markets where Chinese and Indian investors are most prevalent tend to be the most competitive. The analysis also shows that the major source of the competition engendered in the African markets by the presence of Chinese and Indian investors is competition from imports—indeed imports from China and India themselves.

FIGURE 10
Chinese and Indian Foreign Investors Foster Competition in African Markets

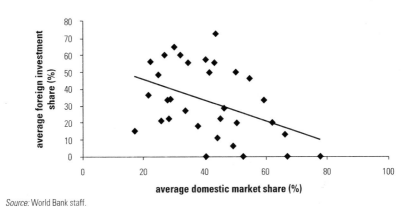

Source: World Bank staff.

As is the case throughout much of the African continent, Chinese and Indian businesses face high transactions costs behind-the-border in the locales in which they operate. The result is diminished attraction of trade and investment by investors from China and India (as well as from other countries) than otherwise would be the case. Four elements of the high cost of doing business in Africa by Chinese and Indian firms stand out:

- poor quality of infrastructure services (power supply, telephone services, Internet access),

- inefficient factor markets (lack of skilled labor, rigidities in the domestic labor market, and limited access to local finance),

- unfavorable regulatory regimes, and

- weak governance disciplines.

Figure 11 illustrates the burden that exporters face from the interruption of electric service from the public grid.

"Between-the-Border" Factors

Africa's trade and investment flows with Asia are affected by the amount of economic or institutional "friction" between-the-borders, as is the case for trade and investment between other regions of the world. As a result, building new trade and investment relations is associated with incurring

FIGURE 11

Exporters in Africa Face Significant Interruption in Electricity Service from the Public Grid, Lowering Their International Competitiveness

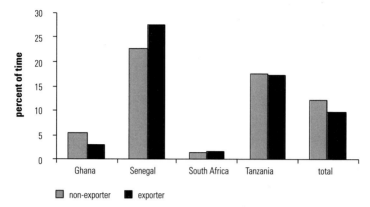

Source: World Bank 2005d, 2005e, and 2004a for Senegal, South Africa, and Tanzania. Teal et al. (2006) for Ghana.

certain—and often, large—costs. Such costs arise from, among other things, assessing new market opportunities, searching for new trading or investment partners, establishing financing and marketing channels, transferring personnel and technology, conforming with customs regulations and technical standards, and determining how best to utilize logistical, transport, and communications systems, especially for landlocked countries, which are prominent on the Sub-Saharan continent.

These costs can be lowered through a variety of means. Search costs, for example, can be reduced through use of either formal channels—whether on a businesses-to-business or a government-to-government basis—or informal "soft" networks, such as ethnic networks and the diasporas.

TABLE 3

Remedying Information Market Imperfections

(percent)

Nationality of owner	Ethnic origin of owner			
	African	Chinese	Indian	European
African	100	4	48	51
Chinese	0	93	0	1
Indian	0	0	45	0
European	0	0	4	41
Other	0	4	3	7

Source: World Bank staff.

Reducing costs arising from logistical bottlenecks can come about through improvement in (or development of) trade facilitation infrastructure and related institutions. The availability of trade finance and risk insurance can help address commercial considerations. In some respects, Africa and Asia are two regions that are still widely apart: there are large gaps of knowledge about each other's markets, and there are only limited direct inter-regional transport services (air, maritime shipping services, and passenger routes). The limited provision of such services could be binding constraints to trade and investment flows between the two regions.

For African, Chinese, and Indian investors, there are significant imperfections and asymmetries in the quality of market information regarding potential cross-border commercial opportunities for the two regions. Ethnic networks are increasingly relied on to facilitate the flow of such information and to compensate for these imperfections and asymmetries. There is a striking difference in the reliance on ethnic networks between Indian and Chinese firms operating on the continent; see table 3. About one-half of the owners of surveyed firms in Africa that are of Indian ethnic origin are in fact African by nationality. (A similar proportion exists for European owners of the surveyed African firms.) These figures suggest that Indian (and European) migrants are substantially integrated into the business community in Africa.

On the other hand, there is near identity in the proportion of owners of surveyed Chinese firms operating in Africa who are Chinese both by nationality and by ethnicity. This underscores the fact that Chinese investors in Africa are relative newcomers and have not, at this juncture, integrated into the African business community to any significant degree; this notion is explored more deeply in chapter 6. Instead, recent Chinese investments in Africa, as evidenced in virtually all of the business case studies carried out for this analysis, have been largely accompanied by temporary assignments of executives to the African continent. As Chinese investment in Africa has grown, it is estimated that some 80,000 migrant workers from China have moved to Africa, creating a new Chinese diaspora.[10]

At the same time, given that impediments to cross-border information flows are inherent in international trade and investment—particularly in the most underdeveloped countries in the world—public information services run by governments or by private firms are proving to be very important. In addition, there has been a growing role for institutional providers of export market information, such as export promotion agencies, and the similar providers of foreign investment information, such as investment promotion agencies.

The adherence by African firms to internationally recognized technical standards and accreditation schemes, such as those governed by the International Organization for Standardization (ISO), is extremely low; see figure 12. Indeed, only 34 countries in Sub-Saharan Africa belong to the ISO. This limits the ability of potential importers in Chinese and Indian markets to readily assess the quality of an African export in comparison to other internationally transacted products.

The flows of technology and labor—line workers as well as professionals—between Africa and Asia are facilitating the formation of business links between the two regions, which then lead to trade and FDI flows. In fact, there is a mutually reinforcing effect between trade and investment on the one hand, and skills and technology transfers on the other. For example, among surveyed Chinese and Indian firms operating in Africa, on average, those that export more from the continent have a higher proportion of workers from their corporate headquarters at home than those who export less.

But Africans and the Chinese and Indian investors operating on the continent face significant challenges in effectively exploiting such synergies. Local technological transfers or skills transfers are compromised when foreign skilled workers, brought in with foreign capital, are not given the

FIGURE 12

Imperfections in the Market for Information: High Transactions Costs

Quality certifications (ISO 9000, 9002, 14000)

received ISO   did not receive ISO

Source: World Bank.

resources, let alone the incentives, to engage in effective skill transfers to local workers. At the same time, because of inadequate education or training, Africans are often ill-equipped to adopt the new skills even when such transfers are being attempted.

Of importance, Chinese and Indian governments are providing or investing in resources for greater technical cooperation with African countries so as to facilitate such technological transfers, among other objectives. Greater participation by African firms in international network production increasingly being carried out by Chinese and Indian investors on the continent is another way for Africans to effectively capture opportunities for the acquisition of advances in technology and modern skills (this will be described in greater detail below).

Chinese and Indian firms (as well as other foreign investors) operating in Africa—not to mention African firms themselves—are being hampered by the inadequate and costly transport and logistics services currently found in Africa; see table 4. Enhancing trade-facilitation infrastructure systems and related institutions could offer tremendous opportunities for reducing the direct and indirect transactions costs of African-Asian trade and investment. Evidence from the business case studies illustrates the point. A Chinese firm in South Africa finds that sending products from Angola to South Africa is as expensive as shipping them to China. An Indian firm in Ghana reports that shipping costs and tariffs *within* the Economic Community of West African States (ECOWAS) are very expensive. It costs $1,000 to send a container from Accra to Lagos. For that reason, the firm decided to do a cross-border investment rather than export. For firms operating in Africa to be able effectively to compete in today's global marketplace will require dramatic improvements in the complex chain of trade-supporting services that include customs and border procedures, management and control of freight movements, transaction documentation, and banking instruments. Indeed, the weaknesses in the continent's trade support services undermine the international competitiveness of African products, and constrain the ability of otherwise internationally competitive African firms to take advantage of new global market opportunities, including those in China and India.

Both domestic and foreign-invested firms in Africa face major problems in accessing local trade financing, which is particularly serious among small and medium enterprises. At the same time, investment by Chinese and Indian firms in Africa is being significantly aided by public

TABLE 4

Trade Facilitation Infrastructure and Institutions: High Transactions Costs

	Export			Import		
	Documents for export (number)	Signatures for export (number)	Time for export (days)	Documents for import (number)	Signatures for import (number)	Time for import (days)
Sub-Saharan Africa average	9	19	49	13	30	61
Ghana	6	11	47	13	13	55
Senegal	6	8	23	10	12	26
South Africa	5	7	31	9	9	34
Tanzania	7	10	30	13	16	51
East Asia and Pacific average	7	7	26	10	9	29
China	6	7	20	11	8	24
South Asia average	8	12	34	13	24	47
India	10	22	36	15	27	43

Source: World Bank 2005.

trade finance programs offered by the export-import banks of the two countries.

FDI-Trade Complementarities and Network Production-Sharing Opportunities

Firms in Africa—both domestic and foreign-owned—have combined international investments and trading relationships for decades. In recent years, however, the globalized marketplace has witnessed the fragmentation of the production process and the formation of new global production and distribution networks that are tightly integrated. The rise of trade in intermediate goods and parts and components constitutes a fundamental shift in the structure of the world trading system. These transformations pose a major challenge to the businesses already operating in Africa, including Chinese- and Indian-owned, as well as those that are contemplating doing so. They also pose a challenge—and opportunity—to African policy makers in their understanding of how their countries fit into today's "international division of labor."

Under traditional notions of international trade, the direction of trade (that is, which countries produce what goods for export) was determined by the principle of "comparative advantage," and a country specialized in the production and export of the good (or goods) for which its relative productivity advantage exceeded that of foreign countries. It is clear, however, that a radically different notion of comparative advantage has now emerged due to the cross-leveraging of investment and trade flows and the significant role that intermediate goods play in overall international trade.

Technological advances in information, logistics, and production have enabled corporations to divide value chains into functions performed by foreign subsidiaries or suppliers and to become more footloose. The availability of real-time supply-chain data has allowed for the shipping for large distances not only of durable goods, but also components for just-in-time manufacturing and—important for developing countries such as those in Africa—perishable goods. The result has been the rapid growth of intra-industry trade—"network trade"—relative to the more traditional interindustry trade of final goods and services. In this environment, it is hard to imagine that the future of Africa's economic development can be isolated from these networks.

"Buyer-driven networks" are usually built without direct ownership and tend to exist in industries in which large retailers, branded marketers, and branded manufacturers play the central role in the organization of the value chain. Buyer-driven commodity chains are characterized by highly competitive, locally owned, and globally dispersed production systems. The products are typically labor-intensive consumer goods such as apparel, footwear, food, and furniture, among others. "Producer-driven networks" are often coordinated by large multinationals. They are vertical, multilayered arrangements, usually with a direct ownership structure including parents, subsidiaries, and subcontractors. They tend to be found in more capital- and technology-intensive sectors, often dominated by global oligopolies, such as automobiles, machinery, and electronics. The manufacturers control "upstream" relations with suppliers of intermediate components and "downstream" or forward links with distribution and retailing services.

New statistical analysis at the country level indicates that in both Africa and Asia there are strong complementary relationships between FDI and trade; in particular, a greater inward stock of FDI is associated with higher exports. For the African countries taken together as a group, these country-level complementarities are more muted than they are for the Asian countries. However, among non-oil-exporting African countries, the complementary effects are actually larger than they are for the Asian countries. Similar results are obtained from a comparison of FDI per GDP and exports per GDP among African countries; see figure 13.

Chinese and Indian firms operating in Africa have been playing a significant role in facilitating these linkages between FDI and trade on the African continent. Indeed, firm-level evidence on these businesses' operations from new survey data and original business case studies developed in the field shows that their trade and FDI flows are complementary activities, rather than substitutes. What gives rise to this behavior?

For one thing, Chinese and Indian businesses in Africa tend to achieve larger-sized operations than do their African counterparts within the same sectors, and this appears to allow them to realize economies of scale. Thus, it is not surprising that the evidence shows that, all other things being equal, Chinese and Indian firms have significantly greater export intensity than do African firms. Moreover, the exports from Africa produced by Chinese and Indian businesses are considerably more diversified and higher up the value chain than exports sold by domestic firms.

The corporate structures of Chinese and Indian firms also differ from those of African businesses. First, the former have more extensive participation in international group enterprises or holding companies (with headquarters in their home countries); see table 5.

FIGURE 13
African FDI and Exports are Complements

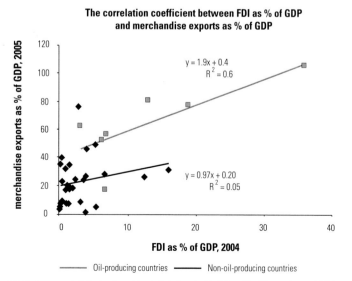

The correlation coefficient between FDI as % of GDP
and merchandise exports as % of GDP

$y = 1.9x + 0.4$
$R^2 = 0.6$

$y = 0.97x + 0.20$
$R^2 = 0.05$

merchandise exports as % of GDP, 2005

FDI as % of GDP, 2004

———— Oil-producing countries ———— Non-oil-producing countries

Source: IMF World Economic Outlook; oil countries include Angola, Chad, Republic of Congo, Equatorial Guinea, Nigeria, and Sudan.

TABLE 5

Extent of Scale and Geographic Spread: Number of Separate Firms Belonging to Holding Companies or Group Enterprises

	African	Chinese	Indian	European
Domestic	8	1	2	3
Other Africa	2	4	1	8
Outside Africa	2	16	5	58

Source: World Bank staff.

Note: Data pertain to median values.

At the same time, Chinese and Indian firms engage more extensively in regional integration on the African continent relative to African firms themselves. They also exhibit more extensive integration into a more geographically diverse set of third country markets outside of Africa than do African businesses; see table 6. These are important findings, suggesting that Chinese and Indian firms are effecting greater integration of the African economy—whether on the continent itself or into the global marketplace—than heretofore has been the case by Africa's own businesses.

There is also strong evidence that Chinese and Indian firms are vehicles for the transmission of advances in technology and skills, as well as new equipment, to the African continent. This is the classic case of spillovers in the host market that often accompany flows of FDI; see table 7.

To be sure, there are significant differences between Chinese and Indian firms operating in Africa. Chinese businesses in Africa tend to have a dif-

TABLE 6

Distribution of Output Sales by Destination Market and Firm Nationality
(percent)

Destination market	African	Chinese	Indian	European
Domestic	85	81	89	76
Other Africa	8	14	10	11
Europe	4	0	0	7
North America	1	0	0	1
India	0	0	0	0
Other South Asia	0	1	0	0
China	0	3	0	0
Other East Asia	0	0	0	2
Other	1	1	0	2

Source: World Bank staff.

Note: Data pertain to 2005 median annual sales.

TABLE 7
Purchases of New Machinery by Import Origin and Firm Nationality
(percent)

Import origin	African	Chinese	Indian	European
Domestic	55	32	15	28
Other Africa	3	1	7	12
China	6	60	13	1
India	5	0	22	2
Other	31	8	44	56

Source: World Bank staff.

Note: Data pertain to 2005 median values.

ferent risk-aversion profile than do Indian firms, as reflected in their foreign investment decisions regarding mode of entry, their degree of vertical
integration, the origin of source markets for their inputs, and the strength
of affiliation with state (as opposed to private) entities in conducting transactions, among other attributes. Chinese businesses in Africa pursue business strategies that yield them greater control up and down the production
chain, resulting in enclave types of corporate profiles, with more limited
spillover effects. Indian firms, conversely, pursue African investment
strategies that result in greater integration into domestic markets and operate extensively through informal channels, indeed even into facets of the
local political economy, surely a result of the fact that there is a longer tradition of Indian ethnic ties to Africa[11] (see tables 8 and 9).

Global value chains offer real opportunities for African countries to use
Chinese and Indian investment and trade activities to increase the volume,
diversity, and value-added of exports from the continent; see table 10.
Indeed, as has happened elsewhere in the world to developing countries
and economies making the transition from central planning to capitalism,
even landlocked countries in Africa—with the right mix of policies—may
well engage in network trade.[12]

Detailed value chain analysis of industry cases in Africa shows that
certain factors are likely to be especially critical for African businesses
wanting to successfully engage in network trade. These include implementing pricing schemes that fully take into account market conditions;
taking steps to enhance product quality, for example, through ISO certification; organizing lines of business to be as flexible and as responsive as
possible to changes in demand and supply; developing the capacity to

TABLE 8
Distribution of Material Input Purchases by Origin Market and Firm Nationality
(percent)

Origin market	African	Chinese	Indian	European
Domestic	60	31	27	40
Other Africa	7	4	9	9
Europe	13	1	13	34
North America	3	5	1	6
India	5	2	26	3
Other South Asia	3	1	4	1
China	4	55	7	3
Other East Asia	2	1	3	3
Other	2	0	11	1

Source: World Bank staff.

Note: Data pertain to 2005 median annual purchases.

TABLE 9
Extent of Vertical Integration by Firm Nationality
(percent)

Indicator	African	Chinese	Indian	European
Output sales to parent firm or affiliate	9	19	0	14
Input purchases from parent firm or affiliate	3	23	9	15

Source: World Bank staff.

Note: Data pertain to 2005 median values.

TABLE 10
Extent of Value-Added in Output Sales and Exports, by Destination Market and Firm Nationality
(percent)

Destination market	Product	Firm nationality			
		African	Chinese	Indian	European
Domestic sales	Finished assembled	88	90	90	89
	Partially finished	5	9	4	4
	Raw material	6	0	5	6
Sales to other	Finished assembled	83	89	100	78
African countries	Partially finished	8	11	0	15
	Raw material	9	0	0	7
Export sales	Finished assembled	77	75	100	90
outside of Africa	Partially finished	10	25	0	10
	Raw material	13	0	0	0

Source: World Bank staff.

Note: Pertains to sales to private firms. Data pertain to 2005 median values.

maximize speed to market; and working to enhance labor productivity through fostering skills and technology transfers as well as requiring training.

There are several industries in Africa that have either already engaged in or have strong prospects for engaging in buyer-driven network trade, including food, fresh-cut flowers, apparel, and fisheries, among others. These are all products where African exports face far tougher competition in international markets than do the continent's traditional raw commodities, and they must meet world-class standards. The prospects for African industries engaging in producer-driven network trade in the short to medium run are far more limited—without implementing concrete and economywide reforms that will attract substantial FDI by international firms plugged into such networks. There are some exceptions, however, such as South Africa's automotive assembly and parts and components industry, a sector in which Chinese and Indian multinational firms are rapidly participating.

There is evidence of significant opportunities for greater African participation in network trade in services exports. And these can engender significant supply chain spillover effects domestically, as well. One possible area is outsourcing and back-office services, such as those already being implemented in Ghana, Senegal, and Tanzania, among others. This is especially relevant to India in light of the commonality of language.

A second concrete opportunity for growth in services network exports is tourism. With rising middle classes in China and India looking to spend a significant part of their increased disposable incomes on holidays, there is clear potential for Africa to reap the benefits. Through positioning itself as a relatively close and attractive holiday destination, the gain for Sub-Saharan Africa would not just be direct (in tourism services, hotels, restaurants, and the like) but also indirect: the fact that more and more flights arrived in African airports would make transport cheaper and Asian markets more readily accessible for African goods and services.

In the main, opportunities are offered by trade in global supply chains, although few African countries have been able to make the leap and exploit these opportunities. To take but one example, India's large exports of diamonds are in part based on the polishing and cutting of unfinished diamonds imported from Africa. Yet the higher value-added process of diamond finishing could well be retained in Africa, possibly by inviting Indian investment.

Investment and trade by China and India could facilitate the African continent's ability to avail itself of such opportunities. Indeed, Africa's rapid export growth to China and India could contribute even more to Africa's export diversification, in terms of products and trading partners, than has already been the case. The strong and intensifying complementarities between the two regions provide African countries with increased opportunities to use FDI and trade flows from China and India to help boost domestic growth by increasing participation in global network trade in nontraditional exports; by developing value-added, local industries through deepening forward and backward linkages to resource-based products; and by enhancing regional economic integration.

If the African continent is to effectively take advantage of the opportunities afforded by China and India's already sizable and growing commercial interests in Africa, it will have to successfully leverage this newfound interest and be a more proactive player in global network trade. Elsewhere in the world, countries' differential performance in terms of network trade can be attributed to the large variation in the amount of FDI received.

FDI inflows are largely determined not only by traditional macropolitical and macroeconomic factors, but also by the quality of the *underlying* domestic business climate and related institutional conditions, both within individual countries and on a regional basis. Thus, the focus of reforms to enhance participation in network trade should be on a set of factors that shape a country's microeconomic fabric at a *deeper* level beyond that touched by the reform of so-called administrative barriers—such as speeding up the pace of business registration or of obtaining a business license—which has become in the conventional wisdom the way in which improvement in the investment climate comes about.

To be sure, there have been visible efforts taken by several African governments in reforming their domestic business environments. However, African countries overall still lag behind other regions with whom they are competing, both in terms of attracting investment and in exporting to foreign markets.

Conclusions and Policy Implications

Market opportunities for trade and investment in the world economy will no doubt continue to grow for the countries of Sub-Saharan Africa. However, as the international economy continues to globalize, market competition from other regions—especially those in the South—will only become stronger. This poses a challenge to African policy makers to make better use of international trade and investment as levers for growth.

China and India's rapidly growing commerce with the African continent presents to its people a major opportunity. In particular, the intense interest by these two Asian economic giants to pursue commercial relations with Africa could lead to greater diversification of Africa's exports away from excessive reliance on a few commodities and toward increased production of labor-intensive light manufactured goods and services. It could also enable Africa to build on the strength of its endowment of natural resources and develop backward and forward linkages to extract more value from processing, and in some cases participate in modern global production-sharing networks. This intense interest could also lead to enhanced efficiency of African businesses through their being more exposed to foreign competition, advances in technology, and modern labor skills; and to greater international integration, not only with other regions of the world, but perhaps most important *within* Africa itself, where most domestic markets are too shallow and small to allow for the scale needed to produce exports that are internationally competitive.

To be sure, there are major imbalances in the current commercial relationships that Africa has with China and India. For example, whereas China and India are emerging as increasingly important destination markets for African exports, from the perspective of these Asian countries, imports from Africa represent only a very small fraction of their global imports. At the same time, FDI inflows to Africa from China and India, although still small in an absolute sense, are growing rapidly. But both the level and growth rate of African FDI going to China and India remains extremely limited.

Absent certain policy reforms, the opportunities presented by China and India's interest in Africa may not be fully realized, while the existing imbalances could continue for the foreseeable future. All other things equal, taken together, these could reduce the likelihood of a boost in Africa's prospects for economic growth and prosperity.

The reform experience in Africa, as well as in other regions of the world, shows that reform success in such an environment requires a *combination* of actions. In particular, the lessons from these experiences are that it is not only important to implement sound, market-based, at-the-border trade

and investment policies, but also to take actions that deal with the impediments to trade and investment that exist behind the border as well as
between the borders. Indeed, these experiences suggest that, if anything,
behind-the-border and between-the-border reforms actually provide for
trade to have greater leverage on growth than do at-the-border formal
trade and investment policies. Moreover, the evidence suggests that these
reforms should be designed in such a way as to exploit the growth-
enhancing complementarities between trade and investment.

The study of which this *Overview* is a part discusses such policy implications based on the empirical findings presented. Below, the principal policy implications that deserve priority attention are summarized. A "division
of labor" for the responsibilities of the various stakeholders with policy-
making roles in furthering Africa-Asian trade and investment is also
suggested.

It is important to emphasize that, because of the significant heterogeneity among the 47 countries of Sub-Saharan Africa, the enunciated policy
reforms should *not* be interpreted as being "one-size-fits-all" actions.
Indeed, in practice, the reforms must be designed to take into account
country-specific circumstances. These circumstances will affect not only
the actual contours of actions to be taken, but also the speed and sequenc-
ing of their implementation.

Summary of Policy Implications

In view of the fact that reforms of formal trade and investment policies
have long been the starting point of negotiations on international commercial relations, the discussion here focuses on them first. However, following this convention should not be interpreted as assigning greater
importance to these reforms relative to those pertaining to behind-the-
border and between-the-border factors and to capitalizing on FDI-trade
linkages. As noted, the contrary is more likely to be the case.

At-the-Border Formal Policy Reforms
Various elements of the policy regimes governing trade and investment
between Africa and Asia are driven by traditional protectionist motives. If
Africa is to take full advantage of trade and investment opportunities with
Asia, especially those arising with China and India, a number of reforms to
these policies will be important.

- For all countries: Lowering the level of tariffs overall. Ideally, this should be done on an MFN basis in the context of WTO negotiations. Should the currently suspended Doha Round terminate, consideration might be given to a pan-Asian-pan-African FTA, but doing so only in a WTO-consistent manner and ensuring that opportunities for "trade diversion" are minimized.

- For China and India: Eliminating the numerous escalating tariffs that limit Africa's leading exports from entering their markets at competitive prices.

- For most African countries: Mitigating elements of the trade policy regime, such as tariffs on imports of certain material inputs, which serve to impart a bias toward exports. Reforms are also needed to reduce the bias in investment decisions across sectors and reduce disincentives for greater product diversification.

- For most African countries, as well as China and India: Eliminating nontariff barriers (NTBs), including not only quotas, but use of technical standards and similar instruments as protectionist measures.

- Primarily for African countries: Rationalizing and harmonizing existing bilateral and regional agreements. The current "spaghetti bowl" of intra-African regional trade agreements provides little, if any, incentive for new trade and investment; in some cases they appear to be more "trade-diverting" than "trade-creating."

- For African countries: Strengthening the role of IPAs and public-private investors' councils to proactively promote FDI opportunities and eliminate bottlenecks for foreign investors interested in African-Asian investment opportunities.

- Primarily for African countries: Based on the experiences of the "East Asian Miracle" countries over the last several decades, there is a legitimate role for using export and investment incentives. But as the evidence shows, use of these incentives must be tailored to country-specific circumstances and even then they entail risks, especially where the requisite institutional and governance capacities do not exist. Such incentives also must be implemented in concert with existing WTO rules.

Beyond Formal Trade and Investment Policy Reforms

Reforms of formal trade and investment policies in both Africa and Asia are certainly necessary to further facilitate the flows of African-Asian commerce and to enlarge the benefits that such commerce brings—and can bring—to both regions. However, they are not sufficient. While high Asian tariffs, for example, clearly curb and shape the contours of African exports to Asia, inefficiencies, distortions, weak market institutions, and lack of competitive productive capacity in Africa appear to be equally if not more critical in limiting the export penetration in Asian markets by African businesses. Thus, even if China and India were to immediately provide open and full market access to African producers, the intended outcomes probably would only materialize if certain reform actions were taken by African policy makers. Indeed, reforms that ameliorate both behind-the-border and between-the-border impediments to African-Asian commerce and that foster the exploitation of complementarities between investment and trade flows so that they leverage one another, would be needed.

BEHIND-THE-BORDER REFORMS

• Primarily for all African countries: Governments should work toward enhancing domestic interenterprise competition by eliminating fundamental economic and policy barriers to new business entry.

• Primarily for all African countries: Barriers to exit of commercially nonviable firms also need to be eliminated to enhance domestic competition, through reducing subsidies and eliminating the practice of tolerating arrears (with the government, banks, and among firms).

• Primarily for all African countries: Sound governance will also require mechanisms to ensure greater transparency and accountability of public officials' conduct. Improving governance will also require efficient institutions that facilitate effective resolution of commercial disputes. Policies for the simplification and cost reduction of formal legal procedures as well as bolstering out-of-court mechanisms will strengthen contract sanctity and property rights and improve the level of investor confidence.

• All African countries: To reduce poverty impacts from changes in prices and outputs engendered by trade flows, measures should be implemented to promote labor mobility (for example, enhancing wage differentiation and adaptability and improving the effectiveness of social safety nets).

BETWEEN-THE-BORDER REFORMS

- Primarily for all African countries: Further development of trade facilitation infrastructure, including improvement and modernization of ports, road, and rail transport, and telecommunications and information technology (IT) capacity. These will foster not only Africa's further integration into the global marketplace, but also regional integration *within* Africa itself. Meeting this challenge will require continued privatization or private-public partnerships to entice new investments.

- Primarily for all African countries: In customs, the priority reforms are to improve coordination among border-related agencies, both in countries and across countries; simplify customs procedures; make customs codes and associated regulations rules-based, transparent, and commercially oriented, with proper incentives for employees; and introduce the use of IT into customs systems.

- Most African countries: Addressing imperfections in the "information market for trade and investment opportunities." Among other measures, this would include adopting international production technical standards, such as those certified by the ISO.

- Primarily for all African countries: Reviewing measures that restrict the movement of professionals (Mode IV reforms) so as to foster transfers of modern skills and technology.

REFORMS FOR ENHANCING FDI-TRADE COMPLEMENTARITIES AND PARTICIPATION BY AFRICAN FIRMS IN NETWORK TRADE

- Most African countries: Bringing the regime governing FDI in line with international best practices so as to attract modern multinational corporate investment and global production- network trade. Typically this would include (i) adhering to "national treatment" for foreign investors; (ii) prohibiting the imposition of new, and the phasing out of existing, trade-related investment measures (TRIMs), for example, local content measures; and (iii) providing for binding international arbitration for investor-state disputes. However, the practical design of these reforms should be tailored to country-specific circumstances. Moreover, it may be desirable to phase in some measures over a longer time than others.

- All African countries: Deregulating services should be the rule rather than the exception, and should include the implementation of market-reinforcing reforms of regulatory procedures and rules, including rate levels and structures. Of course, certain African countries, such as South Africa, are more advanced on this score than are others.

- All African countries: Enhancing flexibility in capital markets so that resources can respond more efficiently to changes in market forces.

- All African countries: Strengthening training and secondary and post-secondary educational programs for workers and managers.

Division of Labor among Policy Makers

International Community (Donors and International Organizations)

- Most, if not all, countries in Sub-Saharan Africa are in need of technical assistance (TA) and capacity building to strengthen trade-related institutions and policy implementation and management. Priority areas of focus for such TA would be in "aid-for-trade" issues, such as trade facilitation, technical standards, and improving customs regimes; harmonization of regional trade agreements; WTO accession (for current nonmembers); and governance reform.

African, Chinese, and Indian Governments

- Much of the reform agenda will largely depend on the implementation efforts of the countries themselves.

- Arguably, the most challenging of such tasks will be the vigorous implementation of economywide behind-the-border and between-the-border reforms, as well as reforms to leverage the complementarities between trade and FDI. These would involve actions to enhance competition in domestic markets and foster greater flexibility in labor markets; improve trade facilitation mechanisms; liberalize the services sectors and reform of associated regulation; and improve the climate to attract FDI.

- In the area of trade policy, actions would include tariff reductions; elimination of escalated tariffs; termination of NTBs; removal of disincentives to exporting; pursuit of WTO accession; and rationalization, harmonization, and modernization of existing regional trade agreements.

Endnotes

1. UNCTAD has estimated that South-South trade accounts for about 11 percent of global trade and that 43 percent of the South's trade is with other developing countries. It also has estimated that South-South trade is growing about 10 percent per year. "A Silent Revolution in South-South Trade," WTO (2004) http://www.wto.org/english/tratop_e/dda_e/symp04_paper7_e.doc.
2. Throughout this study, "Africa" refers to the countries of Sub-Saharan Africa.
3. Between 2000 and 2005, the share of Africa's exports destined for the EU was reduced by almost one-half-from 50 percent to 27percent. Data for 2000 are from World Bank (2004). Data for 2005 are from IMF Direction of Trade Statistics ("IMF DOT"); for details see chapter 2.
4. IMF DOT.
5. UNCTAD 2006.
6. UNCTAD 2005b.
7. The new survey is referred to as WBAATI (World Bank African-Asian Trade and Investment) survey.
8. http://www.fmprc.gov.cn/eng/zxxx/t230615.htm
9. See Broadman (2005).
10. Eisenman and Kurlantzick 2006.
11. This finding of greater integration into African host markets by Indian firms is consistent with the evidence presented earlier regarding the ethnicity and nationality of managers.
12. See Broadman (2005).

CHAPTER 1

Connecting Two Continents

Historical Context

The acceleration of trade and investment *among* developing countries is one of the most significant features of recent events in the global economy. For decades, world trade has been dominated by commerce both among developed countries—the North—and between the North and developing countries—the South.[1] A striking hallmark of the new trend in South-South commercial relations is the massive increase in trade and investment flows between Africa[2] and Asia, especially since 2000. Today, Asia receives about 27 percent of Africa's exports, in contrast to only about 14 percent in 2000. This volume of trade is now on par with Africa's exports to the United States, and only slightly below those to the European Union (EU)—Africa's traditional trading partners; in fact, the EU's share of African exports has halved over the 2000–05 period.[3] Asia's exports to Africa also are growing very rapidly—at about 18 percent per year—higher than those to any other region.[4] At the same time, although the volume of foreign direct investment (FDI) between Africa and Asia is more modest than that of trade—and Sub-Saharan Africa accounts for only 1.8 percent of global FDI inflows[5]—African-Asian FDI is growing at a tremendous rate. This is especially true of Asian FDI in Africa.[6]

The two emerging economic "giants" of Asia's developing countries, China and India, are at the center of this explosion of African-Asian trade and investment. Both nations have centuries-long histories of international commerce, dating back to at least the days of the Silk Road, where merchants plied goods traversing continents, reaching the most challenging and relatively untouched markets of the day. In contemporary times, Chinese trade and investment with Africa actually dates back several decades, with most of the early investments made in infrastructure sectors, such as railways, at the start of Africa's postcolonial era. India, too, has a long history of trade and investment with modern-day Africa, particularly in East Africa, where there are significant expatriate Indian communities. However, the scale and pace of China and India's current trade and investment flows with Africa are wholly unprecedented.

China and India each have rapidly modernizing industries and burgeoning middle classes with rising incomes and purchasing power. The result is growing demand not only for natural resource–extractive commodities, agricultural goods such as cotton, and other traditional African exports, but also more diversified, nontraditional exports, such as light manufactured products, household consumer goods, processed food, and tourism. By virtue of its labor-intensive capacity, Africa has the potential to export these nontraditional goods and services competitively to the average Chinese and Indian consumer and firm.

With regard to investment, much of the accumulated stock of Chinese and Indian FDI in Africa is concentrated in extractive sectors, such as oil and mining. While this has been grabbing most of the media headlines, greater diversification of these countries' FDI flows to Africa has in fact been occurring more recently. Significant Chinese and Indian investments on the African continent have been made in apparel, food processing, retail ventures, fisheries, commercial real estate and transport construction, tourism, power plants, and telecommunications, among other sectors. Moreover, some of these investments are propelling African trade into cutting-edge multinational corporate networks, which are increasingly altering the "international division of labor." China and India are pursuing commercial strategies with Africa that are about far more than resources.

Despite the immense growth in trade and investment between the two regions, there are significant asymmetries. While Asia accounts for one-quarter of Africa's global exports, this trade represents only about 1.6 percent of the exports shipped to Asia from all sources worldwide. By the same token, FDI in Asia by African firms is extremely small, both in absolute and relative terms. At the same time, the rise of internationally competitive Chinese and Indian businesses has displaced domestic sales as well as exports by African producers, whether through investments by Chinese and Indian entrepreneurs on the Sub-Saharan continent or through exports from their home markets.

Nevertheless, these two prodigious countries' newfound interest in substantial international commerce with Africa—home to 300 million of the globe's poorest people and the world's most formidable development challenge—presents a significant, and in modern times, rare, opportunity for growth, job creation, and the reduction of poverty on the Sub-Saharan continent.

Against this backdrop, there is intense interest by policy makers and businesses—in both Africa and Asia—as well as by international development partners, to better understand the evolution and the developmental, commercial, and policy implications of African-Asian trade and investment relations. This interest is reflected, perhaps most notably, in the South-South discussions held during the African-Asian summit in Jakarta in April 2005 celebrating the fiftieth anniversary of the Bandung Declaration, where the dramatic rise in international commerce between the two regions figured prominently, as well as at the July 2005 G-8 summit in Gleneagles, where the leaders of the North underscored the growing importance of South-South trade and investment flows, especially as they pertain to the prospects for fostering growth and poverty reduction in Africa.

Yet despite the sizeable—and rapidly escalating—attention devoted to this topic, especially by some of the world's most senior officials, there is, surprisingly, a paucity of systematic data available on these issues to carry out rigorous analysis, and from which inferences of a similar caliber could be drawn to meet the interest and provide the desired understanding. The vast majority of accessible information is based on anecdotes or piecemeal datasets, which make a well-informed assessment difficult to generate. This study helps fill these gaps.

Scope and Methodology of the Study

As the global marketplace continues to be increasingly integrated, with rapidly changing notions of comparative advantage, much is at stake for the economic welfare of hundreds of millions of people in Sub-Saharan Africa. With this newest phase in the evolution of world trade and investment flows taking root—the increasing emergence of South-South international commerce, with China and India poised to take the lead—Africans cannot afford to be left behind, especially if growth-enhancing opportunities for trade and investment with the North continue to be as limited as they have been. Nor can the rest of the world, including Africa's international development partners, afford to allow Africans to be unable to genuinely participate in—and most important, benefit from—the new patterns of international commerce.

Scope of the Study

Addressing these challenges raises several questions that this study seeks to answer:

- *What* has been the recent evolution of the pattern and performance of trade and investment flows between Africa and Asia, especially China and India, and *which* factors are likely to significantly condition those flows in the future?

- *What* have been the most important impacts on Africa of its trade and investment relations with China and India, and *what* actions can be taken to help shape these impacts to enhance Africa's economic development prospects?

In focusing on these questions the study examines four categories of key factors that are likely to significantly affect trade and investment between Africa and Asia:

- *"At-the-border" trade and investment policies*, including policies affecting market access (tariffs and nontariff barriers (NTBs)); FDI policy regimes; and bilateral, regional, and multilateral trade agreements;

- *"Behind-the-border" (domestic) market conditions*, including the nature of the business environment; competitiveness of market structures; quality of market institutions; and supply constraints, such as poor infrastructure and underdeveloped human capital and skills;

- *"Between-the-border" factors*, including the development of cross-border trade-facilitating logistical and transport regimes; quantity and quality of information about overseas market opportunities, including through expatriates and the ethnic diasporas; impacts of technical standards; and the role of migration;

- *Complementarities between investment and trade*, including the extent to which investment and trade flows leverage one another; the effects of such complementarities on scale of production and ability of firms to integrate across markets; participation in global production networks and value chains; and spillover effects of transfers of technology.

The first set of factors typically has been presumed to be dominant in affecting trade and investment relations between Africa and Asia. This study posits that the effects of formal trade and investment policies are likely to be of equal, if not secondary, importance compared to the latter three sets of factors. Thus, it is hypothesized that behind-the-border and between-the-border conditions, as well as the interactions between investment and trade flows, are the major elements that influence the extent, nature, and effects of Africa's international commerce with China and India, and therefore these are the areas on which the priority for policy reforms likely should be placed.

The assessment undertaken in this study is largely economic in nature. In this regard, the analysis focuses on political economy, governance, and institutional issues insofar as they directly have economic implications. Important as those issues are, however, the intention here is not to focus on them per se; they are topics deserving of separate, dedicated study.

Moreover, the study's prism is largely on the impacts on Africa of China and India's trade and investment flows with that continent, rather than the reverse. To be sure, the analysis does cover lessons that can be drawn from Asia's economic success stories that might be applicable for Africa. But a focus on the implications of African-Asian trade for China and India is beyond the scope of the study.

Finally, Sub-Saharan Africa is not a country: it is a very heterogeneous continent comprising 47 nations with great variations in physical, economic, political, and social dimensions. The bulk of the analysis focuses on those African countries for which new data have been collected specifically for this study, or for which there are systematic data from which economically meaningful analysis, including cross-country comparisons, can be made. The countries that are the subject of the analysis were chosen to be somewhat representative of the continent, but there is no pretense that the study's findings are necessarily applicable to all African countries.

Methodology

To overcome the deficit in the quality and coverage of currently available data, the study makes use of a new database assembled in 2006 for this analysis. Specifically, micro data from a new firm-level quantitative survey and from an original set of individual qualitative business case studies are utilized. These are supplemented by official government statistics at the aggregate level, along with existing firm-level data from Investment Climate Assessments (ICAs). Annex 1A describes in detail the databases utilized. Information from qualitative Diagnostic Trade Integration Studies (DTISs) on 26 African countries carried out under the Integrated Framework (IF) for Trade-Related Technical Assistance was also utilized; see annex 1B for a description of DTISs.

Briefly, the new firm-level survey covers just under 450 businesses operating in Africa having varying degrees of involvement with Chinese and Indian investors, of different sizes and ownership forms, and located in four countries: Ghana, Senegal, South Africa, and Tanzania. The surveys were carried out on a confidential basis; that is, all individual firms' identities have been blinded and they are not revealed in the analysis. The new business case studies were developed in the field, again, on a confidential basis, using 16 firms located in the same four countries.[7] As in the surveyed firms, the firms on which the business case studies were developed have varying degrees of involvement with Chinese and Indian investors, as well as differences in size and ownership form.

The firms covered by the survey and the business case studies are drawn from a consistent set of a variety of sectors in each country, except for the petroleum and petroleum-related sector.[8] Any such firms were excluded in light of the disproportionately large scale of investment required in the sector, which would introduce a significant bias to the data analysis; at the same time, while there is much more known—and understood—about what is driving Chinese and Indian investment and trade in the African petroleum sector, the determinants and effects of these countries' commercial involvement in other sectors is much less appreciated.

Structure of the Study

The core of the study comprises of chapters 2–6. The following pages summarize the focus of each of these chapters' analysis.

Chapter 2: Performance and Patterns of African-Asian Trade and Investment Flows

Chapter 2 systematically documents and assesses regional and national patterns of trade and investment flows between Africa and Asia, with a focus on the roles of China and India. The analysis covers not only historical trends, but also emerging patterns and the contours they will likely take in the medium run. The chapter also quantitatively examines the main determinants of country-level, bilateral African-Asian trade performance. In general, African trade and investment flows with the EU and the United States—the continent's traditional trading partners—are included as comparator cases in the chapter's analysis.

The descriptive analysis focuses on flows of merchandise trade and investment, and, where possible, trade and investment in services. Trade flows are examined according to geography (in terms of origin and destination markets), sector composition, extent of product diversification, and level of processing. Sectoral and geographic concentration are measured using the Herfindahl-Hirschman Index. For FDI flows, bilateral data are more scarce with regard to origin and destination markets ("home" and "host" countries, respectively), as well as on sectoral composition; as a result, in general, the focus is on FDI flows in the aggregate. There are cases, however, where China has more detailed FDI data and thus these receive more in-depth analysis.

A set of gravity models based on bilateral trade flows is estimated to investigate quantitatively the factors that seem to best explain observed differences in the patterns of trade between Africa and Asia. The analysis focuses on the comparative roles in country-by-country trade performance of "at-the-border" formal trade policies, elements of the "behind-the-border" business environment and related institutions, and the extent of "between-the-border" trade facilitation and logistics constraints. The gravity models are then extended to consider the nature of any linkages that may exist between trade and inward FDI.

To set the stage for subsequent chapters, chapter 2 concludes by positing which elements are likely to enhance African-Asian trade and investment flows and help such flows leverage growth in Africa.

Chapter 3: Challenges at the Border: Africa and Asia's Trade and Investment Policies

This chapter assesses the role that "at-the-border" policy regimes play in affecting the extent and nature of trade and investment flows between Africa and Asia, especially China and India. The analysis focuses on market access conditions, including tariffs and nontariff barriers (NTBs); export and investment incentives offered by governments; and bilateral, regional, and multilateral agreements. If Africa is to take full advantage of trade and investment opportunities with Asia, reforms of such policies—by all parties—will be important. There are also valuable lessons that Africa can learn from Asia's experience in trade and investment policies over the past several decades.

The analysis begins with an examination of trade policy regimes in Africa and Asia. An assessment of tariffs that African exporters face in China and India, and that Asian exporters face in Africa, is carried out at both the regional and country levels, as well as on a product-specific basis. The incidence of nontariff barriers in African-Asian trade is also examined. Finally, the role of various export incentive regimes operating in the two regions is assessed.

The discussion then turns to an examination of policy instruments used to influence FDI in Africa as well as in China and India. Various incentive schemes are appraised, as are the use of investment promotion agencies and public-private forums whose objectives are to facilitate FDI flows.

An appraisal of various trade and investment agreements and treaties involving African and Asian countries is then made. The analysis focuses on the impacts of existing bilateral, regional, and multilateral arrangements and discusses new arrangements being contemplated.

The chapter ends by drawing conclusions and discussing policy implications.

Chapter 4: Behind-the-Border Constraints on African-Asian Trade and Investment Flows

This chapter explores how "behind-the-border" conditions in Africa affect the continent's trade and investment flows with Asia, especially

China and India. Unlike chapters 2 and 3, where country-level (or sector-level) data were used, in this chapter, as well as in chapters 5 and 6, the analysis is largely based on firm-level data from the new World Bank Africa-Asia Trade and Investment survey (WBAATI survey) and business case studies, as well as existing Investment Climate Assessments (ICAs) and Doing Business data of the World Bank Group. As such, the primary units of analysis are firms operating in Africa, whether of African, Chinese, or Indian origin (firms of other nationalities are also included as comparators). In addition, the examination focuses primarily on four Sub-Saharan African countries that have significant trade and investment ties with China and India and that were covered by the WBAATI survey and business case studies: Ghana, Senegal, South Africa, and Tanzania.

The basic diagnostics of behind-the-border conditions are first evaluated through the performance of the surveyed firms—in terms of productivity and export performance. These characteristics are compared across sectors, nationality, size, and ownership structure (domestic, joint venture, and foreign-owned).

An assessment of the sources of competition in these African markets is then conducted, first at the country level and then by differentiating among nationalities, with a particular focus on Chinese and Indian firms operating in Africa. At the country level, the assessment looks at various mechanisms through which competition is spurred or constrained. These include foreign import competition, market entry and exit, FDI, vertical dimensions of competition, and transactions with the state. At the nationality level, the chapter discusses whether Chinese and Indian investors play any significant role in fostering domestic competition in African markets or in fostering international integration of Africa's private sector.

In light of the importance that domestic competition appears to play in leveraging the beneficial effects of Chinese and Indian trade and investment in these African markets, the analysis examines the principal behind-the-border factors that are most likely constraining such competition. The discussion focuses on (i) quality of infrastructure services (power supply, telephone services, and Internet access); (ii) factor markets (access to finance, labor market, and skilled labor); (iii) regulatory regimes; and (iv) governance disciplines. The chapter closes with conclusions and a discussion of policy implications.

Chapter 5: Between-the-Border Factors in African-Asian Trade and Investment

This chapter assesses the nature and extent of "between-the-border" barriers to African-Asian trade and investment. It also analyzes a variety of ways that the transactions costs of international trade and investment can be reduced.

The discussion first focuses on the fact that foreign market information on potential demand and investment opportunities is essential in facilitating trade and investment between Africa and Asia. Four mechanisms to reduce asymmetric information are discussed: (i) the role of institutional providers of export market information, such as export promotion agencies; (ii) the role of institutional providers of foreign investment information, such as investment promotion agencies; (iii) the role of technical standards in bridging information gaps; and (iv) the role of ethnic networks and the diaspora in facilitating information flows.

The analysis also discusses how flows of technology and people between Africa and Asia facilitate the formation of business links, which then lead to trade and FDI flows. An emerging agenda for African firms is how to effectively capture opportunities for the acquisition of advances in technology and skills through participating in the international production networks, as discussed in the next chapter.

The analysis concludes with a discussion of the policy implications from the analysis concerning the alleviation of between-the-border constraints.

Chapter 6: Investment-Trade Linkages: Scale, Integration, and Production Networks

This chapter is premised on the fact that the increasing globalization of the world economy and the fragmentation of production processes have changed the economic landscape facing the nations, industries, and individual firms in Sub-Saharan Africa, as they have in China and India—indeed, throughout much of the rest of the world. Firms engaging in trade of intermediate goods (or services) through FDI have been key agents in this transformation. Exploiting the complementarities between FDI and trade, they have created international production and distribution networks spanning the globe and actively interacting with each other. The result has been the rapid growth of *intraindustry* trade—"network trade"—

relative to the more traditional *interindustry* trade of final goods and services.

The chapter assesses the extent to which African countries are involved in network trade centered around or linked to large foreign investors, especially those from China and India. Using new firm-level data from both the WBAATI survey and the business case studies of Chinese and Indian firms in Africa, the analysis details empirically the ways in which firms operating in Africa link investment and trade activities and the implications of these linkages. The assessment focuses on the economic effects of the scale of business operations (for example, economies of scale), vertical integration, and horizontal integration across the African continent (regional integration). The analysis also examines where opportunities for network trade might exist in Sub-Saharan Africa by assessing the characteristics of select country-level industry value chains and comparing their performance with that of direct international competitors.

In addition, and equally important from the perspective of furthering economic development and growth *within* Africa, the chapter examines how the linkages between FDI and trade among Chinese and Indian firms involved in Africa create the possibility for positive "spillovers" on the continent—through the attraction of investment for infrastructure and related services development and through the transfer of advances in technology and managerial skills, which are often the intangible assets that accompany FDI.

If the African continent is to effectively take advantage of the opportunities afforded by the already sizable and growing commercial interest in Africa of China, India, and other economies, it will have to successfully leverage this newfound interest and be a more proactive player in global network trade. This calls for African leaders to pursue certain policy reforms. To this end, the last section of the chapter discusses such policy implications.

Annex 1A
Data Sources

To analyze the determinants and consequences of trade and investment patterns between Africa and Asia with an emphasis on China and India, the study relies on data from several sources. First, data from official sources are used. Second, extensive use is made of originally developed qualitative business case studies of firms in four countries in Sub-Saharan Africa where Asian trade and investment activity (involving China and India) is relatively significant—Ghana, Senegal, South Africa, and Tanzania. Third, data are analyzed from a new firm-level quantitative survey—the World Bank Africa-Asia Trade and Investment (WBAATI) survey. Finally, data from existing World Bank firm-level Investment Climate Surveys are also utilized in the analysis.

Official Statistics

The bilateral trade and FDI data employed in the study, used in the descriptive analysis of the current patterns of trade and investment flows, are drawn from UN COMTRADE, IMF Direction of Trade Statistics, and official government sources such as the Ministry of Finance. The gravity model regressions evaluating the impact of formal trade, constraints between the borders, and behind-the-border policies are also conducted using UN COMTRADE. For data related to trade in commercial services, IMF balance of payments statistics are used. To analyze the extent to which tariff and nontariff barriers in Asian countries affect African export performance in Asian markets and vice versa, the UN TRAINS is used.

Analysis of trade and investment ties between China and India, and Africa, based solely on official statistics could not adequately put forward recommendations that could be implemented to strengthen Asian-African trade and investment flows so as to enhance Africa's economic development prospects. To minimize the risk of being superfluous and single-sighted, the study employs two additional instruments for information: a set of original enterprise-level case studies and the firm-level WBAATI Survey. Both instruments cover the four countries of focus in Africa.

Firm-Level World Bank–Developed Business Case Studies

Sixteen original in-depth business case studies (BCSs)—four enterprises in each of four countries (Ghana, Senegal, South Africa, and Tanzania)—were developed based on extensive field interviews conducted by World Bank headquarters staff in May 2006. To achieve intra- and intercountry comparisons, the selection of the businesses was systematically based on a set of specific criteria such as firm size, sectoral representation, direction of trade, and enterprise ownership structure.

Half of the firms interviewed are domestically owned; the other half are either fully or partially Chinese and Indian invested. Firms were selected from sectors that not only had relative economic importance in Sub-Saharan Africa, but that also allowed for diversity of firms in each country with common characteristics across the countries. The business case studies were conducted in the agroindustry, textiles, construction, and general manufacturing industries.

Table 1A.1 summarizes the sectors and characteristics of the BCSs developed in the four countries.

New Firm-Level World Bank Quantitative Survey (WBATTI Survey)

In addition to the qualitative business case studies, the methodological approach of the study includes the use of data from a new firm-level quantitative survey instrument developed by the World Bank. The WBAATI survey was conducted in the spring and summer of 2006 in the same group of African countries as those used for development of the business case studies. The survey covered 447 firms, including firms that have actual trade and investment ties with China or India or both. The new survey instrument comprises quantitative questions somewhat similar to some of

TABLE 1A.1
Firm-Level Business Case Studies
(number of interviewed firms)

Sectors	Origin of main owner			Size			Main markets		
	Domestic	Chinese	Indian	Small	Medium	Large	Foreign	Domestic	Both
Agroindustry	1	1	2	1	0	3	1	2	1
Textiles	3	0	0	1	2	0	0	1	2
Construction	2	2	0	0	1	3	0	2	2
Manufacturing	1	1	2	1	2	1	0	1	3

Note: Sixteen companies were interviewed in May 2006 in Ghana, Senegal, South Africa, and Tanzania. By agreement, the specific identities of the firms are confidential.

those in the World Bank's Investment Climate Surveys (see below), but focuses in much greater detail on certain topics, especially the extent and nature of competition, network trade, specific attributes of FDI, and ethnicity.

The surveyed enterprises were drawn from *manufacturing* sectors, such as minerals and metals, agriculture, textiles, and chemicals; in addition, firms from the construction and other *services* sectors were also included. The minerals sector *excluded firms in oil-related activities* due to the dominant share that oil holds in Africa's exports and to avoid the biased effects such firms' inclusion would have had on the analysis. The surveyed companies differ also in terms of age and ownership; the majority of the surveyed firms are small and medium, with more than 30 percent foreign ownership representation. Among the respondent firms, there are representatives of state-owned, privatized, and startup firms, and also joint ventures. All of the firms surveyed were located either in the capital cities or the largest business cities of each country. Tables 1A.2 and 1A.3 summarize the sectors and characteristics of the firms included in the WBAATI survey.

World Bank Investment Climate Surveys

Data from a survey instrument developed by the World Bank, the Investment Climate Surveys,[9] covering close to 3,700 firms in 14 Sub-Saharan African countries, were used to complement the survey described above. The Investment Climate Surveys are useful in capturing the magnitude of the institutional barriers faced by enterprises, and thus in providing a quantitative assessment of the overall business environment. These surveys were conducted over the three-year period covering 2001–2004. The firms that took part in the Investment Climate Surveys operate in industrial sectors such as mining, construction, or manufacturing, or are active in services such as transportation, trade, real estate and business services, tourism, or other. In terms of size, the creators of the survey instrument designed the sample frame relying on respondent quotas such that there is an overrepresentation of smaller firms in all of the surveyed countries.

TABLE 1A.2
Firms' Characteristics in WBAATI Survey

(number of interviewed firms, except for Vintage where years are shown)

Survey sample structure	Ghana	Senegal	South Africa	Tanzania
Sector				
Agriculture and food	15	17	7	18
Chemicals	11	7	5	7
Machinery	9	4	11	11
Non-oil minerals and metals	17	2	6	9
Nondurables	10	5	9	21
Textiles	13	23	9	9
Construction	9	12	16	19
Nonconstruction services	16	37	37	33
Size (employees)				
Micro (1–10)	18	20	13	10
Small (11–50)	38	51	19	41
Medium (51–100)	15	19	7	21
Large (101–200)	15	9	9	18
Very large (200+)	14	11	52	37
Ownership structure				
State-owned	1	0	5	3
Domestic	47	69	49	67
Foreign	48	28	24	53
Joint venture	4	13	22	4
Vintage				
Oldest	1931	1931	1887	1947
Youngest	2005	2004	2006	2005
Average age	1990	1987	1971	1989
Median age	1997	1992	1987	1995
Number of firms with Chinese links				
Chinese nationality of principal shareholder	14	4	7	2
Chinese ethnic origin of principal shareholder	14	4	8	2
Parent company headquarters in China[a]	4	0	4	0
Exporting to China	1	7	8	7
Importing from China	35	24	25	26
Number of firms with Indian links				
Indian nationality of principal shareholder	23	1	5	12
Indian ethnic origin of principal shareholder	24	1	12	55
Parent company headquarters in India[a]	7	0	5	4
Exporting to India	1	7	7	8
Importing from India	22	22	14	44

Source: World Bank staff.

a. Applies only if a firm is part of a group enterprise or holding company.

TABLE 1A.3
Sectoral Distribution of Surveyed Firms, by Nationality
(percent)

Sector	African	Chinese	Indian	European
Agriculture and food	14	7	7	17
Chemicals	7	4	17	0
Construction	15	4	5	11
Machinery	7	11	0	13
Non-oil minerals and metals	7	11	24	2
Nondurables	10	7	12	13
Nonconstruction services	24	41	29	36
Textiles	15	15	5	9

Source: World Bank staff.

Annex 1B
Diagnostic Trade Integration Studies

International donors have increased their efforts in providing trade-related technical cooperation to least developed countries (LDCs) under the auspices of the Integrated Framework (IF) for Trade-Related Technical Assistance to LDCs. The IF is supported by six multilateral institutions—the International Monetary Fund, the International Trade Centre, the United Nations Conference on Trade and Development, the United Nations Development Programme, the World Bank, and the World Trade Organization.

The IF has two objectives: (i) to "mainstream" (integrate) trade into national development plans, such as the Poverty Reduction Strategy Papers, of LDCs, and (ii) to assist in the coordinated delivery of trade-related technical assistance in response to needs identified by LDCs. IF implementation comprises three broad stages:

- *Preparatory activities,* which typically include an official request from the country to participate in the IF process; a technical review of the request; establishment of a national IF steering committee; and, to the extent possible, identification of a lead donor

- *Diagnostic phase,* which results in the elaboration of a diagnostic trade integration study (DTIS)

- *Follow-up activities,* which begin with the translation of the diagnostic findings into an action plan to serve as the basis for trade-related technical assistance delivery.

To date, DTISs have been completed on 26 Sub-Saharan African countries: Angola, Benin, Burkina Faso, Burundi, Central African Republic, Chad, the Comoros, Eritrea, Ethiopia, The Gambia, Guinea, Lesotho, Madagascar, Malawi, Mali, Mauritania, Mozambique, Niger, Rwanda, São Tomé and Principe, Senegal, Sierra Leone, Sudan, Tanzania, Uganda, and Zambia. Based on the findings of the DTISs, an action matrix is developed in consultation with all stakeholders.

Endnotes

1. UNCTAD has estimated that South-South trade accounts for about 11 percent of global trade and that 43 percent of the South's trade is with other developing countries. It also has estimated that South-South trade is growing about 10 percent per year. See Puri Lakshmi, "A Silent Revolution in South-South Trade," WTO (2004). http://www.wto.org/english/tratop_e/dda_e/ symp04_ paper7_e.doc
2. Throughout this study, "Africa" refers to the countries of Sub-Saharan Africa.
3. Between 2000 and 2005, the share of Africa's exports destined for the EU was reduced by almost one-half, from 50 percent to 27 percent. Data for 2000 are from World Bank (2004b). Data for 2005 are from IMF Direction of Trade Statistics ("IMF DOT"); for details see chapter 2.
4. IMF DOT.
5. World Bank World Development Indicators.
6. "Economic Development in Africa," UNCTAD (2005a).
7. There is no known overlap between the quantitatively surveyed firms and those firms on which the qualitative business case studies were developed.
8. See annex 1A for a description of the sectors covered.
9. Such surveys conducted before 2006 were known as Investment Climate Surveys; surveys conducted since 2006 are now called Enterprise Analysis Surveys. Those surveys have been conducted to collect firm-level data to prepare the World Bank Investment Climate Assessments (ICAs) for individual developing countries around the world.

CHAPTER 2

Performance and Patterns of African-Asian Trade and Investment Flows

Introduction

This chapter documents and assesses the trade patterns and investment relations between Africa and Asia, with an emphasis given to the roles of China and India. The analysis focuses not only on the historical trend of African-Asian trade and investment flows at the aggregate level, but also on emerging patterns of these flows at the country (or subregional) levels. The chapter also explores the main determinants of trade and investment flows between Africa and Asia, setting the stage for the discussion in subsequent chapters.

To set the context, the chapter begins with a discussion of Africa' and Asia's roles in the world economy, with a focus on those of China and India. Emphasis is given to the fact that Africa is a highly heterogeneous continent of 47 countries, each having different-sized economies, populations, and surface areas, and where GDP per capita ranges from less than $200 to $7,000. It is also a highly segmented continent with extremely inconvenient and costly transportation, contributing to its small role in global trade and investment.

The subsequent analysis of the current patterns of trade and investment between Africa and Asia suggests that the recent boom in international commerce is largely driven by complementarities between the two regions, for example, with Africa's needs for Chinese and Indian manufactured goods and machinery and China and India's needs for Africa's natural resources.[1] This differs from the recent growth in Africa's trade with the European Union (EU) and the United States, which is largely stimulated by preferential treatment in these two markets. The evidence presented points to the fact that the complementarities between the two regions are strong in terms of economic resources, indicating the likely sustainability of the current African-Asian trade and investment boom.

Following the descriptive analysis a quantitative assessment is presented of the roles of "at-the-border" trade policies, "between-the-border" constraints, and "behind-the-border" conditions in shaping the flows of trade and investment between Africa and Asia. The examination also considers the linkages between trade and investment activity. The analysis suggests that, while formal trade policies such as tariffs and regional trade agreements matter, behind-the-border and between-the-border factors also have significant, if not greater, impacts. The findings also suggest that foreign direct investment (FDI) inflows to African countries have a complementary effect on the continent's export flows: greater FDI stocks appear to be associated with an increase in exports.

The chapter concludes by highlighting the policy implications of the key factors contributing to African-Asian trade performance and investment, and how they may leverage domestic growth in African countries in the future.

Africa and Asia in the Global Economy

World trade has dramatically expanded in the last 15 years, the period well-characterized by the term "globalization." Currently, many countries in Africa are experiencing an economic boom, partly due to high prices for their major export commodities. However, not all countries on the African continent have benefited from this boom.

The region is quite diverse in many aspects, including natural resource endowments and economic performance; see figure 2.1, table 2.1, and table 2A.1 in annex 2A. One-third of the world's resource-dependent economies are in Africa.[2] This engenders a high degree of dependence on resource rent and, concomitantly, significant opportunities for corruption. Not surprisingly, and partly as a result, the continent is characterized by a high degree of income inequality and is prone to conflict.

FIGURE 2.1
Africa's Development Pattern is Increasingly Diverse, with More and More Success Stories

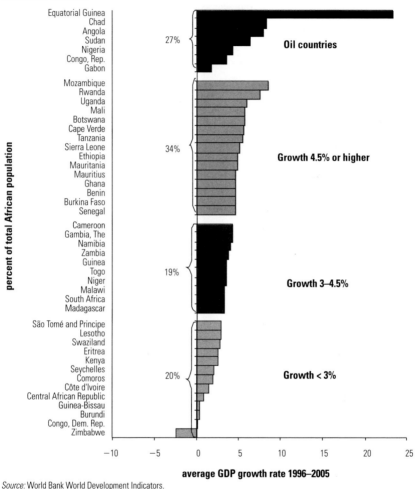

Source: World Bank World Development Indicators.

In Africa, there are 45 small economies and two regional "super powers"—South Africa and Nigeria—that together account for 55 percent of the continent's economic activity. Still, 15 African countries, accounting for 34 percent of the continent's population, have grown in a sustained manner in the last decade; these include Ghana, Senegal, and Tanzania, to name a few. However, 13 African countries, accounting for one-fifth of the African population, have experienced little or negative GDP-per-capita

TABLE 2.1
Heterogeneity of the African Continent

	GDP growth, 1996–2005	GDP per capita, 2000, $	Agriculture as percent of GDP	Industry as percent of GDP	Manufacturing as percent of GDP	Services as percent of GDP
Angola	7.9	799	9	59	4	32
Benin	4.8	324	35	14	9	50
Botswana	5.7	3,671	2	44	4	43
Burkina Faso	4.6	248	31	20	14	49
Burundi	1.2	107	49	19	n.a.	27
Cameroon	4.5	737	43	15	8	40
Cape Verde	6.5	1,292	7	20	1	73
Central African Rep.	0.9	225	56	22	n.a.	22
Chad	7.8	261	59	8	6	29
Comoros	2.0	378	41	12	4	47
Congo, Dem. Rep.	0.0	88	59	12	5	n.a.
Congo, Rep.	3.5	940	6	56	6	38
Côte d'Ivoire	1.5	574	26	18	15	56
Equatorial Guinea	20.9	4,101	5	60	n.a.	3
Eritrea	2.2	174	14	22	10	55
Ethiopia	5.5	132	41	9	n.a.	39
Gabon	1.7	3,860	9	68	5	22
Gambia, The	4.5	327	28	13	5	48
Ghana	4.7	275	35	25	9	40
Guinea	3.6	381	24	35	4	37
Guinea-Bissau	0.6	134	61	12	9	25
Kenya	2.8	427	13	16	11	52
Lesotho	2.7	543	16	36	18	38
Liberia	n.a.	130	61	9	8	120
Madagascar	3.3	229	26	15	13	50
Malawi	3.2	154	36	14	10	40
Mali	5.7	237	33	24	3	35
Mauritania	4.9	437	17	27	8	46
Mauritius	4.9	4,223	5	26	19	56
Mozambique	8.4	276	23	32	14	36
Namibia	4.0	2,035	10	23	11	57
Niger	3.5	155	40	17	7	43
Nigeria	4.0	402	26	48	4	24
Rwanda	7.5	250	40	21	10	38
São Tomé and Principe	3.1	354	17	16	4	67
Senegal	4.6	461	17	21	13	62
Seychelles	2.0	6,688	3	28	16	70
Sierra Leone	1.1	170	n.a.	n.a.	n.a.	n.a.
Somalia	n.a.	n.a.	n.a.	n.a.	n.a.	n.a.
South Africa	3.1	3,346	3	29	18	59
Sudan	6.4	439	28	27	7	39
Swaziland	2.8	1,358	n.a.	n.a.	n.a.	n.a.
Tanzania	5.4	314	41	15	7	35
Togo	3.3	244	41	23	9	36
Uganda	6.1	262	29	19	8	43
Zambia	3.6	339	19	33	11	38
Zimbabwe	−2.4	457	16	21	13	42

Sources: Africa Live Data Base; World Bank 2006a; Goldstein et al. 2006, world conflict map; and World Bank staff.

Note: n.a. = data not available. The diversification indicator measures the extent to which exports are diversified. A higher index indicates more export diversification; see Goldstein et al. (2006) for details.

Oil producers	Land locked	Number of borders	Conflict affected	Population, million	Surface area thousand sqkm	Population density, number of people per sqkm	Export diversification index
✓		3	✓	14.5	1,247	12	1.1
		4		7.1	113	63	2.1
	✓	2		1.7	582	3	n.a.
	✓	6		12.7	274	46	2.2
	✓	3	✓	7.5	28	269	1.6
		6		16.7	475	35	4.4
		0		0.5	4	122	9.2
	✓	5	✓	4.0	623	6	3.4
✓	✓	5	✓	9.1	1,284	7	2.6
		0		0.6	2	282	1.2
	✓	9	✓	56.4	2,345	24	3.0
✓		4	✓	3.9	342	12	n.a.
		5	✓	17.4	322	54	4.0
✓		2		0.5	28	18	1.2
		3	✓	4.6	118	39	5.2
	✓	5	✓	71.3	1,104	65	4.0
✓		3		1.4	268	5	1.6
		1		1.5	11	130	5.2
		3		21.4	239	90	4.0
		6		8.2	246	34	4.2
		2	✓	1.6	36	44	4.8
		5		32.9	580	57	16.0
	✓	1		1.8	30	61	n.a.
		3		3.5	111	32	2.0
		0		17.7	587	30	8.1
	✓	3		11.4	118	96	3.0
	✓	7		12.2	1,240	10	1.3
		4		3.0	1,026	3	3.8
		0		1.2	2	612	11.7
		5	✓	19.5	802	24	2.0
		3		2.0	824	2	n.a.
	✓	7		12.4	1,267	10	1.9
✓		3		143.3	924	155	1.3
	✓	4	✓	8.4	26	320	2.4
		0		0.2	1	171	1.5
		5		10.6	197	54	12.2
		0		0.1	0	189	2.7
		2	✓	5.5	72	77	3.8
		3	✓	10.3	638	16	6.1
		6	✓	45.3	1,219	37	n.a.
✓		8	✓	35.2	2,506	14	1.6
	✓	1		1.1	17	65	n.a.
		7		37.2	945	39	21.7
		3		5.1	57	89	5.3
	✓	5	✓	27.2	241	113	7.3
	✓	7		10.9	753	15	5.0
	✓	4		13.1	391	34	8.1

growth over the last decade; among them are the Democratic Republic of Congo, Eritrea, and Burundi, many of which were affected by conflict.

In addition to this heterogeneity, Africa is also highly segmented geographically. Indeed, Africa is distinctive compared to other developing regions in both its physical and human geography.[3] The continent has the largest number of countries per square area in comparison with other developing regions, with each on average sharing borders with four neighbors. Africa also has a large proportion of its population living in countries with an unfavorable geographic and economic basis for development. Forty percent of its population is in landlocked countries, compared with 23 percent of the population in East and Central Asia. Moreover, the low population density is accentuated by high internal transport costs, estimated at nearly twice the levels of other developing regions. The result, except for South Africa and Nigeria, is small and shallow markets. These endowed conditions make it costly to trade in Africa. In many respects, Africa's geography has shaped it economic fortunes.

Although many countries in Africa have made significant progress in economic development over the last decade, the continent's overall trade performance in the global marketplace has been very disappointing. World trade accounted for 16 percent of global output in 1991; this figure had jumped to 20 percent in 2004. But the trade flows of African economies on the whole have yet to be favorably affected. In fact, Africa's export market shares have continuously fallen over the last six decades (figure 2.2).

FIGURE 2.2
Africa's Share of World Exports Has Been Declining
(percent)

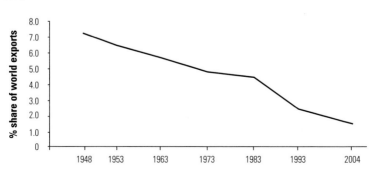

Source: IMF Direction of Trade Statistics

FIGURE 2.3
Prices Have Risen for Many of Africa's Major Export Commodities, Not Just Oil

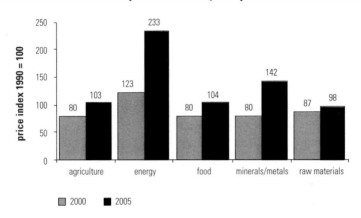

Source: World Bank staff estimates.

Since 1999, Africa has seen price increases for most of its primary export commodities, as illustrated in figure 2.3. With the exception of raw materials, whose prices have been relatively stagnant, other commodities have experienced noticeable increases in their price levels. This is, of course, especially the case for energy prices, driven by the sharp price increase in the worldwide petroleum market. Metal and non-oil mineral prices also have grown substantially.

FIGURE 2.4
Percent Contribution of China and India to the Growth of World Imports of Selected Commodities, 2000–04

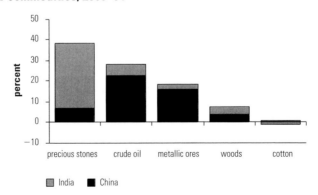

Source: Goldstein et al. 2006.

The worldwide rise of commodity prices has been engendered in large part by the rapid growth of Asian developing countries, especially China and India (figure 2.4). These two countries contributed close to 40 percent of global import growth for precious stones, 30 percent for crude oil, and 20 percent for metallic ores. Their demand for these commodities is likely to grow, or at least not change from current levels, in the foreseeable future.[4]

The recent surge in commodity prices mostly benefits resource-rich countries. Asia has seen little increases in its export commodity prices. The

FIGURE 2.5
Terms of Trade Effects on Gross Domestic Income (GDI), 1997–2003

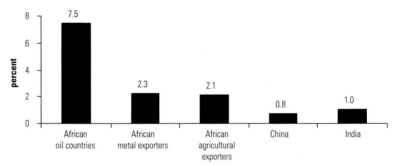

Source: Goldstein et al. 2006.

FIGURE 2.6
The Share of Raw Materials as Percentage of Total Exports, by Region

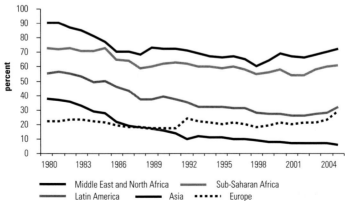

Source: UNCOMTRADE.

Note: Raw materials include agricultural raw materials, crude petroleum, ores, and coal. "Asia" excludes Japan, Republic of Korea, and Singapore. All other regions are restricted to low- and middle-income countries only.

rising prices for major African export commodities have contributed significantly to African countries' Gross Domestic Income (GDI), as illustrated in figure 2.5. In comparison, commodity price increases have contributed little to China and India's GDI growth.

FIGURE 2.7
The Average Shares of Exports by Technology Level

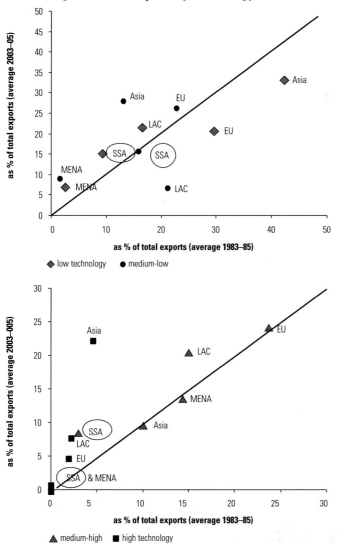

Source: UN COMTRADE.

Note: Technical levels were based on Organisation for Economic Co-operation and Development definition. "Asia" excludes Japan, Republic of Korea, and Singapore. All other regions include low- and middle-income countries only.

African exports are heavily oriented toward raw materials, the share of which is second only to the Middle East and North Africa (figure 2.6). Although Africa made good progress in reducing its dependency on raw materials in the late 1980s, it has not made progress since then.

Figure 2.7 shows the technology content of exports among developing regions. For Asia, the share of low technology and medium-high technology exports has decreased (below the diagonal line) or been stagnant (on the diagonal line) over the last two decades. However, the shares of medium-low and high technology exports have increased drastically (above the diagonal line). There is a clear pattern that Asia is moving up the technology ladder of the world trade.

Africa has also seen some increase in low and medium-high technology exports shares, indicating that it is moving up the technology ladder where Asia is putting less emphasis. However, Africa's shift in the share of medium-high technology exports mainly came from the two regional super powers, Nigeria (refined petroleum exports) and South Africa (machinery and transportation equipment exports). Indeed, overall, Africa's shares of low and medium-low technology exports is at a lower-middle position among all developing regions. Its shares of medium-high and high technology exports are the lowest among all developing regions.

Since 1990, flows of foreign direct investment (FDI) to developing countries have increased rapidly, including those to Africa, China, and India.[5] In

FIGURE 2.8
Regional FDI Share, Percentage of Total World FDI

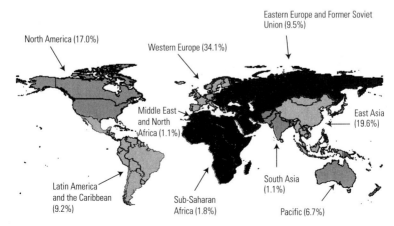

Source: World Bank World Development Indicators.

recent years, the average annual growth rate of FDI flows to Africa was 17 percent, comparable to the 20 percent growth rates of China and India. Still, in spite of Africa's rapid growth of FDI, the continent accounts for 1.8 percent of global net FDI flows. More than half of the world's FDI goes to North America and Western Europe, and 20 percent goes to East Asia (see figure 2.8).

Patterns of Merchandise Trade Flows Between Africa and Asia

During the last 15 years, trade flows between Africa and Asia have been rapidly increasing. This is the hallmark of the recent growth of South-South trade and investment, which is a significant feature of recent devel-

FIGURE 2.9
Africa's Exports and Imports with Asia: 1990–2005

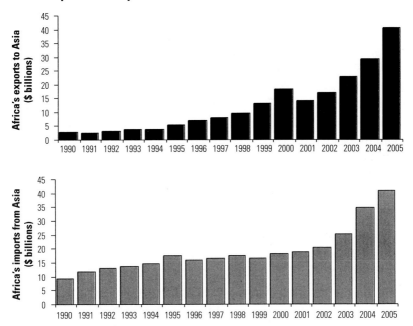

Source: IMF Direction of Trade Statistics.

Note: The 2005 figures were based on data for exports and imports for the first 10 months, adjusting for November and December's exports with the average monthly exports of January to October 2005. "Asia" includes Afghanistan, Bangladesh, Brunei, Cambodia, China (including Hong Kong and Macao), India, Indonesia, Japan, the Democratic People's Republic of Korea, the Republic of Korea, the Lao People's Democratic Republic, Malaysia, Maldives, Mongolia, Myanmar, Nepal, Pakistan, Philippines, Singapore, Sri Lanka, Taiwan (China), Thailand, and Vietnam. Note that the differences in total trade values between these graphs and tables 2.1 and 2.2 result from using different data sources.

opments in the global economy.[6] Africa's exports to Asia have been growing rapidly since 1990 and have accelerated since 2003.[7] Figure 2.9 shows
that, while the 15 percent growth of Africa's exports to Asia during
1990–95 was especially rapid compared to other regions, over the last five
years, total exports of African countries to Asia have grown at an even
faster rate of 20 percent. In fact, since 2003, the annual growth rate has
reached an all-time high of 30 percent.

The Rapid Growth of African-Asian Trade: 1990–2005

Africa's imports from Asia have also grown. However, they have grown
less rapidly than exports, allowing African countries to substantially reduce
their overall trade deficit, which amounted to as much as 50 percent of
their total trade value with Asia in the early 1990s. The rapid growth in
Africa's exports has created financial space for Africa to import. The average annual growth rate of Africa's imports from Asia was 13 percent
between 1990 and 1995, and accelerated to 18 percent between 2000 and
2005. Africa imports one-third of its total imports from Asia, second only
to the EU.[8]

It is easy to see how much the growth of Africa's exports to Asia has been
demand-driven by looking at how the relative share of exports to Asia in
overall African exports to the world has shifted over time. Africa's export
growth to Asia has surpassed that to all other regions over the last decade.
Although exports to the EU and the United States grew much more rapidly
between 2000 and 2005 than they did between 1990 and 1995, the growth
rate of exports to Asia was 20 percent during the last five years (figure
2.10), which is higher than that of exports to any other region during the
same period. Asia is now the third most important export destination, with
a share of 27 percent of Africa's total exports in 2005, lagging only the EU
(32 percent) and the United States (29 percent). Africa's exports to Asia, as
a share of its total exports, have increased from a mere 9 percent in 1990 to
27 percent, while exports to its traditional markets among the EU countries
have decreased from around 48 percent to 32 percent.[9]

Asia has become a significant trade partner for Africa in imports as well
as exports over the last 15 years. As shown in figure 2.11, the average
annual growth rate of Africa's imports from Asia was 13 percent between
1990 and 1995, and accelerated to 18 percent between 2000 and 2005.[10]
Africa imported 33 percent of its total imports from Asia in 2005, second

FIGURE 2.10
Growth and Proportional Change in Africa's Export Destinations: 1990–2005

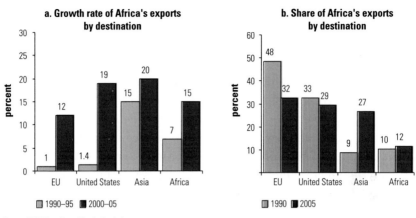

a. Growth rate of Africa's exports by destination

b. Share of Africa's exports by destination

■ 1990–95 ■ 2000–05

■ 1990 ■ 2005

Source: IMF Direction of Trade Statistics.

Note: The growth rate is the simple average of annual growth rates in the respective period.

FIGURE 2.11
Growth and Proportional Change in Africa's Import Origins: 1990–2005

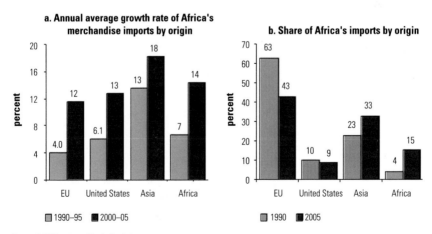

a. Annual average growth rate of Africa's merchandise imports by origin

b. Share of Africa's imports by origin

■ 1990–95 ■ 2000–05

■ 1990 ■ 2005

Source: IMF Direction of Trade Statistics.

Note: The growth rate is the simple average of annual growth rates in the respective period. "Asia" includes Afghanistan, Bangladesh, Brunei, Cambodia, China (including Hong Kong and Macao), India, Indonesia, Japan, the Democratic People's Republic of Korea, the Republic of Korea, the Lao People's Democratic Republic, Malaysia, Maldives, Mongolia, Myanmar, Nepal, Pakistan, Philippines, Singapore, Sri Lanka, Taiwan (China), Thailand, and Vietnam.

only to the EU. In comparison, Africa receives only 9 percent of its total imports from the United States.

Product Composition of the African-Asian Merchandise Trade Structure

Table 2.2 presents the product group-destination matrix of Africa's merchandise exports. The composition of exports is broadly based both for exports to the EU and for intra-African markets, whereas the exports to the United States and Asia are more concentrated in natural resources. Africa's exports to Asia consist mainly of primary commodities, including oil, non-oil minerals, metals, and agricultural raw materials, accounting for 86 percent of exports to Asia. Approximately 47 percent of Africa's exports to Asia comprise oil and natural gas, which represent 12 percent of

TABLE 2.2
Africa's Export Matrix, 2004
(percent)

Product	Africa	EU	United States	Asia	Other	World
Machinery and transport equipment	0.8	3.3	0.7	1.0	0.6	6.0
	(12.9)	(9.7)	(2.7)	(4.0)	(6.7)	(6.0)
Textiles, apparel, and footwear	0.3	1.2	1.3	1.0	0.2	4.0
	(4.8)	(3.5)	(5.0)	(4.0)	(2.2)	(4.0)
Manufactured materials	1.2	5.9	1.3	1.3	0.5	10.0
	(19.4)	**(17.4)**	(5.0)	(5.2)	(5.6)	**(10.0)**
Nonpetroleum minerals and metals	1.1	7.2	2.5	7.2	2.4	20.0
	(17.7)	**(21.2)**	(9.6)	**(28.8)**	**(26.7)**	**(20.0)**
Agricultural raw products	0.7	8.5	1.2	2.5	1.2	14.0
	(11.3)	**(25.0)**	(4.6)	**(10.0)**	**(13.3)**	**(14.0)**
Processed food and beverages	0.3	1.9	0.2	0.2	0.3	3.0
	(4.8)	(5.6)	(0.8)	(0.8)	(3.3)	(3.0)
Oil and natural gas	1.8	6.0	19.0	11.7	3.6	42.0
	(29.0)	**(17.7)**	**(73.1)**	**(46.8)**	**(40.0)**	**(42.0)**
All groups	6.2	34.0	26.0	25.0	9.0	100
	(100)	(100)	(100)	(100)	(100)	(100)
Total export volume (billions $)	9.2	50.7	39.0	37.1	12.8	149.0

Source: UN COMTRADE

Note: Figures are percentage shares in total African exports to the world. Figures in parentheses are percentage shares in total African exports to respective regions or countries (more than 10% are bolded). "Asia" includes Bangladesh, Cambodia, China (including Hong Kong and Macao), India, Indonesia, Japan, the Republic of Korea, Malaysia, Maldives, Mongolia, Nepal, Pakistan, Philippines, Singapore, Sri Lanka, Taiwan (China), Thailand, and Vietnam.

Africa's overall exports to the world. In addition to oil and natural gas, agricultural raw products and non-oil mineral and metal products are also major product groups, representing another 39 percent of Africa's exports to Asia. Cotton, timber, fruits and nuts, and crustaceans and mollusks are the major agricultural products exported from Africa to Asia. The leading non-oil mineral and metal products include gold, silver, platinum, iron, aluminum, iron ore, copper, and pearls. Although almost one-half of total African exports to Asia are from oil and natural gas, the dominance of such products in the export structure is less pronounced than the case of exports to the United States.

Manufactured products (machinery and transport equipment; textiles, apparel, and footwear; and other manufactured materials) are not major exports of African countries in general. In fact, compared to other regions, only Africa has exhibited a stagnant trend in non-oil exports (see figure 2.12). In absolute terms, the EU is the major destination of African manufactured products. Manufactured exports to Asia are approximately one-third of those to the EU in absolute terms. Among exports to Asia, those products constitute only 13 percent (see table 2.2). African exports in manufactured products are also limited. The weak presence of manufactured products in the export structure, or in turn the strong presence of primary

FIGURE 2.12

Africa Is Virtually the Only Region That Has Not Increased Its Share of Non-Oil Exports

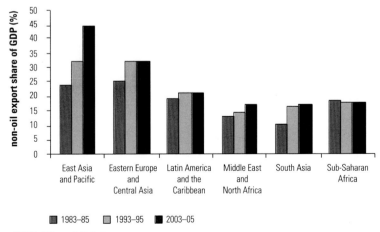

■ 1983–85   ▨ 1993–95   ■ 2003–05

Source: IMF World Economic Outlook.

commodities, is in no way particular to exports to Asia. Only 20 percent of total African exports to the world are from manufactured products.

In regard to the growth rates of Africa's exports, growth is very rapid among petroleum, ores, metals, and gold. However, primary commodities and limited value-added products have not been the only African exports on the rise. Though still in their infancy, high value-added products, such as passenger and transportation vehicles assembled by the FDI-driven automobile industry in South Africa, have also been increasing rapidly, especially in the last two to three years, largely due to increases in sales to Japan (see table 2A.2 in annex 2A for growth rates for more detailed product groups).

The trend of sector-specific exports shown in figure 2.13 indicates that the general patterns of Africa's exports to Asia are quite consistent with the patterns of its exports to the world in general. Oil and natural gas is the leading group of exports from African countries to Asia, and has grown dramatically over the past decade. Crude oil recorded an annual growth rate of 19 percent, while oil products recorded an annual growth rate of 20 percent. The similarity in sectoral composition and growth patterns between Africa's exports to Asia and Africa's overall exports essentially implies that Asian countries have become more representative of Africa's typical export destinations worldwide.[11]

FIGURE 2.13
The Trend of Africa's Exports by Sector, 1999 and 2004

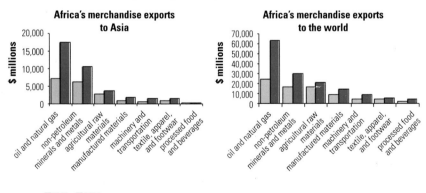

Source: UN COMTRADE.

Note: Export data on Africa are obtained by using Asian countries' reported data on imports from Africa, except for Thailand and Vietnam, where African export information was used. Africa's petroleum exports to India were adjusted for missing values. "Asia" includes Bangladesh, Cambodia, China (including Hong Kong and Macao), India, Indonesia, Japan, the Republic of Korea, Malaysia, Pakistan, Philippines, Singapore, Sri Lanka, Thailand, and Vietnam.

While exporting mostly raw materials to Asia, Africa imports mostly manufactured goods from Asia, including machinery, transport equipment, textiles, apparel, footwear, and manufactured materials. Light industrial products account for 46 percent of Africa's total imports from Asia, including food, pharmaceuticals, electronics, textiles, apparel, and footwear. Cotton fabric is the leading African imported item from Asian countries. The other leading imports are machinery and transport equipment, accounting for almost one-third of all imports from Asia (table 2A.3). The leading products in this category are automobiles and motorcycles. While Africa's primary commodity exports to Asia account for 86 percent of its total exports to Asia, its processed imports, including manufactured products and food products, account for 80 percent of its total imports from Asia.

As in the case of Africa's exports to Asia, the structure of imports from Asia is also similar to the structure of overall African imports from the world. Table 2.3 shows that 62 percent of Africa's merchandise imports

TABLE 2.3
Africa's Import Matrix, 2004
(percent)

Product	Africa	EU	United States	Asia	Other	World
Machinery and transport equipment	2.0	20.0	4.0	12.7	3.0	43.0
	(20.0)	(47.6)	(57.1)	(39.2)	(30.0)	(43.0)
Textiles, apparel, and footwear	1.0	1.0	0.1	3.7	0.2	8.0
	(10.0)	(2.4)	(1.4)	(11.4)	(2.0)	(8.0)
Manufactured materials	2.0	12.0	1.0	3.4	2.0	24.0
	(20.0)	(28.6)	(14.3)	(10.6)	(20.0)	(24.0)
Nonpetroleum minerals and metals	1.0	3.0	0.4	4.1	1.2	7.0
	(10.0)	(7.1)	(5.7)	(12.6)	(12.0)	(7.0)
Agricultural raw products	2.0	3.0	0.0	5.2	2.0	8.0
	(20.0)	(7.1)	0.0	(16.1)	(20.0)	(8.0)
Processed food and beverages	1.0	1.0	1.0	2.5	1.0	7.0
	(10.0)	(2.4)	(14.3)	(7.8)	(10.0)	(7.0)
Oil and natural gas	1.0	2.0	0.1	0.7	0.5	4.0
	(10.0)	(4.8)	(1.4)	(2.2)	(5.0)	(4.0)
All groups	10.0	42.0	7.0	32.0	10.0	100
	(100)	(100)	(100)	(100)	(100)	(100)
Total import volume (billions $)	11.0	49.0	9.0	38.0	10.0	118.0

Source: UN COMTRADE.

Note: Figures are percentage shares in total African imports from the world. Figures in parentheses are percentage shares in total African imports from respective regions or countries (more than 10% are bolded). "Asia" includes Bangladesh, Cambodia, China (including Hong Kong and Macao), India, Indonesia, Japan, the Republic of Korea, Malaysia, Maldives, Mongolia, Nepal, Pakistan, Philippines, Singapore, Sri Lanka, Taiwan (China), Thailand, and Vietnam.

from Asia are manufactured goods (machinery and transport equipment; textiles, apparel, and footwear; and other manufactured materials). The figure is somewhat lower than those products' share in overall African imports, which is 75 percent. Among manufactured products, textiles, apparel, and footwear are more represented in imports from Asia than the average, and less represented for other manufactured products.

Geographic and Product Concentration in African-Asian Trade

By comparing the composition of exports and imports in Africa's trade with Asia, one can easily observe clear complementarities between Africa and Asia. African countries supply raw materials for Asian countries, linked to either industrial growth or emerging consumer populations in Asia. African exports to Asia of oil, natural gas, and other fuels, as well as natural resource–based products, including agricultural raw materials such as cotton and wood, have experienced strong growth as a result of the rising manufacturing sectors in the rapidly developing economies in Asia such as China and India. Food exports to Asia have also increased due to the large populations in Asia with rising income levels. Conversely, Asian manufactured products, likely produced out of Africa's raw materials, are imported into African countries. Those products are not only imported for household consumption, but also for capital goods in the manufacturing sector in the African economy, where growth is much needed; these issues are discussed in greater detail in chapter 6.

The complementarities appear to also exist between Africa and the EU, but they are somewhat different from those between Africa and Asia. Textiles and apparel dominate Asia's exports to Africa, while machinery and transport equipment dominate EU and U.S. exports to Asia. In buying from Africa, the EU is concentrating less on natural resources and more on manufactured products, particularly machinery and equipment. It is likely that the preferential market access to European markets through the Everything But Arms (EBA) initiative or the EU–South African Customs Union (SACU) Free Trade Agreement has facilitated exports of these products to the EU.[12]

In analyzing the structure of African-Asian trade flows, we immediately see that Asia contributes to Africa's export diversification in terms of destination markets (destination diversification). Destination diversification is particularly relevant to primary commodity exports, which are commonly considered to be the traditional exports of most African countries. Decreases in the prices of these commodities over the past decades have lessened the magnitude of export earnings for primary commodity exporters in Africa. Additionally, African countries have experienced difficulty in expanding their exports in real terms because of stagnant demand in existing export destinations. By exploring—and exploiting—markets in Asian countries, where there is unsaturated rising demand for primary commodities, and by establishing new market relations with them, African exporters can find new opportunities to expand their exports of these products; see chapter 6.

However, at present, Asia is not contributing to other aspects of Africa's export diversification, including product diversification and source diversification. Africa's exports to Asia are more sectorally and geographically concentrated than are Africa's imports from Asia. This pattern is quite visible in the Herfindahl-Hirschman Index figures presented in table 2.4. Product concentration is based on how products are concentrated in African exports to and imports from Asia, while geographical concentration is based on how African trade partners (either exporting countries or importing countries) are concentrated in the same trade flows. Behind the figures lies the fact that more than 80 percent of value-added exports originate in only three countries: refined petroleum products are mostly from Nigeria and South Africa, pharmaceuticals are mostly from South Africa and Swaziland, and electronics, machinery, and transportation equipment are also from South Africa.

Figure 2.14 illustrates rather clearly how product concentration in Africa is geographically clustered at the subregional level. Southern African countries are concentrating on non-oil mineral resources, whereas Central-

TABLE 2.4
Geographical and Sectoral Concentration of African-Asian Trade: Herfindahl-Hirschman Index

Indicator	Exports to Asia	Imports from Asia	Exports to world	Imports from world
Geographical concentration of African exporters/African importers	0.19	0.14	0.08	0.04
Product concentration of African exports/African imports	0.25	0.01	0.15	0.01

Source: Authors' calculation based on data from UN COMTRADE.

Note: Figures are based on 2002–04 average trade values. "Asia" includes Bangladesh, Cambodia, China (including Hong Kong and Macao), India, Indonesia, Japan, the Republic of Korea, Malaysia, Maldives, Mongolia, Nepal, Pakistan, Philippines, Singapore, Sri Lanka, Taiwan (China), Thailand, and Vietnam.

FIGURE 2.14

Product and Geographical Distribution of Africa's Trade with the World and Asia

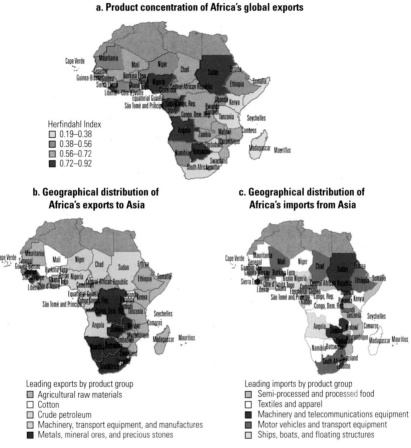

a. Product concentration of Africa's global exports

Herfindahl Index
☐ 0.19–0.38
▨ 0.38–0.56
▦ 0.56–0.72
■ 0.72–0.92

b. Geographical distribution of Africa's exports to Asia

c. Geographical distribution of Africa's imports from Asia

Leading exports by product group
☐ Agricultural raw materials
☐ Cotton
▦ Crude petroleum
▨ Machinery, transport equipment, and manufactures
■ Metals, mineral ores, and precious stones

Leading imports by product group
▦ Semi-processed and processed food
☐ Textiles and apparel
■ Machinery and telecommunications equipment
■ Motor vehicles and transport equipment
☐ Ships, boats, and floating structures

Source: UN COMTRADE.

Note: Figures are based on 2002–04 average trade values. "Asia" includes Bangladesh, Cambodia, China (including Hong Kong and Macao), India, Indonesia, Japan, the Republic of Korea, Malaysia, Maldives, Mongolia, Nepal, Pakistan, Philippines, Singapore, Sri Lanka, Taiwan (China), Thailand, and Vietnam.

Western African countries have high intensity in oil exports. Agricultural products are the dominant exports from Eastern African countries to Asia.

Although Africa's imports from Asia are diversified in comparison, the number of suppliers in Asia is not as high as one would expect if focusing on specific product groups. Only a few Asian countries have large shares of African import markets. Of Africa's total machinery and transport equipment imports from Asia, two-thirds are from Japan and China. Thailand, India, and

Malaysia account for almost 80 percent of Asia's total processed food exports to Africa. While India and China supply 70 percent of Asia's total electronic exports to Africa, China supplies 90 percent of Asia's coal exports to Africa.

Africa's Pattern of Merchandise Trade with China and India

China and India as Drivers of Growth in African-Asian Trade Flows

The high growth of Africa's trade with Asia is largely driven by exports to China and India, the two dynamic economies not only in Asia but also worldwide. The China-India-driven export growth of African countries underpins the earlier observation that Africa's exports to Asia are largely driven by increasing demand in Asia for natural resources and other primary commodities arising from Asia's growing industrial sectors and increasing purchasing power. China and India are the countries where such demand is most visible. While Japan and the Republic of Korea were the most important markets for Africa's exports in the early 1990s, both China and India doubled their annual growth rates of imports from Africa between the periods of 1990–94 and 1999–2004 (figure 2.15). China and India have 40 percent and 9 percent shares, respectively, of Africa's total exports to Asia today.

FIGURE 2.15
Growth in Africa's Exports to China and India

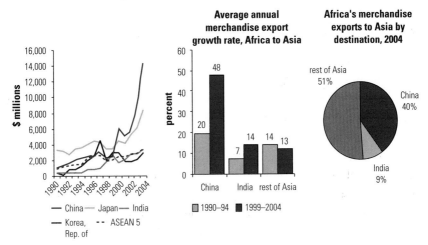

Source: UN COMTRADE.

FIGURE 2.16
Growth in Africa's Imports from China and India

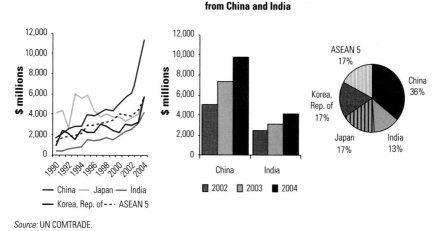

Source: UN COMTRADE.

Note: Imports are based on trade partner's export data, except for 2002 Thailand data, which was based on Africa's export data.

The leading role of China and India in African-Asian trade relations is not limited to Africa's exports. On the import side as well, these two countries have become the major trading partners for African countries. Japan used to be the largest Asian exporter of products that Africa imported from Asian countries. However, China has taken over the leading position from Japan, accounting for more than one-third of Asia's total exports to Africa (figure 2.16).

Product Composition Structure of Africa's Trade with China and India

Africa mainly exports petroleum and raw materials to China, and non-oil minerals to India, while it imports more value-added commodities from both China and India (figure 2.17). Oil and natural gas are the single most dominant category of products exported from Africa to China, accounting for more than 62 percent of total African exports to China, followed by ores and metals (17 percent) and agricultural raw materials (7 percent). In addition, Angola, Sudan, and the Democratic Republic of Congo provide 85 percent of African oil exports to China (box 2.1). Exports to India also show a high concentration in resource-based products. Ore and metals comprise 61 percent, followed by agricultural raw materials (19 percent).

FIGURE 2.17
Product Distribution of Africa's Trade with China and India

a. Africa's exports to China and India

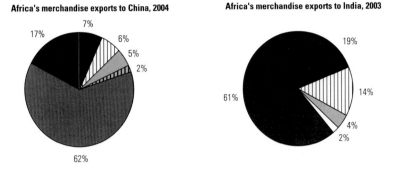

Africa's merchandise exports to China, 2004

Africa's merchandise exports to India, 2003

b. Africa's imports from China and India

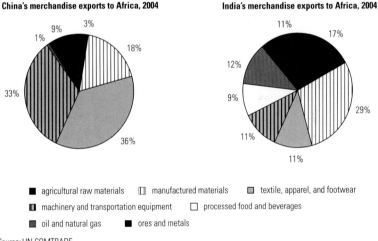

China's merchandise exports to Africa, 2004

India's merchandise exports to Africa, 2004

■ agricultural raw materials   ▥ manufactured materials   ▦ textile, apparel, and footwear
▤ machinery and transportation equipment   ☐ processed food and beverages
▦ oil and natural gas   ■ ores and metals

Source: UN COMTRADE.

Annex 2A provides data on the top 20 African exports to China and India and the leading exporting countries in Africa for those products based on 2002–04 averages (see tables 2A.4 and 2A.5). Oil accounts for 62 percent of total African exports to China. Angola supplies 47 percent of Africa's oil exports to China, followed by Sudan (25 percent), the Democratic Republic of Congo (13 percent), Equatorial Guinea (9 percent), and Nigeria (3 percent). Other leading exports to China include logs, iron ores, diamonds, and cotton. South Africa is almost an exclusive supplier of ore

BOX 2.1

China and India's Oil Imports from Africa

China's oil imports from Africa have been increasing at an annual compounded rate of 30 percent, slightly higher than the growth rate for imports
from the rest of world, which is 26 percent. While China's crude oil imports
from Africa account for more than 25 percent of its total crude oil imports,
its petroleum product imports from Africa are quite insignificant. Among
African oil-producing countries, China imports oil mainly from Angola, Sudan, Republic of Congo, and Equatorial Guinea, with Angola alone accounting for 50 percent of oil imports from Africa.

Share of Chinese Crude Oil Imports from Africa, by Country of Origin

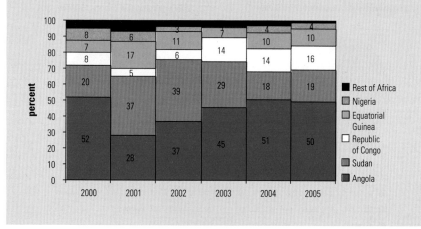

and diamonds to China. Logs and cotton, the two leading agricultural raw
materials for industrial use in China, are supplied by a range of countries
concentrated in West Africa (Cameroon, the Democratic Republic of
Congo, Gabon, Equatorial Guinea, and Liberia for logs, and Benin, Burkina Faso, Cameroon, Côte d'Ivoire, and Mali for cotton).

For India, gold is the major import from Africa, accounting for more
than half of all Indian imports from Africa (52 percent) and almost exclusively supplied by South Africa. Other ore and metal products include
inorganic acid from Senegal and South Africa as well as coal from South
Africa. The leading agricultural products exported to India include logs

Chinese Oil Imports ($ billions)

	2000	2001	2002	2003	2004	2005
Crude petroleum						
Africa	3.6	2.5	3.0	4.9	9.3	13.2
ROW	14.9	11.7	12.8	19.8	33.9	47.7
Petroleum products						
Africa	0.0	0.0	0.0	0.1	0.0	0.1
ROW	5.7	5.8	6.3	9.1	13.4	15.0

Although India also imports a large amount of crude petroleum from Africa, reliable statistics are not available to verify this phenomenon. Since 2000, India has not reported data on oil imports to UN COMTRADE. Based on export data reported by African countries, mainly Nigeria, and by the rest of the world, India imports approximately half of its petroleum from Africa. However, even these data underestimate India's oil imports from Africa. For example, there are no data indicating that India imports oil from Sudan.

Indian Oil Imports ($ billions)

	2000	2001	2002	2003	2004	2005
Crude petroleum						
Africa	3.9	2.1	2.2	2.4	—	—
ROW	1.8	1.9	2.2	2.2	2.4	—
Petroleum products						
Africa	0.01	0.01	0.06	0.03	0.02	0.01
ROW	1.0	0.7	0.7	1.0	1.4	1.4

Sources: UN COMTRADE and World Bank staff estimations.

Note: ROW = rest of world; — = not available.

from West African countries (Benin, Côte d'Ivoire, Gabon, Ghana, and Nigeria) and cotton from Benin, Côte d'Ivoire, Mali, Sudan, and Tanzania. Nuts follow logs and cotton as major exports to India (8 percent), supplied by Benin, Cote d'Ivoire, Guinea, Mozambique, and Tanzania.

African imports from China and India are more broadly based than African exports to those countries (see figure 2.17). Out of all imports from China, 87 percent comprise machinery and equipment, textile and apparel, and other manufactured products. Manufactured products are less represented in imports from India (51 percent). Manufactured products imported from China and India are mainly textile and apparel products, electric machinery and equipment, and consumer products, such as medicine, cosmetic products, and batteries. Tables 2A.6 and 2A.7 provide more detailed lists of top African imports from China and India, respectively, and their destination markets in Africa.

For both China and India, fabrics and yarn are the major exports to Africa. West African countries such as Benin, The Gambia, Ghana, Niger, Nigeria, and Togo, and East African countries such as Kenya and Tanzania are the major buyers of Chinese and Indian cotton fabrics. Cotton yarn from India is bought largely by South Africa and Mauritius. Both China and India export synthetic fibers to countries with relatively more developed light industries, such as Mauritius, Nigeria, and South Africa. One stark difference between China and India is the high prevalence of apparel products (garments) sold to the large African consumer markets, such as South Africa and Nigeria.

Geographic and Product Concentration in Africa's Trade with China and India

Table 2.5 shows the level of geographical and product concentration of African exports and imports with China and India based on the same Herfindahl-Hirschman Index used earlier. Clearly, exports to China and India are more concentrated, both in terms of origin markets in Africa and the range of products, than imports from the two countries. Also, for both geographic and product concentration, and for both exports and imports, Africa's trade with India is less concentrated than its trade with China. For the geographic concentration, this difference is visible in figure 2.18. One

TABLE 2.5
Geographical and Sectoral Concentration of Africa's Trade with China and India: Herfindahl-Hirschman Index

Indicator	Exports to China	Imports from China	Exports to India	Imports from India
Geographical concentration of	0.17	0.09	0.05	0.01
African exporters/African importers	(+0.09)	(+0.05)	(−0.03)	(−0.03)
Product concentration of	0.40	0.02	0.30	0.02
African exports/African imports	(+0.25)	(+0.01)	(+0.15)	(+0.02)

Source: Authors' calculation based on the data from UN COMTRADE.

Note: Figures in parentheses are the difference in index figures from those based on Africa's trade with the world. Figures are based on 2002–04 average trade values.

FIGURE 2.18

Leading African Trade Partners of China and India (as Percentage of Import Values in Importing Country)

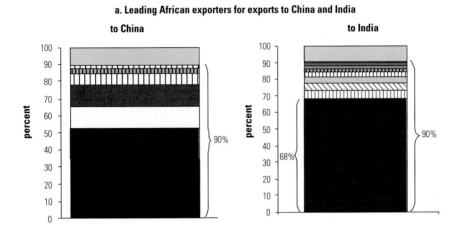

a. Leading African exporters for exports to China and India

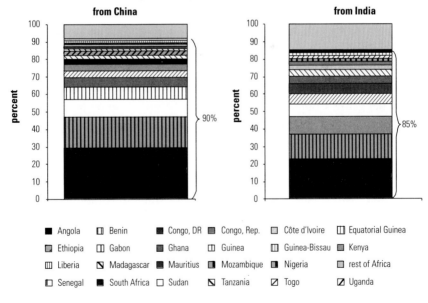

b. Leading African importers for imports from China and India

Source: UN COMTRADE.

plausible explanation for this difference is the historical ties India has with African countries from the colonial period, which have created a large Indian diaspora population across the African continent. Strong ethnic networks are one of the key characteristics of the private sector in African countries.[13] Ethnic networks should work to facilitate trade activities between India and African countries.[14]

Earlier, it was shown that, although African exports to Asia as a whole do not exhibit a significant pattern of product diversification, intersectoral complementarities between Africa and Asia do exist. Similar intersectoral complementarities seem to exist between Africa and China or India. This is true in a general context of Africa as a large supplier of raw materials, including energy resources, and China and India being suppliers of manufactured products to African countries. This pattern is largely driven by factor endowments. The rich resource endowment in Africa provides a natural comparative advantage in raw materials and resource-based products. China and India, on the other hand, have a rich stock of skilled labor compared to Africa and thus have a comparative advantage in manufactured products.[15]

The endowment-based theory of comparative advantage provides a simple but intuitive framework for understanding the trade patterns of African countries. In light of Africa's scarcity in human capital and rich natural resource base, the theory would suggest that it is not economically efficient for African countries to push for manufactured exports. At the same time there is a belief that, with greater trade between Africa and the growing industrial giants China and India, Africa's concentration on primary commodity exports will, if anything, increase, undoing Africa's efforts to promote manufactured exports. However, manufactured exports from Africa to China and India are increasing rather significantly (figure 2.19).

Is this a sign of growing complementarities between Africa and China and India? Three aspects may show positive shifts in complementarities between Africa and China and India. The first concerns the prospects for resource-based, value-added manufacturing exports. There is already evidence of Chinese and Indian imports of resource-based manufactured products. African countries could increase their manufactured exports to China and India based on the existing exports of raw materials. However, there is always a limit to growth based on horizontal diversification. African countries want to avoid being trapped as a "resource basket" for rapidly industrializing economies, such as China and India; they also want to realize dynamic efficiency gains by extracting value from their endowed

FIGURE 2.19

Africa's Exports to China and India by Commodity Groups

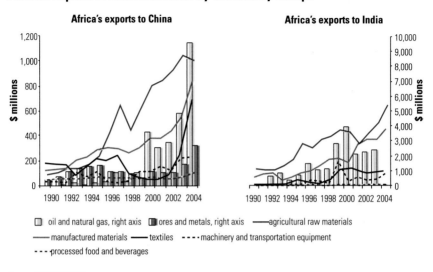

Source: UN COMTRADE.

resources. Natural resources provide a quick launching base for African countries to generate value-added activities. Although still limited to a few countries such as South Africa and Nigeria, resource-based manufactured products such as aluminum, iron, and steel appear among the leading exports to China and India. India's large exports of diamonds, which are likely due to diamond polish work in India using raw diamonds from Africa, raise a clear example of how added processing work could be retained in Africa, possibly by inviting Indian investment.

The second aspect concerns the prospects for broader participation in global value chains. As discussed in detail in chapter 6, there are growing vertical complementarities along value chains between Africa and China and India. Among the top 20 African exports and imports with China and India, there are clear complementarities between African countries and China and India in the cotton-textile-garment value chain (see tables 2A.4 through 2A.7). Raw material (cotton) is supplied by West African countries to China and India, and intermediate materials (fabrics) are supplied by China and India to apparel producers in Mauritius, Nigeria, South Africa, and other countries in Sub-Saharan Africa. Chapter 6 addresses the possibility of African producers participating in global network trade in the apparel sector.

The third aspect is the diversity among African countries and potential benefits from regional integration. Just as African-Asian trade relations encompass various dynamics due to rich variability among Asian countries—from high-income Japan to low-income but dynamically developing economies such as Vietnam—a rich variability is also found among African nations. Particularly, South Africa has evolved as a regional hub of industrial and commercial development in Sub-Saharan Africa and even beyond. The technological complementarities between South Africa and China or India exist at a higher level than is the case for other African countries. This provides scope for more intraindustry trade between South Africa and China and India. Through regional integration, the emerging intrasectoral complementarities between such industrial leaders in Africa and China and India could lead to wider benefits at the subregional markets through further forward and backward linkages; see chapter 6.

Increasing exports to China and India presents both opportunities and challenges to Africa. Africa could benefit from rapidly growing Asian markets in those countries to achieve broadly based economic development, or it could become merely a resource base for Asia's growing economies, benefiting little to its domestic economic development. The agenda for African countries to allow them to benefit from such growth of trade with China and India is really linked to two key questions: how to create an enabling environment for engaging more extensively in value-added production, in natural resources as well as other sectors; and how to effectively participate in global supply chains. These are the focus of chapter 6.

Trade in Services Between Africa and Asia

Since the early 1980s, international services transactions have increased more rapidly than trade in goods. Trade in services amounted to $2,125 billion in 2004, about 24 percent of the figure for trade in goods.[16] Despite the lack of internationally comparable statistics on the direction of international services trade and on South-South trade in particular, figures confirm an increasing volume of South-South services trade. According to UNCTAD (2005f), there is a growing concentration of trade in some developing countries. In 2003, 12 leading developing-country exporters of services—including China, India, Korea, Malaysia, Thailand, Mexico, Egypt, and Brazil—accounted for 71 percent of service exports of all developing countries, compared to 66 percent in 1998.

Services Trade of African Countries

Sub-Saharan exports of services grew from $9 billion in 1990 to $22 billion in 2004. Among Sub-Saharan countries, the largest export sector is travel, accounting for more than half of all Sub-Saharan services exports, followed by financial, construction, communications services, and transport (see figure 2.20). Africa's services export growth in the second half of the 1990s increased, especially since 2003. In recent years, almost three-quarters of recorded Sub-Saharan African exports of services have gone to the EU.

In Kenya, South Africa, and Mauritius, tourism is an important foreign-exchange earner. Benin, Côte d'Ivoire, and Tanzania get revenue from shipments from neighboring landlocked countries transiting through their ports, while Ghana and Mali receive remittances from their citizens working in services sectors abroad. Overall, while Africa's services exports rely heavily on low-skilled labor, under the leadership of South Africa and to some extent Senegal, Mauritius, and Kenya, Africa is engaging in the export of high-skill services. These services include health, financial, and business services.

Sub-Saharan imports of services grew from $18 billion in 1990 to $32 billion in 2004. Africa imports mainly transport, financial, construction, and communication services. In the early 1990s, Sub-Saharan Africa showed rapid services import growth, with imports growing faster than exports. During the second half of the decade, Africa's imports of services slowed down considerably. Sub-Saharan Africa's annual deficit in services trade stands at roughly $10 billion.

FIGURE 2.20

Africa's Trade in Services

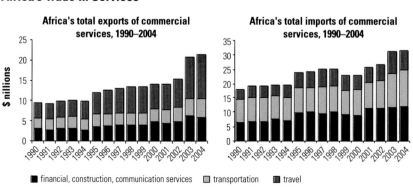

Source: IMF Balance of Payments.

Exports of Services by Asia

In 2004, China and India also sustained high growth rates of services exports. India, in particular, had an average service export growth rate of almost 20 percent. China's services exports for 2003 were about $46 billion. Nearly half of that amount came from travel and tourism, yet all services made up barely 10 percent of China's total exports. China's continued economic growth depends on further development of its services sectors, including services such as banking, insurance, securities, management consulting, telecommunications and information technology (IT), tourism, education, training, and engineering services (see box 2.2). India exported $25 billion in services and $56 billion in goods in 2003. India's services

---

BOX 2.2

Increasing Chinese Trade in Services

Tourism: China has become one of largest outbound tourist markets. There is a sustained Chinese outbound tourism boom. According to the World Tourism Organization, China is projected to supply 100 million travelers by 2020, making it the number one supplier of outbound tourists. In terms of total travel spending, China is currently ranked seventh and is expected to be the second fastest growing in the world from 2006 to 2015, jumping into the number two slot for total travel spending by 2015.

Transport: The Chinese government is in the midst of a massive upgrade of its existing transportation infrastructure. To keep its economy moving forward, China must have an efficient system in place to move goods and people across this 9.326 billion square kilometer land mass. Passenger rail traffic has priority over freight on the many single-track rail lines across China. Rail tracks are now being doubled to alleviate the freight train conflict issues, expressways are being built to cut down on vehicular travel times, sealed roads are being extended to new locations, ports are being improved for greater use of China's waterways, and airports are being improved across the country. This boom in construction will offer opportunities to local and foreign construction services firms.

exports are also more heavily weighted to finance, telecom, call centers, and other "IT-enabled" services than to tourism (see figure 2.21).

Foreign Direct Investment Between Africa and China and India

Patterns of Africa's Inward FDI

As figure 2.22 shows, the volatility of FDI to African oil countries is understandably very high. Another noticeable fact is that the difference between FDI as the share of GDP and domestic investment has been declining for China while increasing for Africa. This could indicate that the multiplier effect of FDI

Distribution services: Foreign companies have been banned from engaging in freight forwarding unless they form a joint venture with local partners. Many have stayed away. With China's accession into the World Trade Organization, these and other structural issues are moving to positions more in line with international standards. These changes are to be fully compliant with negotiated accession terms within five years of the accession date.

Ports: China has 16 major shipping ports with a capacity of more than 5 million tons per year, combined for a total country shipping capacity in excess of 1,400 million tons. The Port of Shanghai is going through a significant upgrade.

Software: China's exports of software were $2.6 billion in 2004.

Energy and natural resources: China's Africa Policy "encourages and supports competent Chinese enterprises to cooperate with African nations to develop and exploit rationally their natural resources." Africa contains about 8 percent of the world's proven oil reserves, 70 percent of which are off the west coast in the Gulf of Guinea. The low sulfur content of West Africa's oil makes it an attractive investment opportunity. China is investing in oil exploration and construction of pipelines. These construction services are creating opportunities for Chinese exports of services in other areas such as restaurants and small stores. Another anticipated benefit of these new investments is that they generate backward linkages with the rest of the economy.

Source: Office of the United States Trade Representative 2005.

FIGURE 2.21
Asia's Trade in Services

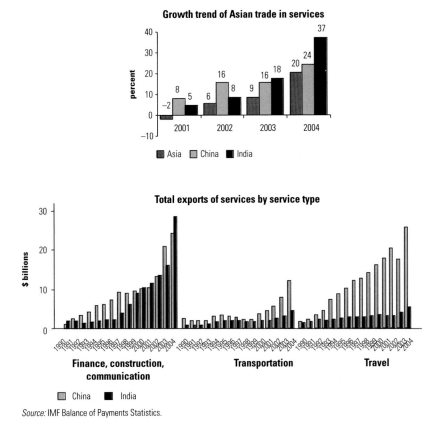

Source: IMF Balance of Payments Statistics.

in China is much higher than it is in Africa. The multiplier effect of FDI is the amount of additional income that one FDI dollar can generate in the host economy. FDI invested in the light manufacturing sector typically has much larger multiplier effects than FDI invested in the extractive sector. While FDI is resources-oriented in Africa, it is manufacturing-oriented in China. FDI as a percent of GDP has been declining in China even though the absolute level of FDI has been increasing. This indicates that GDP grows at a pace that can outweigh FDI growth, very possibly as a result of both a high multiplier effect of FDI and complementary high domestic investment. In comparison, FDI as a percent of GDP has been increasing rapidly in Africa, indicating that GDP grows at a much slower pace than FDI inflows, possibly as a result of a low multiplier effect and low complementary domestic investment.

FIGURE 2.22

Net FDI Flow as a Percentage of GDP and Gross Domestic Investment

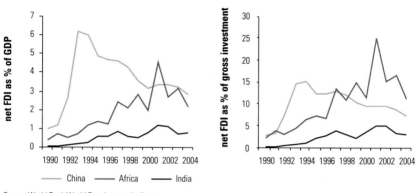

Source: World Bank World Development Indicators.

FDI to Africa is predicted to continue to increase with more diversified investors from different countries (see box 2.3). European countries (the United Kingdom and France) and North American countries (the United States and Canada) have been the main foreign investors in Sub-Saharan Africa, accounting for 68 percent and 22 percent of the FDI stock, respectively. However, FDI from developing countries, particularly from South Africa, China, and India, as well as from Malaysia and Brazil, has increased substantially in Africa. FDI from Asia accounts for 8 percent of total FDI inflows to Africa. South Africa stands out as the major intraregional FDI source country.

Although data on global-sectoral FDI flows are incomplete, by looking at FDI destinations in Africa, one can conclude that a large proportion of FDI goes to the oil sector. Figure 2.23 shows that over the last 15 years, 70 percent of FDI has been invested in five out of the seven African oil-exporting countries as well as in South Africa. South Africa has been able to attract the most dynamic investment among African countries, including in the financial sector after its mid-1990s liberalization reforms. FDI flows to South Africa, however, are quite volatile, affected by large FDI deals.[17]

While in most African countries about 50–80 percent of FDI goes to natural-resource exploitation, some countries are able to attract FDI into the financial, telecom, electricity, retail trade, light manufacturing (apparel, footwear), and transportation equipment sectors (see figure 2.24).

BOX 2.3

Prospects of FDI Flows to Africa

FDI flows to Africa are expected to continue to increase, according to UNCTAD's Global Investment Prospects Assessment 2006–2008 (GIPA). The country sources of FDI are also expected to become more diversified, with China and India to be among the top five leading FDI sources to the Africa region. A number of factors have contributed to the overall increase of FDI flows as well as to the sectoral and source country composition of FDI flows to the region. These factors include

- Rich natural resources in Africa that have always attracted FDI in oil and primary commodities sectors, regardless of the lack of good investment climate conditions.

- Improved macroeconomic and political stability for a number of countries.

- Sector-based reforms. For example, financial sector liberalization and changes in trade policies have encouraged FDI into the financial and automotive sectors in South Africa, and changes in the mining codes in Ghana and other African countries have encouraged mining FDI.

- Simplification of FDI regulations and the establishment of more transparent FDI regimes in a number of countries, including Ghana, Senegal, and Tanzania.

- International agreements, between African countries and the rest of the world, including China and India, increased significantly over last two

Chinese and Indian FDI to Africa

Chinese investors in Africa, like other foreign investors, seek natural resources and local markets, as well as a platform for exporting to Europe, the United States, and throughout the region. In Africa, China has been investing in oil production facilities as well as in light manufacturing. India has invested in an array of sectors, including the financial sector as well as food processing and light manufacturing. Historically, Chinese FDI went primarily to other Asian

years and have facilitated FDI flows and changed the FDI compositions. For example, the African Growth and Opportunity Act (AGOA) and the Multifibre Arrangement (MFA) have attracted FDI into the apparel sector and led to exports growth for Lesotho and Madagascar. AGOA also contributed to the increased FDI to Tanzania's light manufacturing and agribusiness sectors. Bilateral international treaties and double taxation treaties have also led to higher FDI flows.

Even though the above-mentioned factors have encouraged FDI flows to Sub-Saharan Africa, there are still a number of investment impediments that need to be addressed to attract FDI to the region. Such impediments stem from a number of factors, including

- Political instability and conflicts for a number of countries;

- In general, higher tariff barriers among countries in the region than between the region and countries outside Africa, resulting in the balkanization of domestic markets;

- Regulatory and fiscal burden (Africa has the highest taxes compared to other developing countries and the most cumbersome business and customs procedures);

- Corruption is high in the region (African countries dominate the bottom cluster of Transparency International's country ranking);

- Weak, and at times deteriorating, physical infrastructure; and

- Lack of a critical mass of skilled workers in the labor force.

Source: UNCTAD 2005b.

countries, mostly to Hong Kong. Recently, however, Chinese FDI has been targeting Africa, among other areas where natural resources are abundant.

Chinese FDI to Africa represents a small proportion of China's total FDI portfolio (see figure 2.25).[18] However, based on a recent firm-level survey on Chinese outward FDI, Africa in fact is second next to Asia as the major destination of Chinese FDI (box 2.4).[19] China has established its economic and political ties with the region since the Cold War era, but the motivation of Chinese FDI changed drastically before and after the Cold War. China

FIGURE 2.23
FDI to Africa by Destination, Cumulative Between 1990 and 2004

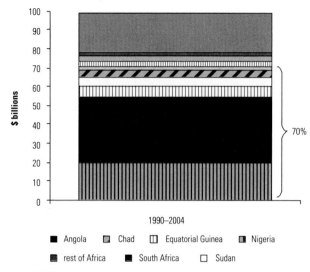

Source: World Bank World Development Indicators.

FIGURE 2.24
Share of Sectoral FDI Inflows to Selected African Countries, 2002–April 2006

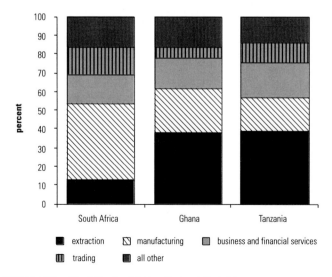

Source: OCO Consulting and Foreign Investment Advisory Services staff calculation.

Note: Greenfield projects.

FIGURE 2.25
Chinese FDI Stock and Flows by Region

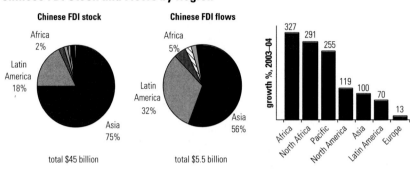

Sources: 2004 Chinese FDI Statistics Bulletin.

participated in various major infrastructure projects throughout Africa during its earlier involvement in Africa and is still very active in investing in infrastructure projects. Globally, 75 percent of China's FDI is in the tertiary sector, including construction and business activities (see box 2.5). More recently, however, a large proportion of Chinese FDI has gone to oil-rich African countries (see figure 2.26). In 2002, some 585 Chinese enterprises received approval by the Chinese authorities to invest in Africa, accounting for 8 percent of the total number of approvals. South Africa had 98 approvals, amounting to $119 million in value. Other important Chinese FDI destinations in Africa include Tanzania, Ghana, and Senegal. Today, it is estimated that there are 700 Chinese enterprises operating in Africa.[20]

As it is in other regions of the world, Indian FDI in Africa is mostly in the services and manufacturing sectors. However, in Africa, India also has significant FDI in natural resources, including the oil sector (in Sudan, for example). Over the period 1995–2004, Africa accounted for 16 percent of India's FDI, at $2.6 billion. Like China, India seeks primarily to secure energy sources from Africa as well as other natural resources such as timber, non-oil minerals, and precious stones to support its dynamic economic growth.

Of course, India has been present on the African continent for decades. In East and Southern Africa, the large Indian diaspora, whose members have business ties to India and a good knowledge of Africa, has played a significant role in attracting new investment to the continent. This is especially true in recent years, given that India is flush with foreign reserves, and the government has lifted regulations and controls allowing firms to go abroad and has removed the $100 million cap on foreign investment by Indian firms.

BOX 2.4

Patterns of Chinese Investment in Africa from Outward Chinese FDI Survey

China's relatively recent Going Global policy has encouraged Chinese firms to invest abroad to seek inputs in support of the country's fast-paced economic development, and to exploit its rapidly developing comparative advantages. While reliable and complete statistics are hard to come by, China's outward foreign investment (OFDI) stock and flows have been estimated at around $50 billion and $5 billion, respectively, in 2005.

Much has been written, often anecdotally, about China's OFDI. Less attention has been directed toward developing a better empirical understanding of the impact of the Going Global policy from the firms' points of view. In mid-2005, the Foreign Investment Advisory Service and the Multilateral Investment Guarantee Agency sponsored a survey of 150 Chinese firms based in eight Chinese cities that had invested or were about to invest abroad. The purpose of the survey was to learn about the motivations, experiences, and perceptions of the firms, and their future investment plans. Defining dimensions of the survey audience include the following:

• The surveyed firms have made 251 overseas investments to date, and of those investments more than half (129) were in developing countries.

• Reasons for investing are similar to those found in overseas investors worldwide—market access, resources, and strategic assets (for example, technology, brands, distribution channels) are the key drivers, across all regions of interest.

• Most are new to investing overseas, and need support to better understand the procedures required, and the opportunities and challenges these markets represent.

With regard to Africa in particular, some specific findings are worthy of note:

- Africa is second only to Asia as the destination of choice of the firms surveyed, accounting for some 18 percent of the overseas projects. (Asia accounted for nearly 40 percent of the total.)

- Reflecting the composition of the firms surveyed, manufacturing was the primary sector of interest of firms investing in Africa (45 percent), followed by construction and services (35 percent), and resource-based investment at 20 percent (focusing on agriculture, oil, gas, and mining).

- Support from the Chinese government was considered to be an important factor driving FDI to Africa relative to other regions.

- Africa was the least attractive environment in the eyes of the Chinese investors with regard to political risk, perceived by 94 percent of the firms surveyed as the riskiest region.

- Some 60 percent of the firms investing in Africa ranked the policy environment there as "good," which was twice the levels achieved by Latin America at 29 percent.

In terms of the future trends and destinations for Chinese outward investment, nearly 60 percent of the firms surveyed had concrete plans for additional overseas projects in the next three years, and an additional 13 percent had plans but no specific projects. Here again Africa fares well, as the intended destination for 21 percent of the planned projects.

It is worth noting that the survey found the firms often lacking information on both sides of the equation—on the procedures required by the government of China for outward investors, and on the investment conditions in the countries in which they were establishing operations. This implies information gaps both behind and across borders that should be addressed.

Source: World Bank Group/MIGA.

FIGURE 2.26

Current Chinese FDI Outflows to Africa are Largely, But Not Exclusively, Resource-Oriented

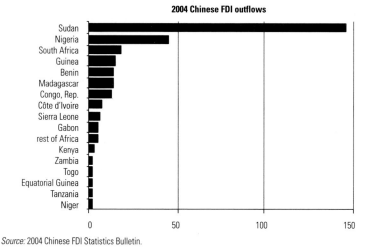

2004 Chinese FDI outflows

Source: 2004 Chinese FDI Statistics Bulletin.

Mauritius is a major Indian FDI destination in Africa, particularly in the financial sector, as well as in the telecommunications and pharmaceuticals sectors (figure 2.27). However, it is difficult to assess the extent to which the investment stays in the country or passes through to take advantage of Mauritius' low tax regime.[21] FDI from India to Africa is set to increase, as the Indian conglomerate Tata Motors has identified South Africa as the next frontier in its globalization policy. It plans to use South Africa as its gateway to Europe by expanding its automotive operations there, taking advantage of South Africa's favorable trade regime with Europe.

Emerging African FDI to China

Official data on Africa's FDI to Asia are largely unavailable. However, data are available on Africa's FDI to China. Based on statistics from the Chinese authorities, African FDI to China reached $776 million in 2004, compared to $565 million in 2002, posting a 17 percent annual compounded growth rate over two years. Mauritius accounted for more than three-quarters of the total flows of FDI from Africa to China in 2004 (figure 2.28).[22] Clearly, a large proportion of that FDI is pass-through, unlikely originating solely in Africa. Worth noting is that South Africa has been actively investing in

BOX 2.5

Dynamic Sectors in Chinese Outward FDI

Worldwide, the largest proportion of China's OFDI stock is in the business sector, including mainly the investment in equity of companies outside China, accounting for 37 percent of the total value. Trade, mainly in the wholesale and retail sectors, amounts for 18 percent of China's OFDI. The mining sector, mainly oil and natural gas exploration and ferrous and nonferrous metal mining and quarrying, attracted $6 billion in Chinese investment, accounting for 13 percent of the total stock. The transport, storage, and communications sector's stock reached $4.6 billion, accounting for 10 percent of China's OFDI, mainly in water transportation. The tertiary sector dominates China's OFDI, accounting for 75 percent of total stock in 2004. It is noteworthy that investment in mining has increased rapidly in recent years.

Chinese Outward FDI Stock by Sector, 2004

Sector and industry	$ millions	percent
Total	**44,579**	
Primary	**6,784**	**15**
Agriculture, forestry, fishery	834	2
Mining, quarrying, and petroleum	5,950	13
Secondary	**4,540**	**10**
Manufacturing	4,540	10
Tertiary	**33,255**	**75**
Electricity, gas, and water	910	2
Construction	832	2
Trade (wholesale and retail)	7,840	18
Transport, storage, and communication	4,580	10
Business activities	16,420	37
Community, social, and personal service activities	1,100	2
Other services	1,573	4

Source: Ministry of Commerce, 2004 Statistical Bulletin of China's Outward Foreign Direct Investment.

China. In 2004, FDI from South Africa to China increased significantly to $109 million, up from $26 million in 2002. In 2005, SAB Miller, the South African food and beverage company, announced plans to invest about $15 million in China. Nigeria is another emerging African investor in China, having more than doubled its FDI to China between 2002 and 2004.

FIGURE 2.27

India's FDI Outflows by Sector and Destination

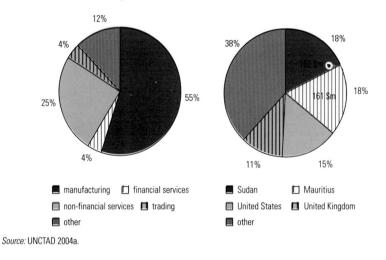

manufacturing	☐ financial services
non-financial services	trading
other	

■ Sudan	☐ Mauritius
United States	United Kingdom
other	

Source: UNCTAD 2004a.

FIGURE 2.28

African FDI to China, Total, 2002 and 2004

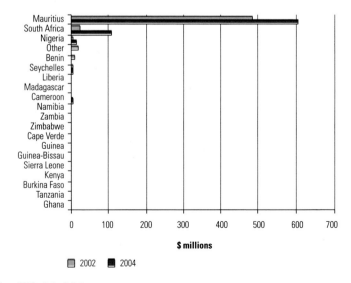

$ millions

☐ 2002   ■ 2004

Source: Chinese FDI Statistics Bulletin.

In summary, the growing FDI from China and India to Africa is consistent with these countries' trade patterns in Africa (see box 2.6). The challenge for Africa is to grasp this opportunity to create an environment for Asian developing economies to invest in the business activities that create high value-added commodities, rather than investing mainly in the extractive sector known to create few backward linkages in the host economy. This is the focus of chapter 6.

BOX 2.6

Summary of Characteristics of Africa's Trade and Investment Patterns with China and India

- Mineral resources, including oil, dominate Africa's exports to China and India and display rapid growth.

- Agricultural raw materials and food are also commodities having high and rapidly growing demand by China and India.

  Complementarities include:

  - Growing demand for raw materials in expanding Chinese and Indian industries and for food by Chinese and Indian consumers with increasing purchasing power

  - Internal pressure for resource reallocation within the domestic economies of China and India

- China and India export manufactured products to Africa.

  Complementarities include:

  - Chinese and Indian firms supply lower-tech and lower-cost products compared to those from industrialized countries; this intensifies competition for and efficiency of African producers—consumers benefit.

  - China and India also provide capital goods and intermediate inputs, enabling African businesses to manufacture products potentially exportable to third regions and countries (for example, EU, United States) and engage in network trade.

Source: World Bank staff.

Key Elements Shaping African-Asian Trade Flows

Roles of At-the-Border, Behind-the-Border, and Between-the-Border Factors

What are the principal factors that account for the differences observed in the patterns of African-Asian trade flows? At-the-border formal trade policies are often at the forefront of negotiations and discussions on international commerce. Obviously, tariff and nontariff barriers (NTBs) are the primary targets of trade liberalization. It is thus important to investigate the impact of such factors on the patterns of Africa's trade flows with Asia. More liberal import policies taken by individual countries (for example, low tariff rates) should facilitate more trade flows among such countries. Preferential market access measures or free trade agreements also should stimulate more trade flows.

However, changes in formal trade policies are only a necessary and not a sufficient condition for engendering cross-border trade. For trade to take place, tradable, internationally competitive goods and services need to be produced. In many developing countries where the private sector base is thin, this translates to enhancing the investment environment behind the border so that both domestic businesses and foreign investors can build an efficient productive (supply) capacity to respond to opportunities created by increased market demand. At the same time, for the goods and services produced to be traded efficiently, sufficient capacity is needed for trade-facilitating infrastructure, institutions, and services to lower between-the-border trade-related transactions costs.

Country-Level Qualitative Studies
A large number of qualitative studies have been conducted to analyze how at-the-border, behind-the-border, and between-the-border factors influence the trade performance of developing countries. Prominent among them are the Diagnostic Trade Integration Studies (DTISs) carried out under the Integrated Framework for Trade-Related Technical Assistance to Least Developed Countries (IF) program. DTISs have been developed for 26 countries in Africa to identify country-specific bottlenecks for promoting trade in those countries (see chapter 1). As illustrated in table 2.6, which summarizes the findings from a sample of 6 of these 26 DTISs, these studies find that these three factors are major parameters affecting African trade performance.

The advantage of these country-specific studies is that they provide rich, qualitative evidence on the nature of the constraints on African trade at the micro level. Moreover, with their detailed analysis they are able to identify complex institutional linkages that may exist among the various constraints, especially where quantitative data do not exist. One such linkage is the interactive effect between formal trade policies and trade facilitation factors. For example, many trade policies such as multiple tariff bands, multiple tariffs for the same products, tariff peaks, nontariff barriers, as well as specific duties, are often creating enormous complexity in customs administration. Those policies not only restrict trade flows but also indirectly discourage trade flows by slowing customs procedures. Eliminating such barriers would have positive spillover effects to other areas, such as improving customs efficiency.

By their country-specific nature, DTISs are difficult instruments to gauge systematically the way in which these various factors impact African countries across the board (beyond the fact that only 26 DTISs have been carried out). Nor do they give a sense of the relative importance of such impacts. To do so requires a quantitative cross-country approach.

Cross-Country Quantitative Analysis: Gravity Model

Gravity models are one of the most popular analytical tools used in the economic study of bilateral trade flows to examine underlying factors that influence the cross-country direction and the volume of such flows.[23] To be sure, such models have shortfalls, in large part due to the lack of necessary data for conducting refined estimation, especially in the case of Sub-Saharan Africa. For example, due to the lack of availability of comprehensive data on bilateral services trade, gravity analysis of African trade necessarily focuses on merchandise trade flows. Careful estimation of interlinkage effects among policy factors is also difficult due to poor data availability. Nonetheless, gravity models provide useful information as to how significant are the various policy factors in influencing the pattern of overall trade flows between Africa and Asia on a cross-county basis. In this regard they are a powerful complement to the qualitative DTISs.

We apply an augmented multivariate gravity model to bilateral trade flows of African countries to and from various countries in the world, including Asian countries as well as African countries themselves.[24] In addition to economic and geographic factors such as GDP, GDP per capita, physical distance, and common language, the augmented gravity model incorporates formal trade policies, domestic behind-the-border business constraints, and between-the-border factors.

TABLE 2.6
Illustrative Findings from a Sample of DTIS Assessments on Six African LDCs

Country	At the border	
Rwanda	• Inadequate export development and diversification • High tariffs on raw materials • Negative tariff escalation on food and textiles	
Zambia	• Inadequate legislation on tariffs and safeguards	
Mali	• Poor promotion of domestically produced exports • Lack of investment promotion policy	
Tanzania	• Urgent need to phase out export taxes • Long waiting periods for duty drawback refunds • Lack of sector-specific foreign investment promotion policy	
Madagascar	• Inadequate assessment of tariff barriers • Poorly functioning investment promotion strategy and lack of an investment code	
Senegal	• Inconsistency between preshipment valuation and import duties • Weak investment promotion strategy • Too many separate Export Promotion Agencies in operation	

Source: World Bank staff.

Note: EPZ = Export processing zone; ICT = Information and communication technology; SME = Small and medium enterprises.

To measure the impact of formal at-the-border trade policies, the model uses several measures, including an index of trade restrictiveness of importers; membership in regional trade agreements; and preferential market access eligibility to the EU and United States markets through EBA and AGOA. Specific between-the-border factors included in the analysis are customs efficiency (in terms of number of documents required); availability of Internet access in exporting and importing countries; and quality of port

Behind the border	Between the border
• Lack of access to electricity constraining rural development and expansion of nonfarm activities • Lack of access to credit for farmers and SMEs • Weak organization of the rural sector and limited role of market activities	• Lack of capacity for standards and quality management constrains diversification into agroprocessed exports • High cost and limited access to rural transport reduces returns to trade and constrains the ability of rural farmers to produce commercial crops • Delays on the main corridors raise the costs of trade • Long border clearance times and uncertainty at customs
• Urgent need to make a thorough assessment of the WTO Government Procurement Agreement	• Long border clearance times, lack of ability to ensure integrity and increased compliance • Insufficient regulatory framework for transport, transit logistics, efficiency, costs • Lack of training for staff in transportation regulation and administration
• Inadequate access to power, water, and telecommunications • Weak regulation of public utilities • Lack of access to finance in specific sectors • Weak supply chain management • Noncompetitiveness of pricing in domestic markets	• Poor customs administration • Long transit delays • Complicated customs procedures
• Insufficient access to power, water, and telecommunications in EPZs • Inadequate competition policy and market access • Inability to use existing trade preferences	• Inadequate transport legislation • Inadequate public-private dialogue in transport and trade facilitation, transit, and border crossings
• Inadequate access to finance for SMEs • Complicated and poorly functioning taxation policy	• Weakly functioning customs administration • Noncompliance with customs practices
• Lack of access to competitively priced infrastructure services • Insufficient investment in the petroleum sector • Lack of a national ICT strategy • Need for reform in the financial sector	• Poor management of customs procedures • Outdated trade facilitation procedures • Lack of investment in cold storage facilities • Delayed implementation of civil aviation legislation

infrastructure (both airport and seaport) of both exporting and importing countries. Behind-the-border factors included in the model are various measures of barriers to doing business and the quality of domestic infrastructure services. The intensity of barriers to doing business is measured by the number of procedures required for starting a new business, registering property, obtaining licenses, and enforcing contracts. The quality of electric power service is used to measure infrastructure service delivery. In general the specific variables and respective data sources used in the model are listed in table 2A.8.

Table 2.7 summarizes the direction of statistically significant impacts from various factors based on the signs of coefficients estimated by Ordinary Least Squares (OLS) regressions. The complete list of estimated coefficients is in table 2A.9 in annex 2A. Although not reported in the table, most of the economic, geographical, historical, and cultural factors have the predicted signs and their coefficients are statistically significant. These variables capture most of the fundamental sources of the heterogeneity among Sub-Saharan countries.

A number of studies using gravity models have shown the significance of at-the-border constraints in impacting bilateral trade flows. Our empirical analysis shows that, on a cross-country basis, in addition to trade policy variables (as well as the standard economic and geographic factors), both behind-the-border and between-the-border factors significantly influence the trade performance of African countries. All of the statistically significant coefficients display the expected sign. Moreover, the results from the estimation procedures show that the same factors are equally important when examining

TABLE 2.7

What Determines Bilateral African-Asian Trade Flows? Relative Roles of At-the-Border, Behind-the-Border, and Between-the-Border Factors

		All merchandise trade		Manufactured trade	
		Exp. from Africa	Imp. to Africa	Exp. from Africa	Imp. to Africa
Formal trade policies	Importer trade testrictiveness	n.s.	n.s.	−	n.s.
	Regional trade agreement	+	+	+	n.s.
	Preferential market access	n.s.	n.s.	+	n.s.
Between-the-border factors	Customs procedure—exporter	−	n.s.	−	n.s.
	Customs procedure—importer	+	n.s.	n.s.	n.s.
	Internet access—exporter	+	+	+	+
	Internet access—importer	n.s.	n.s.	n.s.	n.s.
	Port quality—exporter	−	+	−	+
	Port quality—importer	+	+	+	+
Behind-the-border factors	Domestic business procedure—exporter	−	n.s.	−	n.s.
	Power infrastructure quality—exporter	n.s.	n.s.	+	n.s.

Source: Authors' calculations based on 2002–04 average figures. See table 2A.9 for the table of estimated coefficients and table 2A.8 for the data sources.

Note: Only the signs of significant coefficients are shown (level of significance above 10 percent). "n.s." represents a coefficient not statistically significant.

Africa's trade performance on a global basis or its trade performance vis-à-vis Asia in particular. This indicates the robustness of the estimated model.

At-the-Border Factors

As expected, the estimates show that formal trade policies do matter for exports and imports of African countries. Yet only manufactured exports of African countries seem to be significantly negatively impacted by import trade restrictions and, moreover, only when behind-the-border and between-the-border factors are also taken into account. For (broader) merchandise trade, the multivariate analysis suggests that once between-the-border and behind-the-border impacts are also taken into account, the significance of trade restrictiveness of importing countries tends to diminish significantly. This points to the importance of behind-the-border and between-the-border factors even after allowing for the impact of at-the-border policies.

The finding of a positive regional trade agreement (RTA) effect is consistent with other empirical studies. Through lowering within-bloc trade barriers, RTA participation may cause countries to trade more.[25] Alternatively, intra-bloc trade may grow by diverting flows from extra-bloc trade. In either way, formation of RTAs generates more trade within the blocs.[26] The effect of RTA formation is not only increasing the overall volume of trade but also may likely affect the product composition of exports within and outside the RTAs, partly by diverting trade flows away from countries outside the bloc.[27] This might be one of the reasons why the RTA variable does not have a significant impact on manufactured imports to Africa, while it does for the general merchandise import flows to Africa. The weak manufacturing base in Africa does not cause a diversion of manufactured product flows toward intra-bloc trade. Preferential market access through AGOA and EBA has a positive and significant coefficient only for manufactured exports. This is consistent with the fact that most products benefiting from AGOA and EBA are manufactured products, whereas agricultural products do not receive equal benefits of duty-free market access to those markets.

Behind-the-Border Factors

Our estimated model provides clear empirical evidence that a poor domestic business environment in the form of high barriers to entry and poor power infrastructure substantially restricts exports, particularly for African countries' exports of manufactured products. It is quite straightforward that better power infrastructure improves productivity of domestic producers, thereby strengthening their export competitiveness. Better power infrastructure also attracts foreign investors who would be more prone to produce for export markets. The coefficient estimates from the augmented gravity model underpin this relationship between export performance and power infrastructure.

For exports from Africa, domestic business-related barriers measured in terms of number of procedures for starting and operating a business have a significantly negative impact on exports by African countries. Regulatory burdens in African countries not only increase business transactions costs and reduce productivity, they also pose barriers for new businesses to enter.

Figure 2.29 shows how a 10 percent improvement in some selective between-the-border and behind-the-border factors increases exports of African countries, based on the estimation results of our augmented gravity model (table 2A.9). Improving domestic business-related procedures would visibly improve export performance of African countries. This applies not only to manufactured exports, but also to exports in general. A 10 percent improvement in efficiency of domestic business procedures is associated with 38 percent larger bilateral exports of African countries. Improvement in power infrastructure would also have a high positive impact on exports, particularly on manufactured exports. A 10 percent improvement in power infrastructure–services quality would increase exports by 15 percent.

That there is a relatively strong impact on exports of behind-the-border factors is an important finding. Improvements in domestic business procedures or in power infrastructure–services quality are essentially enhancing domestic production and therefore, in one aspect, should be neutral to exports. Such domestic impacts should be mostly subsumed under GDP and thus already captured in the model. The sizable positive impacts of the behind-the-border factors on exports hint at significant positive spillovers in improving efficiency. A large body of literature shows that there is a clear linkage between productivity and propensity to export both at the country level as well as at the firm level. Exports to each market require certain fixed costs unique to exportation. Firms choose to export and engage in cross-border arm's length transactions only if they are productive enough. Also, several studies point out that higher domestic productivity allows firms to export not only in regional markets but also to geographically more distant markets. The efficiency gain from improving behind-the-border constraints appears to generate sizable improvement in trade flows.

Between-the-Border Factors
The estimated model suggests that customs efficiency is an important

FIGURE 2.29

Predicted Percentage Increase in Africa's Bilateral Exports from Improvement in Factors, Based on Augmented Gravity Model

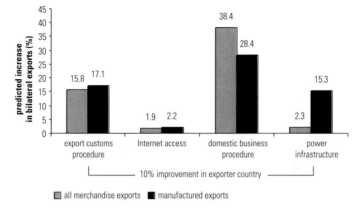

Source: Authors' calculations based on 2002–04 average figures. See table 2A.9 for coefficient estimates.

between-the-border factor affecting Africa's exports. On both general merchandise exports and manufactured exports, the results show significantly negative impacts of poor customs clearance procedures for exporting products. While the number of necessary documents for customs clearance is used here to measure inefficiency of customs procedures, similar results are obtained from using alternative ways of measuring the procedural constraints in customs, such as number of required signatures or total time required to clear customs. Our finding for African trade agrees with evidence from other research that addresses customs efficiency and other trade logistics, both at the country and industry levels as well as at the firm level.[28]

The positive effect of port infrastructure quality, capturing both airport and seaport quality, seems to be much more pronounced in affecting African imports as opposed to exports. For all types of trade flows and for both merchandise trade as well as manufactured trade, higher quality of port infrastructure leads to more imports.[29]

IT infrastructure is found to also significantly affect African bilateral trade flows.[30] Better Internet access in exporting countries is positively related to export flows. The insignificant result for importing countries may suggest that the Internet is increasingly utilized as a tool for suppliers to build their networks with buyers rather than a tool for consumers to source products—at least in the context of African exports and imports. It may also be the case that the use of the Internet goes much beyond simply reducing searching costs of sellers and buyers in cross-border transactions, but reducing more general business-related transactions costs, which improves the productivity level of domestic producers.

Trade and Investment Linkages

What linkages exist between FDI inflows to and exports from African countries? How do these linkages compare with those that might exist for Asian countries? Based on the gravity model incorporating the stock of inward FDI as one of the explanatory variables, FDI in African countries appears to be complementing rather than substituting for bilateral export flows (table 2.8). In the case of the Asian countries, the estimates also suggest complementary effects between FDI and exports. In both cases, greater stocks of FDI are associated with higher exports. While recognizing the variation among individual countries in Africa, for the African countries as a whole, the effect is more muted than it is for Asian countries. However, among non-oil-exporting African countries, the complementary effect is actually stronger than that for the Asian countries.

These findings suggest the existence of an important relationship between trade and FDI flows in Africa as well as in Asia. Not surprisingly, in the context of trade and investment between these two regions, this linkage has various dimensions. In particular, attracting FDI from Asia (as well as from elsewhere) to Africa appears to be an effective route to boosting African exports. Detailed analysis of these types of linkages and their implications for African development is the focus of chapter 6.

Conclusions and Policy Implications

Africa's trade with China and India has grown rapidly in both directions. This is based on high demand for natural resources by China and India and

TABLE 2.8

Trade-FDI Complementary Effects from Gravity Model

Indicator	Coefficient estimate of FDI inward stock on export flows
Exports by Asian countries	0.29
Exports by African countries	0.11
Exports by non-oil-exporting African countries	0.36

Source: Authors' calculations based on 2002–04 average figures. See table 2A.8 for the data sources.

Note: Coefficient estimates are all statistically significant at 5 percent. Non-oil-exporting African countries are all Sub-Saharan African countries other than Angola, Chad, Republic of Congo, Equatorial Guinea, Nigeria, and Sudan.

their industrial advantage in manufactured products against African countries. This reflects complementarities between African countries and China and India based on factor endowment of natural resources in Africa versus skilled labor in China and India.

Africa's exports to China and India have not directly contributed to its export diversification in terms of products and trading partners. Even though the boom of natural resource exports to China and India may provide short-term benefits, African countries need long-term strategies to leverage the current export-boom revenue to create opportunities for long-term economic benefits through export diversification.

Three types of complementarities between Africa and China and India are emerging: (i) vertical complementarities along the cotton-textile-apparel value chain; (ii) exports based on endowed natural resources with greater processing work (aluminum, for example) done locally; and (iii) increased intraindustry trade with emerging African industrial hubs such as South Africa and Nigeria. These complementarities provide opportunities for African countries to increase and diversify their exports by focusing on policies and activities (i) to increase participation in global network trade, (ii) to develop diversified value-added local industries through forward and backward linkages to resource-based products, and (iii) to enhance subregional economic integration and to maximize its benefit.

In addition to trading in goods, Africa-China-India economic relations are deepening in service trade and FDI. Asian FDI in Africa targets various trading opportunities using Africa as the production base; examples include natural resources for overseas markets and construction services for local markets, as well as trade-facilitation service providers. This implies the existence of a strong synergy among trade in goods, trade in services, and FDI, which in turn enhances economic relations between Africa and China and India.

Through quantitatively analyzing bilateral trade flows between Asian and African countries, the evidence presented strongly suggests that, while formal trade policies matter in promoting Africa's exports to Asia (as well as elsewhere), behind-the-border and between-the-border constraints are every bit as, if not more, critical. This means that, if African countries are to enhance their trade performance in Asia, it will take far more than simply liberalizing trade policies to reach that objective. Indeed, the deeper, more complex, and longer-run challenge is to confront the behind-the-border and between-the-border constraints. Improving trade policies is necessary but not sufficient.

Annex 2A

TABLE 2A.1
African Countries' Three Main Exports, with Their Share in Total Exports

Country	Product I	
South Africa	Platinum (11.8%)	
Egypt, Arab Rep. of	Motor gasoline, light oil (15.3%)	
Tunisia	Trousers, breeches etc. (17.1%)	
Morocco	Trousers, breeches etc. (6.5%)	
Kenya	Tea (16.9%)	
Tanzania	Fish fillets, frsh, chilld (12.6%)	
Zimbabwe	Tobacco, stemmed, stripped (30.8%)	
Mauritius	T-shirts, othr. vests knit (16.6%)	
Madagascar	Spices, ex. pepper, pimiento (27.9%)	
Eritrea	Elctrn comp pts, crystals (40.7%)	
Namibia	Fish fillets, frozen (22.5%)	
Senegal	Mollusks (20.2%)	
Uganda	Coffee, not roasted (31.8%)	
Cape Verde	Special trans not classd (19.1%)	
Côte d'Ivoire	Cocoa beans (48.2%)	
Gambia, The	Aircrft etc. ULW >15000kg (40.3%)	
Ghana	Cocoa beans (48.3%)	
Togo	Cotton, not carded, combed (36.7%)	
Zambia	Copper; anodes; alloys (40.7%)	
Ethiopia	Coffee, not roasted (47.2%)	
Sierra Leone	Diamonds. excl.industrial (49%)	
Djibouti	Sodium chloride, etc. (35.2%)	
Cameroon	Crude petroleum (43.1%)	
Guinea	Aluminium ore, concentrat (43.4%)	
Lesotho	Jersys, pullovrs, etc. knit (33.3%)	
Malawi	Tobacco, stemmed, stripped (55.7%)	
Somalia	Sheep and goats, live (27.6%)	
Algeria	Crude petroleum (50.3%)	
Benin	Cotton, not carded, combed (68.7%)	
Burkina Faso	Cotton, not carded, combed (66.9%)	
Central African Republic	Diamonds. excl. industrial (42.7%)	
Congo DR	Diamonds. excl. industrial (54.9%)	
Guinea Bissau	Mollusks (32.8%)	
Mauritania	Iron ore, concntr. not agg (39.8%)	
Chad	Cotton, not carded, combed (57.5%)	
Liberia	Ships, boats, othr. vessels (69%)	

Three main exports, with their share in total exports[a]		No. of products accounting for more than 75 percent of exports
Product II	Product III	
Diamond.exl.industrial (9.6%)	Oth. coal, not agglomerated (7.5%)	44
Crude petroleum (13.4%)		42
Crude petroleum (6.8%)	Insultd wire, etc. conductr (5.4%)	35
Diodes, transistors etc. (5.5%)	Insultd wire,etc. condctr (5.4%)	33
Cut flowers and foliage (11.2%)	Motor gasoline, light oil (9.3%)	25
Coffee, not roasted (8.9%)	Tobacco, stemmed, stripped (6.9%)	21
Nickel, nckl. alloy, unwrgt (8.9%)	Nickel ores, concentrates (8.6%)	13
Sugars, beet or cane, raw (16.4%)	Jersys, pullovrs, etc. knit (11.5%)	10
Crustaceans, frozen (14.6%)	Jersys, pullovrs, etc. knit (11.6%)	9
Electrical capacitors (11.8%)	Drawing, measurg. instrmnt (4.6%)	8
Diamonds.excl.industrial (15.4%)	Radio-active chemicals (10.8%)	8
Groundnut oil, fractions (11.1%)	Fish, fresh, chilled, whole (9.4%)	8
Fish fillets, frsh, chilld (11.0%)	Tobacco, stemmed, stripped (9.7%)	8
Gas turbines, nes (18.2%)	Shirts (9.3%)	7
Cocoa paste (7.7%)	Bananas, fresh or dried (4.8%)	7
Oth. frsh, chll. vegetables (10.4%)	Groundnut oil, fractions (7.3%)	7
Wood, non-conifer, sawn (6.3%)	Alum., alum. alloy, unwrght (5.1%)	7
Natural calc.phosphates (20.9%)	Cocoa beans (5.8%)	7
Copper plate,etc.15mm+ th (10.8%)	Cobalt, cadmium, etc. unwrt (10.4%)	7
Sesame (sesamum) seeds (12.6%)	Sheep skin without wool (6.5%)	6
Convertible seats,parts (10.9%)	Parts, data proc. etc. mch (4.9%)	6
Oth. wheat, meslin, unmlled (11.5%)	Petrolm. bitumen, coke, etc (10.2%)	5
Wood, non-conifer, sawn (13.4%)	Bananas, fresh or dried (9.8%)	4
Alumina (aluminium oxide) (17.2%)	Crude petroleum (10.3%)	4
Trousers, breeches, etc. (18.4%)	Trousers, breeches etc. (15.9%)	4
Tea (10.5%)	Tobacco,not stripped, etc (8.8%)	4
Fuel wood, wood charcoal (20.7%)	Mollusks (17.1%)	4
Natural gas, liquefied (15.1%)	Motor gasoline, light oil (14.8%)	3
Motor gasoline, light oil (5.8%)		3
Sesame (sesamum) seeds (6.4%)	Cigarettes contg. tobacco (4.1%)	3
Wood, non-conif, rough, unt (29.1%)	Cotton, not carded, combed (14%)	3
Industrial diamonds (14.4%)	Crude petroleum (8.8%)	3
Propane, liquefied (21.8%)	Fish, frozen ex. fillets (20.6%)	3
Mollusks (27.8%)	Fish, frozen ex. fillets (15.5%)	3
Crude petroleum (21.1%)	Natural gums, resins,etc. (11.9%)	2
Wood, non-conif, rough, unt (9.5%)	Natural rubber latex (5.9%)	2

(Continues on the following page.)

TABLE 2A.1
(continued)

	Product I	
Mozambique	Alum., alum. alloy, unwrght (70.9%)	
Niger	Radio-active chemicals (71.5%)	
Rwanda	Crude petroleum (61.1%)	
Syechelles	Fish, prepard, presrvd, nes (54.5%)	
Swaziland	Chem. products etc. nes (48.3%)	
Angola	Crude petroleum (94.6%)	
Botswana	Diamonds. excl. industrial (87.6%)	
Burundi	Coffee, not roasted (78.9%)	
Comoros	Spices, ex. pepper, pimento (88.1%)	
Congo, Rep. of	Crude petroleum (78.4%)	
Equatorial Guinea	Crude petroleum (89.6%)	
Gabon	Crude petroleum (77.4%)	
Libya	Crude petroleum (82.8%)	
Mali	Cotton, not carded, combed (86.8%)	
Nigeria	Crude petroleum (86.4%)	
São Tomé and Principé	Cocoa beans (82.2%)1	
Sudan	Crude petroleum (79.6%)	
Africa[b]	Crude petroleum (38.4%) [16.3%]	

Sources: African Economic Outlook 2005/2006, based on African Development Bank Statistics Division; PC-TAS 1999-2003 International Trade UNCTAD/WTO-UN Statistics Division

Note: a. Products are reported when accounting for more than 4 per cent of total exports.
b. Figures in [ ] represent the share of Africa in the world's exports for each product.

| Three main exports, with their share in total exports[a] | | No. of products accounting for more than 75 percent of exports |
Product II	Product III	
Crustaceans, frozen (6.6%)		2
Special trans not classd (12.3%)		2
Ore etc. molybdn. niob. etc (14.8%)	Coffee, not roasted (14.6%)	2
Fish, frozen ex. fillets (27.3%)	Motor gasoline, light oil (4.3%)	2
Yarn, staple fibres, etc. (29.1%)	Othr. organo-inorgan. comp (5.4%)	2
		1
Nickel mattes, sintrs. etc (8.4%)		1
Diamonds. excl. industrial (4.7%)	Ore etc. molybdn. niob. etc (4.4%)	1
Essential oils (8.8%)		1
Motor gasoline, light oil (5.8%)	Wood, non-conif, rough, unt (5.7%)	1
Acyclic monohydric alchl (4.6%)	Wood, non-conif, rough, unt (4.1%)	1
Wood, non-conif, rough, unt (12.3%)	Manganese ores, concentrs (4%)	1
Motor gasoline, light oil (10.4%)		1
		1
Natural gas, liquefied (4.6%)		1
		1
		1
Motor gasoline, light oil (4.7%) [5.5%]	Diamonds. excl. industrial (3.7%) [12.5%]	36

TABLE 2A.2

Composition of Africa's Exports to Asia, 1999 and 2004

Product	Exports in 1999 ($ million)	Share (percent)	Exports in 2004 ($ million)	Share (percent)	Annual growth (percent)
Machinery and transportation equipment	435	2.3	1,383	3.7	26
Ores	804	4.2	2,377	6.4	24
Petroleum products	158	0.8	401	1.1	20
Electronics	19	0.1	47	0.1	20
Crude petroleum	7,136	37.2	17,113	46.1	19
Manufacturing of non-oil minerals	2	0.0	3	0.0	8
Pharmaceuticals	5	0.0	12	0.0	19
Electric machineries	36	0.2	71	0.2	15
Other manufactured goods, paper, pulp, furniture, etc.	490	2.6	904	2.4	13
Nonpharmaceutical chemicals	520	2.7	955	2.6	13
Basic manufactured metals	4,880	25.5	8,201	22.1	11
Cotton, textile fibers and yarns	848	4.4	1,423	3.8	11
Agricultural raw materials, nonedibles	1,525	8.0	1,970	5.3	5
Processed food and beverages	271	1.4	342	0.9	5
Agricultural raw food edibles	1,437	7.5	1,777	4.8	4
Apparel and footwear	30	0.2	25	0.1	−4
Manufacturing of nonminerals	11	0.1	4	0.0	−18
Coal	554	2.9	132	0.4	−25
Total	19,159	100.0	37,141	100.0	14

Source: UN COMTRADE SITC Revision 2.

Note: Asia includes Bangladesh, Cambodia, China (including Hong Kong and Macao), India, Indonesia, Japan, Rep. of Korea, Malaysia, Maldives, Mongolia, Nepal, Pakistan, Philippines, Singapore , Sri Lanka, Taiwan, Thailand, and Vietnam.

TABLE 2A.3
Africa's Imports from Asia—Growth Rate by Commodity Group

Product	Imports in 1999 ($ million)	Share (percent)	Imports in 2004 ($ million)	Share (percent)	Annual growth (percent)
Machinery and transportation equipment	5,241	28.2	12,336	32.3	19
Agricultural raw food edibles	2,075	11.2	3,947	10.3	14
Processed food and beverages	1,426	7.7	2,997	7.8	16
Pharmaceuticals	1,851	10.0	3,529	9.2	14
Electronics	1,457	7.8	2,607	6.8	12
Coal	1,220	6.6	2,586	6.8	16
Cotton, textile fibers and yarns	1,228	6.6	2,283	6.0	13
Apparel and footwear	1,165	6.3	2,087	5.5	12
Agricultural raw materials, nonedibles	1,110	6.0	2,204	5.8	15
Manufacturing of non-minerals	917	4.9	1,525	4.0	11
Basic manufactured metals	286	1.5	559	1.5	14
Petroleum products	269	1.4	825	2.2	25
Other manufactured goods, paper, pulp, furniture, etc.	181	1.0	324	0.8	12
Nonpharmaceutical chemicals	102	0.5	210	0.5	16
Ores	35	0.2	78	0.2	17
Manufacturing of non-oil minerals	27	0.1	71	0.2	21
Electric machineries	13	0.1	19	0	8
Total $m	18,602	100	38,184	100	15

Source: UN COMTRADE SITC Revision 2.

Note: Asia includes Bangladesh, Cambodia, China (including Hong Kong and Macao), India, Indonesia, Japan, Rep. of Korea, Malaysia, Maldives, Mongolia, Nepal, Pakistan, Philippines, Singapore , Sri Lanka, Taiwan, Thailand, and Vietnam.

TABLE 2A.4
Africa's Top 20 Exports to China: Products and Leading Exporters
(2002–04 average)

SITC code: name Share in total African exports to China (US$9,171 m)	Exporting country Share in total export value of the product from Africa to China				
3330: Crude oil 62.20%	Angola 46.80%	Sudan 24.66%	R. Congo 13.00%	Eq. Guinea 9.17%	Nigeria 3.07%
2472: Sawlogs and veneer logs 4.91%	Gabon 41.17%	R. Congo 17.84%	Eq. Guinea 16.31%	Cameroon 8.17%	Liberia 7.21%
2815: Iron ore and concentrates 4.59%	S. Africa 94.03%	Mauritania 3.54%	Liberia 1.31%	Mozambique 1.12%	
6672: Diamonds 3.33%	S. Africa 99.27%				
2631: Cotton (other than linters) 3.28%	Benin 21.54%	Burkina F. 17.26%	Mali 15.14%	C. d'Ivoire 13.70%	Cameroon 8.14%
2879: Ores and concentrat. of other nonferrous base metals 1.75%	S. Africa 30.95%	R. Congo 26.73%	D.R. Congo 26.52%	Rwanda 5.90%	Nigeria 4.10%
1212: Tobacco 1.51%	Zimbabwe 99.56%				
6727: Iron or steel coils 1.38%	S. Africa 100.00%				
6812: Platinum 1.34%	S. Africa 100.00%				
2877: Manganese ores and concentrates 1.31%	Gabon 46.53%	Ghana 25.87%	S. Africa 25.61%	C. d'Ivoire 1.99%	
6821: Copper and copper alloys 1.26%	Zambia 48.36%	S. Africa 29.24%	Namibia 20.41%	R. Congo 1.27%	
6746: Sheets and plates, rolled 0.83%	S. Africa 100.00%				
6841: Aluminium and aluminium alloys 0.46%	S. Africa 99.80%				
5121: Acyclic alcohols 0.41%	S. Africa 100.00%				
3413: Petroleum gases 0.41%	Nigeria 76.12%	Sudan 23.32%			
6716: Ferro-alloys 0.38%	S. Africa 99.99%				
2871: Copper ores and concentrates 0.37%	S. Africa 40.67%	Tanzania 39.74%	R. Congo 13.47%	D.R. Congo 5.42%	
6899: Base metals,n.e.s. 0.36%	Zambia 62.88%	S. Africa 26.08%	R. Congo 5.79%	Uganda 3.39%	D.R. Congo 1.86%
6842: Aluminium and aluminium alloys 0.25%	S. Africa 100.00%				
2483: Wood of nonconiferous species 0.24%	Cameroon 45.58%	Gabon 23.20%	R. Congo 11.92%	S. Africa 7.40%	Ghana 3.09%

Source: UN COMTRADE SITC Revision 2.

TABLE 2A.5
Africa's Top 20 Exports to India: Products and Leading Exporters
(2002–04 average)

SITC code: name Share in total African exports to India (US$3,027 m)	Exporting country Share in total export value of the product from Africa to India				
9710: Gold 52.67%	S. Africa 99.90%				
0577: Edible nuts (excl. nuts used for the extract.of oil) 8.83%	C. d'Ivoire 22.06%	Guinea B. 20.89%	Tanzania 20.52%	Benin 10.95%	Mozambique 9.17%
5222: Inorganic acids and oxygen compounds of nonmetals 8.50%	Senegal 55.46%	S. Africa 43.65%			
2472: Sawlogs and veneer logs 3.73%	C. d'Ivoire 34.55%	Gabon 22.34%	Nigeria 15.67%	Benin 9.55%	Ghana 4.87%
2631: Cotton (other than linters) 2.99%	Mali 20.96%	Tanzania 15.30%	Benin 12.71%	Sudan 9.04%	C. d'Ivoire 8.85%
2820: Waste and scrap metal of iron or steel 2.65%	S. Africa 27.07%	Nigeria 15.40%	C. d'Ivoire 6.68%	Benin 5.66%	R. Congo 4.93%
3222: Coal 2.05%	S. Africa 99.34%				
6673: Precious stones other than diamonds and pearl 1.09%	Zambia 43.75%	Tanzania 34.95%	S. Africa 10.49%	Kenya 6.83%	Madagascar 1.67%
2516: Chemical wood pulp 1.08%	S. Africa 75.14%	Somalia 24.85%			
3330: Crude oil 1.04%	Nigeria 70.76%	S. Africa 9.20%	Angola 7.57%	Senegal 5.87%	Sudan 3.20%
0542: Beans, peas, lentils 0.86%	Tanzania 59.86%	Malawi 12.71%	Kenya 11.88%	Ethiopia 7.55%	Mozambique 6.89%
2713: Natural calcium phosphat 0.74%	Togo 72.03%	Senegal 22.53%	S. Africa 5.44%		
6841: Aluminium and aluminium alloys 0.61%	S. Africa 83.37%	Nigeria 12.78%	Zambia 1.60%	C. d'Ivoire 1.33%	
2871: Copper ores and concentrates 0.48%	Guinea 72.12%	Ghana 26.40%	R. Congo 1.35%		
7932: Ships,boats, and other vessels 0.42%	Liberia 99.90%				
5162: Aldehyde-, ketone-, and quinone-function compounds 0.38%	S. Africa 98.10%	Nigeria 1.71%			
5232: Metallic salts and peroxysalts of inorganic acids 0.37%	Kenya 99.52%				
5121: Acyclic alcohols 0.37%	S. Africa 88.92%	Liberia 6.46%	Sudan 3.21%		
6831: Nickel and nickel alloys 0.36%	Zimbabwe 53.68%	S. Africa 44.62%			
5123: Phenols and phen.-alcohols 0.31%	Senegal 63.03%	S. Africa 34.99%	Nigeria 1.34%		

Source: UN COMTRADE SITC Revision 2.

TABLE 2A.6
Top 20 Imports from China: Products and Leading Importers
(2002–04 average)

SITC code: name Share in total African imports from China (US$7,407 m)	Importing country Share in total import value of the product from China to Africa				
6522: Cotton fabrics,woven 8.45%	Benin 29.73%	Togo 10.67%	Gambia 8.21%	S. Africa 7.52%	Kenya 7.51%
8510: Footwear 5.34%	S. Africa 41.11%	Nigeria 13.47%	Ghana 6.95%	Benin 4.82%	Togo 3.55%
7851: Motorcycles 4.10%	Nigeria 68.48%	Togo 9.71%	Mali 4.38%	Cameroon 3.67%	Guinea 2.38%
7781: Batteries and accumulators 3.08%	Benin 27.88%	Nigeria 10.50%	Togo 7.76%	Ghana 7.12%	Kenya 6.97%
6531: Fabrics, woven of continuous synth. textil. materials 2.94%	S. Africa 23.38%	Nigeria 22.71%	Togo 16.23%	Benin 7.53%	Ethiopia 6.67%
6534: Fabrics, woven, of discontinuous synthetic fibers 2.46%	Benin 18.80%	S. Africa 13.30%	Togo 10.99%	Nigeria 10.00%	C. d'Ivoire 6.54%
0422: Rice 1.64%	C. d'Ivoire 77.16%	Liberia 6.63%	Tanzania 4.10%	Nigeria 3.31%	Ghana 2.22%
8310: Travel goods, handbags, briefcases, purses 1.48%	S. Africa 31.46%	Nigeria 25.14%	Ghana 8.60%	Kenya 6.34%	Tanzania 3.63%
6560: Tulle, lace, embroidery, ribbons, and other small wares 1.32%	Nigeria 45.70%	Benin 22.66%	Togo 14.50%	S. Africa 5.50%	Gambia 3.60%
8459: Outer garments and clothing,knitted 1.32%	S. Africa 58.72%	Nigeria 6.59%	Sudan 5.20%	Ethiopia 5.16%	Madagascar 4.83%
7641: Elect. line telephonic and telegraphic apparatus 1.24%	Nigeria 19.35%	Zambia 15.18%	Ethiopia 13.82%	Angola 10.54%	S. Africa 8.38%
7643: Radiotelegraphic and radiotelephonic transmitters 1.09%	Nigeria 32.01%	S. Africa 30.13%	Ghana 10.87%	Uganda 3.94%	Angola 3.82%
6783: Tubes and pipes, of iron or steel 1.08%	Sudan 94.70%	Nigeria 1.83%	S. Africa 1.17%		
7162: Elect.motors & generators 1.08%	Nigeria 61.71%	S. Africa 9.50%	Sudan 8.16%	Angola 6.27%	Benin 2.60%
6974: Art. commonly used for dom. purposes 1.07%	Benin 30.72%	Nigeria 13.61%	S. Africa 8.62%	Ghana 7.29%	C. d'Ivoire 6.98%
7611: Television receivers, color 1.07%	S. Africa 54.53%	Lesotho 14.03%	Nigeria 11.39%	Sudan 3.38%	Madagascar 2.31%
8423: Trousers 1.02%	S. Africa 51.35%	Nigeria 15.11%	Benin 9.53%	Tanzania 8.17%	Uganda 5.95%
8939: Miscellaneous art. of materials of plastics 1.00%	S. Africa 23.96%	Nigeria 23.74%	Benin 7.63%	Ghana 6.85%	Kenya 5.16%
8124: Lighting fixtures and fittings 1.00%	Nigeria 39.12%	S. Africa 21.11%	Ghana 6.63%	Benin 5.63%	Kenya 5.39%
6991: Locksmiths wares, safes, strong rooms of base metal 0.98%	Nigeria 32.00%	S. Africa 19.18%	Benin 7.38%	Ghana 7.08%	Kenya 5.79%

Source: UN COMTRADE SITC Revision 2.

TABLE 2A.7
Top 20 Imports from India: Products and Leading Importers
(2002–04 average)

SITC code: name Share in total African imports from India (US$3,267 m)	Exporting country Share in total import value of the product from India to Africa				
5417: Medicaments 8.99%	Nigeria 25.97%	S. Africa 8.78%	Kenya 6.26%	R. Congo 5.47%	Ghana 5.05%
0422: Rice 8.77%	S. Africa 35.53%	Nigeria 23.17%	C. d'Ivoire 8.80%	Senegal 6.21%	Somalia 4.97%
6522: Cotton fabrics, woven, bleached 5.15%	Niger 14.02%	Togo 10.84%	Nigeria 10.08%	Benin 8.53%	Ghana 6.86%
6749: Sheets and plates of iron or steel 2.57%	S. Africa 29.36%	Ghana 12.99%	Nigeria 9.40%	Ethiopia 9.27%	Kenya 5.05%
6974: Art. commonly used for dom. purposes 2.25%	Nigeria 31.62%	Ghana 13.83%	Benin 12.97%	S. Africa 6.36%	C. d'Ivoire 4.91%
6513: Cotton yarn 2.20%	Mauritius 81.58%	S. Africa 11.66%			
7853: Invalid carriages, motorized or not 1.98%	Nigeria 19.97%	Tanzania 12.75%	Uganda 10.21%	Burkina F. 9.76%	Kenya 7.88%
6521: Cotton fabrics, woven, unbleached 1.94%	Benin 10.73%	Togo 10.29%	Nigeria 9.62%	Ghana 7.25%	Tanzania 6.82%
6783: Tubes and pipes, of iron or steel 1.87%	Sudan 83.76%	Ghana 3.29%	Ethiopia 1.57%	Nigeria 1.42%	Kenya 1.12%
6531: Fabrics, woven of continuous synth. textil. materials 1.77%	Mauritius 17.51%	Nigeria 14.01%	Togo 10.48%	Malawi 9.28%	R. Congo 8.39%
7284: Machinery and appliances for specialized particular industry 1.26%	Nigeria 31.93%	Kenya 13.56%	Tanzania 10.43%	Ghana 7.72%	S. Africa 7.67%
7849: Parts and accessories of motor vehicles 1.24%	S. Africa 45.38%	Nigeria 20.05%	Sudan 9.24%	Kenya 5.52%	Ghana 2.63%
0111: Meat of bovine animals 1.14%	Angola 59.09%	R. Congo 11.16%	Mauritius 9.13%	Gabon 8.34%	C. d'Ivoire 5.20%
6745: Sheets and plates, rld. thickns 1.01%	S. Africa 29.12%	Ethiopia 20.01%	Nigeria 11.06%	Kenya 7.14%	Ghana 4.36%
7852: Cycles, not motorized 0.89%	Nigeria 25.30%	Mozambique 19.34%	Kenya 9.58%	R. Congo 7.98%	Malawi 5.89%
6672: Diamonds 0.84%	Swaziland 60.04%	S. Africa 29.07%	Mauritius 3.13%	C. African R. 2.26%	São Tomé P. 2.19%
8939: Miscellaneous art. of materials of plastics 0.70%	Sudan 14.56%	Nigeria 13.23%	S. Africa 11.01%	Kenya 10.73%	Tanzania 9.05%
6842: Aluminium and aluminium alloys 0.67%	Nigeria 40.86%	Kenya 27.40%	Ghana 7.99%	S. Africa 6.54%	Ethiopia 2.97%
5530: Perfumery, cosmeticsn and toilet preparations 0.64%	Nigeria 12.95%	Ghana 12.83%	S. Africa 9.53%	Mauritius 8.16%	Sudan 7.65%
5416: Glycosides; glands or other organs and their extracts 0.61%	R. Congo 13.07%	Nigeria 11.36%	Ethiopia 10.32%	Kenya 7.88%	Uganda 5.27%

Source: UN COMTRADE SITC Revision 2.

TABLE 2A.8
Key Variables in Gravity Model and Data Source

Group	Variables	Specific data and sources
Dependent variables	• Bilateral trade flows (aggregate merchandise exports) • Bilateral trade flows (manufactured exports)	UN COMTRADE from World Bank WITS
Base controls	• GDP (EX, IM) • GDP per capita (EX, IM) • Physical distance (PR) • Coastal/landlocked (EX, IM) • Common language (PR) • Colonial past (PR) • Common colonial power (PR)	World Bank, *World Development Indicators* World Bank, *World Development Indicators* CEPII geographical and distance data sets CEPII geographical and distance data sets CEPII geographical and distance data sets CEPII geographical and distance data sets CEPII geographical and distance data sets
Formal trade policies	• Trade restrictiveness in importing market (IM) • Regional trade agreements between exporter and importer (PR) • Exporter's eligibility for preferential market access to importing market (PR)	Heritage Foundation, *Economic Freedom Index* World Trade Organization U.S. Government and European Commission
Trade facilitation	• Port and airport infrastructure quality (EX, IM) • Customs efficiency (EX, IM) • ICT infrastructure availability (EX, IM)	World Economic Forum, *World Competitiveness Report* World Bank, *Doing Business Indicators* (number of documents required for exporting) World Bank, *World Development Indicators*
Domestic business environment	• Business-related administrative barriers (EX) • Power infrastructure quality (EX)	World Bank, *Doing Business Indicators* (composite of numbers of procedures for starting businesses, registering property, obtaining licenses, and enforcing contracts, using Principal Components Analysis) World Economic Forum, *World Competitiveness Report*

Note: CEPII = Centre d'Etudes Prospectives et d'Informations Internationales; WITS - World Integrated Trade Solution. EX (exporting country data), IM (importing country data), PR (exporting and importing countries pair data). All variables except for the variables for coastal/landlocked, common language, colonial past, common colonial power, regional trade agreements, and eligibility for preferential access to importing market are expressed in natural log.

TABLE 2A.9
Coefficient Estimates of Augmented Gravity Model (OLS)

	All merchandise trade		Manufactured trade	
	Exports from Africa	Imports to Africa	Exports from Africa	Imports To Africa
GDP—exporter (i)	1.475 ***	1.210 ***	1.354 ***	1.218 ***
	(0.082)	(0.042)	(0.076)	(0.045)
GDP per capita—exporter (i)	−0.056	−0.581 ***	0.205	−0.280
	(0.144)	(0.169)	(0.136)	(0.182)
GDP—importer (j)	1.078 ***	0.857 ***	0.925 ***	0.801 ***
	(0.044)	(0.071)	(0.043)	(0.075)
GDP per capita—importer (j)	−0.058	−0.059	−0.729 ***	0.035
	(0.161)	(0.104)	(0.152)	(0.111)
Contiguity (ij)	0.642	1.885 ***	1.009 *	1.323 **
	(0.429)	(0.395)	(0.396)	(0.412)
Common language (ij)	0.383 *	0.261	1.041 ***	0.211
	(0.161)	(0.159)	(0.152)	(0.168)
Past colonial relation (ij)	1.229 *	0.659	1.298 **	0.962
	(0.541)	(0.505)	(0.498)	(0.524)
Past common colonial power (ij)	0.128	0.745 ***	−0.106	0.874 ***
	(0.201)	(0.192)	(0.191)	(0.204)
Distance (ij)	−1.763 ***	−1.496 ***	−1.430 ***	−1.610 ***
	(0.147)	(0.135)	(0.139)	(0.145)
Landlocked—exporter (i)	−0.430 *	0.247	−0.866 ***	0.721 ***
	(0.199)	(0.197)	(0.190)	(0.213)
Landlocked—importer (j)	0.189	−0.902 ***	0.322	−0.624 ***
	(0.185)	(0.142)	(0.175)	(0.150)
Importer trade restrictiveness (j)	−0.017	−0.336	−0.451 *	−0.270
	(0.220)	(0.331)	(0.212)	(0.351)
Regional trade agreement (ij)	1.196 ***	0.960 ***	1.220 ***	0.475
	(0.298)	(0.284)	(0.280)	(0.302)
Preferential market access (ij)	0.400		0.956 ***	
	(0.214)		(0.198)	
Export customs procedure—exporter (i)	−1.575 ***	−0.444	−1.711 ***	−0.591
	(0.314)	(0.249)	(0.301)	(0.264)
Import customs procedure—importer (j)	0.366 *	−0.070	0.213	0.083
	(0.175)	(0.234)	(0.165)	(0.248)
Internet—exporter (i)	0.194 **	0.230 **	0.216 **	0.150 *
	(0.072)	(0.074)	(0.068)	(0.079)
Internet—importer (j)	−0.041	−0.036	0.117	−0.085
	(0.081)	(0.068)	(0.076)	(0.072)
Port quality—exporter (i)	−2.975 ***	2.311 ***	−3.158 ***	3.242 ***
	(0.497)	(0.383)	(0.470)	(0.412)
Port quality—importer (i)	2.000 ***	0.889 **	1.507 ***	0.911 *
	(0.343)	(0.336)	(0.330)	(0.356)
Domestic business procedure—exporter (i)	−3.835 ***	−0.249	−2.835 ***	0.230
	(0.549)	(0.274)	(0.526)	(0.292)
Power infrastructure quality—exporter (i)	0.226	−0.295	1.532 ***	−0.789
	(0.350)	(0.383)	(0.335)	(0.411)
No. of observations	1420	1351	1319	1295
R square	0.613	0.651	0.645	0.633

Source: Authors' calculations based on 2002–04 average figures. See table 2A.8 for the data sources.

Note: Standard errors in parentheses. * = Statistically significant at the 10 percent level. ** = Statistically significant at the 5 percent level. *** = Statistically significant at the 1 percent level. All variables except for the variables for coastal/landlocked, common language, colonial past, common colonial power, regional trade agreements, and eligibility for preferential access to importing market are expressed in natural log.

Endnotes

1. Portions of this analysis update earlier work on Africa-Asia trade and investment in World Bank (2004b).
2. An economy that generates more than 10 percent of its GDP in primary commodities exports is classified as a "natural resource economy."
3. See Collier (2006).
4. Goldstein et al. 2006.
5. UNCTAD 2005g.
6. UNCTAD 2005d.
7. Consistently we define Africa to mean Sub-Saharan African countries (Angola, Benin, Botswana, Burkina Faso, Burundi, Cameroon, Cape Verde, Central African Republic, Chad, Democratic Republic of Congo, Republic of Congo, Côte d'Ivoire, Equatorial Guinea, Eritrea, Ethiopia, Gabon, The Gambia, Ghana, Guinea, Guinea-Bissau, Kenya, Lesotho, Liberia, Madagascar, Malawi, Mali, Mauritania, Mauritius, Mozambique, Namibia, Niger, Nigeria, Rwanda, Sao Tome and Principe, Senegal, Seychelles, Sierra Leone, South Africa, Sudan, Swaziland, Tanzania, Togo, Uganda, Zambia, and Zimbabwe. Owing to lack of data, Liberia and Somalia are not in the sample unless otherwise specified. Also, Asia means Eastern and Southern Asian countries (Afghanistan, Bangladesh, Bhutan, Cambodia, China (including Hong Kong and Macao), Indonesia, India, Japan, Vietnam, Thailand, Democratic Republic of Korea, Republic of Korea, Lao People's Democratic Republic, Maldives, Malaysia, Mongolia, Myanmar, Nepal, Pakistan, Philippines, Singapore , Sri Lanka, and Taiwan).
8. EU consists of Austria, Belgium, Cyprus, Czech Republic, Denmark, Estonia, Finland, France, Germany, Greece, Hungary, Ireland, Italy, Latvia, Lithuania, Luxembourg, Malta, Netherlands, Poland, Portugal, Slovak Republic, Slovenia, Spain, Sweden, and United Kingdom.
9. Such a pattern was forecast by several observers in the late 1990s, such as Thomas W. Hertel, William A. Masters, and Aziz Elbehri, "The Uruguay Round and Africa: a Global, General Equilibrium," *Journal of African Economies* 7(2) (1998): 208–34.
10. From the perspective of Asian countries, Africa is the second-fastest growing destination for their products after East and Central Europe and the Commonwealth of Independent States countries (grown by 22 percent during 2000–05).
11. The sectoral patterns of Africa's export growth to high-income countries during the same period (1990–2004) are similar to Asian countries. This implies that African exports to Asia have not necessarily replaced their exports to non-Asian OECD countries.
12. Chapter 3 discusses details of bilateral and regional trade agreements such as SACU or preferential trade arrangements for African countries such as EBA.

13. A number of papers discuss segmentation of the private sector in Sub-Saharan African countries that is based on ethnic communities. See, for example, Easterly and Levine (1997) and Eifert, Gelb, and Ramachandran (2005).

14. Chapter 5 addresses the effect of ethnic networks in trade facilitation in greater depth.

15. Wood and Berge (1997) and Wood and Mayer (2001) compare Africa's endowments with those of other regions. Countries higher up along the spectrum of the skills-resource-endowment ratio export more manufactured products relative to processed or primary goods, and a larger proportion of higher-technology manufactured products. This seems to be a compelling story for trade relations between Africa and China and India.

16. Trade services encompass (i) transportation, including land, air, and maritime; (ii) tourism; (iii) cross-border education; (iv) foreign direct investment in banking and financial services; (v) communications and distribution; and (6) temporary migration of high- and low-skill labor, among others.

17. For example, the 2001 investment by Citibank, the 2005 acquisition of Absa Bank Limited by Barclay's (UK), and the 2003 acquisition of DeBeers by a U.K. concern.

18. It is estimated that by 2005 Chinese FDI reached $1.18 billion in Africa, which, however, may contain FDI to North Africa. "Premier Wen's Africa tour boosts bilateral investment" www.chinaview.cn 2006-06-19 20:32:52.

19. Chinese FDI to Africa increased by 300 percent between 2003 and 2004 due to a large oil investment in Sudan.

20. These estimates are as of mid-2006 based on www.ChinaView.cn, accessed June 19, 2006.

21. Being that Mauritius is a major offshore financial center, it may often be used to pass through investments, particularly those into the financial sector, to take advantage of its low tax regime.

22. Mauritius being a major offshore financial center, it is difficult to determine the actual FDI source country, particularly because of pass-through investment.

23. They allow researchers to measure the gravitational and frictional factors in the bilateral trade flows. The model includes a set of control variables to measure the size of supply and demand (GDP and per capita GDP of exporting and importing countries). There are also a set of control variables to account for various distance factors, such as geographical distance between trading pairs as well as individual exporting and importing countries (physical distance, contiguity, and landlocked); cultural and historical ties between trading pairs (common languages, common past colonial powers, past colonial relations); and economic distance between the two countries (preferential trade arrangements such as regional trade agreements).

24. A critical view toward applying a gravity model to study African export performance is related to the fact that the African countries have very small share in the worldwide trade volume, so that any variation across individual African countries cannot be estimated in any meaningful way when the model is

applied to the global bilateral data. To mitigate this problem, the gravity model is applied to only subsets of the global bilateral trade data, by constraining on either the export or the import side.

26. See Frankel and Rose (2002).

27. There is no strong evidence to support the claim that a preferential trade agreement will be net trade creating or that all members will benefit. Positive outcomes will depend on design and implementation (World Bank 2005a).

27. For example, based on a multi-sectoral gravity model, Kahn and Yoshino (2004) found that formation of RTAs within developed countries are likely to result in more trade in energy-intensive products within trading blocs, and more trade in less energy-intensive products within trading blocs for Southern RTAs.

28. Hausman, Lee, and Subramanian (2005) and Djankov, Freund, and Pham (2006). Both applied the similar indicators of customs efficiency for global bilateral trade flows, and found evidence for significant increases in exports by improving customs efficiency in exporting products.

29. It is somewhat surprising to see that, for both aggregate merchandise trade and manufactured trade, the port quality in exporting countries in Africa has a negative impact on trade flows from African countries. At least in the bivariate setting, port infrastructure quality is positively related to export performance of African countries. Given the fact that customs efficiency matters significantly in exporting African countries, there may be some interactions between customs efficiency and port quality that the model does not capture.

30. The effect of ITC infrastructures, such as the Internet, on exports by developing countries has been increasingly researched recently. The positive effect of exporters' average Internet accessibility found in this analysis is consistent with previous findings by others, including Freund and Weinhold (2004) and Clarke and Wallsten (2006). The latter found that the Internet promotes trade between North and South in particular.

CHAPTER 3

Challenges "At the Border": Africa and Asia's Trade and Investment Policies

Introduction

This chapter assesses the role that "at-the-border" policy regimes play in affecting the extent and nature of trade and investment flows between Africa and Asia, especially China and India. The analysis focuses on market access conditions, including tariffs and nontariff barriers; export and investment incentives offered by governments; and bilateral, regional, and multilateral agreements. If Africa is to take full advantage of trade and investment opportunities with Asia, reforms of such policies—by all parties—will be important. There are also valuable lessons that Africa can learn from Asia's experience in trade and investment policies over the past several decades.

The analysis begins with an examination of trade policy regimes in Africa and Asia. An assessment of tariffs that African exporters face in China and India, and that these Asian exporters face in Africa, is carried out at both the regional and country levels, as well as on a product-specific basis. The incidence of nontariff barriers (NTBs) in African-Asian trade is also examined. Finally, the role of various export-incentive regimes operating in the two regions is assessed.

The discussion then turns to an examination of policy instruments used to influence foreign direct investment (FDI) in Africa as well as in China and India. Various incentive schemes are appraised, as are the use of investment promotion agencies and public-private forums whose objectives are to facilitate foreign direct investment (FDI) flows.

An appraisal of various trade and investment agreements and treaties involving African and Asian countries is then made. The analysis focuses on the impacts of existing bilateral, regional, and multilateral arrangements and discusses new arrangements being contemplated.

The chapter ends by drawing conclusions and discussing policy implications.

Domestic Trade and Investment Policy Regimes

Improvement of market access in world trade for low-income countries has been at the top of the trade agenda in recent years, particularly in the context of the multilateral Doha Round, but also in bilateral and regional forums. This is certainly the case for African countries. Lowering multilateral tariff and nontariff barriers in the North (the developed countries) on African products is estimated to have a substantial impact on increasing African exports.[1] African countries also face such barriers in the South, including in Asia's developing countries. Some African countries also have high tariffs and nontariff barriers, and these similarly restrict trade flows; indeed, in some cases, they impart a bias against exports from Africa. Barriers to foreign investment also exist, in both Asia and in Africa. This section discusses the relevance of formal trade and investment policies Africa and Asia and how these policies affect mutual trade and investment relations.

Asia's Tariff Barriers against African Products: General Patterns

Overall Tariff Barriers
African exports face relatively high tariffs in Asia. Figure 3.1 shows the historical trends of unweighted average tariff rates against Africa's exports.[2] Although Asian tariffs for Africa are gradually declining, the trend is very weak, especially for exports from African least developed countries (LDCs). The overall tariff restrictiveness on African imports in Asian countries is in part a reflection of the lack or limited scope of Asian preferences granted to Africa compared to those granted by the United States and the EU.

FIGURE 3.1

Unweighted Average Tariffs on Exports of African LDCs and Non-LDCs: 1995–2005

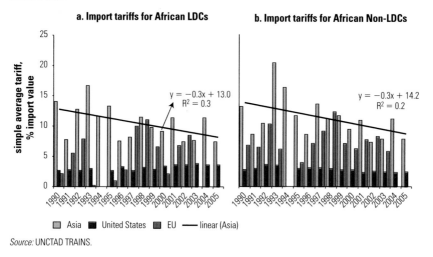

Source: UNCTAD TRAINS.

Note: Asia includes Bangladesh, China (including Hong Kong), India, Indonesia, Japan, Republic of Korea, Lao PDR, Malaysia, Maldives, Mongolia, Myanmar, Nepal, Pakistan, Philippines, Singapore, Sri Lanka, Taiwan, Thailand, and Vietnam. African non-LDCs include Botswana, Cameroon, Republic of Congo, Côte d'Ivoire, Gabon, Ghana, Kenya, Mauritius, Namibia, Nigeria, Seychelles, South Africa, and Swaziland.

An analysis of the rate of tariffs on African exports by product group shows that, on average, the market barriers in Asia's markets for African products are high relative to the United States and the EU (table 3.1). For some specific product groups, Asian tariff rates are *higher* for African LDCs than for non-LDCs (figure 3.2). Those product groups are inedible crude materials and food and live animals, which account for two-thirds of total African LDCs' exports to Asia.

The prevalence of tariff peaks in China and India is at a comparable level to the EU, but stronger than in other Asian countries, such as Japan and Korea (figure 3.3).[3] The tariff peaks in agriculture are particularly high in India.

There is a significant amount of heterogeneity among African products in terms of the tariff barriers they face in Asian markets. Table 3.2 shows the pattern of protection in Asian markets against African exports. There are three discernible characteristics for China and India.

- Among Asian countries, the tariff levels of China and India on African products remain high. Tariff rates on agricultural products are high in both China and India.

TABLE 3.1
Weighted Average Tariff Rates for African Exports by Destination
(percent)

Product group (SITC)	Asia		EU[a]		United States	
	African countries					
	LDC	Non-LDC	LDC	Non-LDC	LDC	Non-LDC
Food and live animals	12.7	9.5	0.0	2.5	0.0	0.1
Beverages and tobacco	2.5	9.3	0.0	66.5	43.3	10.5
Crude materials, inedible, except fuels	9.7	2.5	0.0	1.3	0.0	0.0
Mineral fuels, lubricants, and related materials	0.2	0.7	n.a.	1.5	0.0	0.0
Animal and vegetable oils, fats, and waxes	3.5	19.0	0.0	5.3	0.0	0.0
Chemicals and related products, n.e.s.	14.3	7.2	0.0	5.8	0.0	0.3
Manufactured goods classified chiefly by material	2.3	2.1	0.0	6.5	0.1	0.1
Machinery and transport equipment	11.8	2.6	0.0	6.2	0.0	0.0
Miscellaneous manufactured articles	5.8	6.7	0.0	10.3	11.6	10.0
Gold	14.7	14.8	0.0	0.0	0.0	0.0

Source: UNCTAD TRAINS.

Note: Asia includes Bangladesh, China (including Hong Kong), India, Indonesia, Japan, Korea, Lao PDR, Malaysia, Maldives, Mongolia, Myanmar, Nepal, Pakistan, Philippines, Singapore, Sri Lanka, Taiwan, Thailand, and Vietnam. African non-LDCs include Botswana, Cameroon, Republic of Congo, Côte d'Ivoire, Gabon, Ghana, Kenya, Mauritius, Namibia, Nigeria, Seychelles, South Africa, and Swaziland. n.a. = not available.
a. The EU tariff data are only available for 2003 in the UNCTAD TRAINS database, which were not all zeros for African LDCs. EU tariffs to African LDCs were updated to zeros based on the fact that the Everything But Arms agreement came to effect in 2002. It is possible though that such unilateral preferential treatment is not fully utilized due to rules of origin complexities and administrative costs relative to tariffs elsewhere.

- The prevalence of high tariff rates in India is broadly based.[4] For exports from both LDCs and non-LDCs in Africa, India's weighted average tariff rates are beyond 10 percent in every product category.

- China has zero tariffs for its most highly demanded raw materials, including crude petroleum and ores, but has moderate-to-high tariffs on other imports, especially on inedible crude materials (for example, cotton) from LDCs.

High Asian tariff rates on some African products appear to discourage their export to Asian countries. Contrasting table 3.2 with table 3.3, which shows percentage shares of each product group in total African exports to specific Asian countries, it is clear that high tariffs are associated with low trading volumes in most product categories.

FIGURE 3.2
Weighted Average Tariff Rates of Asian Countries on Exports from African LDCs and Non-LDCs

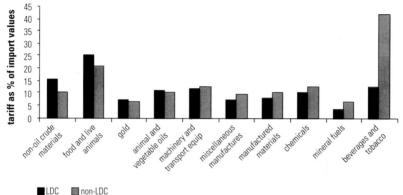

■ LDC   ▨ non-LDC

Source: UNCTAD TRAINS.

Note: The figures are based on 2005 data. Asia includes Bangladesh, China (including Hong Kong), India, Indonesia, Japan, Korea, Lao PDR, Malaysia, Maldives, Mongolia, Myanmar, Nepal, Pakistan, Philippines, Singapore, Sri Lanka, Taiwan, Thailand and Vietnam. Africa non-LDCs include Botswana, Cameroon, Republic of Congo, Côte d'Ivoire, Gabon, Ghana, Kenya, Mauritius, Namibia, Nigeria, Seychelles, South Africa, and Swaziland.

FIGURE 3.3
Average Numbers of Tariff Peaks on Exports from Africa

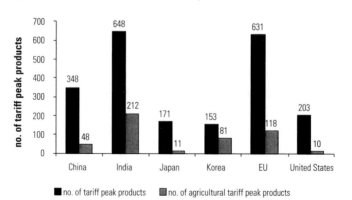

■ no. of tariff peak products   ▨ no. of agricultural tariff peak products

Source: UNCTAD TRAINS.

Note: Tariff peak products are defined as products with tariff rates 15% higher than MFN tariff rates or higher. Based on the latest year of data availability. Asia includes Bangladesh, China (including Hong Kong), India, Indonesia, Japan, Korea, Lao PDR, Malaysia, Maldives, Mongolia, Myanmar, Nepal, Pakistan, Philippines, Singapore, Sri Lanka, Taiwan, Thailand, and Vietnam. African non-LDCs include Botswana, Cameroon, Republic of Congo, Côte d'Ivoire, Gabon, Ghana, Kenya, Mauritius, Namibia, Nigeria, Seychelles, South Africa, and Swaziland.

TABLE 3.2

Tariff Patterns of Asian Countries, Weighted Tariff, 2005

(percent)

Product group (SITC)	China		Hong Kong		Japan		India	
	African countries							
	LDC	Non-LDC	LDC	Non-LDC	LDC	Non-LDC	LDC	Non-LDC
Food and live animals	13	10	0	0	1	6	32	39
Beverages and tobacco		10	0	0	0	6	30	33
Crude materials, inedible, except fuels	15	3	0	0	0	0	11	10
Mineral fuels, lubricants, and related materials	0	0		0	0	0	14	15
Animal and vegetable oils, fats, and waxes		12		0	3	2		45
Chemicals and related products, n.e.s.	8	7	0	0	0	0	15	15
Manufactured goods classified chiefly by material	3	4	0	0	0	1	15	17
Machinery and transport equipment	2	8	0	0	0	0	15	14
Miscellaneous manufactured articles	11	13	0	0	0	5	15	13
Gold						0	15	15

Source: UNCTAD TRAINS.

Note: Figures are rounded to the nondecimal level. Blank cells represent product groups with no imports from Africa so that weighted average tariff rates are null. Korea's tariff schedule was from 2004. Rest of Asia includes Bangladesh, Lao PDR, Maldives, Mongolia, Myanmar, Nepal, Pakistan, Philippines, Sri Lanka, Taiwan, Thailand, and Vietnam. African non-LDCs include Botswana, Cameroon, Republic of Congo, Côte d'Ivoire, Gabon, Ghana, Kenya, Mauritius, Namibia, Nigeria, Seychelles, South Africa, and Swaziland. African LDCs are 33 countries published by UNCTAD in 2005. Shaded cells indicate product groups that have more than 10 percent average tariff rates.

High Indian and relatively high Chinese tariffs on agricultural products are of particular concern because higher tariff rates tend to be applied to the products in which African countries have growth potential. African countries have been traditionally strong in agricultural products and are experiencing high growth in exporting to Asian countries, including China and India (see chapter 2). However, China is a relatively liberalized market, with zero or close to zero tariffs on 45 percent of its imports. China also has plans to further lower its tariffs and bring about lower dispersion in the structure of tariffs by the end of 2007.[5]

In the case of coffee, India imposes a 100 percent tariff on unroasted coffee beans, while China imposes a tariff of 15 percent on roasted coffee.

Although the absolute level of coffee imports of China and India is not comparable to that of more advanced Asian countries, such as Japan, the rise of incomes in China and India has stimulated a much higher growth rate in overall coffee imports from the world (figure 3.4).

Korea		Indonesia		Malaysia		Singapore		Rest of Asia	
African countries									
LDC	Non-LDC	LDC	Non-LDC	LDC	Non-LDC	LDC	Non-LDC	LDC	Non-LDC
10	29	5	5	0	1	0	0	10	11
2	15	5	5	0	0		0	10	19
146	2	1	0	0	0	0	0	2	1
5	5		5		2	0	0	1	1
3	4		8		2		0	0	19
7	7	5	5	0	7	0	0	7	5
0	3	4	3	0	2	0	0	1	1
0	6	7	8	1	4	0	0	11	28
0	8	11	10	2	7	0	0	14	12
0	4								5

Product-Specific Analysis of Chinese and Indian Tariffs on African Products

Detailed product-specific analysis of some of the highest tariffs, specifically those on food, inedible crude materials, and chemicals, shows that although they are applied to a small number of products, in fact they drive up the average tariff rates for African exports (table 3.4). For China, the high tariff on crude materials is a result of the high tariff on cotton. For India, the high tariffs on food, crude materials, and chemicals are the result of high tariffs on cashew nuts, cotton, scrap metals, and phosphorus pentoxide and acids.

Tariff Escalation in Asia on Key African Exports

Asia's tariff structure consists of many peaks and escalations. When higher tariffs are imposed on more processed products to retain higher value-added activities in the domestic market, and raw materials not locally available face lower tariffs, this allows the domestic industry to access

TABLE 3.3

Share of African Exports to Asia by Commodity Group and by Country of Destination, Excluding Petroleum Exports

(percent)

Product group (SITC)	China		Hong Kong		Japan		India	
	African countries							
	LDC	Non-LDC	LDC	Non-LDC	LDC	Non-LDC	LDC	Non-LDC
Food and live animals	2	1	39	24	52	8	33	6
Beverages and tobacco	0	3	0	2	3	0	0	0
Crude materials, inedible, except fuels	83	50	46	9	22	18	32	13
Animal and vegetable oils, fats and waxes	0	0	0	0	0	0	0	0
Chemicals and related products, n.e.s.	0	5	0	3	0	2	23	8
Manufactured goods classified chiefly by material	15	38	13	43	21	53	6	6
Machinery and transport equipment	0	3	1	17	0	18	6	3
Miscellaneous manufactured articles	0	0	1	1	1	0	0	0
Gold	0	0	0	0	0	0	0	63
Total	100	100	100	100	100	100	100	100

Source: UNCTAD TRAINS.

Note: Korea's tariff schedule was from 2004. Rest of Asia includes Bangladesh, Lao PDR, Maldives, Mongolia, Myanmar, Nepal, Pakistan, Philippines, Sri Lanka, Taiwan, Thailand, and Vietnam. African non-LDCs include Botswana, Cameroon, Republic of Congo, Côte d'Ivoire, Gabon, Ghana, Kenya, Mauritius, Namibia, Nigeria, Seychelles, South Africa, and Swaziland. African LDCs are 33 countries published by UNCTAD in 2005. Shaded cells indicate product groups that have more than 10 percent average tariff rates (table 3.2) and more than 10 percent shares in total imports to respective country.

FIGURE 3.4

Growth in Income and Coffee Imports of Asian Countries

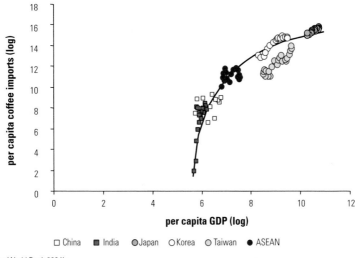

Source: World Bank 2004b.

	Korea		Indonesia		Malaysia		Singapore		Rest of Asia	
	LDC	Non-LDC	LDC	Non-LDC	LDC	Non-LDC	LDC	Non-LDC	LDC	Non-LDC
African countries										
	3	4	5	3	6	25	81	17	6	11
	1	0	2	10	3	1	0	1	1	1
	34	15	86	44	26	28	5	5	63	17
	0	0	0	0	0	0	0	0	0	0
	0	3	7	8	5	4	1	18	0	7
	38	70	0	27	53	37	10	35	29	59
	7	6	0	5	7	3	2	17	0	4
	16	1	0	2	1	1	0	6	0	1
	0	0	0	0	0	0	0	0	0	0
	100	100	100	100	100	100	100	100	100	100

cheap inputs from other countries. The cascading pattern of tariff rates along the level of processing is called "tariff escalation." Figure 3.5 shows the tariff escalation in EU and Asian markets. The reverse escalation tariff on cotton and cotton products in Asia is due to an exceptionally high tariff on cotton imposed by China. Tariff escalation is quite visible in Asian markets on some of the leading exports from Africa (table 3.5).

Tariff escalation discourages processing activities in Africa for the products exported to Asia. A poignant example is an Indian-owned cashew firm in Tanzania seeking to export roasted, rather than simply raw, nuts to India. It does not do so because India imposes higher tariffs on processed nuts than on raw nuts (box 3.1).

Tariff Barriers or Supply Constraint?
One important caveat to the discussion of tariff barriers on African products is the issue of whether there is a supply constraint in Africa. Unless African countries are able to produce such products and identify where demand exists, removal of tariff barriers will not be effective.

TABLE 3.4

Tariffs and Product Shares of African Exports to China and India in Selective Product Groups

SITC code	Product	China				India			
		African countries							
		LDC		Non-LDC		LDC		Non-LDC	
		Tariff (percent)	Percent of category export value	Tariff (percent)	Percent of category export value	Tariff (percent)	Percent of category export value	Tariff (percent)	Percent of category export value
05773	Cashew nuts					30	87	30	79
0721	Cocoa beans, whole or broken, raw or roasted							30	5
0741	Tea							100	4
263	Cotton	27	54	27	10	10	33	10	5
282	Waste and scrap metal of iron or steel							20	26	20	24
52224	Phosphorus pentoxide and phosp.acids, meta/ortho/p.					15	92	15	67

Source: UNCTAD TRAINS.

Note: African non-LDCs include Botswana, Cameroon, Republic of Congo, Côte d'Ivoire, Gabon, Ghana, Kenya, Mauritius, Namibia, Nigeria, Seychelles, South Africa, and Swaziland. African LDCs are 33 countries published by UNCTAD in 2005.

African producers do not effectively capture the benefit of low tariffs for some products in Asian markets due to a lack of production capacity. For example, although the tariff on cotton is high in China, the tariff on cotton yarns is relatively low. Despite this potential opportunity, African countries have not been able to take advantage of low tariffs on cotton products (figure 3.6). The cotton-growing African countries export almost exclusively to China, where the tariffs are excessively high. On the other hand, as illustrated in chapter 2, Africa imports large quantities of cotton yarns, cotton fabrics, apparel, and footwear from China.

Another example is cocoa beans. Figure 3.7 illustrates how Chinese consumers are increasingly importing processed products of cocoa beans, such as cocoa powder, cocoa paste, and chocolate, while their imports of raw cocoa beans have diminished slightly. However, Africa's exports of cocoa beans to China are increasing and dominate its exports of cocoa powder and chocolate.[6] China imposes only a 9 percent tariff on finished

FIGURE 3.5

Tariff Escalation on Major African Agricultural Products

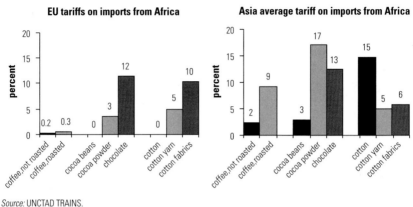

Source: UNCTAD TRAINS.

Note: The average tariff is weighted effectively applied tariff.

chocolate, which is not very different from the duty applied to cocoa beans at 8 percent. But even with a relatively low tariff on chocolate, at present there is little chance for Africa to penetrate the Chinese chocolate market given its constrained supply capacity to produce high-quality chocolate.

African Tariff Barriers Against Asian Products

African tariffs have been lowered significantly in recent times. However, Asian products still face relatively high tariff barriers in Africa. Figure 3.8 presents the trend of the simple average tariff in African markets against the continent's major trade partners. Three patterns are visible. First, African countries, especially non-LDCs, have liberalized their import policies rather quickly. This contrasts with the weak liberalizing trend in Asian markets. Second, Asian exports to African markets are facing higher tariffs than those of the EU and United States, partly because of high tariffs imposed on cheap Asian manufacturing goods such as textiles, apparel, and footwear. Third, Africa's markets on average have higher tariffs against Asian imports than Asian markets have against African imports. This reflects the pattern that Africa mostly imports manufactured goods, which typically have higher tariffs, while Asia imports mostly natural resources and resource-based materials, which typically have lower tariffs.

TABLE 3.5
Tariff Escalation in Asian Countries
(percent)

SITC	Product	African imports			
		China	India	Japan	Asia average
211	Raw hides	6.5	0.1	0	0.8
611	Leather	8.8	14.7	0.7	4.6
612	Manufactures leather	14.6	15.0	1.9	7.9
222	Oil seeds	5.0	30.0	0.4	2.0
423	Vegetable oils	10.0	45.0	—	27.7
07111	Coffee, not roasted	8.0	100.0	0	2.3
07112	Coffee, roasted	15.0	30.0	9.1	9.1
0721	Cocoa beans, raw	8.0	30.0	0	2.8
0722	Cocoa powder	15.0	—	—	0.2
333	Petroleumoils, crude	0	—	—	0.2
334	Petroleum products, refined	7.4	15.0	2.1	0.3
66722	Diamonds, sorted	3.0	—	0	2.2
66729	Diamonds, cut	8.0	15.0	0	6.0
6673	Other precious/semi-precious stones	7.3	15.0	0	9.0
897	Jewelry	26.8	15.0	0.9	15.7
263	Cotton	27.0	10.0	0	14.8
6513	Cotton yarn	5.0	15.0	—	5.0
652	Cotton fabrics, woven	10.0	15.0	1.0	5.6
84512	Jerseys, etc. of cotton	14.0	—	5.7	6.8
8462	Under garments, knitted	14.1	15.0	6.9	5.2

Source: UNCTAD TRAINS.

Note: Darker shades represent higher levels of processing; — = data not available.

The overall tariff structure in Africa has some elements of anti-export bias. Table 3.6 shows that African countries overall have average high tariff rates on many product groups except for machinery and transport equipment and mineral fuels. The low average tariff rates on machinery and transport equipment reflects Africa's high demand for these goods to support its manufacturing sectors. High tariffs on intermediate products, such as textile yarns and cotton, and manmade or knitted fabrics, however, create disincentives for African apparel exports due to high input prices. This is an element of the African tariff structure that is biased against manufacturing exports. In addition, these high tariffs generate inefficiency in the domestic textile industry.

Among African countries, South Africa has very low tariffs on crude materials, crude oil, chemicals, and machinery and transportation equipment, but has relatively high tariffs on food, beverages and

BOX 3.1

**The South's Escalating Tariffs Against African Exports:
The Case of an Indian Cashew Processing Business in
Tanzania Trying to Export to India**

This cashew processing company was established in Tanzania in 1947 by an Indian family. The fourth generation of this family still owns and manages the firm, but today it is part of a large group company (owned by the same Indian family) involved in various lines of the agricultural processing business, including rice mills, seed oil mills, chickpea mills, and maize mills. It recently purchased new machinery from India and is embarking on a new line in its export business: sale of organic cashews, with plans for this line to account for 35 percent of production.

Trade policies constitute some of the most significant challenges facing the firm today, both in Africa and overseas. In Tanzania, the company faces burdensome trade regulations that inhibit its ability to export efficiently. This includes not only burdensome paperwork in customs, but also export taxes, which the company is lobbying to reduce. With respect to its sales outside of Africa, the firm exports 70 percent of its cashews to the United States, Canada, Japan, and the EU. Ironically, only 10 percent of its cashew exports enter the Indian market, the largest cashew market in the world. In large part this is due to India's escalating tariff on processed cashews: while India's imports of raw cashews face a zero tariff, processed cashews face an Indian tariff of 37 percent. This escalation has the effect of providing strong protection for India's domestic cashew firms.

Source: World Bank staff.

tobacco, and manufactured materials and articles (table 3.7). This is a case where local production is protected in sectors that produce finished or semi-finished products, while imports of machinery to support local industrial development are more liberalized. A few African agricultural-based economies have extremely high tariffs against Chinese food imports, including Tanzania, Kenya, Ethiopia, and Uganda at an average rate of above 30 percent.

FIGURE 3.6
Total Cotton Product Imports and Tariff Rates in China

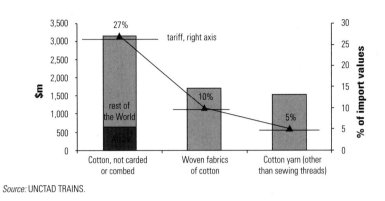

Source: UNCTAD TRAINS.

Figure 3.9 presents tariff schedules of Africa's top 10 items imported from China and India. Textiles and yarn, apparel, and footwear are among the largest imports. They also have the highest tariffs. Other large imports from China and India include manufactured goods such as electronics, machinery and transportation equipment. These items in general have relatively low tariffs.

FIGURE 3.7
Chinese Imports and African Exports of Cocoa and Processed Products

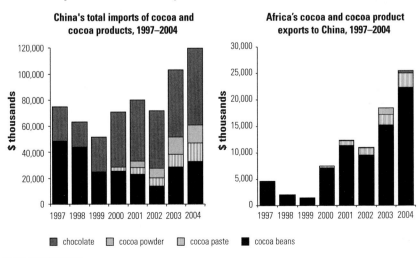

Source: UN COMTRADE.

FIGURE 3.8
Average Tariff Rates of African Countries, Unweighted Simple Average

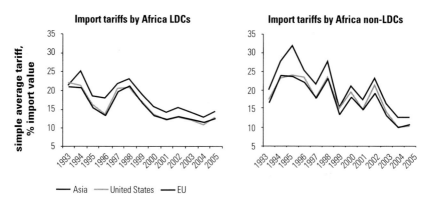

Source: UNCTAD TRAINS.

Note: Asia includes Afghanistan, Bangladesh, Bhutan, Cambodia, China (including Hong Kong and Macao), Indonesia, India, Japan, Lao PDR, Myanmar, Vietnam, Thailand, People's Dem. Rep. of Korea, Rep. of Korea, Maldives, Malaysia, Mongolia, Nepal, Pakistan, Philippines, Singapore, Sri Lanka, and Taiwan. Africa non-LDC includes Botswana, Cameroon, Republic of Congo, Côte d'Ivoire, Gabon, Ghana, Kenya, Mauritius, Namibia, Nigeria, Seychelles, South Africa, and Swaziland.

Chinese exports to African markets on average face higher tariffs than do Indian exports (figure 3.10). Among leading African imports from China and India, coal is the only product for which India on average faces higher tariff rates than does China. For other product groups, such as non-metal manufacturing and electronic machinery, Chinese products face much higher average tariff rates in Africa.

Nontariff Barriers in Asia and Africa

Tariffs were the focus of eight rounds of multilateral trade negotiations to reduce market barriers, resulting in continued tariff reduction worldwide. However, in place of tariff barriers, nontariff barriers (NTBs) have become increasingly common as regulatory instruments to ensure that imports meet the standards of domestic markets. Stringent environmental and technical standards are typical formal NTBs used by industrial countries and increasingly used by developing countries as well. Delays in customs, cumbersome administrative procedures, and bribery are typical informal NTBs, and more present in developing than in developed countries (although they are not nonexistent in the latter). Another example of NTBs, perhaps unintentional, is the burden-of-proof requirement for "country of origin" in preferential tariffs.

TABLE 3.6
Average Tariff on Imports into Africa, Import Values Weighted

Product group	African LDC			African Non-LDC		
	Imports from Asia	Imports from EU	Imports from United States	Imports from Asia	Imports from EU	Imports from United States
Food and live animals	16.0	12.9	11.2	22.0	20.5	8.2
Beverages and tobacco	41.2	26.2	9.6	24.6	24.2	12.4
Crude materials, inedible, except fuels	12.0	17.7	23.1	2.3	10.9	6.3
Mineral fuels, lubricants, and related materials	1.3	7.6	8.6	3.4	11.8	4.3
Animal and vegetable oils, fats, and waxes	13.3	12.3	17.6	8.2	12.2	7.4
Chemicals and related products, n.e.s.	7.2	5.7	5.6	6.0	4.8	3.8
Manufactured goods classified chiefly by material	16.9	13.3	12.6	13.0	8.5	9.0
Individual manufactured product Textile yarn	9.6	8.3	4.1	6.0	4.8	9.9
Cotton fabrics, woven	18.3	19.3	21.7	16.0	13.4	19.2
Fabrics, woven, of man-made fibers	16.8	10.1	19.8	19.9	12.1	20.2
Textile fabrics, woven, other than cotton/manmade fiber	21.9	10.8	20.2	11.5	5.4	9.5
Knitted or crocheted fabrics	21.0	12.8	20.0	16.2	9.5	18.9
Tulle, lace, embroidery, ribbons, and other small wares	20.6	21.0	21.2	19.1	17.1	18.7
Special textile fabrics and related products	12.0	11.3	11.7	14.0	9.1	12.2
Machinery and transport equipment	7.2	8.6	5.7	7.4	6.2	4.4
Miscellaneous manufactured articles	21.4	11.6	10.7	19.0	7.1	3.1

Source: UNCTAD TRAINS.

Note: Asia includes Afghanistan, Bangladesh, Bhutan, Cambodia, China (including Hong Kong and Macao), Indonesia, India, Japan, Lao PDR, Myanmar, Vietnam, Thailand, Korea Dem. Rep., Rep. of Korea, Maldives, Malaysia, Mongolia, Nepal, Pakistan, Philippines, Singapore, Sri Lanka, and Taiwan. African non-LDC includes Botswana, Cameroon, Republic of Congo, Côte d'Ivoire, Gabon, Ghana, Kenya, Mauritius, Namibia, Nigeria, Seychelles, South Africa, and Swaziland.

Both African and Asian countries have significant numbers of NTBs, as shown in table 3.8.[7] The Uruguay Round made most quantity-control measures illegal, especially for agricultural products. Consequently, over the 10-year period between 1994 and 2004, there has been a big decline in applying quotas. However, technical measures have increased significantly among all regions. Africa had the lowest percentage of technical measures in 1994 at 20 percent, but such measures have increased to 60 percent, the highest among all regions. Developed countries and Asia have also doubled their technical measures up to 50 percent. Most technical measures are applied to agricultural products.

Although technical measures aim at controlling the quality and safety of imported products, they effectively constrain trade partners' capacity to export. Not surprisingly, LDCs carry a higher than average burden of NTBs because they export mainly agricultural products. One study estimates that 40 percent of LDCs' exports are subject to NTBs, while only 15 percent of developed and transition economies' exports are subject to NTBs.[8] African countries overall carry a higher NTB burden than any other continent because the majority of LDCs are in Africa. Evidence from the World Bank Africa-Asia Trade and Investment (WBAATI) business case studies of Chinese and Indian firms operating in Africa reveals that NTB-related constraints do significantly affect their business strategies. For example, a Chinese automotive firm in South Africa notes that South Africa requires costly inspections for foreign automobile makers entering the market to ensure compliance with national standards (which are on par with the EU's). For this company, it took one year of testing to complete the procedures for certification. The complicated procedures required to pass inspections increased the cost of selling the company's product in South Africa.

NTBs are also present in African industries where protection of domestic businesses from import surges is sought. Such is the case in the South African textile and apparel sector, which has been buffeted by Chinese imports since the elimination of the Multifibre Arrangement on January 1, 2005 (see below). On September 1, 2006, South Africa announced that it will impose quotas on textile and clothing imports from China for a period of two years starting October 2006.

How much do NTBs compare to tariff barriers in restricting African-Asian trade? Table 3.9 compares marginal impacts of tariff barriers and NTBs on overall trade based on a Trade Restrictiveness Index (TRI).[9] For manufactured goods, the EU, the United States, China, and India have moderate NTBs from 4 to 7 percent. The NTBs of manufacturing goods for African countries, however, vary widely, ranging from 18 to 28 percent for five countries and 0 to 3 percent for others.

For agricultural products, both the EU and the United States have relatively low tariffs, but have high TRIs at 32 and 17 percent, respectively, indicating serious erosion of the effectiveness of the agriculture product preferences embodied in the EUs' Everything But Arms (EBA) initiative and the United States, African Growth and Opportunity Act (AGOA)[10] (see below). India has both extremely high tariffs and NTBs on agricultural products, while China has relatively high tariffs, but less extensive

TABLE 3.7
Average Tariff Rates of African Countries on Imports from China and India

Product Group	China				
	Angola	Côte d'Ivoire	Ethiopia	Ghana	
Food and live animals	5.9	10.2	34.2	14.3	
Beverages and tobacco	30.0	n.a.	20.0	20.0	
Crude materials, inedible, except fuels	2.8	8.1	7.9	14.5	
Mineral fuels, lubricants, and related materials	n.a.	5.2	9.9	46.7	
Animal and vegetable oils, fats, and waxes	n.a.	n.a.	n.a.	20.0	
Chemicals and related products, n.e.s.	5.2	5.7	11.7	11.5	
Manufactured goods classified chiefly by material	10.4	19.0	23.2	13.5	
Machinery and transport equipment	3.9	15.2	14.5	9.8	
Miscellaneous manufactured articles	12.0	18.9	37.9	16.7	
	India				
	Angola	Côte d'Ivoire	Ethiopia	Ghana	
Food and live animals	10.1	10.4	7.6	15.0	
Beverages and tobacco	30.0	n.a.	30.0	20.0	
Crude materials, inedible, except fuels	22.8	5.0	5.5	10.8	
Mineral fuels, lubricants and related materials	20.0	5.0	1.7	87.2	
Animal and vegetable oils, fats, and waxes	2.0	7.5	21.5	17.9	
Chemicals and related products, n.e.s.	4.0	3.5	12.1	7.7	
Manufactured goods classified chiefly by material	6.1	17.5	10.3	12.8	
Machinery and transport equipment	3.1	9.0	11.8	4.1	
Miscellaneous manufactured articles	12.6	15.3	20.2	12.2	

Source: UNCTAD TRAINS.

Note: n.a. = not available.

NTBs. For African countries, the NTBs are very high for some countries, such as Tanzania, Senegal, Nigeria, and Côte d'Ivoire, but very low or nonexistent for many others, such as Chad, Ethiopia, Rwanda, and Madagascar.

NTBs, especially technical standards, can pose triple challenges to LDCs, most of which are in Africa. First, LDCs lack the capacity to regulate based on technical standards, which means that their markets are less protected by NTBs than countries with such capacity. Second, LDCs have less capacity to comply with NTBs imposed by other countries. This means that the actual barriers imposed by NTBs are effectively more binding for LDCs, where the capacity is weaker than for other countries where the capacity is high. Third, a disproportionately large part of LDCs' exports face NTBs due to their concentration on agricultural exports, where the majority of the NTBs lie. For African LDCs, the cost of NTBs can be extremely high relative to the small size of their economies.

China							
Kenya	Mauritius	Nigeria	Senegal	South Africa	Tanzania	Uganda	Africa average
40.7	17.2	18.2	14.6	11.1	71.1	43.7	14.4
25.0	64.8	5.3	5.8	41.3	25.0	25.0	33.0
8.5	2.6	9.3	10.0	1.8	6.7	12.3	3.4
3.7	2.7	6.3	6.8	0.3	2.7	0.2	0.5
18.6	0.0	10.4	16.6	9.4	25.0	19.9	17.7
2.7	6.5	10.5	9.2	2.7	2.6	6.8	6.6
18.0	4.5	17.9	18.9	13.7	15.2	18.3	16.0
7.4	8.7	11.0	13.6	3.5	6.3	14.5	7.6
11.5	10.3	17.5	19.3	24.8	20.3	22.9	22.8
India							
Kenya	Mauritius	Nigeria	Senegal	South Africa	Tanzania	Uganda	Africa average
37.7	2.7	49.7	12.3	1.9	11.3	16.0	20.8
25.0	54.2	12.0	5.9	22.0	25.7	25.0	35.3
3.8	0.3	5.4	5.0	4.1	24.2	40.0	5.3
5.9	7.3	6.2	5.0	4.8	0.1	8.5	5.0
0.7	3.1	11.7	5.0	8.4	1.1	18.1	7.3
6.1	2.6	14.6	3.3	2.1	5.3	8.4	6.8
13.6	2.6	16.8	11.9	9.4	17.2	15.5	12.2
5.0	4.8	5.9	7.3	9.7	4.7	5.0	7.2
17.1	6.4	12.3	17.8	20.8	11.9	16.6	16.4

Domestic Export Incentive Schemes in Africa and in Asia

While the preceding subsections dealt with formal trade policies in the form of tariff and nontariff barriers that restrict trade flows, many developing countries have a number of domestic incentives, fiscal or nonfiscal, granted to exporters for the purpose of promoting exports by domestic producers. Box 3.2 describes such incentives provided by the Indian government. These incentives can be generally categorized as (i) duty relief on imported inputs, such as duty drawback and duty exemption systems; (ii) domestic fiscal incentives, such as value-added tax exemptions; (iii) export processing zones (EPZs) and bonded factories or warehouses; and (iv) trade finance. Clearly, incentive schemes for export promotion are quite diverse and complicated. They are often used to attract foreign investors to produce export products in EPZs or as tools for trade facilitation. Trade finance is discussed in chapter 5.

FIGURE 3.9

African LDCs and Non-LDCs Tariff Rates on Top 10 Imports from China and India, 2004

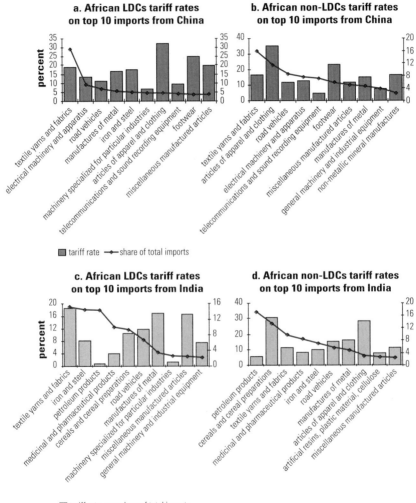

Sources: UNCTAD TRAINS and UN COMTRADE.

The effectiveness of export incentive schemes is widely debated; it also varies among different schemes. Because many fiscal incentive schemes are cumbersome, efficient domestic institutions for fiscal administration are a prerequisite for their effective management. In particular, duty drawbacks are information-intensive and usually utilize cumbersome

FIGURE 3.10

Average Tariff Rates of African Countries on Chinese and Indian Imports

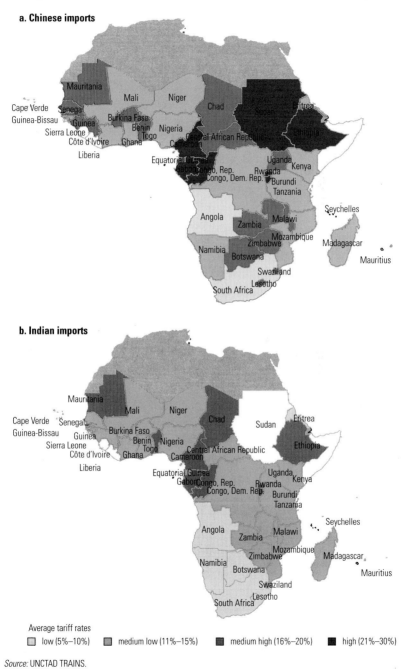

a. Chinese imports

b. Indian imports

Average tariff rates

☐ low (5%–10%)   ▨ medium low (11%–15%)   ▦ medium high (16%–20%)   ■ high (21%–30%)

Source: UNCTAD TRAINS.

TABLE 3.8

Types of NTBs Applied by Region as a Percentage of the Number of Tariff Product Lines

TCM code	TCM description	1994				2004			
		World	Developed	Africa	Asia	World	Developed	Africa	Asia
3	Price control measures	7.1	9.4	15.3	6.9	1.8	2.9	0.5	2.2
4	Finance measures	2.0	0.1	0.0	0.0	1.5	0.3	3.8	0.0
5	Automatic licensing measures	2.8	5.3	0.0	3.7	1.7	7.4	0.7	3.0
6	Quantity control measures	49.2	45.8	62.5	55.6	34.8	34.7	32.0	43.6
7	Monopolistic measures	1.3	1.1	2.5	1.9	1.5	0.7	2.6	2.6
8	Technical measures	31.9	21.9	19.7	23.5	58.5	50.0	60.4	48.4

Source: UNCTAD 2005c.

Note: TCM = Trade Control Measures.

procedures, causing unintended inefficiency in administration and adding extra barriers for the private sector. Duty suspension can be more effective for helping domestic producers to access imported inputs for the production of exports. However, again, without proper administrative capacity, there is the leakage of goods (without being used for exports) into the economy.

Besides efficiency in incentive scheme management, another important question is whether incentive schemes effectively promote participation of exporters in the most appropriate sectors—that is, sectors in which countries have comparative advantages in exporting. Analysis of the WBAATI survey data suggests that export incentive schemes do not generate high participation among the sectors where the African countries in question have comparative advantages, such as textiles, agricultural products, and food industries. Instead, the participation of export incentive schemes is high among the firms producing machinery and nondurable sectors, where those countries lack comparative advantages.

Almost all governments recognize the difficulties that exporters face in entering foreign markets. Different countries choose different combinations of means to encourage exporters to overcome such difficulties. Some used to directly subsidize export activities (direct income tax incentives), but this is no longer allowed under the World Trade Organization (WTO). The effectiveness of domestic export incentive schemes has been rather mixed, however. In many cases, the proper domestic investment climate needs to be in place for the effective management of the schemes (chapter 4).[11]

TABLE 3.9
Market Protection: Trade Restrictiveness Index (TRI)
(percent)

Country	Overall TRI	Marginal TRI of NTB	Over-all TRI tariff only	TRI for manu-factured goods	Marginal TRI of NTB on manu-factured goods	TRI for manu-factured goods, tariff only	TRI for agri-cultural products	Marginal TRI of NTB on agri-cultural products	TRI on agri-cultural goods, tariff only
Burkina Faso	13	3	10	10	0.1	9	38	24	15
Cameroon	18	1	16	17	1	15	24	3	21
Central Afr. Rep.	20	3	17	18	2	16	28	5	23
Chad	16	1	16	15	1	15	23	0	23
Côte d'Ivoire	37	26	11	33	22.9	10	51	38	13
Equatorial Guinea	16	0.3	16	15	0	14	24	0	24
Ethiopia	17	1	16	17	1	16	14	0	14
Gabon	17	0.2	17	16	0	16	21	0	21
Ghana	15	4	12	12	1	11	31	17.5	14
Kenya	10	1	9	7	0	6	31	6	25
Madagascar	13	1	13	13	1	12	18	0	18
Malawi	13	2	12	12	0	11	26	11.9	14
Mali	13	3	10	10	1	9	28	14	14
Mauritius	21	6	15	17	3	15	38	24	14
Mozambique	13	3	10	9	0	9	29	15	14
Nigeria	47	24	23	42	21	21	76	41	34
Rwanda	11	1	10	11	1	10	14	0	14
Senegal	36	27	9	26	18	8	63	51	12
South Africa	7	1	6	7	1	6	12	6	6
Sudan	47	28	19	47	28	19	49	28.6	20
Tanzania	38	28	10	31	23	8	83	59	23
Uganda	7	0.1	6	6	0.0	6	11	1	10
Zambia	11	1	10	9	0.0	9	29	12	17
Zimbabwe	18	5	14	12	1	12	47	23	24
SSA simple average	20	7	13	17	5	12	34	16	18
EU	12	8	4	8	5	3	38	32	6
United States	8	5	3	7	4	2	22	17	5
China	12	6	6	12	6	6	25	8	17
India	24	9	16	20	7	13	65	22	44

Source: Kee, Nicita, and Olarreaga 2006.

Investment Incentive Schemes for Foreign Investors and Other FDI-Related Policies

Many countries compete to attract FDI in the hope that, in addition to capital, it will bring new technology, marketing techniques, and management skills. It is also expected to create jobs and contribute to the overall com-

BOX 3.2

Export Incentives in India

To promote exports and to obtain foreign exchange, the government of India has designed several schemes to grant export incentives and other benefits.

- Free Trade Zones: Several Free Trade Zones have been established in India at various places. No excise duties are payable on goods manufactured in these free trade zones, provided the goods are for export. Goods brought into these zones from other parts of India are also exempted from payments of any excise duties. Similarly, no customs duties are payable on imported raw materials and components used to manufacture goods for export. Because selling the entire stock of goods made in these free trade zones outside of India may not always be possible, the companies are allowed to sell 25 percent of their production in India. Excise duties are payable on such domestic sales at 50 percent of basic plus additional customs duties or normal excise duties payable if they were produced elsewhere in India, whichever is higher.

- 100 Percent Export Oriented Units: Companies can import raw materials without payment of any customs duties provided they export their products. The same rules apply to 25 percent of outputs allowed for sale in the domestic markets.

- Electronic Hardware Technology Parks and Software Technology Parks: This scheme is similar to the Free Trade Zone scheme except that it is restricted to units in the electronics, computer hardware, and software sectors.

petitiveness of the country. The increase in global FDI flows has given more countries an opportunity to participate in global production chains, but the mobility of multinational corporations has also intensified the competition for FDI; see chapter 6.

Attracting FDI is at the top of the agenda for most developing countries. While there are many tools that governments can use to attract FDI, such as tax incentives, economic processing zones (EPZ), investment promotion agencies (IPA), and investment climate assessments

- Advance License or Duty Exemption Entitlement Scheme: Under this scheme, raw materials and other components to be used in goods to be exported against advance license can be imported with the exemption of customs duties. Such licenses are transferable at a price in the open market. The exporter sometimes uses components manufactured in the domestic market. In such cases, the domestic manufacturer can advance an intermediate license for the raw materials required to manufacture and supply intermediate products to the exporter.

- Export Promotion Capital Goods Scheme: In this scheme, under certain export obligations, a domestic manufacturer can import machinery and plant with the exemption of customs duties or at a concessional rate of customs duties.

- Manufacturing under Bond: Under this scheme, if the manufacturer furnishes a bond of adequate amount and undertakes to export its production, the manufacturer is allowed to import goods without payment of any customs duties. Similarly, the manufacturer can obtain goods from the domestic market without excise duties. Production has to be under the supervision of the customs or excise authority.

- Duty Drawback: Drawback means the rebate of duties chargeable on any imported materials or excisable materials used in manufacturing export goods in India. An exporter is entitled to claim drawbacks or refunds of excise and customs duties paid by his suppliers. Drawbacks on materials used for manufacturing export products can be claimed by the final exporters.

Source: Ministry of Commerce and Industry, Government of India.

(ICAs), these tools are only effective within a general good-policy framework. Investment climate improvements in many developing countries with liberalized foreign ownership rules do tend to provide strong incentives for foreign investors to invest. While governments are continuously advised to focus their efforts on improving the investment climate, they also employ the above-mentioned tools, used either as policy instruments in general or to attract prioritized investment projects.[12]

Tax Incentives

In using tax instruments to attract foreign investors, many governments rely on targeted approaches that include reduction of corporate income tax rates, temporary rebates for certain types of investment, and fast-write-off investment expenditures through tax allowances or credits. Such schemes tend to change the FDI composition by attracting certain types of investment rather than raising the level of total FDI. Although a few governments, such as Singapore's, have succeeded with targeted tax incentive schemes, many more have failed. Experience has shown that a nontargeted approach that lowers the effective corporate tax rate for all firms could be more effective than a targeted one. Small economies such as Hong Kong (China), Lebanon, and Mauritius have chosen this option. This approach, however, can be costly by reducing tax revenues in the short run. In the long run, the tax base could be broadened, compensating for the initial reduction.[13]

The degree of attractions offered by fiscal incentives to investors varies depending on a firm's activities and its motivations for investing. For example, tax incentives have been proved to be attractive to mobile firms and firms operating in multiple markets—such as banks, insurance companies, and Internet-related businesses. These firms can better exploit different tax regimes across countries, which may explain the success of tax havens in attracting subsidiaries of global companies. For firms searching to explore strategic resources such as crude petroleum or ores, tax incentives could matter little. Over the past decade a series of studies have shown that tax incentives are not the most influential factor for multinationals in selecting investment locations and are poor instruments for compensating for the negative factors of a country's investment climate.

The costs of tax incentives are multidimensional, including the loss of government revenue in the short run and the creation of incentives for companies to search for short-term profits, especially in countries where basic fundamentals are not yet in place. In addition, targeted tax incentives incur administrative costs and burden administrative capacity in host economies. This might explain why, so far, tax incentives have not been widely successful in attracting FDI to developing countries. Experience suggests that tax incentives do not rank high among the determinants of FDI and that in many instances incentives can be a waste of resources.[14] Harmonization of tax systems within regions has been used by states, such as those belonging to the EU or the Monetary Union of West African States, to avoid costly bidding wars among countries to attract FDI through tax incentives.

Export Processing Zones as an Investment Incentive

Export processing zones (EPZs) are sub-business environments created by governments to attract FDI specifically for the purpose of exporting manufactured goods, and generating local employment and economic development. In a world where an increasing number of governments compete hard to attract foreign investment, EPZs have become a global phenomenon. It is estimated that today there are more than 3,000 EPZs in 116 countries, accounting for more than 40 million direct jobs and more than $170 billion in exports (table 3.10). Developing and transition countries have established nearly 1,000 zones, clustered mainly in Asia and the Americas, with China accounting for about 19 percent of those zones. Sub-Saharan Africa is the region with the smallest number of EPZs.

EPZs have been used to relieve investors of costly hiring and firing provisions in national labor laws and sometimes excessively generous pension requirements. EPZs have been effective in attracting FDI flows, especially in Asia. For example, in the Philippines, the share of FDI inflows going to the country's EPZs increased from 30 percent in 1997 to more than 81 percent in 2000, and in Bangladesh, $103 million of the $328 million of FDI inflows were registered in EPZs. In Malaysia, EPZs have been instrumental in building and developing the electronics sector, started in the early 1970s despite the fact that the country had no particular skills in electronic production. The Chinese Special Economic Zones are often mentioned as a successful case of EPZs (see box 3.3).

TABLE 3.10
Export Processing Zones in Developing and Transition Countries in 2004

Region	Number of zones	Direct employment creation in EPZs		Zone exports ($ millions)
Asia/Pacific	479	Asia	36,824,231	84,500
of which China	173	China	30,000,000	
		Pacific	13,590	
		Indian Ocean	127,509	
Americas	198	C. America and Mexico	2,241,821	44,000
		South America	311,143	
		Caribbean	226,130	
Central/East Europe and Central Asia	98	Transition economies	245,619	14,450
Middle East and North Africa	77	Middle East	691,397	28,700
		North Africa	440,515	
Sub-Saharan Africa	63		431,348	2,400

Source: ILO Database on Export Processing Zones.

Note: Excludes single-factory zone programs and sponsoring countries.

BOX 3.3

Special Economic Zones in China

The biggest success story of economic zones is China. From a largely under-developed, centrally planned economy with poor infrastructure in 1980, China has successfully improved its investment climate to become a primary exporter of manufactured goods—approximately 75 percent of the world's toys and more than 13 percent of the world's clothing supply are manufactured in China. Such a transformation has been achieved mainly through the development of an investor-friendly investment climate in small areas of the country through Special Economic Zones (SEZs). The SEZs can be seen as transitional regimes to better policies throughout the economy.

Chinese SEZs offer an investment structure, labor regulations, management practices, and wage rate policies different from the rest of the economy, with an exclusive package of preferential policies encompassing a much broader array of economic activities than traditional EPZs. In only eight years, from 1980 to 1988, China established the SEZs along its coastline locations, including Shenzhen, Zhuhai, Shantou, and Xiamen cities, and designated the entire province of Hainan a special economic zone, aimed explicitly at attracting foreign investment, especially from nearby Hong Kong. Shenzhen has by far been the outstanding success story. Twenty-three years of growth have transformed Shenzhen from a small, sleepy fishing village into a thriving metropolis. Today, Shenzhen is an export-oriented economy with an export value in 2003 of $48 billion or 14 percent of the country's exports, some $30 billion in FDI, and 3 million direct employments. Shenzhen's per capita income has increased by more than twenty-fold. Shenzhen accounts for one-seventh of China's trade volume, with container throughput ranked fourth worldwide.[a] Shenzhen SEZ has become a model for Chinese economic transformation.

The SEZs in China have facilitated the creation of modern cities and the neighboring areas with well-equipped infrastructures. They have also accumulated sound economic strength and experience in doing business with international investors, creating "economic laboratories" in market practices to attract FDI. The SEZs have accomplished the tasks entrusted to them by the central government to pilot market-oriented reforms, opening to the outside world over the past two decades, and building up a good investment environment useful for their future development. Now, SEZs could consider how to further deepen reforms and expand the opening-up into inland regions, which, in fact, have benefited little from a decade of economic growth.

The Chinese government has already undertaken steps to redefine the role of SEZs in the national economy. In 1994, SEZs had exercised tight controls on approval of foreign investment in labor-intensive and real estate projects. In 1997, Foreign Funded Enterprises were granted national treatment in Shenzhen. These measures are designed to adjust gradually and withdraw the special and preferential treatment granted to SEZs, a necessary step toward achieving balanced regional development while SEZs continue to serve as vehicles in the reform and opening-up process.

In summary, SEZs have proven to give developing countries a window of opportunity for attracting foreign investment by creating pocket areas of experimentation for policy reform that can offset some aspects of an adverse investment climate. The economic impact of free zones has been far-reaching, transforming in some cases entire regions and economies. In an overview of the key investment-related policies that make economic zones successful, ensuring adequate autonomy of the zone authority, and streamlining procedures for business registration, site location, and a rational tax incentive framework are a few key investment policies that would differentiate a successful zone from others. That said, governments need to ensure that their benefits spread to the surrounding economy, including domestic investors; that zones do not absorb too much government technical and managerial expertise while becoming a breeding ground for developing new government skills and processes; and, most important, that zones become a catalyst for reforms nationwide.

Source: FIAS, forthcoming.

a. See Asia Pacific Foundation of Canada (2006).

EPZs, however, tend not to be successful in attracting additional FDI where the basic legal or regulatory framework is inadequate, or where distorted economic incentives in other areas of the economy—such as private property laws—exist. This may partially explain why EPZs' success in Africa has been very limited. In many ways, the poor performance of most African zones—with the prominent exceptions of Mauritius, Madagascar, and Kenya, as shown in box 3.4—mirrors their overall unsatisfactory development records.

There are intrinsic factors in the EPZs that explain their successes or failures. Experience suggests that the failure or success of a zone is linked to its policy and incentive framework and the way in which it is located, developed, and managed. The main reasons behind the poor performance of some zones have been uncompetitive and restrictive policy frameworks. There is potential for African countries to benefit from the EPZ approach. However, a coordinated package of incentives, infrastructure, and services is essential to effectively attract and keep FDI in a country.

EPZs in Asia as well as in Africa continue to be mostly government-run (see table 3.11), usually by central government free-zone authorities (for example, Republic of Korea, Singapore, and Bangladesh), state government corporations (Malaysia and India), or ministerial departments (Taiwan). There is a growing trend toward private zone development, particularly among the Asian and African countries, such as Ghana and Kenya.[15]

Role of Investment Promotion Agencies

The number of investment promotion agencies (IPAs) of national and local governments has grown at least five-fold over the past decade, seeking to attract foreign investment around the world.[16] Forty of the 47 countries in Sub-Saharan Africa have national IPAs; South Africa has over a dozen subnational IPAs. Many other countries, including Kenya, Ghana, and Mauritius, have established other investment promotion intermediaries such as free-zone development bodies and sectoral agencies. Asia is also a focal point for IPA activities. China alone has 31 IPAs, mostly at the provincial level, and hundreds more intermediaries, including economic and technology development zones and municipal promotion offices. India is the host to a similar number of state-based IPAs, where government promotional efforts are also largely devolved at the subnational level.[17]

The nature of investment promotion activities suggests that quasi-government agencies may be best positioned to fulfill the IPA function.[18] Sub-Saharan African IPAs operate within the public sphere but tend to be more autonomous than agencies in other parts of the world. No African IPA is fully private or has joint public-private status. In addition, African IPAs tend to be more reliant on funding from multilateral donors than agencies in other developing countries (figure 3.11).

Recent cross-country analysis suggests that, for each 10 percent increase in IPA promotion budgets, the level of FDI inflows increased by 2.5 percent.[19] African IPAs on average have sufficient funding. The median IPA budget of $626,000 in Africa is twice as high as the median IPA budget in a low-income country and 28 percent higher than a median IPA budget in an upper-middle-income country (figure 3.12). However, the range of budgets in Africa is wide, evidenced by much higher mean budgets.

Beyond the scope of the standard services associated with attracting investors, new activities are being undertaken by IPAs to provide post-investment services. These services are important because they attract new investors and investments through the linkage of existing satisfied investors and encourage the reinvesting of FDI interests. Asian IPAs have been directing their attention toward how to secure and expand existing FDI by improving investor aftercare. By comparison, SSA agencies tend to devote a lower share of resources to investor servicing but more to investment generation. On average, 46 percent of the budget in SSA IPAs is spent on investment generation but only 20 percent on investor servicing. For comparison, the corresponding figures for other developing countries are 33 and 31 percent, respectively.[20]

Experience indicates that assigning IPAs as one-stop-shops is not the best option. The one-stop IPAs have seldom met with success, because regulatory authorities are usually unwilling to fully relinquish their reviewing or approval authority. As a result, what is intended to be "one stop" often turns into an additional complication in the investment process. A far better solution has proven to focus on simplifying the process itself, which argues for IPAs' policy advocacy. Managers of foreign companies can provide first-hand accounts of the investment environment and how it affects their businesses, and IPA staff can channel this feedback to relevant government bodies as part of their policy advocacy efforts.

Another aspect of IPA services that is receiving increasing attention is maximizing the beneficial impact of FDI in the host economy. For exam-

BOX 3.4

Four EPZs in Madagascar, Mauritius, Senegal, and Tanzania

Madagascar started to develop an EPZ in 1989 to attract FDI. EPZ status can be given to companies anywhere in Madagascar. The number of EPZ firms has been growing steadily, from 66 in 1991 to 307 in 2001. The majority of them are engaged in the garment industry, exporting to the EU and the United States under a preferential tariff arrangement. EPZ firms provide about half of all of the secondary sector's employment, although the secondary sector remains small, and account for 50 percent of the country's exports. Although Malagasy EPZs are regarded as a successful story in their own right, from a broader sense, they have been criticized for operating largely outside of the national economy, thus contributing insignificantly to overall economic performance.

Mauritian EPZs, established in 1971, were geared toward separating the EPZ activities from the rest of the economy by reducing the cost of doing business through tax and duty exemptions, concessionary access to finance, fast-track approvals for all administrative procedures, and preferential market agreements and marketing support. EPZ production accelerated from 1984 and performed extremely well until the mid-1990s. However, Mauritian EPZs have been overly dependent on the textile and garment sector, which represented 77 percent of total EPZ exports and 83 percent of total EPZ employment. A Textile Emergency Support Team was set up to address the issues related to the increasing number of closures of EPZs due to the changed dynamics in the international textile and garment markets. The government is also moving toward integrating the EPZ and non-EPZ economies to increase the economic impact of EPZ models.

Currently, Senegal has three EPZ benefits: the Dakar Free Industrial Zone (DFIZ, since 1974), the Free Trade Points (Points Francs, since 1986), and Free Export Enterprises (EFE, since 1996). While the DFIZ and Points Francs have similar benefits, the EFE provides fewer advantages. Altogether there are 197 EPZ firms; 171 of them are under EFE. The recent successes of the Senegalese EPZ program can be attributed largely to the opportunities provided by AGOA. The Senegalese EPZ programs offer a number of features that have enabled Senegal to take advantage of existing market opportunities, including provision of EPZ status to both goods and services exporters, with access to both fiscal and nonfiscal incentives; enabling a framework to allow for private sector development and management of zones; equal treatment accorded to domestic and foreign investors; and streamlined customs procedures largely in line with Kyoto Convention standards and guidelines.

Tanzania has three EPZs with two in Zanzibar and one on the Tanzania mainland. A Free Economic Zone was established in 1992 on Zanzibar, focusing on the development of a manufacturing base in this largely spice and seaweed exports-dependent island region. In 1998, the Zanzibari government introduced a separate "Freeport" regime, essentially a free trade zone regime, to enhance its role as a transport hub on the Indian Ocean. The two zone regimes in Zanzibar, however, have had limited impact on economic development. One of the most significant issues seems to be the lack of an adequately trained workforce for industrial development. In the case of the Freeport, while the legal and institutional environment appears to be favorable, the lack of adequate port infrastructure has and will likely continue to inhibit its growth. The mainland government introduced an EPZ program in 2002, to promote export-oriented industrial investment. So far the mainland EPZ has two garment manufacturers and one used-appliances refurbishing business. Garment exports are largely destined for the U.S. market under AGOA status. The economic impact of this EPZ remains to be seen.

In summary, based on the experiences of African EPZs, several lessons could be drawn. First, an over-reliance on a particular set of exports (for example, garments and textiles) can be unsustainable when market conditions change to a competitor's advantage. Such has been the impact of the repeal of the Multifibre Arrangement on Mauritius' EPZs. The MFA governed world trade in textiles and garments, imposing quotas on the amount developing countries could export to developed countries. By the same token, given the recent erosion of AGOA and EBA's benefits due to the recent repeal of MFA, other African EPZs based on the preferential tariff must restructure themselves to meet the new challenge. Second, good

(Continues on the following page.)

BOX 3.4 (continued)

policy and institutional frameworks must be supported by adequate infrastructure and a trained labor force, as illustrated by Zanzibar EPZs. Third, to
maximize the economic impact of the EPZs, they should be integrated with
the rest of economy to create backward linkages, which has been under
consideration in Mauritius.

Source: FIAS forthcoming.

ple, more than half of 123 IPAs surveyed worldwide, including 16 of 35
African IPAs, are providing some form of linkage program between foreign
investors and small and medium enterprises.[21] The African linkage efforts
tend to focus on agribusiness activities, such as the Oil Palm Outgrower
Scheme shepherded by Ghana's Investment Promotion Centre with
Unilever Corp. Likewise, in Mozambique, the Investment Promotion Centre operates a linkage program that provides megaprojects such as the
Mozal Aluminum Smelter and Sasol gas pipeline with prequalified lists of
some 300 local service providers and suppliers.

Public-Private Responses for Investment Climate Reforms in Africa

Several African countries have established Presidential Investors' Advisory
Councils, including Ghana, Tanzania, and Senegal in 2002, and Mali and
Uganda in 2004 (box 3.5). The objectives of the councils are to provide a

TABLE 3.11

Private and Public Sector Zones in Developing and Transition Economies

Region	Public zones	Private zones	Mixed zones	Total
Americas	53	142	3	198
Asia and Pacific	261	203	15	479
Sub-Saharan Africa	25	38	0	63
Middle East and North Africa	49	28	0	77
Central/Eastern Europe and Central Asia	40	58	0	98
Total	428	469	18	915

Source: ILO Database on Export Processing Zones.

Note: Excludes single-factory programs.

FIGURE 3.11

Sources of IPA Financing by Region, 2004

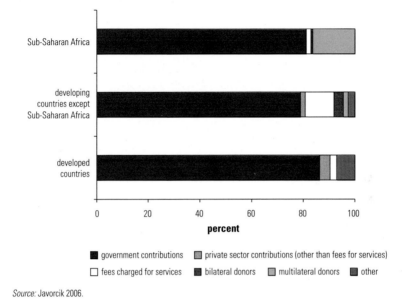

Source: Javorcik 2006.

FIGURE 3.12

IPA Budget by Country Grouping, 2004

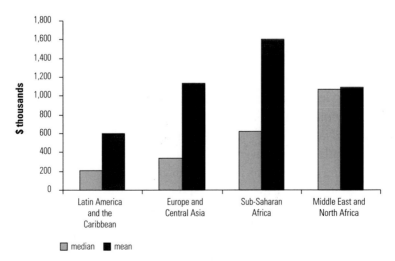

Source: Javorcik 2006.

BOX 3.5

Presidential Investors' Advisory Councils in Africa

Presidential Investors' Advisory Councils in Africa are small, high-level forums, comprising business leaders drawn from the top echelons of (i) international business (both invested and not invested in the country), (ii) local
business leaders, and (iii) key ministers. A small sampling of council members from various countries on the continent includes Unilever, Microsoft,
Diageo, Monsanto, Lafarge, Coca Cola, AngloGold, and Barclays. The councils are chaired by the country president and supported by local secretari-
ats. Local working groups, chaired by private sector representatives, are
arranged around the core issues identified within council meetings. The
working groups are then charged with implementing council actions and
acting as drivers of the reform process.

The councils have widely been regarded as a means to accelerate economic growth. Governments have come to rely on them for expert advice and
to help improve the country's image as an investment destination. To date,
councils have focused on a variety of sectors, such as agribusiness,
tourism, technology, manufacturing, and mining. They also have concentrated on several cross-cutting issues, including labor policies, land access,
taxation, administrative barriers, and infrastructure.

Source: World Bank staff.

direct channel of dialogue for action between investors and political leaders
and to blend the perspective of foreign investors with the knowledge of
local business leaders to create conditions for accelerated growth and investment. The councils aim to identify big-ticket items for policy reforms, and
prioritize and take action on issues to remove obstacles to investment. They
also act as watchdogs for government action on private sector development,
while enabling governments to learn from global corporate experience.

Some of the main achievements of these councils have been the creation of productive and constructive relationships between the private sector and government to accelerate the implementation of difficult reforms.
Some prominent examples include reducing customs clearing time from
two to three weeks to three to five days in Ghana; and enacting legislation

to ease the process for starting a new business and in improving access to land and labor in Tanzania. Progress on more complex strategic priorities, such as identifying and promoting sources of growth, however, has been more elusive.

The Investment Climate Facility (ICF) is another private-public partnership initiated under the New Economic Partnership for Africa's Development, launched on June 1, 2006. The objectives of ICF include (i) encouraging, developing, and working with coalitions for investment-climate reform and supporting business-government dialogues; (ii) supporting governments in creating a legal, regulatory, and administrative environment that encourages businesses at all levels to invest, grow, and create jobs; and (iii) improving Africa's image as an investment destination through a coordinated effort to publicize improvements that have been made in the investment climate.

This initiative, together with the efforts of some African governments, may improve the investment climate of Africa and balance FDI inflows across the world.[22] However, the effectiveness of the agency is still too early to assess.

International Trade and Investment Agreements

Apart from domestic trade-policy regimes, trade and investment flows between African and Asian countries are shaped by various international agreements and treaties. These include arrangements that are multilateral or regional (whether plurilateral or bilateral) in nature.

With respect to trade flows, over the last 30 years, alongside the multilateral trading system, regional trade agreements (RTAs) (or Free Trade Agreements (FTAs)) have proliferated around the world; as of June 2006, 197 RTAs had been filed with the WTO.[23] RTAs include not only reciprocal bilateral and plurilateral agreements but also special preferential arrangements provided by developed countries to facilitate market access for developing countries, including those in Africa. The most notable examples are the Everything But Arms (EBA) initiative, extended by the EU to African LDCs, and the Africa Growth Opportunity Act (AGOA), extended by the United States. Both EBA and AGOA impact the flows of trade between Africa and Asia. Of course, African-Asian trade is also influenced by agreements between countries in the two regions, yet, to date, these remain very limited in number. Regional trade agreements *among* African countries themselves also shape the nature and extent of the continent's trade flows with Asian countries.

While some trade agreements contain provisions related to FDI, the main instruments governing FDI flows are bilateral investment treaties (BITs).

African-Asian Trade under Multilateral Agreements

WTO

At the most macro level, trade between the two regions is governed by multilateral commitments under the WTO. Of the 47 Sub-Saharan African countries, 37 are WTO members. Most of the 10 countries that have not acceded to the WTO are either small island countries or nations that have been subject to conflict over the last decade, since the WTO was founded: Cape Verde, Comoros, Equatorial Guinea, Eritrea, Ethiopia, Liberia, São Tomé and Principe, Seychelles, Somalia, and Sudan. Regarding the Asian countries, China, of course, is a new member of the WTO, while India was a founding member. Of the other developing countries in Asia, Afghanistan, Bhutan, Lao PDR, Timor, and Vietnam do not have WTO membership.

Extensive progress in the lowering of tariffs and other trade barriers was achieved over the half-century life of the GATT (General Agreement on Trade and Tariffs), the WTO's predecessor organization. Indeed, as result, the preponderance of world trade today is governed by a fundamentally liberalized policy regime based on multilateral rules, disciplines, and standards, such as Most Favored Nation (MFN) and National Treatment, that provide for nondiscrimination in international commerce; 149 countries are committed to this policy regime. The founding in 1995 of the WTO marked a watershed by extending multilateral liberalization of trade to cover not only commerce in products but also in services and intellectual property, among other aspects. In the intervening years, however, the WTO has not been able to meet the aspirations of its founders to significantly deepen further what had been accomplished in 1995. The most recent round of multilateral negotiations, the Doha Development Round, which was launch in 2001, has moved in fits and starts. In the summer of 2006, the talks were indefinitely suspended.

The lack of progress in the Doha Round certainly has been disappointing to virtually all of the players, and both Africa and Asia would reap substantial gains—not only from the North but also from each other—if the Round could be concluded in line with the objectives initially envisaged. To this end, much is riding on initiatives to revive the Round and they deserve strong encouragement by African and Asian leaders. Still, the fact remains that the foundation of world trade flows—including those between most countries in Asia and Africa—are still grounded in a multilateral rules-based system. Thus, even if no further progress is made in the Doha Round, the basic contours of trade between Africa and China and India are still subject to WTO rules and standards, including procedures for dispute settlement.

Multifibre Arrangement

In January 2005, the Multifibre Arrangement (MFA), which began in 1974 and governed world trade in textiles and garments, imposing quotas on the amount developing countries could export to developed countries, expired. The expiration of the MFA is engendering inevitable negative consequences and positive effects on both developed and developing countries, including those in Africa and Asia. Positive effects include efficiencies in production and trade of textiles and clothing, saving quota-related expenses, and consumers' benefits from lower prices. Negative consequences include an increase in the unemployed as well as declining exports in least-income countries.

Many analysts predicted that the market shares of China and India in textiles and clothing exports to the United States and the EU would increase as those of Sub-Saharan African and other developing countries with high production costs declined.[24] Evidence from the WBAATI business case studies clearly reveals that such a transformation is already underway in parts of the African textile and garment industry; see below. It is evident that in the short- to medium-run, because Chinese and Indian textile firms have lower cost structures and thus are more efficient than their African counterparts, it will be difficult for African firms to compete in the mass clothing market. Instead, as the business case studies indicate, African textile firms are likely to be more competitive in niche clothing markets. Increasingly these are the markets that African textile firms are targeting.

Regional Trade Agreements Affecting African-Asian Trade

AGOA and EBA

The AGOA and EBA programs add preferences to the existing Generalized System of Preferences (GSP) programs of the EU and the United States.[25]

Most of the countries that have taken advantage of the AGOA apparel and textile benefits are located in Southern and Eastern Africa. In part, the increased inflow of FDI from Asian economies, such as India and China, to these countries has been driven by these preferential arrangements. As illustrated in table 3.12, benefits enjoyed by the apparel sector grew significantly between 1999 and 2002 and exports surged. AGOA's apparel benefits had such visible impacts because general tariff and quota barriers were relatively high for these products in accordance with the MFA.

AGOA and EBA have provided market access for Africa, based on supply capacity largely built by Asian investors. The most well-known case is the sudden surge of Lesotho textile and garment exports to the EU and the United States, facilitated by Asian investors who had capital, technology, and know-how. Textiles were produced locally and exported to the EU and the United States duty free. The repeal of MFA has enabled China to dominate global textile trade and has significantly reduced AGOA's apparel benefits. Many Asian investors abandoned their apparel factories in Lesotho, for example. Non-AGOA countries also suffered. It is reported that South Africa's textile and clothing industry lost 44,000 jobs between 2000 and 2005.

Overall, African textile, apparel, and footwear exports to the United States and EU suffered a big drop in 2005, as shown in figure 3.13. However, the full effect of China's global textile domination remains to be seen. It is still possible that African textile exports could recover from the current

TABLE 3.12
Export Performance of AGOA Countries
(percent)

Categories	Share of United States in total exports (2002)	Growth of total exports (1999–2002)	Growth of exports to United States (1999–2002)
LDCs without apparel benefits	6.4	2.6	−30.2
LDCs with apparel benefits	13.7	19.5	80.1
Non-LDCs non-oil exporters without apparel benefits	8.2	15.4	−16.8
Non-LDCs non-oil exporters with apparel benefits (liberal rules of origin)	6.6	21.5	38.0
Non-LDCs non-oil exporters with apparel benefits (restrictive rules of origin)	13.0	11.1	30.9

Source: Brenton and Ikezuki 2004.

setback if production capacity being built in African countries can be sustained or, more probably, if niche rather than mass markets are targeted.

Cotonou Agreement and Economic Partnership Agreements of the EU

In addition to EBA, the EU has extended to Africa, the Caribbean, and the Pacific (ACP) countries preferential access to its market under the Cotonou Agreement, the successor to the Lomé Convention. Economic Partnership Agreements (EPAs) between the EU and ACP countries are under negotiation to replace the preferential systems embodied in the Cotonou Agreement, which had received a waiver under the enabling clause from GATT Article XXIV; this waiver expires in 2007.

It is envisioned that the EPAs will promote trade and development in the ACP countries compatible with WTO principles by establishing agreements between large groups of countries forming customs unions. By negotiating reciprocal liberalization with existing South-South regional groupings and by providing common rules of origin with cumulative provisions, the intention is to prevent the hub-and-spokes effects that plague many bilateral North-South agreements. Several issues will determine the ultimate effectiveness of any EPAs in promoting development: the degree of additional MFN liberalization in goods and services; the restrictiveness of rules of origin; and the extent of trade diversion that could occur in the event that there is no reduction in MFN border protection. Because tariffs are relatively high and internal barriers within groupings are still prevalent, enacting EPAs without prior action on

FIGURE 3.13

African Textile, Apparel, and Footwear Exports to the EU and the United States

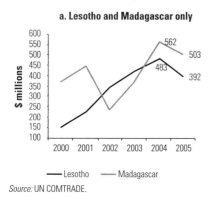
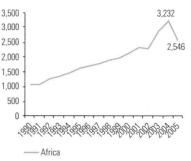

a. Lesotho and Madagascar only

b. African countries

Source: UN COMTRADE.

these issues could result in hub-and-spokes patterns of trade integration, trade diversion, and in a worst-case scenario, net losses of income. Without action on external and internal barriers, giving EU firms preferential access to ACP markets could well divert trade to EU producers from more efficient producers in non-EU countries, including Asian countries.[26]

Agreements between Asian and African Countries

To underpin China's rapid trade expansion with Africa and its intention to consolidate broader economic cooperation, in January 2006 Beijing issued "China's Africa Policy." This white paper pledges further cooperation with Africa in four areas, including politics, economy, cultural exchange, and security (see box 3.6). As a part of its Africa Policy, the Chinese government granted zero preferential tariffs for 24 SSA countries on 190 commodities (see table 3.13).[27] This is a first step to stimulate African LDCs exports to China through a scheme similar to the GSP of developed countries granted to LDCs worldwide. It is still too early to assess the full effect of this preferential treatment.[28]

To date, however, use of Chinese preferential tariffs for African LDCs has been limited. In 2004, African LDCs actually exported products that correspond to only 72 of the 190 lines with zero tariffs. In terms of magnitude, Africa's exports under current preferential tariffs account for only 25 percent of total exports by these countries. The most notable category is "textiles," which includes cotton, cotton yarns, and fabrics. While China granted zero tariffs to 18 lines in this category, African countries only exported products in 7 of them in 2004. In terms of magnitude, the exports under zero tariffs account only for 1 percent of total exports in the textile category. This is because African exports to China under this category are mostly cotton, which has not been granted the preferential tariff. These findings are based on 2004 data, which are the latest currently available. In 2006, after these preferential arrangements came into effect, African producers may have increased exports of the products being covered.

The negotiation of Free Trade Agreements (FTAs) between Africa and Asia is a very recent phenomenon. Table 3.14 gives a list of FTAs that currently are under negotiation or are proposed between the two regions. While AGOA and EBA have the objective of developed countries assisting African economic development, FTAs between Africa and Asia would largely seek mutually beneficial commercial arrangements for their respective domestic economies.

BOX 3.6

China's "Africa Policy"

On January 12, 2006, the Chinese government issued "China's Africa Policy." The occasion was the fiftieth anniversary of the establishment of diplomatic relations between China and the Arab Republic of Egypt, the first such agreement among the countries of the African continent. The policy's purpose is to further promote the steady growth of Chinese-African relations in the long term, and bring the mutually beneficial cooperation to a new stage. The release of the document demonstrates the growing interest of China in Africa and Africa's important role in supporting China's economic growth in the future. In fact, productive and strong relations are of critical importance to both China and Africa. Among Africa's 53 countries, 47 have established diplomatic ties with China, and trade between Africa and China had grown to an estimated $37 billion in 2005.

"China's Africa Policy" is in keeping with China's general foreign policy, which is guided by the "Five Principles of Peaceful Co-existence."[a] In addition, the document sets forth guidelines for future cooperation in the areas of politics, economy, cultural exchange, and security, which are summarized as follows:

- Political cooperation: China will continue to encourage dialogue and exchange with African governments through national executive and legislative bodies and regional gatherings, and support international mechanisms for increased cooperation such as the United Nations.

- Economic cooperation: China will grant duty-free treatment to as yet unspecified exports from the least developed African countries, and will generally facilitate the access of African goods to the Chinese market. In support of outward investment, China will continue to provide preferential loans and buyer credits to encourage Chinese firms to invest in Africa. Moreover, China will expand its economic cooperation with Africa, especially in financial services, agribusiness, infrastructure, tourism, and resource-based sectors (oil, mining, forestry, and so forth). China also pledged to work to resolve or reduce the debts owed by some African countries, both to China and to the broader international community.

(Continues on the following page.)

BOX 3.6 (continued)

- Cooperation in cultural exchange: China will carry out exchange and co-operation programs with African countries in fields of common interest, especially human resources development, education, science and technology, medicine and health, civil service systems, the environment, and disaster reduction.

- Cooperation in security: China will strengthen military cooperation with the continent through technological exchanges and training exercises. In addition, China will work closely with African countries to combat transnational organized crime and corruption, and intensify cooperation on matters regarding judicial assistance, and extradition and repatriation of criminal suspects.

The paper's release coincided with the visit of China's Foreign Minister, Li Zhaoxing to five African countries (Cape Verde, Senegal, Mali, Liberia, and Nigeria). During the trip, Minister Li announced several new initiatives under the policy, including a $25 million interest-free reconstruction loan to Liberia for the construction of hospitals, roads, and other infrastructure projects; cancellation of some $18.5 million in Senegalese debt; and other development efforts.

Source: World Bank Group staff.

a. "The Five Principles of Peaceful Co-existence" refers to the principles of mutual respect for sovereignty and territorial integrity; mutual non-aggression; non-interference in each other's internal affairs; equality and mutual benefit; and peaceful coexistence.

The short-run benefits and costs of any African-Asian FTAs that materialize will depend, in part, on current tariff schedules and, because these vary by sector, so would the benefits and costs. Asian countries, with the exception of India, stand to lose less in the short run than do the African countries because they have comparatively low tariffs on many of their largest import items already. African countries, on the other hand, have comparatively high tariffs on their major imports, such as textiles, apparel, and footwear. All other things equal, then, in the short run, an FTA with Asia could pose significant losses to the African textile and apparel industries.

TABLE 3.13
Chinese Preferential Tariffs to 24 Sub-Saharan African LDCs

Product group	Number of lines in preferential tariffs	Average reduction in tariff rates (percent)	Number of lines exported by African LDCs in 2004	Effectively applied tariff before preferential tariff (percent)	African LDC's export values on preferential tariffs in 2004, $m	As percentage of total category imports from Africa	Tariffs paid in 2004, $m
Agricultural raw materials— non-edible	26	7	15	11	16	28	6.7
Agricultural raw materials— edible	20	10	9	13	10	95	13.4
Processed food	7	14	2	5	26	100	13.0
Petroleum products	2	8	0	n.a.	0	n.a.	0.0
Ores	4	2	3	2	4	2	0.6
Mineral manufactures	1	18	1	18	0.01	100	0.01
Non-metal minerals	2	24	0	n.a.	0	n.a.	0.0
Basic metal	14	8	6	2	147	100	34.7
Textiles	18	8	7	5	2	1	1.2
Apparel/footwear	26	15	9	15	0.04	33	0.1
Machinery and transportation equipment	15	7	1	4	0.003	3	0.001
Electric machines	2	7	0	n.a.	0	n.a.	0.0
Electronics	2	5	0	n.a.	0	n.a.	0.0
Other manufacturing	37	10	14	9	1	77	10.1
Nonpharmaceutical chemicals	11	11	4	8	0	61	0.4
Pharmaceutical chemicals	1	4	1	4	0.005	100	0.002
Live animals—not edible	2	10	0	n.a.	0	n.a.	0.0
Total	190	9.8	72	5.3	$207	25	$80

Source: Chinese Ministry of Commerce, December 2005.

Note: n.a. = not applicable. Categories are based on the conversion of HS code to STIC 2 code.

South Africa, Africa's largest regional economic power, is a natural FTA partner sought by Asian countries. All major Asian countries are seeking FTAs with South Africa or with the Southern African Customs Union (SACU), of which South Africa is a member.

However, the responses of South African domestic industries to some FTAs are mixed. South African mining companies welcome an FTA with China in anticipation of a future increase in exports to China, but local textile and clothing firms largely oppose the FTA, fearing losses due to their inferior competitiveness. While the fear of the South African textile and clothing industry is understandable, due to its currently high tariff of 20 to 40 percent on tex-

TABLE 3.14
Status of Bilateral Trade Agreements Between Asia and Africa

Countries involved	Type of agreement	Status
China–South Africa	FTA	Under negotiation
Japan–South Africa	FTA	Under feasibility study
Korea–South Africa	FTA	Under proposal
India–Mauritius	CECPA (Comprehensive Economic Cooperation and Partnership Agreement)	Under negotiation
India–SACU	Partial scope agreement (leading to FTA)	Under proposal
Singapore–SACU	FTA	Under negotiation

Source: Authors' compilations from various sources.

Notes: SACU (Southern African Customs Union): Botswana, Lesotho, Namibia, South Africa, and Swaziland.

tiles and clothing, the optimism of the mining companies may be overstated, because China's tariff on metallic ores is already close to zero.

To ease the concern of South African textile and clothing companies, China agreed to limit the growth of its textile and garment exports to South Africa, taking a voluntary export restraint measure. South African policy makers are in a dilemma: while some labor-intensive domestic industries might experience revenue reduction and unemployment, consumers can immediately enjoy the benefits of low-priced products imported from China.[29]

Unilateral preferential tariff arrangements such as AGOA and EBA focus on granting market access to goods. However, deeper bilateral and interregional economic integration initiatives, such as FTAs and economic partnership agreements (EPAs), could potentially provide new and additional opportunities for African countries to enhance their trade activities. The fact that African governments in general welcome Chinese investments more than they do Chinese products provides opportunities for Africa and Asia to pursue FTAs on a much broader base, including investments and services trade, such as financial services and tourism.

Regional Trade Agreements Among African Countries

The general benefits of FTAs or RTAs are realized through two main channels: (i) by competition and scale effects, and (ii) by trade and location effects. Not surprisingly, many regional integration agreements (RIAs) are currently in force in Africa to expand the economic and geographic horizons of small African economies. The major RIAs are shown in table 3.15.[30] African economies remain relatively fragmented compared to other regions, which implies that regional integration could significantly improve their economies of scale (table 3.16). However, one distinctive feature of these RIAs is their small economic and population coverage, which implies that the scale effects provided by RIAs could be still limited.

TABLE 3.15
Selected Regional Integration Agreements (RIAs) in Africa

Agreement (founding year)	Full name	Member countries (total number of members)	Population (millions)	GDP ($ billions, ppp)	GDP per capita ($, ppp)
SACU (1910)	Southern African Customs Union	South Africa, Botswana, Lesotho, Swaziland, Namibia (5)	51	541	10,605
ECOWAS (1975)	Economic Community of West African States	Benin, Burkina Faso, Cape Verde, Côte d'Ivoire, The Gambia, Ghana, Guinea, Guinea-Bissau, Liberia, Mali, Niger, Nigeria, Senegal, Sierra Leone, Togo (15)	252	343	1,361
SADC (1980)	Southern African Development Community	Angola, Botswana, Democratic Republic of Congo, Lesotho, Madagascar, Malawi, Mauritius, Mozambique, Namibia, South Africa, Swaziland, Tanzania, Zambia, Zimbabwe (14)	234	737	3,152
ECCAS (1984)	Economic Community of Central African States	Angola, Burundi, Cameroon, Central African Republic, Chad, Republic of Congo, Democratic Republic of Congo, Equatorial Guinea, Gabon, Rwanda, São Tomé and Principe (11)	121	176	1,451
COMESA (1994)	Common Market for Eastern and Southern Africa	Angola, Burundi, Comoros, Democratic Republic of Congo, Djibouti, Arab Republic of Egypt, Eritrea, Ethiopia, Kenya, Libya, Madagascar, Malawi, Mauritius, Rwanda, Seychelles, Sudan, Swaziland, Uganda, Zambia, Zimbabwe (20)	406	736	1,811
CEMAC (1994)	Economic and Monetary Community of Central Africa	Cameroon, Central African Republic, Chad, Republic of Congo, Equatorial Guinea, Gabon (6)	35	85	2,435
WAEMU (1994)	West African Economic and Monetary Union	Benin, Burkina Faso, Côte d'Ivoire, Guinea-Bissau, Mali, Niger, Senegal, Togo (8)	81	101	1,257
EAC (2001)	East African Community	Kenya, Tanzania, Uganda (3)	98	104	1,065

Source: Authors' compilations from various sources (as of December 2004).

Note: ppp = purchasing power parity.

TABLE 3.16
Interregional Comparison of Geographical and Sovereign Fragmentation Indicators

Region	Average number of borders	Proportion of population in landlocked countries (%)	Average intra-regional transportation costs ($)
Sub-Saharan Africa	4	40	7,600
East Asia and Pacific	2	0.4	3,900
Latin America and Caribbean	2	3	4,600
South Asia	3	4	3,900

Source: World Bank staff.

Note: Democratic Republic of Congo, Sudan, and Ethiopia have been treated as "landlocked" countries. Data on average intra-regional transportation costs are based on predicted costs per container using a gravity model regression in Venables and Limao (1999), and are available for East and South Asia regions together.

One prominent feature of Africa's RIAs is the so-called "spaghetti bowl effect," arising from the fact that, at present, each African country is a member of four different agreements (see figure 3.14). Such overlapping arrangements tend to have different rules of origin, tariff schedules, and implementation periods. This engenders complications of customs administration and delays in customs processing, eventually driving up the cost of trade and deterring investment from both domestic and foreign businesses. Indeed, the business case studies revealed clear evidence on this score. Such spaghetti-bowl effects are not unique to Africa: they also exist in other regions, such as South Eastern Europe, where there are 29 bilateral FTAs among eight countries.[31]

In 2003, the EU finalized its financial agreement with ECCAS and CEMAC, conditional on the merging of the two. In 2005, the EU experienced a major challenge in its EPA negotiations arising from overlapping memberships of various regional integration agreements, including those of Eastern and Southern Africa (COMESA, EAC, and SADC).[32]

Implications of RTAs for African-Asian Trade

As Asian countries seek FTA partners with African countries, dealing concretely with specific measures to handle the problem of overlapping RIA memberships will be critical. At the same time, it is critical to recognize that preferential trade agreements may well not be net trade-creating or that all members will benefit. Positive outcomes will depend on the design and implementation of such agreements. RTAs can generate "trade diversion" and thus must be pursued in tandem with reductions in MFN tariffs.

FIGURE 3.14
The Spaghetti Bowl of African RIAs

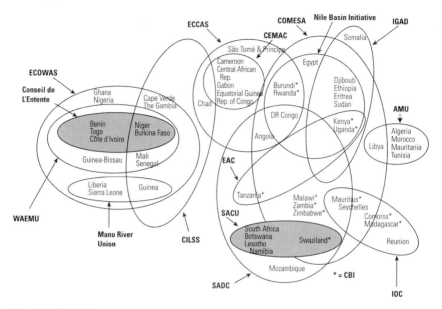

Source: World Bank staff.

Note: AMU: Arab Maghreb Union; CBI: Cross Border Initiative; CEMAC: Economic and Monetary Community of Central Africa; CILSS: Permanent Interstate Committee on Drought Control in the Sahel; COMESA: Common Market for Eastern and Southern Africa; EAC: East African Cooperation; ECOWAS: Economic Community of Western African States; IGAD: Inter-Governmental Authority on Development; IOC: Indian Ocean Commission; SACU: Southern African Customs Union; SADC: Southern African Development Community; WAEMU: West African Economic and Monetary Union.

When embedded in a consistent and credible reform strategy, the key determinant of RTAs' success is low external trade barriers. While many African and Asian countries have reduced tariffs, in some cases, as noted above, they remain high, and the risk of trade diversion remains significant. Further reductions in applied MFN tariffs thus will be required to ensure that RTAs are beneficial for those participating in them and to minimize the impact on the countries that are left out. At the same time, a preferential trading arrangement cannot substitute for an adequate investment climate.

Investment Treaties and Agreements

Bilateral Investment Agreements

Worldwide, the number of bilateral investment treaties (BITs), double taxation treaties (DTTs), and various other types of preferential trade agreements with investment components have increased substantially over the past decade, particularly for developing and transition economies. Asian countries have seen the largest increase of such agreements vis-à-vis other countries within Asia and with other regions. As of 2004, Asian economies had a total of 866 DTTs and 956 BITs with Asian and other countries.

Such agreements encourage and facilitate investment flows through liberalization and protection of foreign investment. In the past, developing countries signed international investment agreements mainly with developed countries, but recently they have been very active in signing such agreements with other developing countries. As of the end of 2004, the number of BITs between developing countries—South-South BITs—stood at roughly 1,046 (about 40 percent of the BIT universe), while South-South DTTs reached roughly 374 or about 19 percent of the total DTTs worldwide; see figure 3.15. Of the existing agreements, roughly 50 percent have been signed and are in force.

China, India, and South Africa are among the top 10 developing countries that have signed the most BITs and DTTs with other developing countries (as well as with developed countries). China at 112 has the highest number of BITs, while India at 83 has the highest number of DTTs. China by far has the most BITs with other African countries, while India tends to have more DTTs with African countries. Table 3.17 provides a detailed look at BITs and DTTs signed between China and India, and various African countries.

Effectiveness of BITs

Some studies show that, despite the significant increase in bilateral investment treaties, the positive impact of those treaties on actual investment flows is not unambiguous. This is the case for both North-North and North-South investment treaties.[33] Empirically, such treaties act more as complements than as substitutes for good institutional quality and protection of property rights, the rationale often cited by developing countries for ratifying BITs. Thus, investors are attracted more by a better investment climate in host countries rather than BITs per se; see chapter 6.

Moreover, given the strong synergies between cross-border trade and foreign investment activities in the global business environment, as discussed in chapter 6, the combination of appropriate trade rules, liberalized market access, and investor protections can have positive effects on FDI flows. Several studies have found that RTAs that formed large markets

FIGURE 3.15
Bilateral Investment Treaties and Double Tax Treaties: 1995–2004

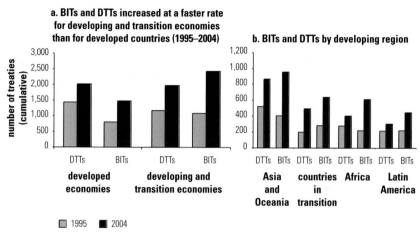

a. BITs and DTTs increased at a faster rate for developing and transition economies than for developed countries (1995–2004)

b. BITs and DTTs by developing region

☐ 1995   ■ 2004

Source: UNCTAD.

Note: These are agreements compared with other countries in the world.

attracted FDI after controlling for other factors that influence investors' location choices. To this degree, RTAs can have a strong positive impact on FDI inflows.[34]

Also, creation of an RTA will not have much effect on investment inflows from outside the region if restrictions on market access are severe and remain unchanged. Thus, open regionalism remains the key to successful attraction of FDI flows.

Conclusions and Policy Implications

Summary of Findings

Tariff structures of African countries as well as China and India still have some unfavorable elements that constrain mutual trade. Some Asian tariff rates are high for many of African countries' leading exports—those that account for about two-thirds of total African exports to Asia. Product-specific analysis of tariffs on African exports to Chinese and Indian markets suggests that in certain cases tariff escalation in these markets has been discouraging the export of higher value-added processed products from

TABLE 3.17

Investment Treaties between China and India, and Selected African Countries

	China		India	
	BITs (112)	DTTs (79)	BITs (56)	DTTs (83)
Benin	X			
Botswana	X			
Cape Verde	X			
Congo	X			
Côte d'Ivoire	X			
Djibouti	X		X	
Ethiopia	X			
Gabon	X			
Ghana	X (25)		X	(7)
Kenya	X			X
Mauritius	X	X	X	X
Mozambique	X			
Nigeria	X			
Senegal	(20)			(12)
Seychelles		X		
Sierra Leone	X			X
South Africa	X (34)	X		(63)
Sudan	X		X	
Tanzania	(12)			X (9)
Uganda	X			X
Zambia	X			X
Zimbabwe	X		X	

Source: UNCTAD.

Note: Numbers in parentheses indicate the number of BITs and DTTs in respective countries relative to the rest of the world.

Africa. However, China is a relatively liberalized market, with zero or close to zero tariffs on 45 percent of its imports. China also has plans to further lower its tariffs and bring about lower dispersion in the structure of tariffs by the end of 2007.

Although African tariff barriers have been lowered significantly recently, Asian products still face relatively high tariff barriers on the African continent. In fact, some high tariffs on intermediate inputs into African countries constrain African manufacturing exports. This bias against exports is an obvious target for reform.

Nontariff barriers, such as inappropriate use of technical standards in African export-destination markets in China and India pose special challenges to African exports. At the same time, most countries in Africa lack the institutional capacity as well as the resources to fully implement or effectively enforce internationally recognized standards. This limits the ability of domestic producers to penetrate certain export markets, not only in more developed countries, but also in Asia, especially China and India.

While export and investment incentives, such as Export Processing Zones (EPZs), to date have been successful in China and India, their potential to stimulate exports has not materialized in African countries, with a few exceptions. The preceding analysis suggests that the ineffectiveness of these incentives in African countries is due in part to significant implementation and enforcement challenges in the face of generally weak institutional capacities, as well as the lack of the requisite infrastructure and labor skills. Export incentives in African countries have also had mixed results in creating backward production linkages.

The proliferation of regional and bilateral trade and investment agreements in recent years on the African continent comprises not only reciprocal agreements among other countries in the South, including those in Asia (China and India among them), but also preferential arrangements provided by developed countries in the North to facilitate market access for exports from Africa. The size of the benefits derived from such preferential treatment diminishes significantly when market barriers for other competitors are lowered. Trade diversion from such regimes challenges their desirability and sustainability. No bilateral free trade agreements are currently in effect between Asian and African countries, with the exception of a few unilateral preferential treatments of limited scale.

RIAs on the African continent are still very much nascent and have yet to significantly foster regional trade. To Chinese and Indian investors, they are not seen as particularly trade- or investment-facilitating. Some Chinese and Indian businesses already operating in Africa complain that these agreements' spaghetti-like character actually inhibits rather than promotes international commerce.

In addition to formal international agreements, African-Asian trade and investment flows are also influenced—in varying degrees—by other instruments. Investment Promotion Agencies (IPAs) and public-private investors councils in African and Asian countries play an important role in facilitating international commerce between the two regions. China and India have also established various other mechanisms in the hopes of stimulating trade and investment with Africa. One of the more recent—and certainly most notable—initiatives is the January 2006 release in Beijing of

"China's Africa Policy," a white paper that identifies a large set of economic issues over which China proposes to cooperate with Africa, including trade and investment.

Policy Implications

Continued reforms of at-the-border trade policies are important for African countries as well as China and India to improve mutual market-access conditions and spur trade and investment. Such reforms would not only help directly reduce the costs of international transactions between the two regions, they would also help to enhance national competitiveness, improve the efficiency of domestic business operations, and lower the prices domestic consumers have to pay for goods.

To this end, reductions of MFN tariffs in India and China would improve Africa's market access to those countries. Equally, MFN tariff reductions in African countries would engender greater access for Chinese and Indian exports to Africa. As part of such efforts, China and India should reduce the escalation in their tariff structures, which serves to discourage higher value-added activities by otherwise competitive African producers, thwarts Africa's ability to diversify its exports, and runs the risk of prolonging Africa's position of being trapped as a raw materials producer.

In lowering the level of their overall tariffs, a phased program could be useful for African countries, such as first lowering tariff peaks—which gets at the most egregious protection, opens up existing domestic monopolies to competition, and reduces current anti-export biases—and then reducing tariff averages. In light of the formidable competitive efficiency of Chinese and Indian producers in certain labor-intensive sectors, such as textiles—especially in the aftermath of the elimination of the MFA—African producers should not only take advantage of this situation and seek joint ventures with Chinese and Indian businesses in the global production networks, as discussed in more detail in chapter 6, they should also focus on building niche markets rather than attempting to penetrate mass consumer markets.

Beyond the need to lower tariffs, eliminating NTBs in both regions is also a reform priority.

All told, countries in both regions have a strong interest in cooperating for a successful completion of Doha Round negotiations. Barring successful multilateral reform, an alternative would be a pan-Asian FTA with Africa or the expansion of existing preferences (or both). But these are second- or third-best approaches, and great caution should be exercised. In light of the risks of creating incentives for trade diversion, the contours of such schemes need to be carefully designed, such as with respect to rules of origin, and they need to be made complementary and mutually reinforcing with other structural and institutional economic reforms.

At the same time, African countries should review their commitments to implementing realistic and substantive regional integration schemes. Rationalizing and harmonizing the "spaghetti bowl" of existing bilateral and regional agreements is clearly needed if they are to accomplish their stated objective, especially because many businesses operating in Africa question the utility of the current arrangements.

The roles of African IPAs and public-private investors' councils could be strengthened to proactively promote FDI opportunities and eliminate bottlenecks for foreign investors. This would require the allocation of more resources to such institutions. Still, IPAs are most effective when operating in an environment with a good investment climate. Countries that do not have these conditions in place should focus on improving them first. By the same token, export and investment incentives appear to be effective only in certain cases where the requisite institutional and governance capacity exists.

Overall, achieving the desirable outcomes hoped for by implementing trade policy reforms will not come only from such actions. While those reforms are necessary to foster trade flows between Africa and Asia, they are not sufficient for trade to leverage growth. Indeed, as suggested by the analysis in chapter 2 and from the assessments contained in the various DTIS diagnostics, relieving domestic supply-side constraints matters a great deal. Thus, for example, while Asian escalating tariffs distort the contours of some African exports, it is the lack of, or the inefficiency in, African countries' domestic production capacity that is likely more critical.

Endnotes

1. While quantitative impacts of tariff reduction are often subject to debate in terms of accuracy, Ianchovichina, Mattoo, and Olarreaga (2001) estimated that fully unrestricted access to all the "QUAD" countries (United States, EU, Japan, and Canada) would lead to a 14 percent increase in non-oil exports.

2. The average rates are separately estimated for tariff rates weighted on the exports from the least developed countries (LDCs) in Africa and non-LDC African countries by destination. Tariff rates for EU are available only up to 2003.

3. The definition of tariff peaks used here is a tariff rate that is more than 15 percent of MFN rate. In large part, the prevalence of tariff peaks reflects the elimination of quantity-control NTBs during the WTO/GATT Uruguay Round, where tariffication of NTBs prompted an increase of very high duties on agricultural products that had previously been quota-constrained.

4. India has not reported petroleum imports from Africa since 1999. India levies a 10 percent tariff on its crude petroleum imports worldwide.

5. Based on World Bank staff estimation.

6. Production of chocolate requires a higher level of technology than producing cocoa paste or powder. Chinese consumers are increasingly fond of high-quality chocolate from Europe and the United States over low-quality domestically produced chocolate.

7. Many efforts have been taken to measure the trade impact of formal NTBs in a systematic manner, including (i) directly trade-related measures such as import quotas, surcharges, and anti-dumping measures; (ii) trade-related measures at the border, including labeling, packaging, proof of compliance with regulations, and sanitary standards; and (iii) general public policy such as government procurement procedures, investment restrictions, and intellectual property rights protection. Based on UNCTAD Coding System of Trade Control Measures (TCMCS), over 100 different types of NTBs are classified. They are broadly lumped into core measures, used primarily for quantity control, and noncore measures, used primarily for automatic licensing and technical measures.

8. UNCTAD 2005c.

9. Kee, Nicita, and Olarreaga (2006) have calculated Ad-Valorem Equivalent (AVE) of NTBs, directly comparable to a tariff, at tariff level for price and quantity control measures, technical regulations, monopolistic measures, and agricultural domestic supports. It is worth noting that their estimation of AVE applies only to merchandise NTBs. Because NTBs affect trade in addition to the existing tariff structure, the impact of NTBs is estimated over the impact caused by tariff, thus marginal impact.

10. Everything But Arms (EBA) is extended by the EU to African LDCs and the Africa Growth Opportunity Act (AGOA) is extended by the United States to eligible countries. Both programs have added additional preferences to the existing Generalized System of Preferences (GSP) programs of the EU and the United States.

11. Using the World Bank Investment Climate Surveys data of seven African countries, Yoshino (2006) showed that among export incentive programs, trade financing schemes were only effectively promoting firms' exports, after controlling for domestic investment climate factors such as infrastructure qual-

ity and customs efficiency. The role of duty relief measures and domestic fiscal incentives were found to be insignificant.

12. According to the United Nations Conference on Trade and Development (UNCTAD) as many as 67 countries offered tax holidays in 1995, one of the most used fiscal incentives among developing countries. Also, surveys indicated that the number of countries granting investment incentives and the range of possible measures is on the rise (UNCTAD, 2004b, pp. 11).

13. The tax incentive section is largely based on the work done by Morissett (2003).

14. See, for example, Morisset (2003).

15. It is difficult to establish whether privately owned and operated zones perform better economically than public ones.

16. UNCTAD 2002b.

17. India's investment promotion intermediaries take many different forms, including industrial development corporations, economic development zones, economic development councils, and the like, all active at the state level.

18. Wells and Wint 2000.

19. Morisset and Andrews 2004.

20. Javorcik 2006.

21. It should be noted that the definition of linkage program in the UNCTAD study is quite broad, and that while the survey did ask the IPAs to self-evaluate their linkage programs, it does not include empirical data on program effectiveness (UNCTAD 2006b).

22. Source: IFC website.

23. WTO members are required to notify the organization concerning any RTAs they participate in.

24. Nordas 2004.

25. For a comprehensive description of AGOA see http://www.agoa.gov/. For the EBA, see http://ec.europa.eu/comm/trade/issues/global/gsp/eba/index_en.htm.

26. See World Bank (2005b) and Hinkle, Hoppe, and Newfarmer (2005)

27. The Chinese government granted the access to 25 African countries, but we excluded Djibouti from our analysis.

28. Based on Chinese government statistics, African LDCs exports on the preferential tariff items have increased by 100 percent since their implementation (Liu 2006).

29. With regard to the current surge of Chinese inexpensive imports in South Africa, what Neva Seidman Makgelta, an economist for the Congress of South African Trade Unions in Pretoria, mentioned is of significance: "There is no question that, for upper classes, it's a boon. The problem is any lower class South Africans who would rather have a job."

30. As of now, examples of other RIAs are as follows; Liptako-Gourma Authority (LGA, since 1970, three members of West Africa), Economic Community of the Great Lakes Countries (CEPGL, since 1976, three members of Central Africa), Mano River Union (MRU, since 1973, three members of West Africa),

Intergovernmental Authority on Development (IGAD, since 1986, seven members of East Africa).

31. See Broadman et al. (2004).

32. Some SADC members are negotiating an EPA with the EU under the SADC framework; meanwhile other members are negotiating under the COMESA framework.

33. Blonigen and Davies (2000) studies the impact of bilateral tax treaties on foreign direct investment using data from OECD countries over the period 1982–92. Hallward-Driemeier (2003) analyzed bilateral flows of OECD members to 31 developing countries from 1980 to 2000. Also, UNCTAD (1998) found that the number of BITs signed by the host countries was uncorrelated with the amount of FDI it received.

34. See, for example, Lederman, Maloney, and Serven (2004), Levy Yayati, Stein, and Daude (2004).

CHAPTER 4

"Behind-the-Border" Constraints on African-Asian Trade and Investment Flows

Introduction

This chapter explores how "behind-the-border" conditions in Africa affect the continent's trade and investment flows with Asia, especially China and India. Unlike chapters 2 and 3, where country-level (or sector-level) data were used, in this chapter, as well as in chapters 5 and 6, the analysis is largely based on firm-level data from the new World Bank Africa-Asia Trade and Investment (WBAATI) survey and business case studies, as well as existing Investment Climate Assessments (ICAs) and Doing Business data of the World Bank Group. As such, the primary units of analysis are firms operating in Africa, whether of African, Chinese, or Indian origin (firms of other nationalities are also included as comparators). In addition, the examination focuses primarily on four Sub-Saharan African countries that have significant trade and investment ties with China and India and that were covered by the WBAATI survey and business case studies: Ghana, Senegal, South Africa, and Tanzania.

The basic diagnostics of behind-the-border conditions are first evaluated through the performance of the surveyed firms—in terms of productivity and export performance. These characteristics are compared across sectors, nationality, size, and ownership structure (domestic, joint venture, and foreign-owned).

An assessment of the sources of competition in these African markets is then conducted, first at the country level and then by differentiating among nationalities, with a particular focus on Chinese and Indian firms operating in Africa. At the country level, the assessment looks at various mechanisms through which competition is spurred or constrained. These include foreign import competition, market entry and exit, foreign direct investment, vertical dimensions of competition, and transactions with the state. At the nationality level, the chapter discusses whether Chinese and Indian investors play any significant role in fostering domestic competition in African markets or in fostering international integration of Africa's private sector.

In light of the importance that domestic competition appears to play in leveraging the beneficial effects of Chinese and Indian trade and investment in these African markets, the analysis examines the principal behind-the-border factors that are most likely constraining such competition. The discussion focuses on (i) the quality of infrastructure services (power supply, telephone services, Internet access), (ii) factor markets (access to finance, the labor market, and skilled labor), (iii) regulatory regimes, and (iv) governance disciplines. The chapter closes with conclusions and a discussion of policy implications.

Performance of Firms Behind-the-Border

The WBAATI survey data show that, among Chinese and Indian firms operating in Africa, there is significant heterogeneity in their performance, evaluated in terms of productivity and export intensity. This section discusses the observed variations in firm performance, by sector, nationality, size, and ownership structure.[1]

Sector

The nondurable, construction, and nonconstruction services sectors have relatively high labor productivity, measured as value-added per worker (see figure 4.1 (a)). The nondurable sector has the highest median value-added per worker ($16,000). The textile, non-oil minerals and metals, agriculture and food, and chemicals sectors exhibit relatively low labor productivity. The chemicals sector has the highest capital productivity,

FIGURE 4.1

Firm Performance by Sector

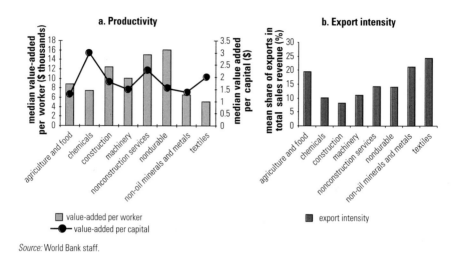

Source: World Bank staff.

measured as value-added per unit of capital stock valued in dollars, followed by the nonconstruction services sector.[2]

The sectors that show high export intensity are agriculture and food, non-oil minerals and metals, and textiles, reflecting comparative advantage in such sectors (figure 4.1 (b)). The construction services sector has low export intensity due to the sector's intrinsic nature.

Nationality

Productivity varies across firms of different nationality (figure 4.2 (a)). African, Chinese, and Indian firms differ only marginally in terms of labor productivity, while in terms of capital productivity, Chinese firms are much more productive than African or Indian firms. The survey data show that Chinese firms have significantly less capital per worker (that is, they are more labor intensive) than firms of other nationalities, which may explain the difference between the labor and capital productivity of Chinese firms relative to others.

A comparison of export intensity provides another pattern. Chinese firms are more intensive in exports than African and Indian firms, as are European firms (figure 4.2 (b)). The surveyed Indian firms are found to be less export intensive than African firms.

FIGURE 4.2
Firm Performance by Ownership Nationality

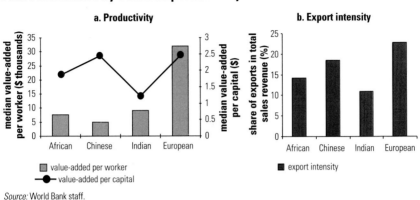

Source: World Bank staff.

Size

There is a large volume of literature explaining how size is a determinant of firm performance.[3] This is true for firms around the world. Consistent with this literature, both labor productivity and export intensity increase with size among the surveyed firms in Africa (figure 4.3). It is likely to be the case that larger firms are more productive or more efficient in production due to economies of scale as well as economies of scope. This is in turn reflected in their export intensity. Because exporting requires certain fixed costs, larger firms can expand their overseas marketing networks more easily. As discussed in detail in chapter 6, scale is also relevant for the geographical orientation of exports, particularly in terms of exports to the global market vis-à-vis intraregional exports.

The figure also shows that, unlike labor productivity, capital productivity declines with size. Among surveyed firms, larger firms tend to have more capital per worker than do smaller firms. It may be the case that larger firms are already facing diminishing returns to capital while still enjoying increasing returns to labor.[4]

Ownership Structure

Among the surveyed firms, domestic businesses are not performing on par with joint venture firms or foreign-owned firms, either in terms of productivity or export performance (figure 4.4).[5] Interestingly, in the case of labor productivity, joint venture firms are found to be more productive than for-

FIGURE 4.3

Firm Performance by Size

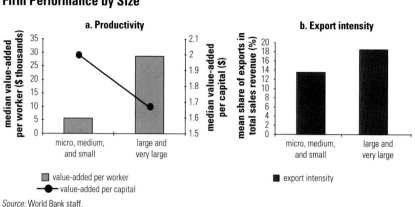

Source: World Bank staff.

eign firms, while they are equally productive based on capital productivity. Joint venture firms also export more intensively than do foreign firms.

Superiority of performance of joint ventures relative to foreign firms is at variance with some findings in other regions.[6] In certain cases, joint ventures are imposed by host-country governments as a condition for foreign investment. In general, it is believed that requiring a local partner weakens the export performance of joint venture firms relative to firms wholly owned by foreigners.[7] On the other hand, particularly in the context of African countries, where business transaction costs and business-related risks are often perceived to be high, joint venture firms may enjoy certain advantages. Unless firms intend to operate in isolated enclaves entirely detached from local economies, linking with local partners could mitigate risks associated with local transactions, making joint ventures a preferred option for many foreign investors.[8] This has been the case in other countries, such as in Latin America. The fact that such advantage in local transactions is often embodied in labor rather than capital may help explain the observed contrast in productivity between joint ventures and foreign-owned firms; that is, while there is little difference in capital productivity, joint ventures exhibit superior performance in terms of labor productivity.

Role of Domestic Competition in Promoting International Integration

A competitive environment in domestic markets is one of the most significant factors promoting the international integration of nations'

FIGURE 4.4
Firm Performance by Ownership

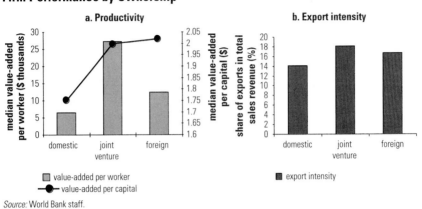

Source: World Bank staff.

Note: State-owned firms are not shown since very few of them reported their revenue data.

industries. This is the case found in many developing economies and economies in transition.[9] Surprisingly, there is only a limited literature focusing on the topic of domestic competition in Sub-Saharan African countries.[10]

Domestic competition propels international integration of domestic firms in two ways. First, it increases firm productivity, as the natural market mechanism forces out inefficient firms from the market while inviting new efficient firms to enter (*allocative efficiency*). An increase in productivity generates an improvement in the international competitive position of firms, hence improving their overall export performance.

Second, a competitive domestic market structure facilitates international integration of firms by inducing imports and competition through foreign entries. Import competition and foreign entries through direct investment could then encourage domestic firms to innovate and thus improve their efficiency (*dynamic efficiency*).

This section discusses the role of competition in promoting international integration at the country level, looking at the following dimensions: (i) foreign import competition, (ii) market entry and exit, (iii) foreign direct investment, (iv) vertical dimension of competition, and (v) transaction with the state. The section then quantitatively shows how competition improves firms' productivity and international integration.

State of Competition in Domestic Markets of Four African Countries

Average domestic market share among firms in a sector is one measure of intensity of market competition in that sector.

Table 4.1 lists the average domestic market share by sector and country, as perceived by the firms surveyed. According to the data, the construction, nonconstruction services, and non-oil minerals and metals sectors appear to be least concentrated or most competitive. The chemicals sector appears to be the most concentrated sector in Senegal, South Africa, and Tanzania. Overall, the sectors in Senegal tend to be more concentrated than the sectors in the other three countries.

As shown in figure 4.5, domestic market shares are greater for firms of larger scales, which is to be expected. For any sector, there is generally a positive correlation between size and average market share. Number of competitors that firms face is another dimension to measure intensity of market competition.[11] The competitors here include overseas competitors through imports.[12] The figure shows that larger firms on average face fewer competitors in the majority of the sectors. The only exceptions are the chemicals, construction, and nondurable sectors.

Foreign Import Competition
Typically, the most immediate channel through which competition is introduced to domestic markets is imports from other countries. In Africa, import competition appears to have differentiated impacts. In the survey

TABLE 4.1
Average Domestic Market Share, by Sector and by Country
(percent)

Sector	Ghana	Senegal	South Africa	Tanzania	All four countries
Agriculture and food	32	49	52	41	42
Chemicals	22	78	62	46	47
Construction	28	28	40	26	31
Machinery	34	67	43	38	41
Nonconstruction services	22	55	34	25	36
Nondurables	27	50	45	40	39
Non-oil minerals and metals	30	50	59	29	36
Textiles	17	66	44	43	44
All sectors	26	57	42	34	39

Source: World Bank staff.

FIGURE 4.5
Size and Domestic Competition

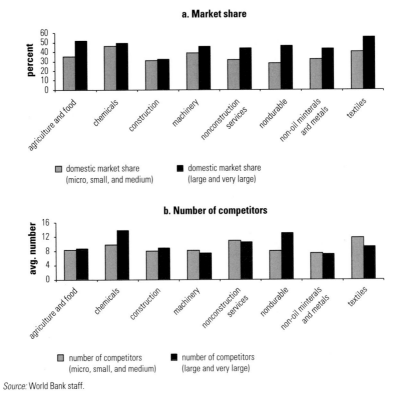

a. Market share

domestic market share
(micro, small, and medium)

domestic market share
(large and very large)

b. Number of competitors

number of competitors
(micro, small, and medium)

number of competitors
(large and very large)

Source: World Bank staff.

data, only in South Africa do firms on average appear to be exposed to more foreign import competition than to competition from local rivals. In the other three countries, competition from local rivals appears to be more dominant (figure 4.6).[13]

The reason South African firms appear to face more foreign import competition than local competition is partly related to the fact that there is relatively large representation of large and very large firms in the survey sample from South Africa. The survey data show that larger firms face more import competition than do smaller firms, while smaller firms face more local competitors than do larger firms (figure 4.7). This size-related difference is intuitive because large firms often have relatively greater technological prowess and tend to produce products that are more comparable to the products made by overseas producers.

FIGURE 4.6

Local and Foreign Import Competitors by Country and Sector

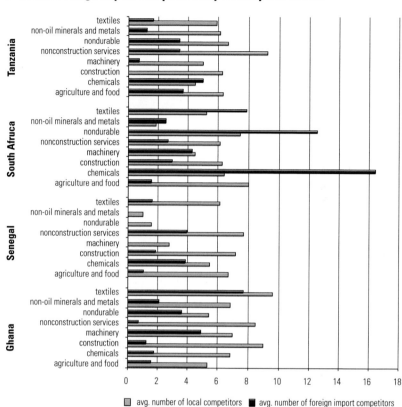

Source: World Bank staff.

Market Entry and Exit

Barriers to entry and exit in domestic markets are fundamental impediments to competition in Africa. Such barriers arise from different sources. Some are formal policy-based barriers, either for an intentional purpose of deterring new entrants to protect domestic incumbents or hangovers from the past command-and-control domestic economic regimes (for example, state-owned enterprises). The privatization efforts in African countries that have taken place in the past decades have created conditions for lowering entry and exit barriers.

Still, certain types of government-generated entry and exit barriers continue to constrain firm turnover in Africa. Some of these are cumbersome administrative procedures that make entry and exit costly. The height of

FIGURE 4.7
Local and Foreign Import Competitors by Size

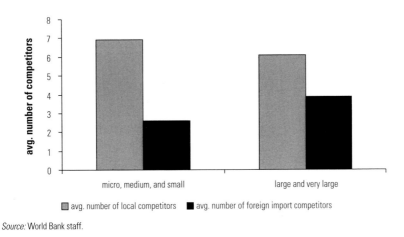

Source: World Bank staff.

so-called administrative barriers in Africa is appreciable (table 4.2). In some instances, however, China and India actually have higher entry and exit barriers.

The bulk of empirical research in many regions around the world points to more fundamental barriers to entry and exit. These include weak market-supporting institutions, especially those assuring a competitive

TABLE 4.2
Administrative Barriers to Starting and Closing a Business

	Starting a business				Closing a business		
Country	Procedures (number)	Time (days)	Cost (% of income per capita)	Min. capital (% of income per capita)	Time (years)	Cost (% of estate)	Recovery rate (cents on the dollar)
Sub-Saharan Africa avg.	11.0	63.8	215.3	297.2	3.3	19.5	16.1
Ghana	12.0	81.0	78.6	27.9	1.9	22.0	23.7
Senegal	9.0	57.0	108.7	260.4	3.0	7.0	19.1
South Africa	9.0	38.0	8.6	0	2.0	18.0	34.0
Tanzania	13.0	35.0	161.3	6.0	3.0	22.0	22.4
East Asia avg.	8.2	52.6	42.9	109.2	3.4	28.8	24.0
China	13.0	48.0	13.6	946.7	2.4	22.0	31.5
South Asia avg.	7.9	35.3	40.5	0.8	4.2	7.3	19.7
India	11.0	71.0	61.7	0	10.0	9.0	12.8

Source: World Bank 2005a.

business environment; legal protection and enforcement of property rights; sound governance; and market-reinforcing regulatory regimes governing the provision of basic infrastructure services. They constitute the set of serious business barriers in Africa. Reforms in these areas—those that shape a country's microeconomic fabric at a *deeper* level beyond what is touched by reform of so-called administrative barriers, such as speeding up the pace of business registration or of obtaining a business license—would significantly facilitate domestic competition in the region.

There are also less visible barriers in Africa to business growth. Such invisible barriers include ethnic networks. Ethnic networks often facilitate business transactions in the private sector in African countries, where businesses and consumers incur high transaction costs. As discussed in chapter 5, ethnic networks in fact facilitate cross-border trade and investment, linking nonindigenous ethnic groups in Africa with their countries of ethnic origin (for example, the Indian diaspora in African countries and their ties with India). However, closely integrated ethnic networks can also work as an implicit barrier to entry for parties outside of the networks. Due to network externalities, market entry is easier for members of a particular group but not for others. Parties who receive information from their own community that helps them screen each other become less willing to spend additional resources screening individuals from outside their communities.[14]

Business turnover in Africa appears to vary with firm size.[15] Figure 4.8 shows that smaller firms in the survey data are much younger than larger firms. They also generally face more local competitors and have smaller domestic market shares than larger firms. This indirectly suggests a higher turnover rate among smaller firms than larger firms.

Foreign Direct Investment

Entry and exit barriers in Africa impinge not only on firm turnover among domestically owned local firms but also on foreign entry through direct investment. Foreign investors seek opportunities to penetrate domestic markets in Africa not only through exporting their products from their factories in the home countries but also through establishing *de novo* greenfield operation bases in Africa or through acquiring existing African firm; see chapter 6.

Restrictions on foreign investment, either explicit or implicit, lead to a less competitive market environment, thus also limiting other beneficial elements of foreign investment such as generating incentives among

FIGURE 4.8
Age, Market Share, and Numbers of Competitors by Size

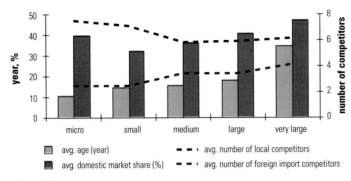

Source: World Bank staff.

domestic firms to innovate. However, depending on the way in which the foreign investors enter the market, they can either enhance the competition or limit it.[16]

Among surveyed firms in Africa, greater foreign capital involvement appears to be more procompetitive than anticompetitive.

Figure 4.9 suggests that, the more foreign investment sectors attract, including Chinese and Indian investment, the more competitive the environment in which they operate. Of course, other factors also play a role in affecting the size of market shares.

FIGURE 4.9
Domestic Market Share and Foreign Ownership Share

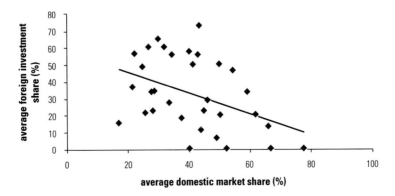

Source: World Bank staff.

Note: Each plot represents an individual sector in a country among the four African countries covered by the WBAATI survey.

Vertical Dimensions of Competition

Buyer-supplier relations can have prominent effects on domestic competition. There are several dimensions in which competition can be affected. The survey data suggest an association between the degree of competition on the sales side and on the purchase side (figure 4.10). Firms that face more diversified suppliers of material inputs appear to have less concentration of business customers to whom they sell their products. Similarly, firms that are more sensitive to price differences among those suppliers (in other words, firms that buy from more competitive input markets) appear to face customers' demand that is more sensitive to price changes (that is, they are selling to more competitive output markets).

A closer look at value chains reveals a deeper dimension of competition in the relationships between buyers and suppliers.

Table 4.3 shows that, among the firms surveyed, firms' sales are more price sensitive when firms sell unfinished products for further processing by their buyers, such as raw materials or partially assembled products, than when they sell completely finished products.[17] This is suggests that, by adding value, products become more differentiated and less homoge-

FIGURE 4.10

Competition in Input and Output Markets

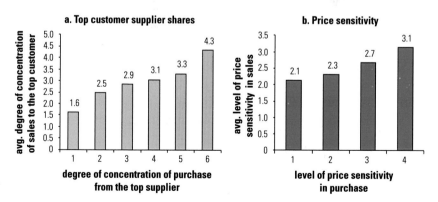

Source: World Bank staff.

Note: The degree of concentration of top supplier (buyer) is measured on a scale of 1–6, where 1 = share in the total purchase (sales) is less than 5 percent; 2 = if between 5 and 10 percent; 3 = if between 10 and 25 percent; 4 = between 25 and 50 percent; 5 = between 50 and 99 percent; and 6 = 100 percent. Price sensitivity in sales (purchases) is based on the expected responses in quantity sold to existing buyers (quantity purchased from existing suppliers) from a hypothetical increase of 10 percent in the price of main outputs (inputs). It is measured on a scale of 1–4, where 1 = no quantity change or *not sensitive*; 2 = a small quantity reduction with limited switch to competitors or *moderately sensitive*; 3 = major quantity reduction with significant switching to competitors or *sensitive*; or 4 = complete switching to competitors or *very sensitive*.

TABLE 4.3

Price Sensitivity in Sales and Proportions of Finished and Unfinished Products Sold

(percent)

Price sensitivity in firm's sales	Domestic sales		Export sales (Africa)		Export sales (outside Africa)	
	Finished product	Unfinished product	Finished product	Unfinished product	Finished product	Unfinished product
1 (Not sensitive)	94.9	5.1	90.5	9.5	92.3	7.7
2 (Moderately sensitive)	92.5	7.5	92.6	7.4	83.9	16.1
3 (Sensitive)	90.7	9.3	86.9	13.1	84.1	15.9
4 (Very sensitive)	85.8	14.2	76.1	23.9	75.6	24.4

Source: World Bank staff.

Note: For each group of firms with a different level of price sensitivity, the figures show percentage of finished and unfinished products in total sales to three types of market. Price sensitivity in sales is based on the expected responses in quantity sold to existing buyers from a hypothetical increase of 10 percent in the price of main outputs. It is measured on a scale of 1–4, where 1 = no quantity change or *not sensitive;* 2 = a small quantity reduction with limited switch to competitors or *moderately sensitive;* 3 = major quantity reduction with significant switching to competitors or *sensitive;* or 4 = complete switching to competitors or *very sensitive.*

neous, thus facing more inelastic demand. At the same time, this observation hints that by engaging in the production of upstream products in value chains, firms would be exposed to tougher competition.

Among the firms surveyed, firms' relations with buyers of their products are found to be less concentrated than firms' relations with their suppliers of inputs (table 4A.2). This suggests that firms in Africa are more selective in their relationships with input suppliers because they need to ensure the quality levels of the inputs they use. Exposure to competition is more evident when such products are sold to geographically distant markets through exports. This implies that by selling raw materials to geographically more distant markets, firms operating in Africa are facing more competitive pressure (see chapter 6 for a detailed discussion of value chains and international integration).

Transacting with the State

Purchases of goods and services by national governments—through participation in "state orders" or other forms of public procurement—constitute a significant portion of business transactions for many firms operating in Africa and, as a result, can have a significant impact on competition in the market. In turn, this can have an influence on the extent and pattern of the region's international integration. Privatization in African countries has reduced the prevalence of state-owned enterprises, which once occupied the lion's share of economic activities. However, given the thinness of

FIGURE 4.11

Dependence on Sales and Purchase Relations with Government by Country, Sector, and Size

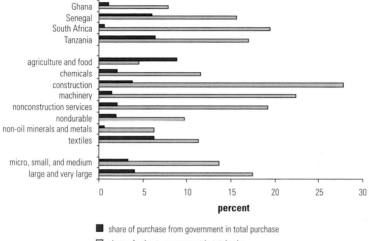

percent

■ share of purchase from government in total purchase
□ share of sales to government in total sales

Source: World Bank staff.

the private sector in Africa, sales and purchase relations with governments remain a significant part of many firms' business transactions.

Based on the WBAATI survey, the construction sector has the largest share of sales to governments (figure 4.11). This is consistent with findings in the other regions of the world. Larger firms generally rely more on government sales and purchases. With the exception of the agriculture sector, the survey data show that transactions with governments are more intensive on the sales side than on the purchase side across the board, regardless of sector and size.

Dependence on government sales and purchases appears to make firms in Africa less competitive. The sectors that have higher shares of sales to governments in their total sales revenues tend to have fewer competitors in their national markets (figure 4.12). Also, the degree of intensity in sales to or purchase from government is associated with the degree of concentration in firms' buyer or supplier relations (figure 4.13).

Minimizing the anticompetitive nature of transactions with government is important for fostering overall domestic competition in Africa. Adherence to World Trade Organization (WTO)–based rules regarding government procurement that provide for open competition, transparent

FIGURE 4.12

Sales to Government and Domestic Market Share

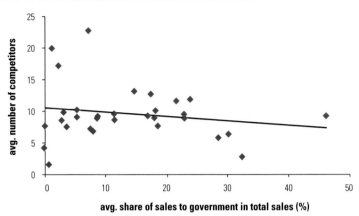

Source: World Bank staff.

Note: Each plot represents an individual sector in a country among the four African countries covered by the WBAATI survey. One sector, which has only two firms represented, has not been included.

procedures, and nondiscriminatory treatment to domestic and foreign firms alike can be an important reform in minimizing existing distortions in international trade and investment in Africa and in fostering international integration on the continent.

FIGURE 4.13

Top Supplier-Buyer Concentration and Government Sales and Purchase

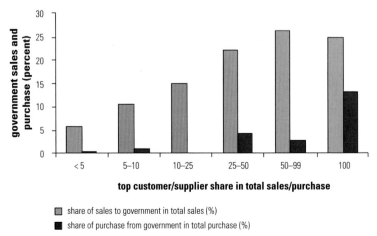

share of sales to government in total sales (%)

share of purchase from government in total purchase (%)

Source: World Bank staff.

Quantifying Impacts of Competition on Firm Performance

Analysis of firms operating in Africa suggests a linkage between firms' performance and the degree of competition as measured by price sensitivity in output and input markets as well as by concentration in buyer-supplier relationships. Price sensitivity negatively correlates with market power. For example, if firms face buyers that are more sensitive to price changes (that is, with more elastic demand), firms have less market power in the output markets in which they operate. Concentrated buyer-supplier relationships also limit the extent of competition in respective markets. Based on the WBAATI survey data, table 4.4 shows that, in general, firms facing more competitive input and output markets and operating with less concentrated buyer and seller relationships have higher average labor and capital productivity.

Higher productivity places firms in more competitive positions in international markets. Sectors with more competitive environments for input purchases and output sales or with less concentrated buyer-seller relations exhibit better average export performance among firms in the sectors (figure 4.14).

Role of Chinese and Indian Firms in Affecting Africa's Competition and International Integration

The preceding discussion centered on dimensions of behind-the-border competition in Africa at the country level, without differentiating among the nationality of the firms. How does competition coming from Chinese and Indian firms, either through exports to African markets or through investment, affect the competitiveness of African markets?

Import Competition from China and India

The WBAATI survey data show that import competition from China and India is felt differently among sectors and countries (figure 4.15). Labor-intensive sectors seem to face more Chinese and Indian import competition. Sectors such as agriculture and food, machinery, nondurable, nonconstruction services, and textiles face tougher competition from Chinese and Indian imports than do other sectors.

TABLE 4.4

Market Competition, Concentration in Buyer-Supplier Relationship, and Productivity

Competitiveness and concentration		Median value-added per worker ($)	Median value-added per capital (ratio)
Competitiveness in sales market (Price sensitivity in firms' output sales)	**Less competitive market** (Firms face buyers not sensitive or moderately sensitive to changes in price of firms' products)	12,424	1.08
	More competitive market (Firms face buyers sensitive or very sensitive to changes in price of firms' products)	15,114	2.53
Competitiveness in input market (Price sensitivity in firms' input purchase)	**Less competitive market** (Firms are not sensitive or moderately sensitive to changes in price of material inputs)	13,677	1.50
	More competitive market (Firms are sensitive or very sensitive to changes in price of material inputs)	12,447	2.40
Concentration in buyer relations	**Less concentrated relations** (Firms sell 50% or less of output to largest buyer)	14,455	2.40
	More concentrated relations (Firms sell more than 50% of products to single buyer)	11,098	1.00
Concentration in supplier relations	**Less concentrated relations** (Firms buy 50% or less of inputs from largest supplier)	14,160	1.71
	More concentrated relations (Firms buy more than 50% of inputs from single supplier)	11,930	1.41

Source: World Bank staff.

Note: Firms with 10 or fewer workers or age less than 5 years are not included. Price sensitivity in sales (purchases) is based on the expected responses in quantity sold to existing buyers (quantity purchase from existing suppliers) from a hypothetical increase of 10 percent in the price of main outputs (inputs). It is measured on a scale of 1–4, where 1 = no quantity change or *not sensitive;* 2 = a small quantity reduction with limited switch to competitors or *moderately sensitive;* 3 = major quantity reduction with significant switching to competitors or *sensitive;* or 4 = complete switching to competitors or *very sensitive.*

Competitive pressure coming from import competition may likely reduce the profitability of firms. However, this does not imply that import competition affects firms in Africa only in a negative way. Import competition can motivate firms to differentiate their products from imported

FIGURE 4.14

Competition and Export Intensity

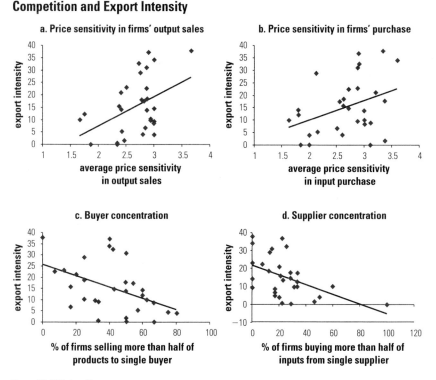

a. Price sensitivity in firms' output sales

b. Price sensitivity in firms' purchase

c. Buyer concentration

d. Supplier concentration

Source: World Bank staff.

Note: Each plot represents an individual sector in a country among the four African countries covered by the WBAATI survey. Firms with 10 or fewer workers or age less than 5 years are not included. Price sensitivity in sales (purchases) is based on the expected responses in quantity sold to existing buyers (quantity purchase from existing suppliers) from a hypothetical increase of 10 percent in the price of main outputs (inputs). It is measured on a scale of 1–4, where 1 = no quantity change or *not sensitive;* 2 = a small quantity reduction with limited switch to competitors or *moderately sensitive;* 3 = major quantity reduction with significant switching to competitors or *sensitive;* or 4 = complete switching to competitors or *very sensitive.*

goods to capture a market niche. For example, one South African blanket manufacturer that was the subject of a case study focuses on producing blankets at the higher end in the quality range so that it can effectively differentiate itself from low-quality blankets imported from China, locally referred to as "Wash and Cry." The term "Wash and Cry" comes from the fact that those low-quality Chinese blankets are not dyed properly, so the colors of the blankets can be easily lost when such blankets are washed. Import competition also enables local producers to access a variety of imported raw and intermediate materials, including those from China and India (see chapter 6).

FIGURE 4.15
Origins of Foreign Import Competitors by Sector

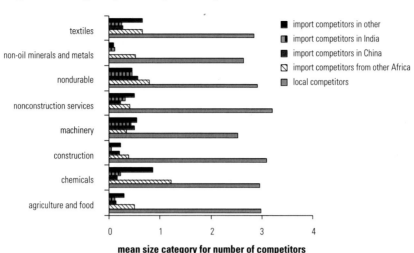

Source: World Bank staff.

Note: The number of competitors is measured on a scale of 0–4, where 0 = no competitor; 1 = one competitor; 2 = 2 to 3 competitors; 3 = 4 to 10 competitors; and 4 = more than 10 competitors.

Foreign Investors and Import Competition from China and India: Two-Way Street in Competition and International Integration?

There is no doubt that the increasing penetration of Chinese and Indian businesses in African national markets has intensified competition. However, is the competition generated by Chinese and Indian businesses helping the private sector in Africa to be more internationally competitive and become more integrated in the global economy?[18] The WBAATI survey data indicate that business transactions with Chinese and Indian firms play a pivotal role in linking domestic competition with international integration of Africa's private sector. The analysis shows that the major source of the competition engendered in African markets by the presence of Chinese and Indian investors is competition from imports—indeed, imports from China and India themselves. The survey data reveal that import competition from China and India is faced more by Chinese- or Indian-owned firms operating in Africa than by African indigenous firms (table 4.5).[19]

Figure 4.16 looks into sector-specific patterns of Chinese and Indian import competition. The figure suggests that, in the machinery and nondurable sectors in the four African countries under examination, Chinese

TABLE 4.5

Mean Category for Number of Competitors in Domestic Market, by Nationality and by Source of Competition

Nationality of firms in Africa	Local competitors	Sources of import competition:			
		Other African countries	China	India	Other, including European
African	3.0	0.5	0.2	0.2	0.4
Chinese	3.3	0.7	0.6	0.3	0.3
Indian	3.2	1.1	0.2	0.6	0.5
European	2.5	0.6	0.4	0.3	0.5
Other	2.9	0.6	0.1	0.3	0.8

Source: World Bank staff.

Note: The number of competitors is measured on a scale of 0–4, where 0 = no competitor; 1 = one competitor; 2 = 2 to 3 competitors; 3 = 4 to 10 competitors; and 4 = more than 10 competitors.

and Indian firms face more intense competition from imports from China and India than African firms face. At the same time, such competition is more intense than or at least on par with what Chinese and Indian firms operating in Africa face from local rivals. Chinese construction firms that participated in the business case studies indicate that their pricing decisions are more dependent on the behavior of other Chinese construction firms in Africa than on the firms of other nationalities.

Competition between foreign *investors* from one country and foreign *exporters* from the same country serving the same overseas markets is quite plausible, given the fact that firms choose foreign investment as an alternative to serving the overseas markets through imports due to high transportation costs or tariff barriers against imports.[20] Firms choose to export rather than invest if the investment climate in the destination market is not favorable and transactions costs in the destination market are high. In turn, a more competitive environment in the destination market would encourage firms to invest rather than export, because the more intensive domestic market competition would reduce local transactions costs relative to cross-border trade costs, which firms incur only when they export. Chapter 6 presents a more detailed discussion on such choices between exports and foreign direct investment (FDI).

The observation from the WBAATI survey that Chinese- and Indian-owned firms in Africa are facing relatively fierce import competition from China and India themselves implies a mutually reinforcing relationship. African firms that face more competitive markets at home have greater

FIGURE 4.16

Numbers of Domestic Competitors and Import Competitors from China and India by Nationality of Firm Owners

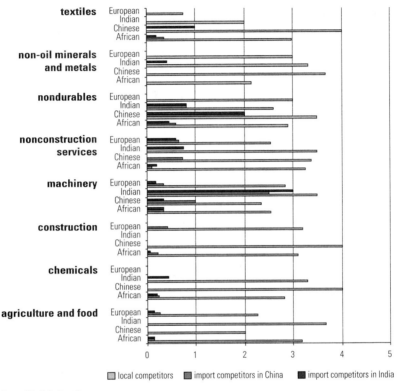

Source: World Bank staff.

Note: The number of competitors is measured on a scale of 0–4, where 0 = no competitor; 1 = one competitor; 2 = 2 to 3 competitors; 3 = 4 to 10 competitors; and 4 = more than 10 competitors.

involvement with Chinese and Indian capital, while the African markets where Chinese and Indian investors are most prevalent tend to be the most competitive. As shown in chapter 6, the WBAATI survey data suggest that Chinese and Indian investment, relative to European investment in Africa, tends to take the form of *de novo* greenfield investment rather than acquisition of existing national firms or joint ventures with national firms. In this regard, Chinese and Indian investments have a salutary effect on behind-the-border competition in Africa.

There is also a two-way relationship between import competition from China and India and firms' export performance. Based on the survey data, average export intensity of a sector appears to be positively associated with import competition from China and India, while no particular association is observed with local competition (figure 4.17).

Competition from Chinese and Indian Investment and Local Linkages
In addition to invigorating competition in Africa through their exports and investment, Chinese and Indian firms operating in Africa are engendering competition in the informal sector. Building working relationships with informal firms is important for Chinese and Indian firms to survive in African markets.

The WBAATI business case studies reveal a number of experiences of Chinese and Indian firms operating in both formal and informal sectors in Africa (box 4.1).

Like foreign investment from other countries, Chinese and Indian investment in Africa also creates opportunities for backward and forward linkages with local indigenous industries. Thus, while facing competition from Chinese and Indian rivals, local indigenous African firms are at the same time finding ways in which they can engage Chinese and Indian firms through subcontracts and joint ventures (box 4.2).

Sources of Competition in Africa's Market

If the degree of competition in African markets faced by Chinese and Indian firms is important to engendering Africa's international integration, what are the main ingredients that give rise to a competitive business environment? Numerous studies on the investment climate in African countries point to the critical factors.[21] Among them, perhaps the most prominent approach has been taken by the Investment Climate Assessments (ICAs) and the Doing Business reports by the World Bank Group. Box 4.3 summarizes the principal findings of the ICAs on the investment climate constraints faced by firms, including Chinese- and Indian-owned businesses, operating in the four African countries under examination.

Quality of Infrastructure Services

Infrastructure is often cited as the most immediate source of the high cost of doing business in Sub-Saharan Africa. Among various dimensions of

FIGURE 4.17
Number of Competitors and Export Intensity

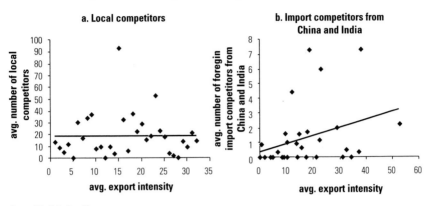

Source: World Bank staff.

Note: Each plot represents an individual sector in a country among the four African countries covered by the WBAATI survey. Firms with 10 or fewer workers or age less than 5 years are not included. The average number of competitors is based on the actual number of competitors and not on the scale used in other tables and figures.

infrastructure-related constraints, the poor quality of power services is the leading bottleneck, causing interruptions in production and thus revenue losses. (Owning generators only adds production costs.) The limited availability of communications networks also costs firms marketing opportunities. Transportation costs are also excessively high in Africa due to poor road, port, and aviation services quality, as discussed in chapter 5. Economic sparseness is a considerable obstacle to the quality of infrastructure services in the region, but it is clear that the quality of management of infrastructure systems is also questionable. The most recent progress in infrastructure in Sub-Saharan African countries has been made in the area of telecommunications, where the successful incorporation of private providers of cellular infrastructure has enhanced the overall accessibility of telecommunications networks. The least progress has been made in electricity, where effective reforms of national companies still lag.

Electricity

Based on the ICA data in Senegal, South Africa, and Tanzania, as well as a comparable data set for Ghana, figure 4.18 presents reported average interruptions of electricity as a percentage of production time and average revenues lost due to electricity outages from public grids, by size category and

(*Text continues on page 218.*)

BOX 4.1

Informal-Sector Competition and Chinese and Indian Firms in Africa

The informal sector in West Africa is geared almost exclusively toward producing final consumer goods. Even in manufacturing, final consumption products, such as garments, leather products, furniture, and foodstuffs are by far the most important. Some manufacturing firms in Senegal are selling their products to distributors working in the informal sector. As such, there is a high volume of cash-based transactions, without formal contracts with their distributors. There is a high rotation of distributors for these firms. This is in part due to the low survival rate of firms in the informal sector. One manufacturing firm that participated in the WBAATI business case studies reported that 25 percent of new dealings with distributors in one year do not continue the next year. There is no repetition of future sales with bad informal distributors. In South Africa, the informal sector is not highly representative, as it is in West Africa. However, informal firms are present in the manufacturing sector, such as textiles and the food and beverages sectors.

The WBAATI business case studies provide some evidence that Chinese and Indian businesses operating in Africa interact with the informal sector in various ways. The informal sector is a significant competitor for Chinese and Indian firms. For example, the biggest agenda for an Indian beverage company in South Africa (sorghum beer) is how to gain the share of the market currently served by the informal sector producing a competing product (household back-yard production of sorghum beer). They try this by influencing both the supply and the demand sides. For the supply side, they try to absorb the informal sector by providing them production licenses for their branded sorghum beer. For the demand side, they lobby the government on the negative health impact of informally brewed sorghum beer due to sanitary and health quality conditions.

Source: World Bank staff.

BOX 4.2

Competition and Complementarities in the Construction Industry in Africa: Chinese and African Firms

Competition

Construction services procured by governments represent the largest share of the construction markets in African countries. Outsourcing and subcontracting services are the trend in this market. Based on the government procurement policies and the procurement policies of the donors, in line with the WTO Agreement on Government Procurement, the international bidding process is required for public construction projects in Sub-Saharan African countries above certain threshold values of contracts. Cost-efficient Chinese construction firms now dominate large-scale infrastructure construction projects in Sub-Saharan African countries by winning such international bids. The lack of capacity in this sector in African firms is undermining their ability to bid for implementation of the construction projects domestically and compete with international firms, particularly those from China. The majority of African firms are small and do not have the level of experience required to compete in large bids financed by multilateral organizations. In several cases they do not even fulfill the prequalification requirements requested for international bids and larger infrastructure projects. For example, firms in Tanzania cannot compete in the market above $2 million based on the WBAATI business case studies. Local firms cannot meet requirements for equipment, cash flow, and other items for this level of bid. African firms are unable to compete with the subsidies or other policies that may indirectly subsidize Chinese firms.

Complementarities

While international contractors from other regions such as European countries, Japan, and the Republic of Korea face serious setbacks from Chinese penetration in the construction market in Africa as they directly compete against Chinese firms in construction projects of similar scale, local African contractors are impacted somewhat differently. While facing competitive pressure as mentioned above, local African contractors still have some complementarities with Chinese firms. Based on the WBAATI business case studies, there seem to be three ways in which local African firms seek complementarities with Chinese construction firms in the construction industry.

Market specialization. Because small contracts are not subject to international bidding, African contractors can still obtain small-scale contracts for public work. At the same time, Chinese contractors prefer to specialize in large-scale contracts to capture economies of scale because they still rely on a sizable technical workforce brought from China for each project. The procurement thresholds for international open tenders, coupled with Chinese contractors' strategies of specializing in large-scale contracts, have led to a natural division of labor between African and Chinese contractors in terms of scale of projects.

Joint venture opportunities. Several African contractors seek opportunities to form joint ventures with Chinese contractors. For example, a Senegalese construction firm that participated in the business case studies has a joint venture project with a Chinese contractor. The firm has a company strategy to form joint ventures with Chinese firms rather than compete with them. For this firm, if Africans *"cannot beat Chinese, then,"* Africans should *"join them."*

Backward and forward linkages. Chinese firms subcontract services to local firms. This provides opportunities for the acquisition of experience and access to technology for developing-country firms. A road paving and equipment company in Ghana that participated in the business case studies receives subcontracts from a Chinese construction firm that is engaged in road construction work in Ghana and in neighboring countries. However, it is still the case that the benefit African firms receive from subcontracts in terms of acquisition of experience and technology is limited.

Source: World Bank staff.

BOX 4.3

Firms' Perceptions of the Domestic Investment Climate

Ghana. The predominant constraints that firms in Ghana face are access to credit, the cost of and access to domestic raw materials, insufficient demand, and high inflation and interest rates. The obstacle identified as the most severe problem is access to credit; this is stated as being a major problem by 50 percent of firms. As is the case for most firms in Africa, smaller firms in Ghana were far more likely to rank access to finance as a problem in comparison to larger ones; almost 70 percent of small firms identified this as a constraint, whereas only 20 percent of larger firms perceived it as a serious problem. A large percentage of firms are reported to be either discouraged by the procedural requirements for obtaining credit or the cost of obtaining it, such as high interest rates. Following access to finance, insufficient demand is ranked second as the most severe problem by over 20 percent of the firms. Ranked third, with 20 percent of firms identifying it as a major constraint, is the cost of domestic raw materials. When broken down by firm size, it is reported that, while large firms find access to domestic raw materials to be a serious constraint, small firms focus on the problem of cost. This can be explained by export orientation and the different cost structure that larger firms have.

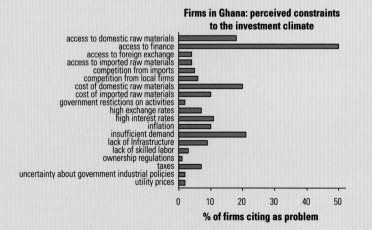

Firms in Ghana: perceived constraints to the investment climate

access to domestic raw materials
access to finance
access to foreign exchange
access to imported raw materials
competition from imports
competition from local firms
cost of domestic raw materials
cost of imported raw materials
government restictions on activities
high exchange rates
high interest rates
inflation
insufficient demand
lack of Infrastructure
lack of skilled labor
ownership regulations
taxes
uncertainty about government industrial policies
utility prices

0   10   20   30   40   50

% of firms citing as problem

Senegal. For enterprises in Senegal, finance is ranked as the biggest problem; access to and cost of finance were more likely to be identified by enterprise managers as a major or severe constraint to the investment climate than any other constraint. Smaller firms in Senegal have much less access to finance; only 20 percent of small firms reported having access to formal bank credits compared to 90 percent of large firms. Following the constraint of finance, tax rates and anticompetitive practices rank highest as serious constraints. Fifty-five percent of enterprises perceived tax rates as a major or severe constraint, whereas 54 percent stated anticompetitive practices (informality) as a serious problem. The tax system in Senegal is more complex than those other countries in the region with higher corporate and local taxes levied on enterprises. Compared to the other three focus countries, firms in Senegal are more likely to perceive informality as a major or severe constraint.

Firms in Senegal: perceived constraints to the investment climate

South Africa. Worker skills, macroeconomic instability, labor regulation, and crime and theft stand out as the most important problems for the investment climate in South Africa. However, when compared with the other three focus countries, relatively few firms rated the constraints as major or severe problems. For firms in South Africa, 35 percent of managers were more likely to rate worker skills as the most serious obstacle to their

(Continues on the following page.)

BOX 4.3 (continued)

enterprises, suggesting that firms find it difficult to hire skilled workers. This could be explained by higher wages for skilled workers and managers relative to other countries in the region. Following worker skills, macroeconomic instability and labor regulations are pointed out as the second and third most serious constraints. Although growth has been increasing steadily and inflation has remained low for the last decade, exchange rates have been very unstable, with the rand depreciating against major currencies. Labor regulation in South Africa appears to be more rigid than in most of the comparator countries, and the cost of firing and hiring workers is higher than in most Organisation for Economic Co-operation and Development countries. Another important obstacle identified as a serious problem is crime and theft. Direct losses due to crime and robbery and security costs in South Africa are a lot higher than they are in other middle-income countries.

Firms in South Africa: perceived constraints to the investment climate

Tanzania. Firms in Tanzania point out tax rates and administration, electricity, interest rates, and corruption as the leading constraints to the investment climate. Over 70 percent of firms were more likely to perceive tax rates as a serious problem than any other constraint. Despite being ranked the biggest concern, corporate income tax rates are similar to rates in other developing countries; however, value-added rates are slightly higher than those of comparator countries. Electricity came in second as the highest-ranked constraint to the investment climate. Sixty percent of firms rated the power sector as a serious problem, even though the cost of power is not excessively high in Tanzania compared to other countries in the region. When broken down by firm size, concern was more widespread among larger enterprises; the median firm reported losing 5 percent of production due to power shortages. Despite considerable progress achieved in developing the Tanzanian financial sector, access to and the cost of finance continue to be reported as important constraints. Interest rates in Tanzania are very close to those in neighboring countries; however, access to finance seems to be more of a problem in this country. Another highly ranked constraint is the problem of corruption. In comparison to other countries in the region, Tanzania does well on most measures of governance; however, in terms of corruption, it lags behind most comparator countries.

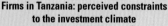

Firms in Tanzania: perceived constraints to the investment climate

% of firms citing as problem

Sources: World Bank 2005d, 2005e, and 2004a for Senegal, South Africa, and Tanzania. Teal et al. 2006 for Ghana.

FIGURE 4.18

Electricity Service Interruptions from Public Grids, Percentage of Time

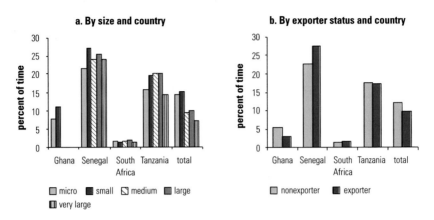

Source: World Bank 2005d, 2005e, and 2004a for Senegal, South Africa, and Tanzania. Teal et al. 2006 for Ghana.

by exporter status. The figure shows that Senegal and Tanzania have the highest average electricity interruption time, accounting for close to 25 and 20 percent of production time, respectively. South Africa has the best electricity supply, with only about 2 percent of interruption time. In terms of firm size, there is no particular pattern within each country that indicates a consistent correlation between the size of the company and the electricity supply. On average, however, micro and small firms suffer more electricity interruptions than do large firms.

There are no consistent patterns among the four countries in terms of electricity interruptions between exporters and nonexporters. However, the average of the four countries shows that exporters experience fewer power outages than do firms that sell products domestically.

Figure 4.19 shows the average percentage revenue lost due to electricity outages. The average revenue loss is consistently higher for nonexporters than for exporters. This is an especially interesting case for Senegal, where exporting companies experience more frequent average incidents of electricity outages but a lower percentage of average revenue loss. Also, although Senegal has the highest percentage of electricity interruption time among the four countries, its average revenue loss due to the electricity outages is much lower than that of Tanzania. One reason is that Senegal has better facilities and capacity to monitor electricity outages so that firms can report outages more accurately.[22]

FIGURE 4.19

Loss of Revenue Because of Electricity Outage, Percentage of Sales Revenue

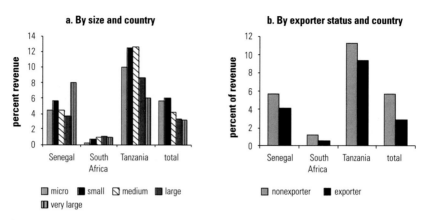

Source: World Bank 2005d, 2005e, and 2004a for Senegal, South Africa, and Tanzania.

To compensate for the shortage of electricity, firms operating in Africa often need to own generators to supplement the electricity supply (figure 4.20). Generator ownership is more prevalent in Senegal, at 64 percent, than it is in Tanzania, at 56 percent. In all three countries, there is a clear pattern that the ownership of generators increases with size. There is not a visible difference between exporters and nonexporters in terms of generator ownership in Senegal. In Tanzania, while over 85 percent of exporters own generators, only about 50 percent of nonexporters do.

Telephone and Internet

In terms of telephone services, Senegal and South Africa have far fewer interruptions—only around 1 to 3 percent—than Senegal and Ghana (figure 4.21). In Ghana and Tanzania, micro companies experience much higher telephone interruptions—on average at above 20 percent—than larger-sized companies. In all countries except Tanzania, nonexporters experience a higher percentage of telephone interruptions than exporters.

In terms of Internet access, South Africa has almost 100 percent access for all firms while Senegal and Tanzania have much less (figure 4.22). While about three-quarters of Senegalese firms have access to the Internet, only half of Tanzania firms have access. The Internet divide, not surprisingly, is most pronounced in Tanzania where Internet access is low,

FIGURE 4.20
Proportion of Firms with Generators

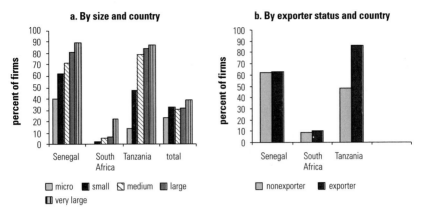

Source: World Bank 2005d, 2005e, and 2004a for Senegal, South Africa, and Tanzania.

Note: Ghana is not included in the figures owing to lack of comparable data.

with only 10 percent of micro companies having Internet access compared to more than 80 percent for the medium or larger companies. The Internet divide between exporters and nonexporters is also most pronounced in Tanzania. An increasing number of studies have addressed the trade-facilitating role of the Internet. Use of the Internet is particularly relevant for African manufacturers to access the global market.[23]

FIGURE 4.21
Telephone Service Interruption, Percentage of Time

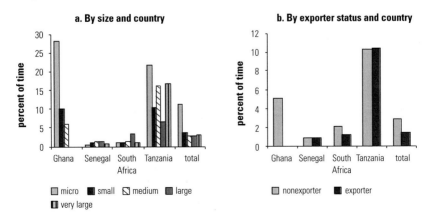

Source: World Bank 2005d, 2005e, and 2004a for Senegal, South Africa, and Tanzania. Teal et al. 2006 for Ghana.

FIGURE 4.22

Proportion of Firms with Internet Access

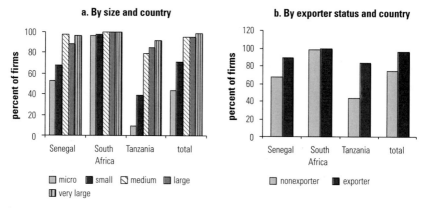

Source: World Bank 2005d, 2005e, and 2004a for Senegal, South Africa, and Tanzania.

Note: Ghana is not included in the figures owing to lack of comparable data.

Efficiency and Accessibility of Factor Markets

Access to Finance

Another serious bottleneck for firms operating in Africa is the lack of access to reliable and inexpensive financing (see box 4.3). The demand for trade finance in Africa far exceeds supply from commercial or noncommercial sources, foreign or local. Paradoxically, in many African markets, capital is not in short supply. For example, in the single-currency, eight-nation West African Economic and Monetary Union more than $2 billion in excess liquidity lies dormant in the central bank.

When compared with firms operating in China and India, firms operating in Africa have less access to loans and overdrafts, use more internal funds and retained earnings to fund investments and operating costs, pay much higher interest rates, and are required to register much more assets as collateral. Market failures are rampant. Small firms are less likely to get loans; relationships and ethnic connections are very important in access to credit; and outstanding debt is positively related to obtaining future lending.

Figure 4.23 consistently shows that, in each country, access to finance improves with firm size. South African, Tanzanian, and Senegalese firms reported relatively high access to financial credit or overdraft facility (at 75, 70, and 60 percent, respectively). Access to financial services is the lowest in Ghana (at only 30 percent). In addition, the financial divide is

FIGURE 4.23

Proportion of Firms with Access to Financial Services (Overdraft Facility or Loan)

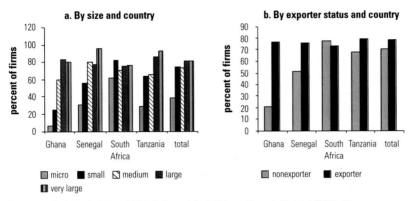

Source: World Bank 2005d, 2005e, and 2004a for Senegal, South Africa, and Tanzania. Teal et al. 2006 for Ghana.

the most pronounced in Ghana, with micro and small firms having little access to financial services, but large and very large firms having access equivalent to that of South African companies. The difference in access to financial services between exporters and nonexporters is also the largest in Ghana, visible in Senegal, and not very significant in Tanzania.

Labor Market Rigidities and Shortages in Skilled Labor

Restrictive labor regulations can limit flexibility and increase operating costs. Sub-Saharan Africa suffers from very large regulatory burdens on labor markets, which translates into excessively high rigidity in workers' mobility (see table 4.6).

A highly skilled labor force is critical for firms operating in Africa, including firms owned by Chinese and Indians, to build export competitiveness. The shortage of skilled labor is the most significant constraint reported by the majority of the firms that participated in the WBAATI business case studies (see box 4.4). The types of skills that are in short supply vary among countries and sectors. In some cases, the scarcity of skilled labor (for example, technicians) is acute. In other cases, firms claim that there is not a sufficient supply of skilled engineers and managers with experience in export-oriented business and modern commercial practices.

TABLE 4.6
Cost of Hiring and Firing

Country	Rigidity of employment index	Hiring cost (% of annual salary)	Firing cost (weeks of wages)
Sub-Saharan African average	53.1	11.8	53.4
Ghana	34.0	12.5	24.9
Senegal	64.0	23.0	38.3
South Africa	52.0	2.6	37.5
Tanzania	69.0	16.0	38.4
East Asia average	26.2	8.8	44.2
China	30.0	30.0	90.0
South Asia average	39.9	5.1	75.0
India	62.0	12.3	79.0

Source: World Bank 2005a.

Regulation, Governance, and Judiciary System

In addition to insufficient infrastructure and financial services as well as rigidities in the labor market, large regulatory burdens and weak discipline on governance constitute significant impediments to business development among firms operating in Africa, including those owned by Chinese and Indians.

Figure 4.24 shows that Tanzania has the highest incidence of inspections per year at an average of 27 days, compared to 19 days in Senegal and 14 days in South Africa. For all three countries, larger firms tend to be inspected more often, as do exporters. The number of inspections could be correlated with the scope and the scale of the firms' activities. Nonetheless, the excessively high frequency of government inspections places serious constraints on them.

Corruption remains a serious issue in African countries. Small companies as well as nonexporting companies in Ghana, Senegal, South Africa, and Tanzania chronically report the burden of having to make unofficial payments (figure 4.25).

Enforcement of property rights and contracts is at the heart of a properly functioning market economy. However, many African countries have serious deficiencies in their judicial systems, due to lack of resources and human capital, weak institutional capacity, as well as lack of transparent administration. Therefore, business disputes tend to be

BOX 4.4

Shortage of Skilled Labor in Africa

In South Africa, the problem of skilled labor shortage seems to be pervasive. Among firms that participated in the business case studies, a shortage of engineers was reported in the large export-oriented apparel manufacturing industry. A few graduates of South African universities from the "previously advantaged group" (white) are moving to Australia and New Zealand because it is difficult for them to find jobs after graduation due to the government's Black Economic Empowerment program, which favors employment of people in "previously disadvantaged groups" (for example, black, colored, and Indian). The country also lacks productive workers for the assembly of vehicles. There is also a shortage of specialized mechanics and engineers. Firms look for qualified labor nationwide. They subcontract to specialized engineers (from three companies) some specific tasks such as detailing and tools drawing. In the automotive sector, qualified workers may likely go to their foreign competitors, like Toyota, Nissan, Daimler-Chrysler, and Mazda. So their strategy for obtaining qualified workers is to pay more. In the apparel and textiles sector, firms that provide training lose their most qualified employees to their competitors. In Senegal, there is a lack of specialized engineers. A Chinese firm in Senegal has found it very difficult to employ local managers and technicians that have experience operating in large construction projects.

The shortage of skilled workers is voiced by Chinese and Indian firms, as well as local indigenous companies, as one of the major constraints they face in Africa. Chinese firms cope with this problem by either bringing skilled workers from China (construction firms) or by limiting the manufacturing component of their operations in Africa. As an example of the latter case, one Chinese automobile maker operating in South Africa decided to shift from Complete-Knock-Down (CKD) to Complete-Build-Up (CBU) in automobile manufacturing to reduce manufacturing components in their operation in South Africa.

Source: World Bank staff.

FIGURE 4.24
Average Number of Days of Inspections per Year

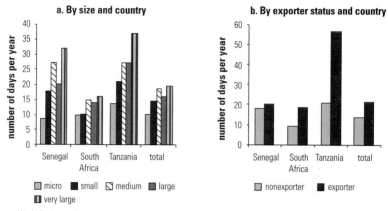

a. By size and country

b. By exporter status and country

micro   ■ small   ▧ medium   ■ large
■ very large

nonexporter   ■ exporter

Source: World Bank 2005d, 2005e, and 2004a for Senegal, South Africa, and Tanzania.

Note: Ghana is not included in the figures owing to lack of comparable data.

costly and lengthy in the Sub-Saharan Africa region. In the case of Ghana, Senegal, South Africa, and Tanzania, contract enforcement is costly in terms of the time it requires if not the number of procedures or cost (table 4.7).

FIGURE 4.25
Unofficial Payments as Percentage of Sales

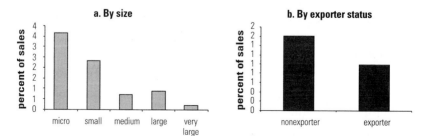

a. By size

b. By exporter status

Source: World Bank 2005d, 2005e, and 2004a for Senegal, South Africa, and Tanzania.

Note: Ghana is not included in the figures owing to lack of comparable data.

TABLE 4.7
Contract Enforcement

Country	Procedures (number)	Time (days)	Cost (% of debt)
Sub-Saharan African average	35.9	438.5	41.6
Ghana	23.0	200.0	14.4
Senegal	33.0	485.0	23.8
South Africa	26.0	277.0	11.5
Tanzania	22.0	242.0	35.3
East Asia average	29.8	406.8	61.7
China	25.0	241.0	25.5
South Asia average	29.9	385.5	36.7
India	40.0	425.0	43.1

Source: World Bank 2005a.

Conclusions and Policy Implications

Summary of Main Findings

The basic diagnostics of behind-the-border conditions, based on the WBAATI survey data, find that surveyed larger firms outperform surveyed smaller firms both in productivity and exports. Among the surveyed firms, export propensity is lower for domestically owned firms than for Chinese or Indian firms.

An assessment of the sources of competition in these African markets at the country level suggests that, not only do imports play an important role, but so do low domestic entry and exit barriers, the incidence of FDI in the market, and access and integration into global production networks. Not surprisingly, firm turnover is found to be more prevalent among smaller businesses, while larger firms enjoy longer tenure and higher market shares. Again, this is true regardless of firm nationality. The data suggest that entry via FDI is an important channel through which competition is introduced into these surveyed African markets, a finding consistent with research on other regions of the world. International integration into production networks—the focus of chapter 6—particularly upstream in the value chain, appears to stimulate competition among the surveyed firms.

The evidence from the degree of competition among different nationalities of firms indicates a clear role played by Chinese and Indian investors in fostering domestic competition in African markets. In fact, a mutually reinforcing effect is found: African firms that face more competitive markets at home have greater involvement with Chinese and Indian capital, while the African markets where Chinese and Indian investors are most prevalent tend to be the most competitive. The analysis also shows that the major source of the competition engendered in the African markets by the presence of Chinese and Indian investors is competition from imports—indeed imports from China and India themselves. Chinese and Indian investment also provides opportunities for indigenous African firms to form joint ventures or backward-forward linkages with such investment. The question is whether skills and technology are effectively transferred from such business relations.

African countries continue to face high business transactions costs due to poor infrastructure quality, inefficient and insufficient factor markets such as shortages in credit access and skilled labor, labor market rigidity, and heavy regulatory burdens and weak governance and judiciary systems. As is the case elsewhere in the world, the analysis suggests why such factors constitute integral roles in Chinese and Indian (as well as other) investors' location choices in Africa. To be sure, there have been visible efforts made by several African governments in reforming their domestic business environments. But African countries overall still lag other regions with whom they are competing, both in terms of attracting investment and exporting to foreign markets.

Policy Implications

Proper conditions for greater domestic competition and sound governance in the domestic market are of high priority on the reform agenda of African countries to enhance the prospects that trade will engender growth in those countries. It is important to emphasize that strong policy initiatives are critical for supporting Africa's private sector to effectively link competition and international integration.

For competition to work, the countries need to implement more rigorous policy reforms to encourage competition by providing necessary institutional frameworks to foster entry and exit and eliminate inefficient barriers. Governments should work toward eliminating economic and policy barriers to entry and establishment of new businesses. Stronger efforts among policy leaders are needed to reduce administrative barriers and remove underlying economic barriers to entry. At the same time, barriers to exit of commercially nonviable firms need to be eliminated. Exit barriers can be lowered through reduction of publicly provided subsidies to businesses. National competition policies in Sub-Saharan African countries are still at an early stage of development and need to be properly institutionalized to build competitive markets at home.

African countries continue to face high business transaction costs, due to inferior quality of infrastructure, insufficient access to credit, rigid labor markets, heavy regulatory burdens, lack of transparency in public administration, and weak judiciary systems. For competition to work and to develop a mutual reinforcing linkage with international integration, more comprehensive improvements in the investment climate are in order. African countries must reinvigorate their efforts toward investment-climate reforms in those countries in all aspects. It is important, in this regard, to promote more active public-private dialogue in such forms as investor councils, thereby allowing the governments to absorb concerns from the private sector (see chapter 3).

Private markets in Africa need to be sufficiently large relative to procurement-based markets with governments so that business transactions with the government do not crowd out the incentives for private firms to compete in the private market. Government procurement policies need to be transparent and market-oriented. Improving quality of institutions, strengthening governance, and reducing incentives for corruption are critical components of behind-the-border reforms to engender the international integration of African countries. This will require greater transparency and accountability of public officials' conduct, a reorientation of the public sector incentive framework (for example, through civil service and public administration reform), and establishment of a stronger system of checks and balances.

Improving governance will require strengthening well-functioning institutions that facilitate contract enforcement. Efficient settlement of commercial disputes is generally limited by lengthy procedures, lack of qualified and independent judges, and weak enforcement mechanisms. Policies toward the simplification and cost reduction of formal legal procedures will strengthen contract sanctity and property rights and improve the level of confidence that businesses have in the investment environment of the region.

Last, policy initiatives to foster domestic competition have to be in tandem with various supports for scaling-up private sector capacity in expanding value-added activities along the value chains and absorbing skills and technology through interacting with foreign investors, including Chinese and Indian investors. Thus, the African governments, in support of international donors, need to implement more comprehensive capacity building-programs of small and medium enterprises (SMEs), encompassing improvement in credit access, skills development among workers, and supporting their market access both domestically and internationally.

Annex 4A

TABLE 4A.1
Average Market Share in Domestic Market, by Sector and by Country
(percent)

Sector	Ghana	Senegal	South Africa	Tanzania	All four countries
Agriculture and food	32.0	49.1	52.4	41.4	42.4
Chemicals	21.6	77.6	62.0	46.4	47.2
Construction	28.4	28.0	40.3	25.9	31.4
Machinery	34.3	67.0	43.5	37.6	41.4
Nonconstruction services	22.1	54.7	33.7	24.9	35.5
Nondurable	26.9	50.3	45.1	40.1	38.8
Non-oil minerals and metals	30.1	50.0	59.2	28.9	36.1
Textiles	16.9	66.2	44.2	43.1	44.4
All sectors	26.3	57.1	42.0	33.9	38.8

Source: World Bank staff.

TABLE 4A.2
Top Buyer and Supplier Shares: Joint Distribution

Top buyer share in total sales	Top supplier share in total purchase						All % level of top supplier share
	< 5%	5–10%	10–25%	25–50%	50–99%	100%	
< 5%	24	10	8	11	15	3	71
5–10%	8	17	13	21	22	5	86
10–25%	7	15	13	29	14	8	86
25–50%	1	3	9	26	18	3	60
50–99%	0	4	5	10	26	9	54
100%	0	0	1	1	4	16	22
All % level of top buyer share	40	49	49	98	99	44	379

Source: World Bank staff.

Endnotes

1. Productivity measures how efficiently firms produce their products and services using one unit of factor input, either as labor or capital. Value-added per work and value-added per a unit of capital are used to show labor and capital productivity of the firms. Export intensity is measured as the share of export sales revenue in the total sales revenue and indicates how well firms perform in terms of exports. For both labor and capital productivity, productivity for services has to be interpreted carefully because services require substantive amounts of nontangible material inputs that are not captured by materials in the sense of raw and intermediate materials for manufactured products.

2. In the survey, the capital value is measured in terms of replacement cost of capital firms.

3. See Tybout (2000) for the survey of the literature on this topic.

4. Total factor productivity is in fact found to be higher among medium firms while lower among small and large firms.

5. State-owned enterprises are excluded here due to the small number of firms that provided revenue and cost information in the survey.

6. See Moran (1998).

7. The technology employed is not as current as in the wholly owned foreign counterpart, partly due to fear of having the technology misappropriated. Concerns about quality control inhibit integration of local production into the parent's global networks. See Moran (1998).

8. Based on the Brazil data in the 1970s, Evans (1979) found supporting evidence for foreign investors choosing joint ventures as their optimal strategy. Using Ghanaian firm-level data, Acquaah (2005) found that the enhancement in manufacturing efficiency and quality improvement in privately owned enterprises could be traced to the activities of foreign-domestic joint venture enterprises. However, as market competition increases, wholly domestic-owned enterprises emphasize manufacturing efficiency and quality improvement more than foreign-domestic joint venture enterprises.

9. For example, Broadman (2005) provides a comprehensive analysis of how domestic competition effectively promotes integration of East European countries and the former Soviet Union.

10. The existing studies on the role of competition in the African private sector are often conducted for individual countries. For example, Azam et al. (2001) for Côte d'Ivore, Hajim (2001) for Tanzania, Reinikka and Svensson (1999) for Uganda, and Frazer (2005) for Ghana.

11. Another measurement of intensity of domestic competition is average domestic market share by individual firms. In this case, domestic competition is more intensive if average market share is smaller. See table 4A.1 in annex 4A.

12. For the remainder of the chapter, "numbers of competitors" in the WBAATI survey data always refers to the numbers of competitors in reference to national markets of the four African countries the survey covered.

13. Note that "local competitors" includes firms owned by foreign nationals but operating in Africa as opposed to "foreign import competitors," who are physically located outside of the market and compete with local firms through imports.

14. Fafchamps 1999.

15. Formal policy-based barriers as well as nonpolicy institutional barriers would have different impacts on firm turnovers depending on the size of the firms. Nonpolicy institutional barriers such as ethnic networks would have a stronger impact on smaller-sized and informal sector firms. There are several studies that have examined firm turnover patterns in Sub-Saharan African countries. They are consistently reporting higher turnover rates among smaller firms. Based on the data from firm-level surveys conducted in the 1990s through the Regional Program on Enterprise Development (RPED), Harding, Soderböm and Teal (2004) report that more than 40 percent of firms existed in Tanzania and Kenya between 1993–94 and 1998–99 and 20 percent in the case of Ghana. For both Ghana and Kenya, they found that the exit rate decreases with the firm size. Using similar data for Ghana, Frazer (2005) also found larger firms are less likely to exit. The finding that smaller firms have high turnover rates is consistent with the data from the WBATTI survey.

16. Entry can occur through several channels. Each channel would have a different impact on domestic market concentration. Entry can affect market structure not only by altering the relative market shares of sales, but also the number of producers; thus, the effects of foreign business entry on domestic market structure and competition may vary. Entry through imports as well as greenfield investment decrease market concentration in host countries. However, mergers would increase domestic market concentration (Broadman 2005).

17. Although it is not as clear as the sales side, a similar pattern exists on the purchase side.

18. This linkage is clearly shown in the case of East Europe and the former Soviet Union per Broadman (2005).

19. Because the data on competitors are not measured in a perfectly objective manner, the numbers of competitors from the same home countries can be biased upward, particularly among foreign-owned firms. However, the table shows that, comparing across different origins of competitors (rather than comparing across different firm nationalities), local competitors and competitors from neighboring African countries are the leading origins of competitors for any nationality group. Thus, potential upward bias should not change the basic pattern in any significant manner. Even with the bias being corrected, it appears that Chinese and Indian import competition is felt more by Chinese and Indian firms operating in Africa than by indigenous African firms.

20. Recently, Helpman, Melitz, and Yeaple (2004) both theoretically and empirically showed that more efficient firms would choose FDI to serve a foreign market while less-efficient firms serve the market by exporting their products.

21. Macroeconomic data show that African countries in general are high-cost countries relative to income and productivity. In addition, several recent studies based on firm-level data show that manufacturers in Africa also experience high transaction costs at the micro level. For example, Eifert, Gelb, and Ramachandran (2005) show how high indirect costs reduce the productivity and competitiveness of manufacturers across Africa. These costs are reducing productivity for the region's manufacturers. Indeed, the combination of high regulatory costs, unsecured land property rights, inadequate and high-cost infrastructure, unfair competition from well-connected companies, ineffective judiciary systems, policy uncertainty, and corruption makes the cost of doing business in Africa 20-40 percent above that for other developing regions, according to the World Bank Doing Business Indicators.

22. See Eifert, Gelb, and Ramachandran (2005).

23. Using industry-level data, Clarke and Wallsten (2006) found a strong effect of the Internet in promoting North-South trade. Using firm-level ICA data of African manufacturing firms, Yoshino (2006) found that the use of the Internet has much more significant effect for firms to export outside of Africa than to export within Africa.

CHAPTER 5

"Between-the-Border" Factors in African-Asian Trade and Investment

Introduction

The friction arising from "between-the-border" barriers to international commerce between Sub-Saharan Africa and Asia limits the flows of trade and investment between the two regions. These barriers make firms in both regions incur high transactions costs. These costs arise in a variety of dimensions and in both direct and indirect forms. For instance, there are costs associated with compliance with procedures for the collection and processing of international transactions; transport costs; and search costs associated with imperfections in the "market for information" about trade and investment opportunities.

This chapter assesses the nature and extent of such between-the-border barriers to African-Asian trade and investment and analyzes a variety of ways that these costs can be reduced. We first focus on the fact that foreign market information on potential demand and investment opportunities is essential in facilitating trade and investment between Africa and Asia. Four mechanisms for reducing asymmetric information are discussed: (i) the role of institutional providers of export market information, such as export promotion agencies; (ii) the role of institutional providers of foreign investment information, such as investment promotion agencies; (iii) the role of technical standards in bridging information gaps; and (iv) the role of ethnic networks and the diaspora in facilitating information flows. Given imperfect cross-border information flows, which are inherent to international trade and particularly so among developing countries, public information services run by government or by private firms can be effective. The use of standards and accreditation schemes may reduce difficulties in assessing the quality of a product by enhancing the availability of reliable, accessible information on aspects of quality considered important by exporters, importers, and consumers. Ethnic networks that operate across national borders can help overcome between-the-border barriers as well.

The analysis also discusses how flows of technology and people between Africa and Asia facilitate the formation of business links, which then lead to trade and foreign direct investment (FDI) flows. There is a mutually reinforcing effect between trade and investment flows on the one hand and technology transfers and migration on the other. The World Bank Africa-Asia Trade and Investment (WBAATI) survey, as well as business case studies, clearly suggest the presence of such two-way links in the context of China and India's trade and investment ties with African countries. The complementary relationship among migration, trade, and capital flows suggests that removal of certain between-the-border barriers can facilitate all of these flows. Increases in these three flows are likely to accelerate the pace of technological diffusion throughout Africa and Asia.

Of course, Africa faces significant challenges in the adoption of advances in technology. Perhaps most visible is the fact that the workforce in most countries on the continent have very weak, although improving, skills. Local technological transfers can be compromised when foreign skilled workers are simply brought in with foreign capital and without any effective means of transferring the requisite skills to local workers. An emerging agenda for African firms is how to effectively capture opportunities for the acquisition of advances in technology and skills through participating in the international production networks, as discussed in chapter 6.

Finally, enhancing the capacity for trade facilitation could offer tremendous opportunities to reduce direct and indirect costs. African, Chinese, and Indian firms all have been hampered by inadequate and costly transport and logistics services in Africa. The ability to compete in today's global marketplace depends on a complex chain of trade support services that include customs and border procedures, management and control of freight movements, transaction documentation, and banking instruments. African firms continue to face problems in accessing trade finance, which is particularly serious among small and medium size enterprises. At the same time, evidence shows that investment by Chinese and Indian firms in Africa has been significantly aided by public trade finance programs by the export-import banks of those two countries.

The chapter concludes with a discussion of the policy implications from the analysis concerning the alleviation of between-the-border constraints.

Remedies for Imperfections in the Market for Information

Information on overseas markets is critically important for firms to make decisions on exporting their products and services, sourcing their inputs outside of domestic markets, and investing in other countries. One of the major constraints African firms face in penetrating the export markets is their limited access to global market information, including information on prices and consumer tastes. The problem of poor market information in Africa is particularly acute among small and medium enterprises (SMEs), as well as local farmers. There are several mechanisms through which these constraints can be reduced. This section discusses four such mechanisms: (i) institutional providers of export market information; (ii) institutional providers of FDI information; (iii) the role of standards in mitigating information gaps; and (iv) the role of ethnic networks in facilitating market information flows.

Institutional Providers of Export Market Information

The current level of market information inflows to private firms in African countries is not sufficient to allow them to effectively respond to the emerging demands in overseas markets. There are three types of information-related bottlenecks: (i) lack of general knowledge of foreign markets; (ii) lack of knowledge as to how to identify foreign agents or buyers in destination markets; and (iii) lack of credential information on those foreign agents or buyers, which results in increased uncertainty, including fears of delinquency.

Information flows on export markets are in fact endogenous to actual flows of exports. While market information facilitates exporting, exporting itself enables a firm to obtain knowledge about foreign markets ("learning-by-exporting"). Firms collect market information directly or indirectly from overseas business partners through their exporting activities. This learning process allows firms to further expand their exports by adding new product lines to their exports or into new markets by entering (or both). There is a mutually reinforcing effect between exporting and acquisition of export market information.

Firms can also receive market information indirectly from their customers or from suppliers of their inputs. In their search for low-cost, quality products among various suppliers, buyers often tacitly transmit to a supplier proprietary knowledge obtained from another supplier. Or a supplier may transmit such knowledge to a buyer as well. This type of implicit knowledge transfer is more common in simple production sectors such as clothing and footwear. The business case studies of African firms developed for this analysis have many examples where this true. For instance, a South African blanket firm obtained from its Italian supplier of fabric new information about who in Italy manufactured a particular type of machinery.

Export market information could well be kept as *private information* in the sense that it is collected in an implicit form and kept closely held. However, when a firm has little or no export experience to begin with, it has to rely on outside knowledge. Just like firms in other regions, firms in Africa seek market information from public or private suppliers. It is common for governments to sponsor trade missions and to run export promotion agencies (EPAs) (see box 5.1 for Uganda's EPA).

Typically, EPAs are agencies providing four broad categories of services: (i) image building; (ii) export support services (that is, information on trade finance, logistics, customs, packaging, pricing, and the like); (iii) marketing services (for example, trade fairs and commercial missions); and (iv) market research. As discussed in chapter 3, African governments provide various forms of export incentives to domestic firms for the purpose of promoting exports. As a part of the incentive programs, government-run EPAs assist domestic exporters in identifying new market opportunities for exporting their products by providing them with information on the types of products that are demanded in different overseas markets as well as the necessary steps for firms to take to initiate export transactions. Export market information, if only supplied privately, tends to be undersupplied. The rationale for these agencies is to provide export market information as public goods rather than private information.

In Sub-Saharan Africa, the presence of export promotion agencies is relatively rare. However, recent research suggests that for every U.S. dollar in an EPA budget, there are an additional $137 of exports from Sub-Saharan Africa.[1] The few EPAs in Africa concentrate their budget resources on export support services (exporter training; technical assistance; capacity building, including regulatory compliance; and information on trade finance, logistics, customs, packaging, and pricing).

In addition to governmental agencies, market information is supplied by private firms in the form of consultancy services. Private companies sell market information to their clients. The information gap between supply and demand could generate profitable business opportunities for entrepreneurs if it were properly packaged.

Information Flows for Foreign Direct Investment

While there are many academic discussions as to how to compare the attractiveness of countries for FDI, the perspective of the actual investors has been less explored. International firms faced with choosing the next location for their operations generally focus on a few, narrowly defined criteria, based on the particular needs of their industry. Broad dissemination of investor-relevant information in a timely fashion is an issue that needs to be addressed if African countries are to feature on the radar screen of international investors. One way is to make use of benchmarking exercises that compare different countries in terms of their FDI attractiveness (see box 5.2).

In addition to the compiled information to be disseminated to potential investors, proper information intermediaries also need to be in place. As discussed in chapter 3, one of the fundamental roles of investment promotion agencies (IPAs) is collecting and providing accurate information on linkage opportunities to investors. According to a recent UNIDO study on IPAs, the most common activity undertaken by IPAs with business linkage programs is the provision of information services that are conducted in collaboration with the private sector and international agencies.[2]

IPAs seek to provide up-to-date information on local laws, regulations, and the characteristics of the local economy and markets, positioning the country or province high on the "long list" of a potential investor. The critical first step in the corporation selection process is now increasingly implemented online. Those IPAs that could provide tailored services online are even more effective in bridging the information gap, leading their locations for follow-up investigations and site visits. In a continent known for

BOX 5.1

The Uganda Export Promotion Board and the Role of Exporters' Associations

Trade promotion is experiencing radical changes. Technology, economic integration, and instant communications have transformed the way in which products are made and distributed. Furthermore, as a consequence of lower barriers on trade, investment, and technology, products are being increasingly broken down into components—not only in terms of goods, but of services—produced or delivered in the most advantageous locations. The model in the twenty-first century is one of global supply chains, with linkages between investment and trade, and the leverage of outbound FDI to open up new markets. This new reality is the international competition for capital, technology, and markets.

In October 2004, the International Trade Centre of the UNCTAD/WTO declared the Uganda Export Promotion Board (UEPB) the best trade promotion organization in the least developed countries. Trade Promotion Organizations were created in response to the strong advice and support of the International Trade Centre. These institutions are used by many countries to promote their exports by delivering commercial intelligence, market research, services to foreign buyers, group promotions, and advice on shipping, transport, and packaging. The Ugandan board provides services in the following areas: conducting market studies to support exports; providing market information and training to the business community; supporting companies to participate in trade fairs and exhibitions; organizing trade missions; helping exporters overcome trade barriers, especially in the regional markets; and counseling SME exporters. To continue the upward trend in exports, the UEPB is focusing on the following activities during the period 2005–09:

- Promoting market standards

- Diversifying the export base. Programs such as promoting trade in biodiversity and natural ingredients and promoting trade opportunities in organic agriculture with the support of UNCTAD are already being implemented. The board will develop more of these alternatives.

- Establishing a strong presence in emerging markets. Market studies and contract promotion programs will be undertaken, especially in markets where trade preferences have been offered to Uganda, including China and Canada.

- Overcoming supply-side constraints. The board will implement tested concepts such as export production villages, nucleus farming, and clustering as the existing practices in overcoming supply-side constraints associated with fragmented agriculture in Uganda.

Trade promoting agencies have come under a lot of scrutiny, especially the ones that are supported by state funds. However, sometimes the job of export promotion can be conducted by private associations such as Chambers of Commerce or Exporters' Associations. Trade promoting agencies are becoming more client oriented and provide more specialized services to their clients. The Uganda Trade Board is working with SMEs to support them in export services. SME coalitions now are helping in trade negotiations. The Uganda Services Exporters' Association is a small private sector association working on trade in services through the Private Sector Foundation Uganda, an apex body whose members include all organized groups for industry, professionals, and trade in Uganda. This has allowed Ugandan services firms, even small ones, to contribute to Uganda's negotiating proposals. It also serves as a basis to select private sector representatives to a number of WTO and regional negotiation forums.

Source: World Bank staff.

BOX 5.2

Benchmarking FDI Competitiveness

At the most basic level, the Enterprise Benchmarking Program (EBP) methodology aims to answer questions such as, "How much would it cost to run my operations in Location A, given these specific operating parameters? How does this compare with Locations B and C?" It should be stressed that the benchmarking framework does not attempt to determine "absolute" competitiveness. Rather, it seeks to identify the location that provides the most suitable mix of cost and operating conditions to meet the specific needs of a particular investor in a particular industry. Through the EBP program, it is hoped that these investors' perspectives will be conveyed to client governments, to assist in identifying industries in which these countries can be attractive destinations for foreign investment.

The initial EBP study in 2003 considered the relative attractiveness of electronics manufacturing and offshore office operations in four countries in East Asia. The recently completed Africa EBP encompassed research in 11 countries—Ghana, Kenya, Lesotho, Madagascar, Mali, Mauritius Mozambique, Senegal, South Africa, Tanzania, and Uganda—and covered six sectors for the majority of the countries: apparel, textiles, call centers, tourism, horticulture, and food and beverages processing. An important lesson that has been learned through the EBP in Africa is that there is a lack of quality information, which hinders many international firms from even considering Africa in the first place. Given the scarcity of reliable and up-to-date information available at the desktop level, the benchmarking in Africa could not have been conducted without field work. In other words, field work would have been required even to make a company's initial list of potential candidates. This is a significant cost for a firm to assume simply to be able to consider an African country as a candidate for its operations. Broad dissemination of investor-relevant information in a timely fashion is an issue that needs to be addressed if African countries are to feature on the radar screen of international investors, when compared to leading investment locations, such as China and India.

Source: World Bank Group/MIGA staff.

its infrastructural shortcomings, African IPAs are remarkably well-connected to the online community. Although the content and quality vary greatly, there are 35 countries with national IPA Web sites listed in the World Bank Group's Multilateral Investment Guarantee Agency's (MIGA's) online investment promotion "yellow pages" in IPAnet; see annex 5A.

IPA's Role in Facilitating Network Production

Given the new trend toward international network production—the focus of the next chapter—as well as the research and development (R&D) networks of multinational corporations, IPAs can serve as a bridge between the private and public sectors, helping to improve the understanding of what is required to benefit from international production networks. Indeed, IPAs can be used to draw the attention of policy makers to areas that are important for making a location more attractive for knowledge-based activities. In Africa, only a minority of IPAs (only nine) promote R&D-related FDI.[3] Computer and information and communication technology (ICT) services are the industries most commonly targeted by IPAs in developing countries that promote R&D-related FDI. Costa Rica is a good example of a developing country that tapped into the R&D networks through FDI. R&D investment by multinational corporations is likely to be found among already-existing foreign affiliates. The experience of Costa Rica with Intel, for example, suggests that close collaboration with existing investors can pay off if supported by other policies to make the country environment more conducive to such investments.

Bilateral Market Information Between African Countries and China and India

In the case of trade and investment between Chinese and African firms, there are some private firms providing information on mutual trade and investment opportunities, which range from information related to sourcing in China and Africa to basic business contacts and investment advisory services. Also, they arrange business travel and product exhibitions; help African delegations to contact Chinese government, enterprise associations, and factories; promote Chinese products in the African markets and vice versa; and provide logistics and shipping consultancy, among others (see box 5.3).

BOX 5.3

Private Companies Promoting China-Africa Trade and Investment

Africaccess Consulting Company Limited is a Sino-African trade and investment consulting company based in Beijing. This company is helping Chinese companies set up business operations in Africa. It has been collaborating with the China State Development Bank, the Cameroon Chamber of Commerce and Industry, and the China Center for the Promotion of International Trade. As part of its activities, the company has organized identification mission trips to Africa for Chinese businesses and also arranged for African businesses to explore business opportunities in China.

The company was created by a Cameroonian businessman, who studied at a graduate program in Beijing, in partnership with a Chinese woman. He realized that Chinese companies did not possess accurate information about Africa, while many African firms also lacked sufficient knowledge on business opportunities in China. This motivated him to create this company to close this information gap.

One of the company's initiatives includes cooperation with the Cameroon Ministry of Post and Telecommunications on a project to set up 400 mul-

In addition to private consulting companies, the governments of China and India, as well as African countries, are equally active in facilitating information flows on bilateral trade and investment opportunities between China and Africa as well as between India and Africa. The Chinese government has set up centers for "investment and trade promotion" in various locations in the world. There are 10 centers located in Sub-Saharan Africa (Cameroon, Côte d'Ivore, Gabon, Guinea, Kenya, Mali, Mozambique, Nigeria, Tanzania, and Zambia).[4] Those centers provide business consultation services to Chinese enterprises in Africa. They also provide special funds and simplified procedures to encourage Chinese enterprises to invest in Africa.

Moreover, trade and investment ties with Africa are being strengthened through various bilateral and multilateral public-private initiatives

timedia centers throughout the country. The company also facilitated the exports of Beijing Tianzhushengjie sunshade coverings to Botswana. In addition, the firm is working with the Cameroon Real Estate Company (SIC) to find reliable business partners in China for low-cost housing schemes.

Africa-Invest.Net, created by Beijing Yeaco Investment Consulting Co., Ltd. in 1999, is the largest Web site in China featuring information on Africa. Beijing Yeaco Investment Consulting Co., Ltd. is a professional company, specialized in promoting economic and trade exchange between Africa and China. During 2006, Africa-Invest.Net opened a new country-business on-line portal called Lesotho Business Online (www.invest.net.cn/swzx/lesotho/index.html) and renewed another called Nigeria Business Online (www.invest.net.cn/swzx/Nigeria/index.htm).

Before he set up the company, the general manager of the company worked at the Department of West Asia and Africa of the Ministry of Commerce of China for 11 years, and worked in African countries for more than five years. Up to now, the company has received more than 50 African business and government delegations. The company has also arranged for more than 50 Chinese delegations to visit Africa.

Source: Corporate Web sites.

between China and African countries. For example, the China-Africa Business Council, a joint initiative of China with the United Nations Development Programme, aims to support China's private sector investment in Cameroon, Ghana, Mozambique, Nigeria, South Africa, and Tanzania. China also uses summits and informal meetings to reach out to African business leaders. The firms' Sino-African business conference was held in Ethiopia in December 2003. It resulted in agreements on 20 projects with a total value of $680 million. In August 2004, China held a China-Africa Youth Festival in Beijing.

As to India-Africa bilateral information, as part of India's Ex-Im Bank's 2002–07 policy program, the government of India launched "Focus Africa" to boost Indian exports to the Sub-Saharan Africa region. The program seeks to reduce the uncertainty in doing business with Africa. During the first phase of the program, Nigeria, South Africa, Mauritius, Kenya, Ethiopia, Tanzania, and Ghana were selected as the target countries. The scope of the program was further extend in 2003 to cover all of the other Sub-Saharan countries where India has diplomatic missions: Angola, Botswana, Côte d'Ivoire, Madagascar, Mozambique, Senegal, Seychelles, Uganda, Zambia, Namibia, and Zimbabwe, along with six North African countries.

Several industry associations in India also play a pivotal role in disseminating market information. In November 2005, the Confederation of Indian Industry and the Export-Import Bank of India, in collaboration with the Ministry of External Affairs and the Ministry of Commerce and Industry, organized the Conclave on India-Africa Project Partnership 2005 "Expanding Horizons." It was attended by 160 delegates from 32 African countries and led to over 600 meetings between African and Indian entrepreneurs.[5] Over 70 projects were discussed. Also, the Federation of Indian Chambers of Commerce and Industry prepared a study titled "Destination Africa: India's Vision." The study identified the top seven destinations in Sub-Saharan Africa for India's exports markets, which are Nigeria, South Africa, Kenya, Mauritius, Ghana, Tanzania, and Sudan. In the study, the sectors of pharmaceutical and health care, information technology, water management, food processing, and education were identified as those that could act as "engines of growth" to boost Indo-African trade.

Role of Technical Standards in Bridging Market Information Gaps

Technical standards applied to products and services have both positive and negative effects on trade. In chapter 3, it was discussed how standards could become barriers to trade. In fact, standards and technical regulations in overseas markets are increasingly mentioned by African firms as barriers to exporting to those markets. However, standards have a very potent role as facilitators of international trade and investment. The use of standards and accreditation schemes alleviates difficulties that firms face in export markets in relation to asymmetric information on their products vis-à-vis their buyers in export markets.

As their primary function, standards are expected to enhance reliability and accessibility of information on the quality aspects of products, which are deemed essential by buyers. Thus, standards could play an important role in international markets by reducing information costs. This is the case for both exporters and importers. For importers, standards reduce the uncertainty about product quality. For exporters, standards lower production costs, facilitate the exchange of information, and reduce the imitation costs.

In fact, this positive effect of standards is present for Chinese and Indian firms in Africa. Unlike developed countries, developing countries often lack effective and efficient consumer organizations as well as governmental product-approval and surveillance mechanisms. In such cases, quality and safety standards have an even more important role as instruments of self-regulation. Box 5.4 illustrates how Chinese firms utilize standards as a tool to communicate the quality of their products and services in African countries.

BOX 5.4

Local Standards in Africa and Chinese Construction Firms

Foreign firms entering into Africa, including Chinese construction firms, need to pass the "quality" test to satisfy consumer demands on road construction. The WBAATI business case studies covered several Chinese companies operating in Senegal and Tanzania that reported that their companies complied with domestic standards in the respective countries.

A Chinese construction firm in Tanzania indicated that it needed to keep its operation license current. The firm has met requirements on health and safety regulations. The firm has not had any accidents. The firm pays $20,000 per year to be certified properly, which is a significant expense for the firm. However, the firm is aware of building its reputation in African markets.

Construction standards in Senegal are aligned with French standards. A Chinese construction firm in Senegal said it had been applying Senegalese standards. According to the firm, these standards are comparable to Chinese standards. The firm recognizes the importance of gaining a reliable reputation as a provider of high quality products in construction services in Africa.

Source: World Bank staff.

Capacity building among African firms in complying with international standards is an urgent agenda item for private sector development in African countries. Only a small percentage of firms in Africa have obtained ISO certification (figure 5.1). Many surveyed firms in Africa report that product quality and low demand are the most important factors that affect their firm's ability to export.[6] African countries can increase their exports if firms in those countries have sufficient capacity to comply with global technical standards. However, standards and regulations raise production costs for firms seeking to export from developing countries. In Africa, the costs to get certified under ISO 9000, ISO 9002, and ISO 14000 are particularly high among small and medium enterprises.

Apart from the issue of capacity shortage in meeting global standards, African firms are also short on access to updated information on standards. For example, Sub-Saharan countries are not well represented in international standards meetings and relevant processes. Only 34 countries from Sub-Saharan Africa belong to the International Organization for Standardization (ISO). As such, only the local standards bureau and development agencies in individual countries provide firms with relevant information on standards for their products. Lack of information on the new standards potentially affects firms' ability to market their products in international markets. There is a clear need for a high-impact awareness campaign and information centers from which information about standards and quality is readily accessible.

FIGURE 5.1
Firms with ISO 9000, 9002, and 14000 Certification

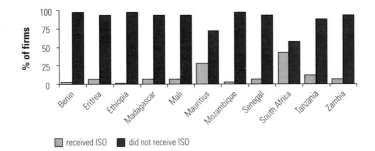

Source: World Bank Investment Climate Assessments.

Market Information Through Ethnic Networks and Migration

Ethnic Networks

Worldwide, increasing attention is being paid to the role of ethnic networks in overcoming inadequate information about international trade and investment opportunities, and there is evidence that ethnic networks promote bilateral trade by providing market information and supplying matching and referral services to their members.[7] To be sure, as discussed in chapter 4, ethnic networks in Africa can cause market segmentation and reduced competition by deterring market entry by parties outside a group. But it is also the case that such networks have a catalytic role in cross-border exchanges of market information. In a foreign market, ethnic networks facilitate a range of business-to-business contact, including between producers of consumer products and their distributors, assemblers, and component suppliers, as well as foreign investors and their local joint venture partners.

Migrants usually maintain personal connections with their families and with other personal contacts in their home countries. These groups form what are called diasporas. Chinese and Indian diasporas are serving as vehicles for diffusion of information about investments and trade opportunities between the countries where they reside and the countries of their ethnic ancestries. Benefits from ethnic networks are particularly large in an environment in which formal networking opportunities are limited. Contacts among expatriate communities across international boundaries play a crucial role in exchanging market information for international trade. Chinese entrepreneurs use their diaspora to overcome the constraints they face from the lack of formal channels available to them.

Speaking a common language or sharing similar cultural backgrounds eases communication and allows better understanding of documentation, procedures, and regulations related to cross-border trade. Chinese expatriates are widely used by "outsiders" to facilitate their business relations in China (see box 5.5).

Ethnic networks bring a valuable reservoir of knowledge and information on trade and investment opportunities. India is one notable example of a country that is using its diaspora to enhance bilateral trade and investment expansion.[8] China also benefits from its diaspora. In one estimate, as much as 45 percent of its total $41 billion in FDI came from the Chinese diaspora in 2000.[9]

BOX 5.5

Using Chinese Ethnic Networks to Help African Firms Find Suppliers in China

The WBAATI business case studies found that one South African firm imported blankets from China. The firm, which was originally started by a European family, engages a Chinese trader or what is called in the literature an "ethnic network intermediary" who sells access to and use of his network in China. The firm has paid a commission on the value of the involved transactions. This ethnic intermediary has knowledge of the capabilities and preferences of the sellers of blankets in China. The manager of this South African firm had never been to China. The firm chose the fabrics from a catalogue that the trader provided. In this way, the Chinese trader connected the South African firm with the suitable Chinese retailers of fabrics.

Source: World Bank staff.

In Africa, there is a striking difference in the reliance on ethnic networks between Indian and Chinese firms operating on the continent; see table 5.1. About one-half of the owners of surveyed firms in Africa that are of Indian ethnic origin are in fact African by nationality. (A similar proportion exists for European owners of the surveyed African firms.) These figures suggest that Indian (and European) migrants are substantially integrated into the business community in Africa.

TABLE 5.1
Ethnicity versus Nationality of Business Owners
(percent)

Nationality of owner	Ethnic origin of owner			
	African	Chinese	Indian	European
African	100	4	48	51
Chinese	0	93	0	1
Indian	0	0	45	0
European	0	0	4	41
Other	0	4	3	7

Source: World Bank staff.

Conversely, there is near identity of the proportion of owners of surveyed Chinese firms operating in Africa that are Chinese both by nationality and by ethnicity. This underscores the fact that Chinese investors in Africa are relative newcomers and have not, at this juncture, integrated into the African business community to any significant degree, a notion that is explored more deeply in chapter 6. Instead, recent Chinese investments in Africa, as evidenced in virtually all of the business case studies carried out for this analysis, have been largely accompanied by temporary assignments of executives to the African continent. As Chinese investment in Africa has grown, it has been estimated that some 80,000 migrant workers from China have moved to Africa, creating a new Chinese diaspora.[10]

Table 5.2 shows that, among surveyed firms, Chinese firms hire the largest percentage of workers from China or other East Asian countries, accounting for 17 percent of total employees. Indian firms hire about half as many of their workers from India (9.8 percent).

By differentiating between firms that export more than 10 percent of their output (exporters) and those that do not (nonexporters), it becomes clear that exporting firms tend to have higher proportions of employees hired outside of the countries where firms are located, regardless of firm nationality (table 5.3). In the case of Chinese, Indian, and European firms, exporters have a significantly higher proportion of employees brought from the firms' home country or home region. In the case of African firms, exporters also hire a greater proportion of employees from other African countries than do nonexporters. Taken together, this is clear evidence that foreign workers, particularly those from foreign firms' home countries,

TABLE 5.2

Sources of Labor Force by Location of Employee's Previous Residence
(percent)

Firm nationality	Previous location of employees before hiring						
	Domestic	Other Africa	Europe and N. America	India	Other South Asia	China	Other East Asia
African	96.3	1.6	0.4	1.4	0.0	0.0	0.0
Chinese	80.8	0.6	0.0	0.4	0.1	9.5	7.4
Indian	89.5	0.1	0.2	9.8	0.1	0.0	0.1
European	92.5	3.1	1.1	2.2	0.2	0.3	0.0

Source: World Bank staff.

TABLE 5.3

Sources of Labor Force by Location of Employee's Previous Residence: Exporter versus Nonexporter Firms

(percent)

Firm nationality	Exporter	Previous location of employees before hiring						
		Domestic	Other Africa	Europe and N. America	India	Other South Asia	China	Other East Asia
African	Nonexporter	97.3	0.6	0.2	1.8	0.0	0.0	0.0
African	Exporter	93.8	4.1	1.0	0.6	0.0	0.1	0.0
Chinese	Nonexporter	82.6	0.0	0.0	0.0	0.1	6.5	8.8
Chinese	Exporter	77.6	1.7	0.0	1.0	0.0	14.7	5.0
Indian	Nonexporter	93.4	0.2	0.0	6.0	0.1	0.0	0.2
Indian	Exporter	77.3	0.0	1.0	21.7	0.0	0.0	0.0
European	Nonexporter	94.1	4.5	0.7	0.7	0.0	0.0	0.0
European	Exporter	90.4	1.3	1.5	4.3	0.5	0.6	0.0

Source: World Bank staff.

play a catalytic role in facilitating firms' exports from Africa. However, locally hired workers contribute to local sales. This is also quite intuitive because of their comparative advantage in knowledge of local markets and commercial practices.

Migration and Mode IV

Reducing between-the-border barriers to African-Asian trade and investment is also coming about through the flow of people. Indeed, there is increasing evidence that the cross-border movement of people is a complement to rather than a substitute for trade and investment flows.

The temporary movement of persons for delivery of services, so-called Mode IV services delivery, was negotiated under the General Agreement on Trade in Services (GATS); see box 5.6. The agreement defined four possible modes for which services can be traded between members of the World Trade Organization (WTO). The four are Mode I: "cross-border supply" (for example, the provision of architectural blueprints via fax); Mode II: "consumption abroad" (for example, tourism); Mode III: "commercial presence," which typically, though not always, means that FDI is part of the provision of the service (for example, establishment of a foreign law practice in the host country); and Mode IV: "presence of natural persons" (for example, a foreign computer software consultant).

Some free trade agreements (FTAs) contain provisions allowing the temporary entry of business professionals into the other country for the

BOX 5.6

The General Agreement on Trade in Services (GATS)

The GATS accord was part of the Uruguay Round negotiations, which began in 1986 under the auspices of the GATT and concluded with the establishment of the WTO in 1995. The GATS represents the first attempt to devise a multilateral, legally enforceable understanding covering trade and investment in the services sector. Like the GATT, which was updated as part of the Uruguay Round and still forms the WTO's principal rule book for trade in goods, the GATS provides a legal basis on which to negotiate the multilateral elimination of barriers that discriminate against foreign services providers and otherwise deny them market access. The GATS differs from the GATT in several respects. Perhaps the most important difference is the principles of national treatment (that is, nondiscrimination) and market access (that is, freedom of entry and exit) are provided automatically under the GATT, but are negotiated rights and obligations in the GATS. The negotiations on national treatment and market access for services in the GATS constitute the equivalent of tariff negotiations for goods in the GATT. In services trade there is effectively no "border," as there is in goods trade. The restrictions on international transactions in services are embedded in countries' domestic laws, regulations, and other measures. Under the GATS obligations these restrictions are liberalized (in varying degrees), thus creating for services a regime that is the equivalent of a duty-free regime for goods.

The GATS is composed of two principal components. The first is a textual framework that sets out general multilateral rules governing trade and investment in services. The second complements the rules framework. It is the set of binding commitments to market access and national treatment of individual services industries; countries append these commitments to the agreement in the form of a "schedule." Like tariff negotiations in goods, these multilateral services commitments result from iterative bilateral "request and offer" negotiations conducted seriatim on a country-by-country basis. Supplementing the rules framework are sectoral annexes and understandings that contain specific rules dealing with, among other

(Continues on the following page.)

BOX 5.6 (continued)

things, issues affecting financial services, aviation services, and access to telecommunications networks. While some of the provisions of the overall rules framework apply to all services industries, regardless of whether they are "scheduled," many only pertain to industries for which market access or national treatment commitments are assumed. As a result, on balance, the GATS employs what has become known as a "positive list" approach: unless an industry is scheduled, it is, in the main, automatically excluded from the most meaningful terms of the agreement.

The mechanism fundamental to the GATS that engenders the agreement's multilateral liberalizing character is the rule that also serves as the basis of the GATT: Most Favored Nation (MFN) treatment. Like the GATT, the MFN principle—that a signatory treat all countries in a manner no less favorable than its treatment of a particular country—generally applies for all services included in the GATS regardless of whether a particular industry is included in a country's schedule of commitments. However, the GATS allows for flexibility in the application of MFN. In particular, it permits exemptions to MFN for specific laws, regulations, and administrative practices. Such flexibility is essential because of the need to be able to maintain existing regulations or agreements not consistent with MFN, or the need to preserve the prospective use of reciprocal or unilateral measures, particularly when a country has concluded, as a tactical matter, that the GATS commitments offered by other countries for a specific industry generally are not sufficiently liberalizing.

In addition to the negotiated rights and obligations of market access and national treatment as well as the MFN rule, other core provisions of the GATS include the requirement for countries to publish all domestic laws and regulations affecting services; assurances for due process in notifying interested services providers of the status of license applications; disciplines on public monopolies; rights governing the mutual recognition and harmonization of regulatory standards; consultation procedures on competition matters; and exceptions for national security, safety and health, and the enforcement of tax laws.

Source: Broadman 1994.

purpose of facilitating trade in services.[11] As services become one of the driving forces in trade, cross-border mobility of business professionals, particularly those providing professional services, has gained considerable attention from countries as an important aspect of expanding market access for suppliers of such services. Facilitating the movement of professionals allows trade partners to more efficiently provide each other with services such as architecture, engineering, consulting, and construction. However, in the case of the FTA being discussed between South Africa and China, trade in services, including Mode IV–related issues, are not yet on the agenda; see chapter 3.

As in other regions, there are still barriers to the movement of people in Africa. Most countries in Africa have enacted or retained a series of laws that in effect restrict "foreigners" from participating in certain kinds of economic activities. However, with some variation in terms of degree of liberalization, several regional economic communities in Sub-Saharan Africa have made progress in liberalizing the movement of people among their member countries. For example, Economic and Monetary Community of Central Africa (CEMAC), Economic Community of West African States (ECOWAS), and West African Economic and Monetary Union (WAEMU) have recently introduced the use of intraregional passports. However, the level of liberalization varies. The Common Market for Eastern and Southern Africa (COMESA) has adopted the Protocol on the Free Movement of Persons, Labor, and Services.

Some foreign companies operating in Africa face significant impediments to relocating staff and families. Immigration services, including processing of work permits, study permits, and visitors permit applications, have become a significant concern for Chinese and Indian firms in Africa. The business case studies reveal that several Chinese and Indian firms in South Africa and Tanzania face serious difficulties in obtaining study permits for the children of their expatriate staff, either because the process of obtaining a working permit takes a long time, or because the process is not clear. In one case, one firm that located in Tanzania had to pay $600 for a two-year work permit. In another case, Chinese expatriates were also requested to show a return ticket to China at the point of entry.

South Africa has become the predominant platform for the entry of multinational corporations, including from China and India, with plans for regional integration on the Sub-Saharan continent. The result is the attraction of thousands of non-African expatriates. But for the compa-

nies to effectively operate in South Africa, there is a need to institution-
alize simplified procedures for facilitating cross-border movements of
professionals. Despite the two changes in the country's immigration legislation in the past three years designed to simplify the procedures,
obtaining work permits still requires a lengthy process. A bilateral immigration arrangement can facilitate the movement of people. For example, as of summer 2006, Indian nationals transiting through South Africa
no longer are required to obtain transit visas. This policy change is part
of South Africa's strategy to forge closer trade and investment ties with
India.[12]

Trade Facilitation in African-Asian Commerce: Transport, Logistics, and Finance

Interest among countries to reduce direct and indirect costs related to
international trade has placed trade facilitation at the forefront of the
global trade dialogue. Trade facilitation aims to make trade procedures as
efficient as possible through the simplification and harmonization of documentation, procedures, and information flows.[13] Trade facilitation issues
generally include (i) physical movement of consignment (transport and
transit) and border-crossing procedures; (ii) import and export procedures,
including customs; (iii) information and communications technology; (iv)
payment systems, insurance, and other financial requirements that affect
cross-border movements of goods in international trade; and (v) international trade standards.

The high transactions costs of engaging in international trade—such as
those arising from gaps in transport infrastructure, inefficiency in customs
procedures, and poor quality in logistics services due to weak (or nonexistent) competition by service providers—are increasingly outweighing the
costs of tariffs in global trade. A number of empirical studies on various
regions of the world have estimated these costs and the potential impacts
specific policy reforms in trade facilitation can have on increasing trade
flows.[14] In most cases, the net benefits are huge. The African continent is
particularly affected by a "trade facilitation deficit," with only a few exceptions. The gravity model analysis in chapter 2 confirmed such findings in
the context of assessing the factors that shape the extent of aggregate trade
flows between African and Asian countries.

Transport and Logistics

Poorly developed transport, communications, and logistics systems lie at the core of the trade facilitation problem in Sub-Saharan African countries. These countries' limited capacity to meet the growing demand of an increasingly complex global economy hampers trade and investment both within and outside the region. Indeed, the weaknesses in the continent's trade support services undermine the international competitiveness of African products, and constrain the ability of otherwise internationally competitive African firms to take advantage of new global market opportunities, including those in China and India; see box 5.7.

On average, freight costs for all developing countries worldwide are nearly twice as high as those for developed countries. Including costs related to conveyance, storage, and handling of goods, Africa has the highest transports costs among developing countries. A recent study by UNCTAD indicates that the freight cost as a percentage of total import value was 13 percent for Africa in 2000, compared to 8.8 percent for all developing countries and 5.2 percent for developed countries.[15] Some African countries have made some improvements in reducing freight costs, largely due to improvements in terminal handling that offset insufficient infrastructure facilities and inefficient practices for transit transport, and terminal equipment. However, that is not sufficient to change the position of African countries as high-transport-costs countries. As figure 5.2 shows clearly, among select African countries relatively little progress has been made in reducing transport costs.

Maritime Transport

Port-related bottlenecks include poor rail-to-road interfaces, inadequate shunting locomotives, insufficient cargo-handling equipment, absence of reliable shipper information, and port congestion. As a result, transport time takes longer than in other region. For example, the average port turnaround time in South Africa tends to be up to five times longer than that of competitor countries.[16] Many firms that are part of the business case studies report that they did not export *within* Africa because of high intraregional maritime transport costs. Indeed, some Chinese firms operating in Africa report that such transport costs to ship on the continent from South Africa are greater than shipping from South Africa to China.

BOX 5.7

Trade Facilitation, Customs, and Logistics Barriers in Africa

Many of the firms covered in the WBAATI business case studies report logistical obstacles in exporting. The key bottlenecks include: inefficient trucking and transport services; low export volume that results in higher costs; burdensome customs procedures; and inefficient cross-border transit procedures, among others.

For example, there are serious bottlenecks at the border between South Africa and Zambia, where the border control documentation seems to be quite cumbersome. South African firms reported that they used trade logistics companies for moving products between Zambia and South Africa. Even with utilizing service from a trade logistics company, communication between its South Africa and Zambia offices remains a problem, hindering the firms' ability to ship their products from Zambia and South Africa.

In fact, a few firms feel that intra-Africa exports are very expensive given the physical proximity of neighboring countries. For example, sending products from South Africa to Angola is as expensive as sending products from China to Angola. Maritime shipment seems to be three times as costly as road shipment due to the monopolized shipping line market in Africa. A Ghanaian firm reported that shipping costs and tariffs within ECOWAS are very expensive. It costs $1,000 to send a container from Accra to Lagos. For that reason, the firm decided to do a cross-border investment rather than export.

Road Transport

Costs of road transport are also high, attributed in part to low volumes of cargo, imbalanced trade flows between origins and destinations, and long travel time. Moreover, there are serious impediments at borders due to a lack of harmonization in customs procedures; see below. The costs are the highest in Africa's landlocked countries; see box 5.8.[17] Table 5.4 shows that inland freight rates faced by importers and exporters in landlocked Zimbabwe are significantly higher than those faced by their counterparts in coastal Mozambique or South Africa. On average, it is estimated that

Due to such high costs in shipping, firms devise some mechanisms to internalize shipping costs so that they can remain competitive. For example, one construction firm operating in South Africa reported that it bears shipping costs when the firm bids for the entire project. Before posting its bids, the firm makes sure to obtain quotations from shipping companies to see if they can be competitive in the bid.

The firms perceive that inefficiency in customs often involves lack of transparent management. For example, a firm in South Africa hired a private investigator to detect whether other companies were smuggling goods through the Port of Durban. The private investigator detected 11 smuggled containers sitting at the port of Durban. After the firm contacted the authorities regarding the smuggled containers, the containers disappeared without a trace. Most goods imported by small traders for sale in local markets are smuggled in without paying duties. This is the case of blankets in South Africa. Several blankets from China and Turkey are smuggled by informal traders. There are still a lot of undervalued and undeclared imports of finished products. In Tanzania, there are several bureaucratic processes for imports and exports. Underinvoiced imports and smuggling are continuing problems. Firms report that they need to make informal payments to get their products from the port.

The firms commonly voiced the opinion that removing these types of impediments associated with bureaucratic red tape increases productivity, helps reduce corruption, and encourages investments in infrastructure.

Source: World Bank staff.

landlocked countries incur 50 percent higher transport costs than those countries with coastal access. Goods transported to and from landlocked countries generally must travel longer distances, which may entail varying road conditions, border crossings, and greater opportunity for breakdown.

Air Cargo

Air transport services are inefficient and charges for freight remain high. Given the low cargo shipping volumes, companies in Africa tend to rely on

FIGURE 5.2
Africa Has Made Little Progress in Lowering Transport Costs:
Freight Transport Rates of Selected Countries

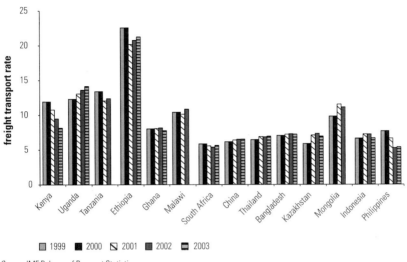

■ 1999   ■ 2000   ◩ 2001   ■ 2002   ▦ 2003

Source: IMF Balance of Payment Statistics.

Note: Freight transport rate is defined as the ratio of the sum of freight credit, freight debit, other transportation services credit, other transportation services debit, insurance credit and, insurance debit to the sum of merchandise exports and merchandise imports. Data are not available for Tanzania, Malawi, and Mongolia.

the freight capacity of passenger airlines instead of chartered freighters or cargo planes. This lowers the efficiency of air cargo transport.

Although countries in Africa differ greatly, a large percentage of the total lift capacity in Sub-Saharan African countries is handled by passenger airlines, either through their national carriers (such as South African Airlines, Kenya Airways, or Air Senegal) or through the carriers of countries that have signed bilateral air service agreements. Reliance on passenger airlines to carry the majority of cargo has several impacts.

In the East Africa region, Kenya Airways (and its Tanzanian affiliate Precision Air) has emerged as the leading carrier. In the Southern region, South Africa exports the largest amount of air transport services to it neighboring countries and the rest of Africa. It handles about 87 percent of the region's passengers. In addition, South Africa also dominates the share of the region's cargo. However, Air Mauritius, Kenya Airways, and Air Zimbabwe also play important roles. In West Africa, some countries do not have their own fleet aircraft (Sierra Leone specifically).

BOX 5.8

Logistics and Transport Issues in East African Countries

The international trade routes in East Africa mostly use the Northern and Central transport corridors, which link the ports of Mombasa and Dar es Salaam by road and rail to the landlocked countries. The main Northern Corridor route runs inland from Mombasa via Nairobi to Kampala, with extensions to Democratic Republic of Congo, Rwanda, and Burundi. The Central Corridor runs from Dar es Salaam via Dodoma to Northwestern Tanzania, with extensions to Democratic Republic of Congo, Burundi, Rwanda, and Uganda. Road infrastructure in the two major transport corridors has improved substantially over the last few years, while the performance of the railway networks has deteriorated considerably.

Transport costs are estimated at 35 percent of the value of exports for Uganda and more for the other Great Lakes countries. Some World Bank studies found that the costs per ton-km to/from Rwanda to Mombasa through the Northern Corridor are twice the cost per ton-km between Nairobi and Mombasa, which stresses the large impact of border crossing and trade volumes on logistics costs.

Transport delays and uncertainty contribute to higher transportation costs. On average, it takes almost three weeks for a container between the day it lands in the port of Mombasa and the day it arrives in Kampala: almost two weeks for dwell time in the port and six days for road transport between Mombasa and Kampala. Along the Central Corridor from Dar es Salaam to Kampala, it normally takes eight days, which means that the return trip should take less than 20 days. Nevertheless, some freight forwarders acknowledge that it takes longer. The return trip takes 45 days (20 days to go, 5 days for clearance, and 20 days to return).

Current operating conditions in Tanzania Railways cannot allow predictions to be accurate at four or five days for any shipment, and the situation is also complicated in Kenya Railways. Locomotive shortages, as well as wagon mismanagement, may explain transport uncertainty. Due to this uncertainty, exporters prefer to send goods by road, despite the increased risk of theft and higher freight costs. Frequently, departure times are missed and goods remain at the port for an extended period. In an uncertain environment, transport companies strive to cope with these problems by investing in costly information systems or employing additional people in charge of smoothing transactions.

Source: World Bank East Africa Trade Facilitation Project 2005.

TABLE 5.4
Comparative Intra-African Road Transport Costs
($ per TEU dry container)

Origin	Destination	Cost $/TEU
Harare, Zimbabwe	Durban, South Africa	1,362
Harare, Zimbabwe	Beira, Mozambique	775
Durban, South Africa	Harare, Zimbabwe	1,297
Beira, Mozambique	Harare, Zimbabwe	1,522

Source: Quotes from freight forwarders and shipping agents, CARANA.

Note: TEU = Twenty-foot equivalent unit.

Almost all the private airlines in the region rely more on passenger traffic than on cargo traffic for their operations. Cargo is often left behind in favor of passenger and baggage carriage when there is competition for space. Cargo generally flows one way. As a result, airlines are subject to the same economics as maritime carriers in the case of empty backhauls, which leads to highly divergent inbound and outbound cargo rates.

Table 5.5 shows cargo rates according to the Air Cargo Tariff (TACT) list published quarterly by the International Air Transport Association. The TACT rates indicate clear differences for inbound and outbound rate structures. The cost for 400 kgs from Singapore to Dakar is $19.78 per kilo, while the rate for Dakar, Senegal to Singapore is $16.43 per kilo.

Liberalization and Competition in Services
Competition among providers of transport services is largely absent on the

TABLE 5.5
Inbound and Outbound Air Cargo Rates
($ per kilo)

Destination	Origin						
	Dar es Salaam, Tanzania	Dakar, Senegal	Hanoi, Vietnam	New York	Singapore	Amsterdam	La Paz, Bolivia
Dar es Salaam, Tanzania	—	8.77	10.08	11.98	11.12	13.35	14.42
Dakar, Senegal	5.93	—	16.37	8.01	19.78	7.96	9.15
Hanoi, Vietnam	7.51	16.20	—	5.94	3.06	17.77	10.88
New York	5.20	4.91	6.94	—	7.49	3.87	2.99
Singapore	6.52	16.43	2.97	4.88	—	4.52	9.83
Amsterdam	3.61	4.75	10.55	2.49	4.74	—	6.76
La Paz, Bolivia	15.10	11.23	12.58	5.66	17.44	11.26	—

Source: CARANA 2003.

African continent. Due to policy-based barriers to entry, private service companies have only a weak commercial presence in Africa. Where they do exist, incumbent providers—often monopolies created or sanctioned by the government—have the upper hand in the market. This has adversely affected the rate of investment in, and the maintenance of, the transport infrastructure. The result is either incomplete (or nonexistent) transport connections or poor service quality where facilities do exist.

Where regulatory reform has taken hold, such as in South Africa, and there has been liberalization in the provision of such services, especially allowing for the entry of foreign vendors who have skilled personnel and more advanced technologies, competition has led to substantial improvements in service delivery. With the rise of global trade networks engendering a premium to countries that exhibit greater economic flexibility and mobility in international commerce, it is increasingly clear that such improvements are critical ingredients of a successful economic development and growth strategy. Not only would they help to facilitate trade, they would be trade creating themselves, such as in tourism; see chapter 6. Box 5.9 illustrates what is at stake in this regard for Mauritius.

Customs and Border Procedures

Inefficiency in most African countries' customs severely affects cross-border trade and investment between Africa and India and China. This finding was expressed by virtually all firms that were part of the business case studies. Customs in African countries faces a host of problems that include complicated and excessive documentary requirements; outdated official procedures; insufficient use of automated systems; a lack of transparency, predictability, and consistency in customs activities; and inadequate modernization of, and cooperation among, customs and other governmental agencies. Table 5.6 presents evidence on this score in the four countries in which the WBAATI survey and business case studies were conducted, as well as in China and India. Compared to exporting, importing overall takes much longer and incurs more procedures, both in terms of signatures and documents. The four African countries have efficient ports and customs relative to the Sub-Saharan African average. However, they are still less efficient than China.

According to Chinese and Indian firms covered by the business case studies, the problem of distance for landlocked African countries is com-

BOX 5.9

Promoting Competition in Air Transport Services in Mauritius

Protection of the air transport market has been justified on the basis that Air Mauritius provides an essential service to an island nation, because carriers making decisions on a purely commercial basis could decide to no longer serve the Mauritian market, cutting critical trade and transport links. As a high-end tourist destination, Mauritius believed it did not need to provide service to the low-cost mass transport market. Yet as the global tourism market has become more competitive, in part due to "open skies" policies in other destinations, there is increasing recognition that, in order to grow, the Mauritian tourism industry requires expanded capacity, new routes, and lower costs. Beyond benefits to the tourism sector, increasing air access to Mauritius would also enable greater competition in the air cargo sector, with benefits for Mauritian exporters in other sectors. Cost-effective air cargo is becoming increasingly important to the textiles sector, for example, where restructuring is requiring the industry to move into higher-end products for which rapid delivery is critical.

In balancing these factors, Mauritius has moved toward a policy of gradual liberalization, which involves selective opening of particular routes, including by third carriers (for example, Corsair from France to Mauritius, ComAir to South Africa); adoption of a more flexible approach to capacity increases for existing carriers; additional flights by existing carriers in peak seasons; and opening new markets, including direct flights from Spain and China, and special flights targeting markets in Central and Eastern Europe.

There is some evidence that the relatively modest increases in capacity to date have released pent-up demand. Year-on-year December growth in passenger arrivals was relatively steady at between 2,000 and 4,000 per year between 2000 and 2004. Introduction of further capacity in 2005 (via additional flights from Air Europe) saw arrivals in December 2005 increase by 13,000, or 16.3 percent, over the previous year, and increases in arrivals for 2006 to date of 15–18 percent over 2005. Price competition remains an issue on major routes served by two carriers. With around 80 percent of Mauritius' tourism taking the form of packages, the air component is considered to be higher than for competing routes (some tour operators claim that the UK-Mauritius route is around £200 (approximately $360) too high in comparison to the UK-Thailand route). Price competition is also not assisted by the presence on the Air Mauritius Board of airlines that ostensibly compete with Air Mauritius on its major routes—Air France, British Airways, and Air India. Introduction of third carriers (such as Corsair on the French route) is expected to assist in reducing prices.

While there appears to be a degree of consensus on gradual liberalization, disagreements persist over whether the emphasis should be on "gradual" or on "liberalization." In either case, some additional complementary measures are critical to its success.

- *Gradual liberalization requires ongoing monitoring and assessment of the sector* to ensure that the goals of increased capacity, lower prices, and greater connectivity are being met and to provide market participants with clear direction of policy in the sector. A well-resourced and expert—and independent—regulator is required. While the present policy consensus and the desire to group air transport and tourism under one roof have led to consideration of an Air Access Policy Unit under the Ministry of Tourism and External Communications, an independent regulator provides a greater degree of confidence to potential market entrants of a level playing field, particularly in view of the government's continuing share in Air Mauritius.

- *The requirement for Air Mauritius to operate in a more competitive environment* necessitates changes to its present governance structure to remove its competitors from the Board. One solution would be to create a holding company, under which competing airlines with a presence on the Board would be able to receive shareholder value but would be separated from strategic and operational aspects. While the presence of these airlines has in the past been argued to provide international credibility and reduce potential government interference, these goals may be better met by an independent regulator and quality management. Efforts by the new management of Air Mauritius to reduce costs and improve competitiveness should not be impeded by the governance structure and should be encouraged by a sufficient level of competition in the market.

(*Continues on the following page.*)

BOX 5.9 (continued)

- *Reforms to introduce a penalty for late (15 days or less) handing back of seats by tour operators* would also strengthen the ability of Air Mauritius to compete, including in the fast-growing market of last-minute online bookings made by individuals. Online bookings currently account for around 60 percent of the global market.

Source: World Bank 2006b.

pounded by the multiple regulatory environments through which cargo has to go. In addition, the crossing of the drivers and their vehicles is also subject to various cross-border regulations. Immigration services and vehicle inspection stations often do not allow for predictable and timely border crossings. For example, requirements for drivers to leave their vehicles and process visa papers slow down border crossing significantly. Adding to the delays are the manual processes for visa record keeping and issuance. Delays are often so significant that shippers are often forced to pass cargo on to local haulers, incurring additional cargo handling costs.

TABLE 5.6
Trade Facilitation Infrastructure and Institutions: High Transactions Costs

Region or country	Export			Import		
	Documents for export (number)	Signatures for export (number)	Time for export (days)	Documents for import (number)	Signatures for import (number)	Time for import (days)
Sub-Saharan Africa average	9	19	49	13	30	61
Ghana	6	11	47	13	13	55
Senegal	6	8	23	10	12	26
South Africa	5	7	31	9	9	34
Tanzania	7	10	30	13	16	51
East Asia and Pacific average	7	7	26	10	9	29
China	6	7	20	11	8	24
South Asia average	8	12	34	13	24	47
India	10	22	36	15	27	43

Source: World Bank Doing Business 2006.

Trade Finance

Poor access to trade finance also significantly increases nonmodal costs of trade and investment in African countries by Chinese and Indian firms. Many such firms—as well as African firms—report they do not have sufficient access to private trade finance or instruments to support their operations in Africa related to international trade and investment. However, some government agencies and financial institutions do make trade finance available.[18] Limited use of political risk insurance by Chinese and Indian investors in Africa—despite its availability—compounds the problem arising from poor access to trade finance; see box 5.10.

Three patterns of trade finance among firms operating in Africa are revealed from the WBAATI survey and business case studies; see box 5.11.

• First, informal trade credit is more common among micro and small firms. The pattern was particularly visible in the case of Senegal.

• Second, private external sources of finance are generally most used by larger firms. Letters of Credit are more expensive than supplier credit.

• Third, public assistance in export financing for their own companies operating in Africa is offered by the government of India and the government of China. Both governments provide export credits for working capital and acquisition of capital goods and machinery. Depending on the type of ownership, Chinese firms in Africa follow the same pattern of financial funding as those operating in China. The majority of the Chinese construction firms operating in Africa are state-owned enterprises (SOEs). Chinese SOEs receive funding from the Chinese financial system and from the Export-Import Bank of China, while Chinese private companies operating in Africa resort more to private or informal lending markets.

Domestically Provided Trade Finance in Africa

In general, access to finance among businesses in Africa is particularly limited among smaller firms, as noted in chapter 4. Extending financial services to SMEs and the rural sector, each of which could become effective drivers for overall trade expansion and economic growth in Africa, remains constrained. However, larger firms have access to credit from importers, the banking system, or other nonbank financial institutions. These firms

BOX 5.10

The Availability of Political Risk Insurance for Trade and Investment with Africa

The tendency to portray Africa in a less-than-favorable light is echoed in broadcast media, according to DFID research.[a] The steady stream of news about political instability in Africa—civil strife, contested elections, and so forth—often makes investors wary of political risk. With regard to Chinese firms in particular, in a 2005 FIAS/MIGA study of outward investment from China, 94 percent of the companies surveyed believed Africa to be the region of the world most beset by political risk.[b]

Political risk insurance is coverage intended to mitigate the perceived or demonstrated risk associated with a particular investment. It generally includes four types of coverage—transfer restriction; war and civil disturbance; expropriation; and breach of contract. While these political risks are considered "noncommercial" in nature, the line between political and commercial risks is increasingly blurred in today's business environment.

There are significant gaps in the private political and credit risk insurance market when it comes to the assumption of risk in cross-border transactions involving African countries. Political risk coverage from commercial sources or export credit agencies is not available at all for some African countries, and where coverage is available it is usually very costly and on unfavorable terms.

To address the problem resulting from the lack of political risk coverage, the Multilateral Investment Guarantee Agency (MIGA) of the World Bank

are able to provide trade credit to their suppliers (small suppliers), who in many cases do not have access to credit.

The ways in which firms operating in Africa secure financial sources varies with ownership, size of firm, and location on the continent. The WBAATI survey data indicate that use of formal bank credit is low among firms operating in Africa. For both working capital and investment pur-

Group provides guarantees to private investors investing in developing countries, including those in Africa. Since its inception, MIGA has issued more than 750 political risk guarantees worth $14 billion in coverage for projects around the developing world. Of this, 150 contracts totaling $1.64 billion in coverage have been issued in support of projects in Sub-Saharan Africa.

The Africa Trade Insurance Agency (ATI) was establish by African states in 2001, bringing together a growing group of countries that are willing to address the market's perception by setting up a credible insurance mechanism against losses caused by political risks. ATI provides a broad range of innovative and competitively priced insurance products and services customized to support African-related investments and trade transactions.

While OECD investors only occasionally use such coverage in selective circumstances, at least it is known to them, and, with varying skill and adroitness, they can effectively utilize it. This is not the case for Chinese and Indian investors, for whom there are several factors at work. While there are relatively new nationally funded programs of political risk investment insurance in both countries, they are not even well known to most national investors. National insurers and guarantors have not done an appreciable volume of business and thus often lack the experience to respond flexibly and swiftly to investor needs. Additionally, most Indian and Chinese companies are not well-known to private international insurance brokers. Hence the ability of these firms to access the private insurance market is limited.

Source: World Bank staff.

a. DFID 2000.
b. MIGA-FIAS forthcoming.

poses, surveyed firms use primarily retained earnings or other internal funds, across different nationalities. As shown in table 5.7, among firms surveyed, African firms are financing more of their working capital and new investments through the formal banking sector in Africa relative to Chinese or Indian firms, which is what would be expected. These survey findings are consistent with the data gathered in the business case studies.

BOX 5.11

Access to Trade Finance in Africa: Experiences of African, Chinese, and Indian Firms

Among firms covered by the WBAATI business case studies, experience in the use of trade finance is rather diverse.

African Firms. Many firms in Africa do not have access to finance or do not have the ability to choose from a variety of trade instruments. The availability of trade finance to African firms has implications for their supply sourcing. Firms decide where to acquire inputs depending on the financing terms to which they have access. In some instances, foreign suppliers offer better terms than local banks. Despite the fact that there are a series of short-term trade instruments and banking institutions that offer trade finance in South Africa, firms in the country on average still face higher costs due to the perceived greater risk. For example, a South African textile firm commented that it preferred to choose suppliers that offer them open accounts for 90 days. Mexico and Thailand request them to open a Letter of Credit, which is very costly.

Chinese Firms. Chinese construction firms operating in Africa received export credit for feasibility studies, government guarantees for bank loans, export credits for financing the operational cost of projects, and lines of credit for capital goods and machinery. In Tanzania, a Chinese construction firm reported that all its machinery needed for a construction project was acquired new. The firm's headquarters purchased the equipment. It also reported that it obtained 100 percent credit for its working capital needs from its parent company.

Indian Firms. An Indian firm reports on the use of supplier credit from India for 60 days.

Source: World Bank Group/ MIGA staff.

In the construction sector, for example, Chinese firms use African banks only to receive payments from host governments as part of their public procurement contracts, to receive money transfers from their headquarters, or to make payments to the workers—both local and expatriates.

TABLE 5.7

Average Share of Finance for Working Capital and New Investments Provided by Private Commercial Banks

(percent)

Element financed	Firm nationality				
	African	Chinese	Indian	European	Other
Working capital	14.0	9.6	11.3	12.4	8.2
New investments	20.0	8.0	17.0	15.0	20.5

Source: World Bank staff.

They do not use the local banking system for investment financing. Where Chinese and Indian firms operate in the retail sector or in the informal sector in Africa, they engage in mainly cash transactions and rely on informal channels for finance.

The share of working capital financed by trade credit is significantly smaller than formal banking sector loans and overdrafts. Among firms surveyed, only 3 percent of working capital is being financed through trade finance in the form of supplier or customer credit. When broken down by firm nationality, survey results show that Chinese and Indian firms finance less of their working capital through trade credit in comparison to African or European ones. The same pattern is evident for the financing of new investments (see table 5.8).

Chinese and Indian Government-Provided Trade Finance and Economic Assistance

The Chinese government, through the China Export-Import Bank, supports Chinese firms' investments and business operations in Africa. The scope of its activities includes provision of export credit (including export seller's credit and export buyer's credit); loans to overseas investment and

TABLE 5.8

Average Share of Working Capital and New Investments Composed of Trade Credit

(percent)

Element financed	Firm nationality					
	African	Chinese	Indian	European	Other	Overall
Working capital	3.0	0	2.3	5.2	2.9	3.0
New investments	1.8	0	0	0.6	0	1.2

Source: World Bank staff.

construction projects; Chinese government concessional loans; and international guarantees. The Chinese ExIm Bank is playing a significant role in promoting bilateral trade and economic assistance between China and Africa; see box 5.12. To take two examples, the ExIm Bank is supporting a major Chinese telecommunications investment in Nigeria. It also has extended a credit line to the Angolan government for the amount of $1 billion to assist the country in the rebuilding of infrastructure. As a part of the agreement, public tenders for the construction and civil engineering contracts are to be awarded primarily to Chinese state-owned enterprises approved by the Chinese government. The ExIm Bank has compiled a list of 35 Chinese firms approved by both the ExIm Bank and the Chinese government to tender in Angola.

Like its Chinese counterpart, India's Export-Import Bank plays a significant role in facilitating trade and investment between Indian and African countries. The Export-Import Bank of India launched a program called "Focus Africa" to increase interactions between the two regions by identifying priority areas for bilateral trade and investment.

The total operative Line of Credit (LOC) extended by India's Ex-Im Bank to Sub-Saharan African countries amounts to $558 million (table 5.9). The ExIm Bank extended an LOC of $250 million to the ECOWAS Bank for Investment and Development (EBID) in May 2006 to finance India's exports to the 15 member countries of EBID, namely Benin, Burkina Faso, Cape Verde, Côte d'Ivoire, The Gambia, Ghana, Guinea, Guinea-Bissau, Liberia, Mali, Niger, Nigeria, Senegal, Sierra Leone, and Togo. Another LOC was signed in 2005 between the ExIm Bank and the Eastern and Southern African Trade and Development Bank (PTA Bank) for a line of $5 million to promote India's exports to 16 Eastern and Southern African countries. This was the sixth LOC extended by the ExIm Bank to the PTA Bank.

Transfers of Technology and Skills

Formal Market Channels for Technology Transfers

There are several channels for technology transfer. These include purchasing of new equipment, transferring of nonproprietary technology, licensing, information from customers, knowledge from returning nationals, and domestic research. For firms in Sub-Saharan African countries, there is little scope for acquiring technology besides importing technology either by importing foreign technologies through licensing and imports of machinery and capital goods, or from foreign parent companies through their FDI; the latter is discussed in chapter 6.

Licensing of existing technologies, both rights to proprietary equipment and details about production processes, offers African countries opportunities for improving their levels of best practice. However, there is evidence that licensing is decreasing as an option for closing the technology gap. As shown in figure 5.3, the use of licensing technology as a channel for technology transfer is not very prevalent among firms in African countries. The most direct relation between trade and technology transfer lies in the direct imports of machinery goods.[19] Chapter 6 discusses the pattern of machinery imports among firms participating in the WBAATI survey.

Drivers Behind Transfers of Skills and Technology

We focus on two mechanisms that facilitate cross-border transfers of skills and technology: adherence to international technical standards and the movement of professionals.

Adherence to Standards as a Method for Technology Transfer

With most incremental improvements in products and processes, manufacturers follow existing industry production standards. This can lower production costs and facilitate the exchange of information (as discussed earlier). At the same time, an effort to meet foreign standards can trigger transfers of technology from overseas partners to firms operating in Africa. Evidence from the business case studies shows that when technical assistance is received by firms operating in Africa to meet technical standards required for them to export into higher positions in the value chain, the results are often positive. One example is an Indian-owned food processing firm in Tanzania (see box 5.13). Of course, simple importation of capital goods alone does not necessarily lead to an appropriate use of the machinery because it requires transfers of tacit knowledge. Nevertheless, it is difficult to learn new technologies through these mechanisms. The way that developing countries are learning new technologies more effectively is through their participation in the global production networks, as discussed in chapter 6.

BOX 5.12

Chinese Government-Sponsored Economic Support to Africa

The Chinese government began giving financial support to African countries in the 1970s. At the outset, the objectives of support were largely ideological in nature—to demonstrate China's "solidarity" with the developing world. With the advent of its economic reforms in 1978, China's government stepped up its aid to Africa and such assistance began to serve multiple purposes, including economic objectives. In the last several years the Chinese government has dramatically boosted its economic support to Africa. At the same time, the assistance has become both more sophisticated, in terms of instruments utilized, and more geographically diverse.

In the 1980s, China's government provided much of its economic aid in-kind—in the form of building large non-commercially oriented projects, such as sports stadiums and government office buildings, such as those in The Gambia and Sierra Leone, among other countries. In the 1990s, support began to shift from in-kind to grants. Today, the provision of in-kind and grant support is a decreasing proportion of China's aid to Africa, with loans accounting for the vast majority of Chinese government-sponsored African assistance.

China's Export-Import Bank, which was established in 1994 as a state policy-bank directly under the leadership of the State Council (China's "Cabinet"), is the sole state-owned entity the Chinese government uses to dispense official economic aid worldwide, including to Africa. The Ex-Im Bank indicates it provides not only "concessional" loans—akin to those provided by the multilateral aid institutions, such as the World Bank or the African Development Bank—but also "non-concessional" loans—support given on terms that are more in line with commercial lending. The Ex-Im Bank also provides export credits; international guarantees; on-lending of foreign governments and financial institutions; and other functions.

Data on the precise nature and extent of the Chinese government's aid to Africa—including loan duration and interest charges—are not generally available. The last officially reported flows are for 2002. For that year, China's government reported that it provided $1.8 billion in economic support to all of Africa (that is, support pertaining to countries on the African continent regardless of whether or not they are Sub-Saharan). Although a systematic breakdown of how much of this support was in the form of concessional versus non-concessional loans is not known, it is generally believed, based on anecdotal evidence, the bulk was in the form of non-concessional loans.

The recent explosion of China's official economic support to Africa has been largely in the form loans by the Ex-Im Bank. The Ex-Im Bank indicates that, as in earlier years, most of these loans are made on non-concessional rather than concessional terms (although the specifics of the terms are not disclosed). The Ex-Im Bank reports that as of end-2005, its concessional loans to the African continent covers 55 projects in 22 countries, with an accumulated commitment of $800 million. China is also using debt relief to assist African nations, effectively turning loans into grants. Since 2000, Beijing has taken significant steps to cancel the debt of 31 African countries. That year China wrote off $1.2 billion in African debt; in 2003, it forgave another $750 million. Beijing's new "China's Africa Policy" white paper, released in early 2006 foresees more debt relief as part of the country's economic assistance strategy with the continent (see chapter 3).

Preliminary estimates compiled from public sources by World Bank staff suggest that *total* China Ex-Im Bank loans to Sub-Saharan Africa—that is, non-concessional *as well as* concessional loans—amounts to over $12.5 billion as of mid-2006 in the *infrastructure* sector. These loans finance projects in the power, telecom, transport, water and sewerage sectors, but exclude projects in the petroleum and mining sectors. These loans are highly concentrated in five countries: Angola, Nigeria, Mozambique, Sudan and Zimbabwe, which account for over 80% of the total. Moreover, support to the power sector makes up about 40% of total commitments, followed by "general" or multiple sector commitments (24%), transport (20%), telecom (12%), and lastly water (4%). However, without knowing what proportion of these loans is made on concessional versus non-concessional terms, let alone the duration and interest rates for these loans, it is difficult to compare meaningfully these China Ex-Im Bank financing commitments to Sub-Saharan Africa's infrastructure to more traditional forms of such aid. Overseas Development Assistance (ODA) from OECD countries to Sub-Saharan Africa's infrastructure—which generally is made on concessional terms—amounted to just over $4 billion in 2004, the most recent date for which data are available.

Sources: World Bank staff estimates, China Export-Import Bank website and Eisenman and Kurlantzick (2006).

TABLE 5.9
Export-Import Bank of India—Operating Lines of Credit in Africa

Country or institution	Amount (millions)
Burkina Faso	31.0
Côte d'Ivoire	26.8
Gambia, The	6.7
Ghana	15.0; 27.0; 60.0 (3 LOC)
Senegal	15.0; 17.8; 27.0 (3 LOC)
Mali	27.0
Mali and Senegal	27.7
Niger	17.0
West African Development Bank (BOAD)	10.0
ECOWAS Bank for Investment and Development (EBID)S	250.0
Total amount operative LOC	558.0

Source: Export-Import Bank of India.

Skills Transfer Through the Migration of Professionals

Migration of professionals or diasporas can be effective resources for skills transfers. For a sending country, diaspora can be an important source as well as a facilitator of research and innovation, technology transfer, and skills development. Technology transfer through migration can take several forms. Those include (i) licensing agreements to provide transfers of technology and know-how between diaspora-owned or managed firms in host countries and firms in sending countries; (ii) knowledge spillovers when diaspora

FIGURE 5.3
Imperfections in the Market for Information: High Transactions Costs

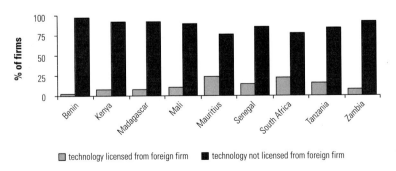

Usage of licensed technology

□ technology licensed from foreign firm   ■ technology not licensed from foreign firm

Source: World Bank Investment Climate Assessments.

BOX 5.13

Foreign Firms in Africa Use International Standards to Boost Higher-Value Exports from the Continent

An Indian-owned firm in Tanzania decided to export organic cashew nuts as a new product. The company made the necessary investments in processes to comply with the requirements of food quality and safety standards for organic cashew nuts. For organic products, informational requirements are high, and standards help to reduce the information costs to produce goods that require more sophisticated technology such as the production of organic food products.

The process of gathering information is costly for this type of firm in Africa. Firms trying to export to China, Europe, and India have to research technical specifications and preferences that prevail in those countries. To get information on how to establish a new organic product line, this firm contacted its machinery supplier, who provided the firm with all the required standards to establish it. A Swiss company has helped the firm to implement the process and provided technical assistance.

In addition, the firm is finalizing the setting of the new process line to produce this organic cashew nut, following the standards of the buyer as well. Thus, the firm complements the information on production standards from the supplier of the machinery with the additional health and safety standards from the buyers.

Source: World Bank staff.

members assume top managerial positions in firms in their countries of origin; (iii) networks of scientists or professionals to promote research in host countries directed toward the needs of sending countries; (v) virtual return, through extended visits or electronic communications in professional fields such as medicine and engineering; and (vi) return to permanent employment in the sending country after work experience in the host country.

The functioning of the Indian diaspora is a clear example of how skills transfers have come about in that country's software sector. Table 5.10 summarizes various stages of growth in the information technology (IT)

TABLE 5.10
Evolving Roles of the Indian Diaspora

Stage of growth	Characterization of the stage of growth of IT industries	Role of diaspora
1970s	Building a foundation for "first movers" Key role for the very few entrepreneurs who created initial entrepreneurial projects (both within established and new firms)	Exposure of Indian talent to U.S. firms. Executives of Indian origin start to outsource through "body shopping" contracts.
1980s	Emergence of a software cluster in Bangalore and a critical mass of professional entrepreneurs	Continuation of business linkages and "body shopping" contracts.
1990s	Emergence of high value-added outsourcing (R&D and consulting)	Diaspora is engaged in a concerted effort to promote an image of India as an attractive outsourcing location. Diaspora firms provide the specifications for the software to be manufactured as well as a market for the products.
Present day	Emergence of knowledge-process outsourcing	Highly placed executives of Indian origin pioneer knowledge-intensive outsourcing (R&D and professional services).

Source: Pandey et al. 2004.

industry in India, and the role the diaspora played in its evolution. A group as small as 200 professionals can provide reliable business and technologies linkages with the rest of the world. Replication of successful experiences in smaller countries will be more difficult, however, because they may be unable to reach a critical mass of influential people in any given sector (for example, medicine, engineering, large corporations, and so forth).

However, migration in the form of foreign investors' hiring of workers from their home countries may slow down the transfer of technology in the host country. As more skilled workers are transferred to host countries, foreign investors operating there have diminished incentives to be engaged in skills and technology transfers to local businesses or employees through either subcontracts or hiring (see box 5.14).

Chinese Bilateral Initiatives for Technology Transfers to Africa

The China-Africa Cooperation Forum was established in 2000 as a framework for dialogue between China and African countries. During the First China-Africa Cooperation Forum in Beijing (October 2000), the forum established a series of long-term economic partnerships in the fields of agriculture, light industry, infrastructure construction, and information technology. In January 2006 the Chinese government issued an official white paper on "China's Africa Policy", calling for further strengthening of the traditionally friendly relations between the continent and China (see chapter 3). Among other areas, the white paper highlights the possibilities for deeper bilateral cooperation in technical knowledge for development. In this regard, the current focus of China is to encourage the use of an appropriate level of technology to be transferred to Africa. Their cooperation programs include (i) forming joint commissions on issues of economy, trade, and science and technology between China and Africa; (ii) providing technology training in agriculture and processing sectors; (iii) sending experts, teachers, and technologists to African countries; and (iv) bringing experience in telecoms, road construction, and power networks to African countries, such as supporting an electricity modernization program in Kenya.

There are a number of important initiatives by China in the human resources development area in Africa as well. For example, China has offered 1,500 scholarships to African students, providing them opportunities to gain skills and knowledge from Chinese universities. China's African Human Resources Development Fund has sponsored a variety of training courses geared to African professionals and has trained nearly 7,000 African personnel in different areas. The country also provides seminars and training classes given by senior African diplomats and economic and financial officials.

Indian Bilateral Initiatives in Technical Cooperation with Africa

India and Africa have an old relationship that is in the process of being given a new focus by closer collaboration in the areas of technology, trade, and training. There are a series of Indian initiatives to enhance economic and political cooperation with Africa. India has announced an LOC of $200 million to assist the New Partnership for Africa's Development (NEPAD). Mali, Niger, Senegal, and the Democratic Republic of Congo have received project funds under this initiative.[20] The Indian government has also extended a $500 million LOC for TEAM-9, a new initiative for a group of Francophone countries of West Africa including Burkina Faso, Chad, Côte d'Ivoire, Equatorial Guinea, Ghana, Guinea Bissau, Mali, and Senegal.

In 2005, India became the first Asian country to become a full member of the Africa Capacity Building Foundation. Indian engineers, doctors, accountants, and teachers are present in Africa. India is actively engaged in Africa's telecommunications, IT, and development of transport infrastruc-

BOX 5.14

Construction and Engineering Services and Foreign Workers: China in Africa

The construction industry comprises design services (architects and engineers), construction services (general and subcontractors, skilled and unskilled labor), and consulting services related to the others (including management and training personnel). One factor that makes firms competitive in the industry is related to the availability of low-cost professional staff rather than unskilled manual labor. In addition, government support is an important factor in cost competitiveness abroad. It seems that this is the strategy of China in exporting construction services to Africa. Foreign companies offering services in construction and engineering may face some nontrade barriers. Restrictions on Mode IV are one of the barriers in the construction sector in Africa.

In China, state-owned enterprises (SOEs) and construction collectives (run by local governments or communities in urban and rural areas) are the main providers of construction work. Prior to 1984, most SOEs were general construction companies, carrying out all of the trades needed for construction work. These were huge organizations with a permanent workforce with fixed-worker status. Several of these SOEs are now exporting construction services to other parts of the world, including Africa.

Chinese firms are operating mainly in the physical construction services sector in Africa. They participate in road construction, water and sewerage, and construction of government buildings and bridges. In the WAATI business case studies, the majority of the professional staff of Chinese construction firms were from China. Companies explained that managers

ture (see box 5.15). It is also exploring possible collaboration in biotechnology.

India is also involved in a number of significant initiatives in human resources development in Africa. For example, more than 1,000 officials from Sub-Saharan Africa receive training annually in India under the

needed to communicate effectively with workers about complex tasks in Chinese. However, the vast majority of nonskilled labor is Africans.

Chinese firms subcontract services to local firms. This provides opportunities for acquisition of experience and access to technology for developing country firms. However, African firms are not equally benefiting from acquisition of experience and access to technology through subcontracting. In the case of Angola, Chinese firms import all materials, technology, and staff from China, partly due to the high cost of local materials and lack of skilled labor. This results in little skill being transferred. A Chinese firm in Senegal only uses nominal local content in subcontracting services. For example, they subcontract drawings but not engineering services such as structural engineering, which provides opportunities for acquisition of experience and technology. In Tanzania, construction methods employed by Chinese firms are becoming more sophisticated. There are 14 Chinese firms registered in the country. The majority of the materials are procured locally and suppliers across the construction industry are increasingly using Chinese fittings and materials. The transfer of skills, technology, and work practices to Tanzanians and subcontractors is increasing as Chinese firms use new construction methods in the country.

Greater regional and global integration could also alleviate some of the constraints of the small African countries' services sector due to its limited endowments of capital and skills. In addition, weaknesses in the business environment are hampering the development of services in Africa. Several of these countries can export more services if they improve their business climate, infrastructure, and complementary services.

Source: World Bank staff.

Indian Technical and Economic Cooperation Program. India spent more than $1 billion on such assistance, including training, deputation of experts, and implementation of projects. Over 15,000 African students study in India. Seminars and training classes are given to senior African diplomats and economic and financial officials.

BOX 5.15

India's Contribution to the Pan-African E-network Project

Ethiopia has been selected as the first country to benefit from the pilot phase of the Pan-African E-network Project, a joint initiative between the Indian government and the African Union to develop ICT infrastructure across the continent. Under the initiative, the Indian government will donate $1 billion to connect 53 African countries through satellite and fiber optic networks to promote telemedicine and tele-education programs. The project is at "an advanced stage of implementation" in Ethiopia, and South Africa, Mauritius, and Ghana have also been short-listed for the pilot phase. The e-network initiative is being heralded by the local press as the largest infrastructure project in Africa's history, and the e-education and e-medicine programs are particularly expected to extend ICT infrastructure to certain rural communities and underserved areas. This announcement came during the recent "International Conference on ICT for Development, Education, and Training" in Addis Ababa, Ethiopia, and follows a major India-Africa trade summit in Accra, Ghana, dubbed the "Making India a Partner of Choice" meeting.

Source: The Observatory on Borderless Higher Education http://www.obhe.ac.uk/cgi-bin/news/article.pl?id=561

Conclusions and Policy Implications

Summary of Findings

This chapter assessed various between-the-border factors that facilitate trade and investment, particularly in the context of Africa's trade and investment ties with China and India. First, foreign market information on potential demand and investment opportunities is essential in facilitating trade and investment. Given the imperfect information flows now in existence for trade and investment with African countries, public information services, run by both the government or by private firms, have proven to be very important. While they also may work as a barrier to trade (chapter 3), standards and accreditation schemes may also reduce difficulties in assessing the quality of a product by enhancing the availability of reliable, accessible information on aspects considered important by exporters, importers, and consumers. Also, although they run the danger of restricting domestic competition by segmenting markets (chapter 4), ethnic networks that operate across national borders can help overcome between-the-border barriers by providing efficient circulation of market information within the networks that link African countries and India and China.

Also presented was how flows of technology and people between Africa and Asia facilitate the formation of business links that lead to trade and FDI flows, and how the latter two enhance technology transfers and migration simultaneously. The WBAATI survey as well as business case studies clearly suggest such two-way links in the context of China and India's trade and investment ties with African countries. For example, Chinese investors operating in Africa tend to bring their workforce from China. Also, exporting firms tend to rely more on foreign workers, whose skills and knowledge help firms to link themselves with overseas markets. The complementary relationship among people flows, trade, and capital flows suggests that any removal of between-the-border barriers should facilitate all of these flows. Increases in these three flows are likely to accelerate the pace of technological diffusion throughout Africa and Asia.

However, local technological transfer or skills transfer is also somewhat compromised when foreign skilled workers are simply brought in with foreign capital without effective skills transfer to local workers either through subcontracts or employment opportunities. Furthermore, the emerging agenda for African firms is how to effectively capture opportunities for acquisition of technology and skills through participating in the international production network as discussed in chapter 6. At the same time, this chapter also showed how Chinese and Indian governments have increasingly invested their resources in providing technical cooperation to African countries to foster technological transfer to African countries.

The ability to enhance trade facilitation could offer significant opportunities to reduce direct and indirect costs in Africa. African, Chinese, and Indian firms have been hampered by inadequate and costly transport and logistics services in Africa. African firms continue to experience difficulty in accessing necessary trade financing tools, which is a particularly acute issue among small and medium enterprises. At the same time, it was found that investment by Chinese and Indian firms in Africa has been significantly aided by public trade finance programs by the Export-Import Banks of those two countries.

Policy Implications

The WBAATI business case studies suggest that one area of emphasis in improving trade facilitation should be dealing with customs and reduction of transport costs. Many government departments are involved in trade facilitation processes. For example, improving coordination among institutions to better link trade and transport initiatives, both within and across countries, will facilitate harmonization of customs reforms. Furthermore, implementation of already-agreed decisions on regional trade (particularly on documents requirements and implementation of regional transit systems) will reduce the delays and the unpredictable application of rules across borders.

African countries face significant constraints to trade facilitation stemming from their market size, the situation of their landlocked countries, and their lack of financial and capacity resources to reduce direct and indirect costs. Hence, considering alternative solutions—such as adopting a regional approach to trade-related infrastructure investments, and requesting technical assistance from donors on these issues—is worthwhile. Without significant support from national governments, international organizations, and donors in resources, technology, and capacity building, no accomplishments can be made in trade facilitation. It is quite clear from the experience of developed countries, India, and China, that capacity building is essential for streamlining various processes and institutional mechanisms. It is important that each of the African countries work out a comprehensive strategy on trade facilitation for a more focused, coordinated, and well-resourced approach. Regional cooperation between Africa and Asia may also play an important role.

In the emerging structure of global production systems, participating in the production network, building forward and backward linkages of foreign capital and technology, and expanding the area of services are increasingly relevant for Africa. Technology diffuses in the receiving country mainly through the purchase of new equipment, direct foreign investment, the transfer of nonproprietary technology, licensing, information from customers, knowledge from returning nationals, and domestic research. Thus, African countries should emphasize Mode III and Mode IV when they liberalize their services sectors.

Given the suspension of the Doha Round WTO negotiations, apart from bilateral efforts to promote Mode IV in liberalizing trade in services, African countries should encourage unilateral reforms to trade in services. India is a good example of a successful technology transfer in services. IT services and telecommunications were among the sectors that were the most liberalized in the 1990s. A liberal regulatory and policy framework encouraged investment by multinationals and temporary movement of skilled labor. These people flows enabled technology transfers. However, services reforms are complex and resource-intensive. Experience in services liberalization around the world suggests that the design of efficient regulation that could allow foreign providers to access the market while maintaining a competitive environment in which public policy objectives are enforced is key to success.

The WBAATI business case studies showed in very concrete terms how Chinese networks living in Africa help to overcome between-the-border barriers in doing business with China. Ethnic networks promote bilateral trade and investment by providing market information and by supplying matching and referral services. Equally, the transfer of knowledge and experiences transmitted by the African diaspora living in Europe and Asia has improved export opportunities and increased information to new markets. Following the experiences of Taiwan, India, and Ireland, actions should be taken to foster further interactions between African diaspora and professionals in the home country. For example, a combination of Internet-based and relationship-based networks should be developed and linkages with the Chinese and Indian diaspora should be established to serve as bridges for doing business.

Annex 5A

For more than a decade, the World Bank Group's Multilateral Investment Guarantee Agency (MIGA) has offered free online services to give investment promotion intermediaries a platform to effectively disseminate information on investment opportunities and to market their respective locations. The objective has been to provide information on investment opportunities and facilitate investment flows in emerging markets.[21] MIGA's online information dissemination services provide an interesting snapshot of the supply side of the FDI-information market. In terms of the number of FDI-information resources supplied through MIGA's online services, Sub-Saharan Africa is well represented compared to other regions. Out of nearly 8,400 investment-related information resources contained in the online services, 22 percent refer to Sub-Saharan Africa. Of the 55 national and provincial investment promotion agencies listed for Sub-Saharan Africa in MIGA's directories, 21 agencies supply content to the online services. South Africa, Tanzania, and Ghana appear consistently among the top countries in Sub-Saharan Africa in terms of the number of investment information resources available under each of the four subjects (legal, markets, business, opportunity). Also, South Africa tends to feature more prominently than the other countries.

An analysis of the number of users by region shows a very significant increase in the number of registered users based in East Asia, South East Asia, and South Asia who have selected Sub-Saharan Africa as a region of interest for investment. Sub-Saharan Africa ranks second to Latin America and the Caribbean in terms of generating the most interest from Asian users (see figure 5A.1). Specifically, the number of FDI Xchange registered users who have selected Sub-Saharan Africa as a region of interest has increased 20 times during the period between June 2002, when the service was first launched, and December 2005.

The snapshot of investment information that is contained in MIGA's online services suggests that Sub-Saharan Africa overall is well represented. However, the "on-average" good picture of the continent hides significant asymmetries across countries in terms of investment information availability. Important gaps in the availability of information for many countries in Sub-Saharan Africa still exist. It should be noted that this analysis only points to a snapshot of the *quantity* of documents available in MIGA's online services database. Only a third of the investment promotion

FIGURE 5A.1
Demand for FDI Information on Sub-Saharan Africa by Region

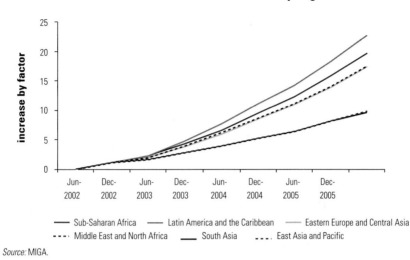

Source: MIGA.

agencies from the continent listed on MIGA's online services supply content directly. These issues indicate the need to improve not only the quantity but also the quality of information resources focused on investor demands.[22] On the demand side, the evidence based on users' interests strongly suggests growing attention to Sub-Saharan Africa by potential investors from Asia.

Endnotes

1. Lederman, Olarreaga, and Payton 2006.
2. UNIDO 2006.
3. UNCTAD 2006b.
4. See the Web site of the Ministry of Foreign Trade and Economic Cooperation of China. There is also a center in Egypt. (www.cofortune.com/cn/moftec_cn/tzkfzx/tzkf_menu.html).
5. This was second in the conclave series organized by the Confederation of Indian Industry. The first one was held in March 2005. About 178 projects were discussed and 12 Memoranda of Understanding were signed. Regional mini-conclaves were held in 2006, including one in Lusaka, Zambia (April 2006), targeting Southern African countries, and another in Accra, Ghana (May 2006), targeting Western and Central African countries.
6. World Bank Global Technical Barrier to Trade Survey.

7. Rauch 2001; Gould 1994; and Rauch and Casella 1998.

8. See http://indiandiaspora.nic.in/contents.htm.

9. Wei 2004. A recent strand in the literature emphasizes that trade and migration might appear as complements as opposed to substitutes (Gould 1990, 1994). Rauch (2003) and Rauch and Trindade (2002) also find that trade and migration are complements.

10. Eisenman and Kurlantzick 2006.

11. When FTAs are formed among developing countries or between developed and developing countries, they have generally limited their coverage to temporary location of skilled workers, if any, as illustrated in the case of the Chile and the Singapore agreement with the United States.

12. Announcing this at a meeting organized by the Southern Indian Chamber of Commerce and Industry, South African High Commissioner to India Francis Moloi said orders in this regard were issued in July 2006. He said South Africa must re-examine its visa regulations, particularly in the context of forging closer ties and trade and business between the two countries. http://www.the-hindu.com/2006/07/11/stories/2006071107960500.htm.

13. See Roy and Bagai (2005).

14. See Walkenhorst and Yasui (2003); Cudmore and Whalley (2004); Wilson, Luo, and Broadman (2006); Djankov, Freund, and Pham (2006); Soloaga, Wilon, and Mejia (2006).

15. Naude, Gilroy, and Gries 2005.

16. Naude, Gilroy, and Gries 2005.

17. Amjadi and Yeats 1985.

18. Based on the World Bank Investment Climate Assessments, trade finance programs are most effectively facilitating manufactured exports among African firms, compared to other export incentive schemes African governments extend to firms such as duty drawback, bonded warehouse, and VAT exemption programs. See Yoshino (2006).

19. Eaton and Kortum (2001) and Navaretti and Soloaga (2001).

20. "India, Africa ready to embrace global destiny." An Article by Minister of State for External Affairs Rao Inderjit Singh. In http://meaindia.nic.in/ interview/2006/01/25in01.htm. January 25, 2006.

21. MIGA's online services for foreign investors comprise IPAnet, Privatization-Link, and FDI Xchange. When MIGA launched IPAnet in 1995, it was considered a pioneer in the use of the Internet for disseminating information on investment opportunities and the business environment in developing countries. Subsequently, MIGA diversified its information services by launching PrivatizationLink (1998), FDI Xchange (2002), and the FDI Promotion Center (2004).

22. Although a recent evaluation of MIGA indicated that the services appeared to be providing reliable, accurate, timely, and current information, in Africa there is a quality deficit. Independent Evaluation Group-MIGA 2006 Annual Report.

CHAPTER 6
_____

Investment-Trade Linkages in African-Asian Commerce: Scale, Integration, and Production Networks

Introduction

The increasing globalization of the world economy and the fragmentation of production processes have changed the economic landscape facing the nations, industries, and individual firms in Sub-Saharan Africa, as they have in China and India—indeed, throughout much of the rest of the world. Firms engaging in trade of intermediate goods (or services) through foreign direct investment (FDI) (or through subcontracting) have been key agents in this transformation. Exploiting the complementarities between FDI and trade, they have created international production and distribution networks spanning the globe and actively interacting with each other. Technological advances in information, logistics, and production have enabled multinational corporations to divide value chains into functions performed by foreign subsidiaries or suppliers. The availability of real-time supply-chain data has allowed for shipping large distances not only durable goods, but also components for just-in-time manufacturing and—important for developing countries such as in Africa—perishable goods. The result has been the rapid growth of *intraindustry* trade—"network trade"—relative to the more traditional *interindustry* trade of final goods and services.

One manifestation of the rise in network trade is the increasing expansion of production "downstream" into finished or semifinished products, where greater value can be extracted, as compared with the "upstream" production of raw materials alone. Many of the countries in the world that have grown rapidly in the last 15 years, especially Asian countries, including China and India, have done so through such integration and the exploitation of the associated economies of scale and scope. They have moved progressively from production and trade in labor-intensive, low-value-added products (for example, unprocessed agricultural products and primary commodities, such as cotton) to production and trade in higher stages of the value chain, that is, capital-intensive, high-value-added products (automotive parts, for example). Even many "transition countries" in the former Soviet Union, making the jump from central planning to capitalism, have recognized that, to take advantage of globalization and foster economic growth through international trade, it is increasingly important for their firms to reap the benefits of scale economies and have access to and be integrated within international production networks.[1]

This chapter shows that to date the participation of most African countries in network trade centered around or linked to large foreign investors—not only those from China and India, but also multinational firms from elsewhere, including the most advanced economies—has been very limited. As discussed earlier in this study, oil still dominates exports from Sub-Saharan Africa, together with primary agricultural commodities and minerals, such as platinum and diamonds. There are notable exceptions, however. African network trade is being carried out in food, apparel, and automotive assembly and parts, the latter largely concentrated in South Africa. Another is horticulture, especially fresh-cut flowers. All are exported to international markets where the competition is much tougher than in the export of traditional, raw commodities, and standards are world-class.

Yet outside of these relatively few products, there is little trade in intermediate goods, let alone clear signs of major participation in coordinated global value chains. Exports of Sub-Saharan African firms hardly figure into Chinese or Indian markets, let alone the United States, the European Union (EU), or Japan. For example, there are no African countries represented in the top 25 apparel exporters to either the United States or the EU. In fact, in both Europe and America, African producers have seen growing competition from Asia—especially China, India, and Bangladesh—even after taking into account the preferential trading agreements, Cotonou Agreement and African Growth and Opportunity Act (AGOA), that African firms enjoy.[2] The same picture emerges when considering the world's main exporters of automotive parts. The only Sub-Saharan African country represented in the top 50 exporters is South Africa.

The analysis in this chapter suggests that if African countries want to move up in the value chain and increase overall value-added, they will have to diversify their exports, move out of traditional primary commodities into manufactured goods and services, and become part of global production networks. To this end, the mounting commercial interest in Africa by China and India creates an important "South-South" opening for Africa to take these steps and create new high-value export opportunities. Both Asian giants, China and India, have a growing middle class with increasing purchasing power and with an increasing appetite for imported goods.[3] This means that China and India are not just big *potential* markets for higher value-added goods and services from Africa, but *real opportunities*, especially compared with Africa's traditional export markets in the "North." For example, China's imports as a percentage of GDP are more than 25 percent, while for the United States, EU, and Japan they are only 15 percent, 14 percent, and 11 percent, respectively.

Using new firm-level data from both the World Bank Africa Asia Trade Investment (WBAATI) survey and the World Bank's newly developed business case studies of Chinese and Indian firms in Africa, this chapter details empirically the ways in which these businesses operate in Africa, with a focus on the linkages between their investment and trade activities.[4] The chapter also examines where opportunities for network trade might exist in Sub-Saharan Africa by assessing the characteristics of select country-level industry value chains in Africa and comparing their performance with that of direct international competitors. The analysis suggests that in the short-run such network trade opportunities are likely to remain concentrated in only a select group of relatively labor-intensive products and services, such as food, horticulture, apparel, and tourism, with the South African automotive assembly and parts sector standing out as an exception, where network trade is more capital- and skilled-labor intensive. Only in the medium- to the longer-run, with significantly more investment—not only from foreign but also domestic sources—as well as implementation of structural and institutional reforms that facilitate infrastructure development and regional integration, will it be likely that African producers are able to effectively enter global value chains in capital- and skilled-labor-intensive products beyond what already exists in South Africa's automotive sector.

In addition, and equally important from the perspective of furthering economic development and growth *within* Africa, the chapter examines how the linkages between FDI and trade among Chinese and Indian firms involved in Africa create the possibility for positive "spillovers" on the continent—through the attraction of investment for infrastructure and related services development and through the transfer of advances in technology and managerial skills, which are often the intangible assets that accompany FDI.

If the African continent is to effectively take advantage of the opportunities afforded by China's, India's, and other economies' already sizable and growing commercial interest in Africa, it will have to successfully leverage this newfound interest and be a more proactive player in global network trade. This calls for African leaders to pursue certain policy reforms. To this end, the last section of the chapter posits that, as is the case elsewhere in the world, African countries' differential performance in terms of network trade can be attributed to the large variation in the amount of FDI received across the continent (whether considering oil-producing countries or not). The analysis suggests that the FDI inflow differentials observed across African countries are largely determined not only by traditional macropolitical and macroeconomic factors, but by the quality of the *underlying* domestic business climate and related institutional conditions, both within individual countries and on a regional basis. Thus, the focus of the policy implications at the close of the chapter is on a set of factors that shape a country's microeconomic fabric at a deeper level beyond that touched by the reform of so-called administrative barriers—such as speeding up the pace of business registration or of obtaining a business license—which has become the conventional wisdom as the way in which improvement in the investment climate comes about.

Determinants of Linkages Between Trade and Foreign Direct Investment

Trade-FDI Integration in the Global Context

Complementarities Between Investment and Trade
Although traditional economic theory often assumes that firms choose between either supplying a foreign market through exports or establishing production facilities in a host country, the overwhelming bulk of empirical

evidence in regions worldwide broadly suggests the opposite. Although there clearly are cases of "tariff-jumping" FDI,[5] most empirical studies at the aggregate country or industry level find that increases in FDI tend to be positively correlated with a rise in exports; chapter 2 provides such evidence in the case of both African and Asian countries.[6] Similarly, most firm-level empirical studies also point to the complementary effects between FDI and exports, a finding that is also corroborated in the case of Asian investors in Africa below.

Indeed, even a decade ago the *World Investment Report* stated

> . . . the issue is no longer whether trade leads to FDI or FDI to trade; whether FDI substitutes for trade or trade substitutes for FDI; or whether they complement each other. Rather it is: how do firms access resources—wherever they are located—in the interest of organizing production as profitably as possible for the national, regional or global markets they wish to serve? In other words, the issue becomes: where do firms locate their value added activities? . . . increasingly, what matters are the factors that make particular locations advantageous for particular activities, for both domestic and foreign investors.[7]

The increasing complementarity between FDI and trade throughout the world marketplace has been the result of the growing fragmentation of production, combined with the creation of distribution networks spanning across continents. The information revolution and new technologies have made it possible to divide an industry's value chain into smaller functions that are performed by foreign subsidiaries or are contracted out to independent suppliers. This global diffusion of productive activity has led to increased international trade in both final goods and parts and components. Thus, it comes as no surprise that about one-third of world trade consists of intrafirm trade (that is, international trade among constituent entities within a single corporation), and the importance of intrafirm trade has been growing over time. Estimates also suggest that about two-thirds of world trade today involves multinational corporations in one way or another, whether intrafirm trade or arms-length transactions in intermediate goods. In fact, intermediate goods trade has risen more rapidly than trade in final goods.[8]

The result has been that, although producers from developing economies may not possess the intangible assets or services infrastructure developed at a level sufficient to have a competitive advantage in the manufacturing of final goods, thanks to production fragmentation, they may be able to join the production chain by specializing in the labor-intensive fragment of the manufacturing process.[9] Thus, production fragmentation not only enables firms from developing countries to access foreign markets without large outlays on advertising and market research, but it also may lead to an additional benefit in the form of knowledge spillovers, which will be discussed later in the chapter.

Fragmentation of production also offers a unique opportunity for producers in developing countries to move from servicing small local markets to supplying large multinational firms and, indirectly, their customers all over the world. This phenomenon is accompanied by an evolution in the nature of competition, with a growing emphasis on customization of products, rapid innovation, flexibility, and fast response to changes in demand. In many cases, the managerial and technological skills required to successfully compete in global markets make it impossible to rely on the resources of one country. Under these circumstances, integration into the production and marketing arrangements of multinational corporations, rather than the pursuit of an autarchic national development strategy, has become the most efficient way of taking advantage of growth opportunities offered by the global economy.

However, fragmentation of production also means that foreign investors have become more sensitive to changes in the investment climate. In some cases, multinational corporations can relatively easily shift their production from one geographic location to another in response to changes in the cost of production, market access, regulatory conditions, or perceived risks. Noteworthy to developing countries, such as in Sub-Saharan Africa, relocation is easier to accomplish in labor-intensive industries, where low capital investments are required and thus disinvestment does not represent a large loss for the investor; the ability to shift production tends to diminish with the technological intensity of exports. The difference in the extent of footlooseness is clearly visible when distinguishing between the different types of production and distribution networks, an issue to which we now turn.

Rise of Buyer-Driven and Producer-Driven Global Networks

International production and distribution networks, also known as global commodity chains, refer to production systems that are dispersed and integrated on a worldwide basis. Typically, four main dimensions of such chains are identified: their internal governance structure, their input-output structure, the territory that they cover, and the institutional framework that identifies how local, national, and international conditions and policies shape the process at each stage. In terms of internal governance structures, it has become customary to distinguish between "buyer-" and "producer-driven" global networks or commodity chains.[10]

Buyer-driven networks are usually built without direct ownership and tend to exist in industries in which large retailers, branded marketers, and branded manufacturers play the central role in chain organization. Buyer-driven commodity chains are characterized by highly competitive, locally owned, and globally dispersed production systems. Profits do not come from scale, volume, and technological advantage, but rather from market research, design, and marketing. The products are designed and marketed by the buyer and are typically labor-intensive consumer goods, such as apparel, footwear, and furniture.

However, there are successful cases of natural resource–based industries successfully entering into buyer-driven networks. One such example especially applicable to Africa because it is landlocked, poor, and small, is Armenia; it has been very effective in selling its diamonds through the global value chain.[11] In fact, there are reasons to believe that Africa can effectively build on its endowment of natural resources, enhance export competitiveness, and climb the value chain; see box 6.1.

Producer-driven networks are often coordinated by large multinationals. They are vertical, multilayered arrangements, usually with a direct ownership structure including parents, subsidiaries, and subcontractors. They tend to be found in more capital- and technology-intensive sectors, often dominated by global oligopolies, such as aircraft, automobiles, and heavy machinery. The manufacturers control "upstream" relations with suppliers of intermediate components and "downstream" or forward links with distribution and retailing services. Examples of such developments can be found in East Asia and Eastern Europe and the former Soviet Union, where network trade has been the driving force behind economic growth and has enabled producers in these regions to access foreign markets without large outlays on advertising and market research. East Asia's recent experience perhaps epitomizes the success that countries can have entering into production-driven network trade; see box 6.2.

BOX 6.1

Building African Competitiveness and Value-Added from Natural Resources: Aluminum and Diamonds

Many African countries continue to depend on a few primary commodities for their export earnings (see chapter 2). A number of economic studies support the hypothesis that Africa's comparative advantage is in natural resources. This often leads to a pessimistic view that, because Africa does not have a highly skilled workforce, with only a few exceptions, manufactured exports are likely to remain unprofitable in Africa for the foreseeable future. The recent rapid increase in trade and investment between Africa and Asia is largely driven by economic complementarities between the two regions based on factor endowments—skilled labor and more advanced technologies in Asia, and the abundance of natural resources and unskilled labor in Africa. Can Africa build competitiveness based on its endowed natural resources?

International experience shows that developing local value-added activities can indeed help countries build competitiveness based on natural resources. Supported by stable and sound economic policies, several resource-rich developing countries, ranging from Chile to Malaysia, have been successful in developing value-added resource-processing industries in the early stages of industrialization and then using these as a springboard to even higher value-added resource-processing activities. These natural resource success stories stem in large part from the establishment of favorable behind-the-border investment climates—analogous to what has been behind other developing countries' successes in building higher value-added competitive manufacturing sectors.

Commodity processing requires significant investment. FDI can alleviate the domestic shortage of financial resources. Such investment can also bring the technology required. Equally important, a competitive domestic market environment engenders the development of local backward and forward linkages to the extractive process. Quality of infrastructure services, particularly power and transport, is also critical to building export competitiveness. The following two cases highlight how these factors have been influencing the development of natural resources processing in Africa.

Aluminum Smelter in Mozambique

Mozal, one of the largest aluminum smelters in the world, is located near Maputo, the capital of Mozambique. It was constructed in two phases with approximately $2 billion in funding and $1.1 billion in nonrecourse project funding from international enterprises. Shareholders in the enterprise are BHP Billiton of Britain (47 percent owner, and the smelter operator), Mitsubishi Corporation of Japan (25 percent), Industrial Development Corporation of South Africa (24 percent), and the government of Mozambique (4 percent). The factors that have led to Mozal's success include a competitive and inexpensive power supply, based on Mozambique's connection to neighboring countries through the intraregional power grid; training of efficient labor; and a good supply of raw materials. Mozal has contributed to a doubling of Mozambique's exports, providing in excess of $400 million in foreign exchange earnings per year and adding more than 7 percent to GDP. Moreover, a goal of Mozal is to recruit and train staff directly from the local community. At its peak, it is anticipated that 65 percent of the Mozal labor force will be Mozambican. The Mozal project has also contributed to significant spillovers. These include upgraded roads, bridges, water lines, and hazardous-waste facilities. In addition, numerous contracts have been awarded to local small and medium enterprises (SMEs).

Diamond Polishing

Today, most commercially viable diamond deposits are in Africa, notably in South Africa, Namibia, Botswana, the Democratic Republic of Congo, Angola, Tanzania, and Sierra Leone. The diamond value chain is highly concentrated. De Beers runs most of the diamond mines in South Africa, Namibia, and Botswana that long produced the bulk of world supply of the best gemstones. The Diamond Trading Company (DTC) is a subsidiary of De Beers and markets rough diamonds produced both by De Beers, who produces more than half of worldwide production of rough diamonds, and other mines. DTC performs sophisticated sorting of rough diamonds into over 16,000 categories, and then sells bulk lots of rough diamonds to a limited number of invited clients or "sightholders" at nonnegotiable prices. Once purchased by sightholders, diamonds are cut and polished in preparation for sale as gemstones. The cutting and polishing of rough diamonds is a

(Continues on the following page.)

BOX 6.1 (continued)

specialized skill that is concentrated in a limited number of locations world-wide. Traditional diamond cutting centers are Antwerp, Amsterdam, Johannesburg, New York, and Tel Aviv. Recently, diamond cutting centers have been established in China, India, and Thailand. Cutting centers with lower costs of labor, notably Surat in Gujarat, India, handle a larger number of smaller carat diamonds. India, where 900,000 people are working as basic polishers, produces 90 percent of all cut and polished diamonds by number.

Partly in an effort to break the market concentration, several diamond trading companies have started establishing polishing plants in Africa. In June 2004, Lev Leviev Diamonds, the Israel-based second-largest diamond trader in the world, opened Africa's first diamond-polishing factory in Namibia, employing 550 workers. In September 2004, Eurostar Diamond Trader, a Belgian-based diamond company, broke ground in Botswana for the construction of a new diamond cutting and polishing factory, employing more than 1,000 workers. However, the viability of such polishing plants in Africa is still in question. In Namibia, for example, just a few hundred people work as polishers and cutters. There are few skilled workers, the scale of production is small, and wage costs are roughly 10 times those of India. In South Africa, because skilled labor is in relatively short supply, the estimated cost of cutting and polishing diamonds there is $40–60 a carat, compared with $10 a carat in India and $17 a carat in China.

However, there is also a new movement from India to make it the global hub for the diamond market. The Indian Department of Commerce set off in August 2006 a series of initiatives with major diamond producing countries, including South Africa, Namibia, Ghana, and Angola. The shortage of skilled workers in South Africa has hampered the country's advantage in diamond polishing. However, India's policy makers identify this as a potential for providing skills training to South Africans so that South Africa could move up the value chain. Two models were suggested to South Africa under which a joint venture of diamond jewelry (including cutting and polishing of diamonds) could be set up in Mumbai with roughs coming up from South Africa and jewelry being exported to South Africa. The second one pertains to setting up a joint venture in South Africa.

Source: World Bank staff.

BOX 6.2

Producer-Driven Network Trade: The Case of East Asia

Producer-driven network trade in East Asia experienced remarkably high growth during the last two and a half decades, much higher than that in either Europe or North America. Exports of parts and components from East Asian countries increased more than 500 percent over the 1984–96 period, as compared to a 300 percent increase in total exports. Trade in parts and components recorded the fastest annual growth rate in both regional as well as global exports, exceeding by 5 to 6 percentage points the export growth of all other goods, and significantly increasing in relative importance. By 1996, parts and components accounted for approximately 20 percent of the region's total exports and imports of manufactures.

Source: Ng and Yeats 2001.

Worldwide, there appears to be a natural progression in a country's participation in networks, reflecting the country's development path.[12] Because buyer-driven commodity chains usually involve less capital- and technology-intensive production processes, they are typically the networks through which developing countries enter the global production system. Developing countries often start with unskilled-labor-intensive exports, such as apparel, agricultural products, and natural resources. Over time, rising wages and improved human and physical capital allows them to move up the value chain. Ideally, this process of upgrading shifts the export mix toward skilled labor- and capital-intensive exports conducted through producer-driven networks, such as those in the automotive and information technology industries. This has important implications for understanding the evolution of the linkages between trade and FDI flows by China and India with Africa.

Trade-FDI Integration in the African-Asian Context

The phenomenon that FDI by Asian countries in Africa is being accompanied by trade flows—both exports and imports—with those countries has only recently begun to be systematically documented.[13] It exemplifies how, as in much of the rest of the world, trade and investment activities on the African continent are becoming more integrated, and that firms are pursuing such strategies in a complementary fashion. However, unlike other regions of the world, where it is foreign firms from advanced countries in the North, such as the United States, the EU, and Japan, that have tended to be dominant in integrating investment and trade, in Africa, especially in the last few years, it is increasingly foreign firms from the South, especially China and India, that are exhibiting the most rapid growth in combining investment and trade.

To a certain extent, the integration of FDI and trade flows in Africa has been fostered by special market-access incentives engendered by trade preferences the African countries have been receiving from certain industrial countries, such as the Untied States' AGOA program, the EU's Everything But Arms initiative, and country Generalized System of Preference schemes (see chapter 3).[14] Beyond the objective of exploiting such incentive regimes—which pertain essentially only to *exports* from Africa and only to *designated* markets—the evidence from the WBAATI firm-level survey and business case studies points to the fact that Chinese and Indian firms operating in Africa are also engaging in such integration—albeit on a limited scale, as discussed below—as a means of strategically diversifying their production channels in *global* supply chains, and they are doing so in both *export as well as import* transactions. In other words, the emergence of network trade between Africa and China and India is being driven by more than taking advantage of trade preference schemes.

A useful way to analyze how trade and FDI flows are becoming integrated in the business relations between Africa and Asia is to categorize such integration according to the markets being targeted by Chinese and Indian businesses operating in Africa in the *selling* (exporting) of their products and services.[15] (An analogous categorization could be done regarding where Asian firms operating in Africa are *purchasing* (importing) their inputs.) This categorization gives rise to the following tripartite taxonomy.

Host Country–Targeted Investment

FDI in Africa in which the goods (or services[16]) produced are sold primarily in the markets where they are made—either within a single African country or subregionally (that is, among several African countries)—can be thought of as host country–targeted investment. It would be rare in the

African case, except for perhaps South Africa, for host country–targeted investment to engender, or be associated with, network trade, and if such trade did arise, it would likely be of the buyer-driven variety.

From the 1960s through the 1980s, Asian firms making such investments were mostly (but not exclusively) Japanese businesses in the light manufacturing sectors, for example, the home electronic appliance and textile sectors. These investments were aimed at supplying manufactured products to Africa's domestic markets, which were protected by high tariffs under African governments' import substitution policies during this period. In subsequent years, African import liberalization reforms (see chapter 3) eliminated some of the competitive advantages that local sales from such investments may have had vis-à-vis direct importation of the product in question. For example, some Japanese electronic firms such as Matsushita Electric-Côte d'Ivoire and Sanyo Electric-Kenya were forced out of the market by a growing wave of cheaper imported products (some of which were imported through a black market). As a result, the recent rapidly growing Asian investors in Africa—the Chinese and Indians—that operate in such manufacturing industries and sell output locally (or subregionally) face direct competition from imports (as discussed in chapter 4), far more so than did the earlier Asian investors in Africa.

At the same time, the export prospects for the Chinese and Indian firms invested in these host-country sectors are also limited—at least at this juncture—especially in today's fiercely competitive global marketplace. This is because such investments and any intra-African regional trade associated with them are generally bound by the constraints of most African countries' small local markets and high transactions costs: the limited size of the typical African domestic market limits economies of scale and thus the pursuit of the mass-production manufacturing business model commonly used in larger country markets, whether in the South or the North. In part, that is why intraregional trade on the African continent, while growing, remains small at present; see figure 6.1. Other reasons include policy barriers to intraregional trade, such as tariffs and nontariff trade barriers (NTBs); these are discussed below. If the various initiatives fostering regional trade integration in Africa (described in chapter 3) are successful, they could help achieve economies of scale and reduce production costs. This could enable the output from such manufacturing investments to become more competitive vis-à-vis imports, thus making subregional trade

FIGURE 6.1

African Intraregional Trade is Increasing but Small

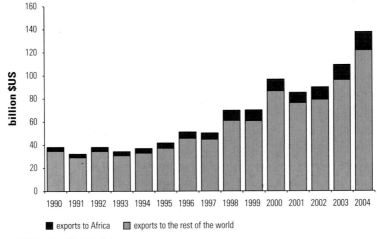

Source: IMF Direction of Trade Statistics.

more cost effective, and possibly, vis-à-vis international production in global markets, fostering exports.

To be sure, there are cases where such constraints may not greatly impinge on business viability and thus small and medium scale is sustainable. One instance is where the foreign presence by Asian firms is made not through direct investment per se or long-term contracting, but rather by manufacturing through local licensing or franchising. Although there were cases of this mode of entry into Africa by Japanese businesses in the past few decades, for example, in the chemical sectors, at present, based on the latest available evidence from the WBAATI survey and business case studies, existing Chinese and Indian manufacturing firms in Africa appear to use this mode in a more limited fashion; see chapter 5.[17] One prominent example of this is an Indian investment in a locally owned brewery in South Africa; see box 6.3.

In many ways, this example epitomizes one difference between Chinese and Indian firms in the way in which they operate in Africa: whereas Indian firms integrate relatively deeply into local African economies—including, in some cases, business managers becoming involved in municipal government—and operate through informal networks, Chinese firms have a tendency to operate as enclaves. In part, no doubt, these differences stem from the longer history that ethnic Indians have living in Africa as compared with the Chinese. Indeed, as one CEO of an Indian-owned firm in Africa that was part of the business case studies remarked: "We want to be thought of as an African business."

A greater number of cases where small and medium enterprises (SMEs) are sustainable in Africa come from various services sectors—for example,

---

BOX 6.3

The Africanization of Indian-Owned Businesses

This company is a producer of sorghum beer, a traditional beverage drink of South Africa. The firm was originally a state-owned enterprise, but in the mid-1990s, after its ownership was ceded to private black management, the majority of its capital was acquired by a large brewery group with headquarters in India, which was seeking to penetrate the South African beer market. Sorghum beer accounts for about 25 percent of the South African beer market, with 75 percent of the market held by lager beer. Within the sorghum beer market, this firm is the only formal producer; it has 10 breweries, and its sales account for about one-third of the market. The remaining two-thirds of the market is supplied by about 1,000 informal individual local producers. While the company distributes its products by trucks through its long-standing distribution network, most local producers do not transport their products and sell them on the spot. Because sorghum beer is highly perishable and there is a lack of infrastructure to ensure adherence to the health standards of such products, the company does not export to other African countries; instead, it is planning to produce in-country (plans are underway to build a brewery in Botswana). There are complaints about some of the informal breweries not maintaining health standards. While the company pays value added taxes and excise duties, the informal sector does not. Although these differences present serious competitive and hence financial challenges to the profitability of the company, because of the traditional position that the beverage holds in South African society, including the convention of having many local "mom and pop" producers, the company is reluctant to seek redress for these problems. The senior management of the company—although only four of them are Indian—does not want the firm to be perceived as an Indian business, but rather as a local one.

Source: World Bank staff.

construction, retail, or tourism, among others—as well as in the light manufacturing sector, such as textiles, apparel, and furniture. Here, today,
small- and medium-scale Chinese and Indian businesses are operating in
Africa—at a very rapid pace—serving local or subregional markets. These
investors—especially Chinese firms, who are generally substantially newer
to Africa than Indian firms—are, in some respects, following in the foot-
steps of earlier Asian firms. In the past, investors in this sector came from
Asian countries where SMEs were active, such as the Republic of Korea
and Taiwan. For Africa, these Chinese- and Indian-invested SMEs are
proving to be significant sources of job creation.

To be sure, much of the Chinese and Indian FDI in Africa is concentrated in extractive sectors, such as oil and mining, which grabs most of
the headlines. These are more properly thought of as "home country–targeted investments" (see below). But, in fact, greater diversification of
these countries' African FDI has been occurring, and they increasingly fall
into the "host country–targeted investment" category. Significant Chinese
and Indian investments on the African continent have been made in
apparel, retail ventures, fisheries, commercial real estate and transport
construction, tourism, power plants, and telecommunications, among
other sectors. To cite a few examples, Huawei, a major Chinese telecommunications firm, has won contracts worth $400 million to provide cell
phone service in Kenya, Zimbabwe, and Nigeria. In Zambia, the Chinese
are building a $600 million hydroelectric plant at Kafue Gorge. And in
South Africa and Botswana, hotels and other elements of the tourist infrastructure are being built by Chinese investors.[18] China and India are pursuing commercial strategies with Africa that are about far more than
resources.

Home Country–Targeted Investment

The objective of home-country-targeted investment is to produce African
goods (or services) that are to be exported and sold primarily in the
investors' home countries in Asia. Typical examples include Chinese and
Indian investments in Africa in natural resource–extractive industries,
such as oil and mining, and increasingly, agricultural primary commodities
and (to a still-limited extent) processed foods. An example of the latter is a
large Indian-owned cashew-processing company in Tanzania, which, ironically, faces escalating tariffs on its imports into its home market; see chap-

ter 3. Where such investment is taking place in Africa, any network trade that has arisen generally has been buyer-driven.

On a global basis, where Chinese firms are engaged in home country–targeted investments, such investments are most often conducted by SOEs.[19] On average, 88 percent of Chinese firms engaging in FDI abroad are owned by provincial governments.[20] In fact, in the African setting, new survey data suggest that Chinese firms investing in Africa rank "Chinese government support" as the second most important determinant of their investment decision, following "market seeking."[21]

Needless to say, investments in extractive industries are large scale and capital intensive, and in Africa, not surprisingly, the recent oil-industry investments by China are also relatively large (see chapter 2).[22] They have been often initiated by government-to-government agreements followed by corporate engagement, frequently by SOEs. Although Asian (and other nationality) firms have invested in Africa's extractive-industry sectors for many years, the investments by China in African oil production over the past decade, and especially in the last few years, have garnered the most public attention.[23]

Still, even after accounting for China's comparably sizeable investments in Africa's oil sector, with a few exceptions, in the aggregate the African countries that possess the greatest accumulation of Chinese FDI differ from those generating the greatest exports to China; see figure 6.2. This suggests that, outside the oil sector, home country–targeted investments in Africa, at least in the case of those made by Chinese firms, are at present not a significant phenomenon. This implies relatively limited substitution of trade for FDI. Indeed, if anything, the data suggest growing *complementarities* between Africa and China, a theme that emerges from the data in chapter 2.

China, however, is substantially dependent on its oil imports from Sub-Saharan Africa—regardless of whether these imports are the direct product of Chinese investment on the continent. More than a quarter of China's global imports of oil come from African countries (see figure 6.3). If anything, this suggests that these African oil-exporting countries—as a whole—may well have market power in their crude oil exports to China, which might allow for higher prices to be charged, all other things equal. Of course, to exercise market power would require these exporting countries to cooperate in some joint fashion in their production and sales activities, an unlikely event. It also would require other oil-exporting countries in the world to not lower their prices.

FIGURE 6.2
How Home-Targeted Are China's Investments in Africa?

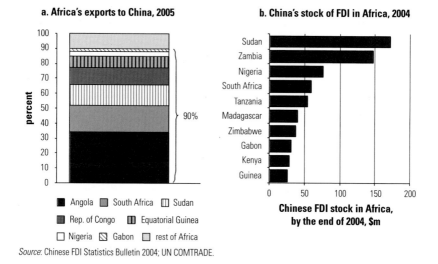

a. Africa's exports to China, 2005

b. China's stock of FDI in Africa, 2004

■ Angola ■ South Africa ⊞ Sudan
▨ Rep. of Congo ⊞ Equatorial Guinea
□ Nigeria ⊠ Gabon ▢ rest of Africa

Chinese FDI stock in Africa,
by the end of 2004, $m

Source: Chinese FDI Statistics Bulletin 2004; UN COMTRADE.

Global Market–Targeted Investment

Global-market-targeted investment is focused on exporting goods produced in Africa to third-country markets. At this juncture, except for some
special cases such as the network trade emerging in South Africa's automotive industry (see below), these investments are almost always based

FIGURE 6.3
Does China's FDI in Oil Engender African Market Power?

China is substantially oil import–dependent on Africa

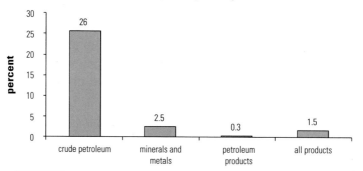

Source: UN COMTRADE.

Note: China's imports from Africa as a share of China's global imports.

on buyer-driven, as opposed to producer-driven, global-supply-chain considerations. Over the past few decades, most of the Asian businesses in Africa engaging in these types of investments, such as Japanese and Korean firms, have been primarily targeting industrial regions, such as the EU and the United States.

The recent, rapid, significant entry by Chinese and Indian firms engaged in this mode of investment is changing things. A substantial portion of their target export markets tends to be other countries in the South, especially (but not exclusively) in Asia. However, there are also cases in which such investments by Chinese and Indian firms are facilitating African exports into other markets, including the North, and furthering even more so the continent's global integration.

One prominent example is Chinese firms' involvement in the African textile and apparel sector—especially in the wake of the expiration of the Multifibre Arrangement in 2005, which unleashed fierce global competition—a clear illustration of how China's foreign investment in Africa is linked to the future of the continent's trade patterns. Investment in these sectors has been accompanied by imports of textile materials (for example, cotton fabrics) from China to African countries that have growing apparel sectors. In turn, partly as a result of the trade preference schemes noted earlier, this is linked to African exports of garment products to the global market, most notably to the EU and the United States.[24] Like other places in the world where global market–targeted investment and the associated network trade are occurring, the focus of Chinese and Indian firms pursuing this business strategy has been on "footloose" industries.

The emerging network trade is being motivated by the low labor costs in Africa, especially in sectors that are displaying relatively higher and rising labor costs in Asia. The result is that global market–targeted investments by China and India—as well as others—can create important opportunities for Africa to not only expand the volume of exports, but also diversify them away from traditional sectors. In fact, network trade has been creating export opportunities for Africa in newer, higher value-added industries, such as telecommunications and electronic parts and components, which are proving to be the domain for Chinese investors.

In other sectors, such as data services, call centers, and telemarketing—so-called back-office support—Indian investors in Africa have shown a greater interest. Indeed, while India itself has become a center for outsourcing services for more advanced countries, such as the United States and the EU, it is now outsourcing its own services to Africa, especially in the software sector. Data from the WBAATI business case studies suggest that countries such as Ghana, Senegal, and Tanzania, among others, have the ability to compete globally in such services markets. For example, HCL Enterprises, Ltd., a $3 billion Indian software company, is working on a $400 million multiyear outsourcing contract with Old Mutual, South Africa's largest insurance company. In many cases, although by international standards the size of these investments in Africa may be limited, they nonetheless can generate significant employment opportunities for local economies.

More advanced global market–targeted investments by Asian firms investing in Africa are emerging, resulting in (limited) producer-driven network trade. These investments are fostered by the promise of substantial productivity increases that could be engendered by subregional integration of the continent. If such regional integration were to succeed—and the challenges are appreciable (see box 6.4)—ultimately, it could provide a platform for exports to global markets. To seize on such prospects, beginning in the 1990s, major Japanese and Korean automobile companies, for example, established plants in South Africa, which is rapidly becoming an important regional economic hub. More recently, Chinese and Indian automotive and truck assembly operations made significant investments in Africa—not only in South Africa, but also in Tanzania, with plans for exports to Uganda, Rwanda, Burundi, and the Democratic Republic of Congo. Importantly, as the WBAATI business case studies suggest, these newer investments are targeting export markets inside—and ultimately outside—the Africa region.

Evidence on FDI-Trade Linkages of Chinese and Indian Firms in Africa

Country-Level Evidence

Aggregate statistical evidence—at the country level, that is, regardless of firm nationality—on the strength of linkages between FDI and trade flows among African countries yields mixed findings; see figure 6.4. When relating the growth of merchandise exports to the growth of FDI, there appears to be a positive association for the oil-producing countries, but none for the non-oil-producing countries. In the case of the relationship between

BOX 6.4

Barriers to Regional Integration Are Barriers to Africa's Export Prospects: Evidence from Chinese and Indian Business Case Studies

The WBAATI business case studies of Chinese-owned and Indian-owned firms in Africa point to a number of difficulties enterprises face in realizing the benefits that regional integration can bring to the continent. Without regional integration, the many small, landlocked countries of Africa will not be able to create unified economic spaces sufficiently large to achieve economies of scale. Without economies of scale, unit production costs will unlikely be low enough to allow for the successful penetration of export markets. Every Chinese and Indian business study noted the poor quality and high cost of transport services, the long shipping times, and the lack of effective logistics services such as insurance and transport intermediaries, all of which limited the commercial viability of intra-African trade. One Chinese firm operating in South Africa indicated that sending a product from South Africa to Angola costs as much as sending the product from China to Angola. An Indian firm in Tanzania noted that intra-African maritime shipping costs are three times because high as road shipping costs, in part due to the lack of competition. Another Indian firm, in Ghana, stated flatly that "ECOWAS does not work," as there are still high tariffs among ECOWAS countries. The firm reported that it costs about $1,000/TEU to send a container from Accra to Lagos, a distance of just over 200 miles. In fact, the high tariffs on trade induced this firm to make cross-border investments instead, an example where intraregional trade barriers gave rise to intraregional investment.

Source: World Bank staff.

Note: TEU = twenty-foot equivalent unit, a measure of container capacity.

merchandise exports as a percentage of GDP and FDI as a percentage of GDP, there is a much stronger positive association for the oil-producing countries than for the non-oil-producing countries. Of course, other variables beyond the growth of FDI and FDI as a percentage of GDP affect export growth and exports as a percentage of GDP.

Fortunately, there are new firm-level data from the WBAATI survey of Chinese and Indian firms operating in Africa that permit a more disaggre-

FIGURE 6.4
Country-Level Statistical Evidence on FDI-Merchandise Trade Linkages in Africa

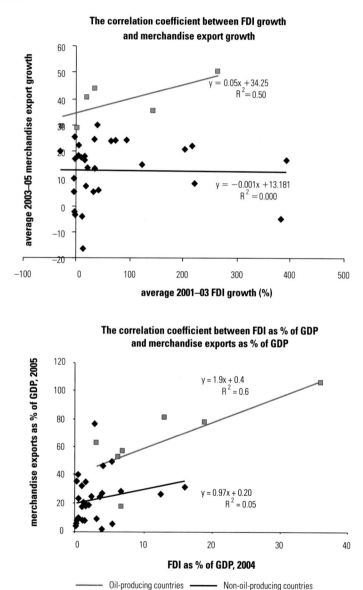

Source: IMF World Economic Outlook; oil countries include Angola, Chad, Congo, Equitorial Guinea, Nigeria, and Sudan.

gated analysis of the extent to which trade and FDI flows are related to one another on the continent. We now turn to assess the findings from these data.

Firm-Level Evidence

Modes of Foreign Investment Entry

The initial conditions of Chinese and Indian foreign investors' entry into the African economy influence the scale and pattern of integration attained by these businesses. As chapter 2 shows, FDI in Africa by Chinese and Indian firms is not a wholly recent phenomenon; indeed, in some cases Chinese and Indian FDI in Africa dates back several decades. Nonetheless, according to new firm-level data from the 2006 WBAATI survey, a snapshot of a large sample of the *stock* of Chinese and Indian firms currently operating in Africa reveals that the median Chinese firm began its African operations in 2002, and its Indian counterpart began its operations in 1999; see table 6.1. This finding at the firm level is consistent with that suggested by the aggregate data presented in chapter 2, which showed a rapid increase in the last few years of *flows* of FDI to Africa by firms from these countries. Overall, today, a substantial portion of Chinese and Indian foreign investors in Africa are of a relatively young vintage, especially compared with European firms currently operating on the continent.

Initial conditions are also shaped by the form of entry that firms pursue in their FDI. Worldwide there is much diversity in the way in which firms engage in FDI, depending in no small measure on the sector in question and the degree of economic and political stability of the country, among other factors. Still, it is often the case that firms that are newer to a market—and thus less familiar with the local investment climate—tend to

TABLE 6. 1
FDI Entry to Africa by Start-Up Vintage

Firm nationality	Vintage
Chinese	2002
Indian	1999
European	1993

Source: World Bank staff.

Note: Data refer to median year.

enter in ways that reduce risks, such as through acquiring an existing operation. With greater familiarity of a market or greater willingness to incur
risk, foreign investors have felt more comfortable entering by establishing
greenfield (or de novo) operations. Of course, in settings where existing
firms are either very limited in number or insufficiently commercially
attractive for buy-outs or joint ventures, the options for entry will be more
limited.

In the case of Chinese and Indian investors in Africa, surveyed firms
exhibit a strikingly different pattern of entry; see table 6.2. In contrast to
entrepreneurs from India, who, like their European counterparts, have had
relatively longer commercial ties with Africa and tend to initiate investments
in the African market through both de novo entry as well as acquisition of
existing businesses, the vast majority of Chinese firms have entered Africa
through greenfield investments. To some extent, these differences might be
explained by the variance in sectoral orientation between the surveyed Chinese and Indian firms, although such variance is relatively limited, and it
also does not appear to break along sectoral lines where inherent risks differ
significantly or potentially acquirable African businesses are unlikely to exist;
see table 6.3 and table 1A.3 in the annex to chapter 1.[25] Instead, that an
overwhelming portion of surveyed Chinese firms investing in Africa have
done so through de novo entry may suggest that such enterprises simply do
not pursue a relatively strong risk-averting business strategy or perhaps they
find fewer benefits to rapidly integrating into African markets than do Indian
firms, a notion that other evidence appears to support.[26]

Scale of Investment and Corporate Structure

The ability of firms in Africa to achieve lower production costs to better
exploit export opportunities and climb the value chain through network

TABLE 6.2

Form of FDI Entry to Africa

(percent)

Firm nationality	De novo	Joint venture	Acquisition
Chinese	82	9	9
Indian	68	9	23
European	50	26	25

Source: World Bank staff.

Note: Data pertain to median values.

TABLE 6.3
Form of FDI Entry to Africa by Sector
(percent)

Product group	De novo	Joint venture	Acquisition
Agriculture and food	63	13	25
Chemicals	60	20	20
Construction	100	0	0
Machinery	56	44	0
Non-oil minerals and metals	86	0	14
Nondurables	63	13	25
Nonconstruction services	57	10	33
Textiles	40	40	20

Source: World Bank staff.

Note: Includes Chinese, Indian, and European firms. Data pertain to median values.

trade can, in part, depend on the scale of operations attained through FDI. This is likely to be true to the extent that the underlying technology and the organization of production inherent in the sector in question provide for decreasing unit costs as production increases. Among businesses covered by the WBAATI survey, in comparison with Chinese and Indian firms

FIGURE 6.5
Business Size Differences (Relative to African Firms) for Selected Sectors

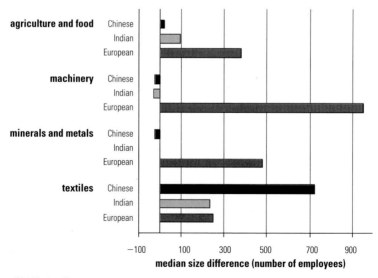

Source: World Bank staff.

Note: Difference in median size, by number of employees, relative to median African firm. "Minerals" excludes non-oil minerals.

operating in Africa, the scale achieved by domestically owned enterprises in certain sectors, for example, agriculture and food and textiles, is considerably smaller (see figure 6.5).[27] Especially in the textile sector, the scale of Chinese firms, and to a lesser extent Indian firms, greatly dominates that of African-owned firms. In contrast, in the machinery and the non-oil minerals and metals sectors, there is relatively little difference between the scale of African firms and their Chinese or Indian counterparts. These scale variations across sectors are likely to have a significant influence on the reasons why Chinese and Indian firms in Africa are better able to engage in network trade than are domestic businesses.

One obvious dimension of scale that can play a key role in the ability of firms to integrate investment with trade activities and engage in international production sharing is the extent to which a business is part of a larger holding company or group-enterprise corporate structure. It has been widely documented that some of the larger businesses in China and India—including some of the largest (and most well-known) companies in the world, such as SINOPEC (primarily in the chemical sector) and Tata (a conglomerate), respectively—have group structures.[28] In fact, a recent survey of FDI outflows from China on a global basis finds that on average 97 percent of Chinese firms investing abroad are affiliates of a parent firm in China.[29] As investors in Africa, survey data reveal that both Chinese and Indian (as well as European) businesses have a higher incidence of belonging to a holding company or group enterprise than do African firms; see figure 6.6. In fact,

FIGURE 6.6
Extent of Scale: Incidence of Holding Company or Group Enterprise

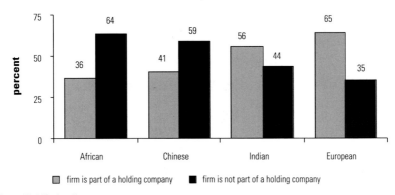

Source: World Bank staff.

the survey data suggest that a greater proportion of Indian firms operating in Africa are part of a group structure than are stand-alone enterprises.

Effects of Scale on Regional Integration and Geographic Diversification Outside Africa

Beyond the issue of whether a firm is part of a larger corporate group structure is the degree to which variation in this dimension of scale engenders differences in the facility for effectively integrating investment and trade activities. In part, this will likely depend greatly on how extensive is the geographic spread of the group structure. The presumption is that the greater the corporate geographic diversification, the higher the payoff from investment-trade linkages, hence the stronger the tendency for firms to exploit opportunities to be able to undertake them.

In this regard, the pattern of geographic diversification of the number of group member firms is quite notable in the WBAATI survey; see table 6.4. Not surprisingly, African-owned firms tend to exhibit by far the greatest geographic spread within their "home" countries. But in terms of geographical diversification across the African continent as a whole, Chinese-owned (and to a much greater extent, European-owned) businesses appear to engage in significantly more intra-African regional integration than do African firms themselves. As Chinese and Indian firms participating in the business case studies revealed, intraregional barriers to trade, in part the result of de facto lingering high tariffs and NTBs, despite de jure regional trade agreements, actually have had the effect of engendering intraregional (cross-border) investments rather than trade (recall figure 6.1).

The contours of regional integration undertaken by foreign investors in Africa sometimes result in market segmentation of the pan-African mar-

TABLE 6.4
Extent of Scale and Geographic Spread

Location of firms	Number of separate firms belonging to holding company or group enterprise			
	Firm nationality			
	African	Chinese	Indian	European
Domestic	8	1	2	3
Other Africa	2	4	1	8
Outside Africa	2	16	5	58

Source: World Bank staff.

Note: Data pertain to median values.

ket. The WBAATI business case studies focused on a large state-owned Chinese construction firm operating on the continent in Tanzania, Uganda, Kenya, and Zambia, doing so largely through competing for public procurement contracts in each of the four countries. Although the firm possesses the capacity to engage in construction contracts in other, neighboring countries on the continent, its management follows a business strategy dictated by headquarters in China: the firm will operate only in its current four markets; other construction firms belonging to the same holding group will bid on contracts in other African markets. All other things equal, the effect of such market segmentation is to reduce the extent of competition in Africa's construction sector.

A similar, but even more striking, pattern emerges in table 6.4 among the surveyed firms when the focus is on geographic diversification of the number of group-member firms in markets outside of Africa altogether. Again, and not surprisingly, given the relative nascence of their international corporate development, African businesses that are part of a group structure are much less extended to other continents than are their Chinese and Indian counterparts also operating in Africa.

Impacts of Scale on Exports

Based on the foregoing analysis of differences in scale of businesses operating in Africa as a starting point for assessing the nature of the investment-trade linkages exhibited by such firms, it is useful to gauge the extent to which firm size is related to overall export performance. The analysis then focuses on an assessment of the differences in export—and import—patterns at a more disaggregated level.

Whether in terms of comparing (i) domestic sales versus exports, (ii) exports to regional markets within Africa versus exports to global markets, or (iii) exports to specific markets all wholly outside Africa, new empirical evidence from firm-level survey data on such businesses suggests that firm size and export propensity—measured by exports as a percentage of total sales revenue—are positively related, all other things equal; see figures 6.7a–6.7c. In the first case, the data indicate that while, *within* either of the two size classes—micro, small, and medium or large and very large[30]—domestic sales exceed exports, on average, larger firms exhibit greater export propensity than do smaller firms.

In comparing the propensity to export regionally (that is, within Africa) versus the propensity to export globally, smaller firms export more to regional markets than they export outside the continent, consistent with the findings on domestic sales versus exports above. The larger firms not only export more than smaller firms to regional markets but also to international markets; in fact, the data suggest that larger firms export to regional and global markets with about the same intensity.

Finally, in comparing the propensity to export to different international markets—whether China and India, Europe and North America, or the rest of the world—larger firms register more exports per unit of sales than their smaller counterparts.

FIGURE 6.7

Scale and Export Propensity: Intra-African, Global, and Asian Trade

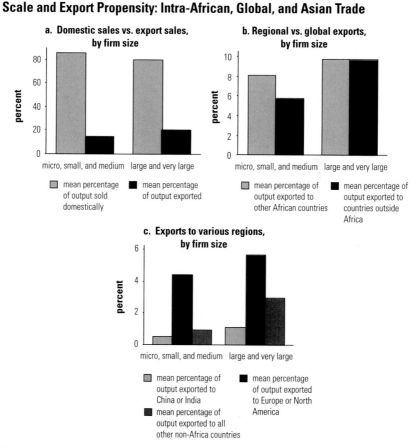

a. Domestic sales vs. export sales, by firm size

b. Regional vs. global exports, by firm size

c. Exports to various regions, by firm size

Source: World Bank staff.

Note: Data pertain to 2005 median annual sales and exports.

Patterns of Firm-Level Exports and Imports by Businesses in Africa

In light of the significant heterogeneity among firms with operations in Africa, whether in terms of nationality, mode of entry, scale of investment, or geographic diversification, among other factors, one would expect to observe significant differences in the patterns of the exports and imports at the firm level. In fact, the 2006 survey data indicate, even from the most aggregate perspective, substantial variation; see table 6.5. On the sales side, for the totality of the sample of surveyed firms, the geographic distribution of sales is rather skewed, with almost 70 percent of output produced in 2005 being sold within Africa (either in the local market or in other markets on the continent; see below for further disaggregation on this specific point). The EU is the next largest destination market, accounting for 15 percent of the surveyed firms' aggregate sales in 2005. By contrast, total exports to China and India among all the firms taken together accounted for only about 2 percent of sales. These findings are not terribly surprising, considering the fact that, as noted earlier, the survey deliberately omits coverage of firms in the oil-related sectors, which account for the lion's share of Africa's exports, and instead, by design, concentrates on general manufacturing and various service industries.[31]

On the input purchase side, the distribution across source markets is more balanced. While the EU market supplies about one-quarter of the inputs used in Africa by the surveyed firms in the aggregate, only a slightly lesser amount—about one-fifth—is procured in Africa. Goods from China

TABLE 6.5
Geographic Distribution of Output Sales and Input Purchases in the Aggregate

Destination market	Percent	Origin market	Percent
Africa	68.0	Africa	19.1
China	1.0	China	13.2
India	1.0	India	12.6
EU	15.0	EU	26.8
Other Asia	4.0	Other Asia	9.1
North America	4.0	North America	7.7
Other	6.0	Other	11.5
Total	100.0	Total	100.0

Source: World Bank staff.

Note: Data pertain to 2005 median annual sales and purchases.

and India also account for a substantial portion of inputs—each locale supplies about 13 percent of total input purchases by the surveyed firms.

The geographic distribution of output sales and input purchases varies significantly across surveyed firms according to nationality. Particularly noteworthy in table 6.6 is the fact that both Chinese and Indian businesses operating in Africa sell a significantly larger amount of output in other African markets *outside* the local market than do their African business counterparts. This finding is consistent with data presented above suggesting that non-African firms operating in Africa appear to engage more in regional integration on the continent than do domestic firms. Interestingly, the median African firm surveyed indicates that its sales to Europe and North America account for 4 percent and 1 percent, respectively, of total sales in 2005, whereas the median Chinese and Indian firms indicate they sell none in those two markets.

The observed pattern of origin markets used by firms of different nationality operating in Africa to procure inputs is considerably different than that of destination markets for output sales; see table 6.7. Not surprisingly, all surveyed firms, regardless of nationality, substantially tap their home markets for inputs. But there is a surprisingly significant heterogeneity. At one extreme, African firms tend to rely very heavily on local markets for inputs, with such purchases constituting 60 percent of total inputs bought; at the same time, 13 percent of African firms' inputs are bought in Europe.

TABLE 6.6
Distribution of Output Sales by Destination Market and Nationality
(percent)

Destination market	Firm nationality			
	African	Chinese	Indian	European
Domestic	85	81	89	76
Other Africa	8	14	10	11
Europe	4	0	0	7
North America	1	0	0	1
India	0	0	0	0
Other South Asia	0	1	0	0
China	0	3	0	0
Other East Asia	0	0	0	2
Other	1	1	0	2

Source: World Bank staff.

Note: Data pertain to 2005 median annual sales.

TABLE 6.7
Distribution of Material Input Purchases by Origin Market and Nationality
(percent)

Origin market	Firm nationality			
	African	Chinese	Indian	European
Domestic	60	31	27	40
Other Africa	7	4	9	9
Europe	13	1	13	34
North America	3	5	1	6
India	5	2	26	3
Other South Asia	3	1	4	1
China	4	55	7	3
Other East Asia	2	1	3	3
Other	2	0	11	1

Source: World Bank staff.

Note: Data pertain to 2005 median annual purchases.

At the other extreme are Chinese firms: like their Indian (and European) counterparts, African markets account for about 30–40 percent of total inputs purchased. But Chinese firms indicate they buy 55 percent of their inputs in China, almost twice the level purchased in Africa, whereas Indian (and European) firms purchase an almost equivalent level of inputs in their home markets as they do in Africa.

Extent and Geographic Distribution of Intraindustry and Network Trade
The intensity of intraindustry and network trade being undertaken by firms operating in Africa can be gauged across several dimensions. One is the extent to which firms engage in vertical integration—that is, the buying and selling of outputs or inputs by different business units that operate under one corporate roof, resulting in common ownership and control. This practice is in contrast to "arms-length transactions," where the buying and selling of outputs or inputs is done with independent and privately owned corporate entities. Worldwide, firms generally engage in vertical integration (as opposed to transacting in the open market) when they want to avert undue exposure to market risks or there are genuine technical economies of scale (or economies of scope) that can be realized by combining successive stages of the production process in a single corporate unit. The latter condition is often largely determined by the basic technology underlying the industrial production process in question. A classic case is manufacturing steel, where it would make little economic sense to have

TABLE 6.8
Extent of Vertical Integration by Nationality
(percent)

Intrafirm transactions	Firm nationality			
	African	Chinese	Indian	European
Output sales to parent firm or affiliate	9	19	0	14
Input purchases from parent firm or affiliate	3	23	9	15

Source: World Bank staff.

Note: Data pertain to 2005 median values.

TABLE 6.9
Extent of Arms-Length Transactions with Private Firms
(percent)

Outside transactions	Firm nationality			
	African	Chinese	Indian	European
Arms-length output sales to private firms	49	24	42	57
Arms-length input purchases from private dirms	92	75	89	83

Source: World Bank staff.

Note: Data pertain to 2005 median values.

one firm heating up iron ore ingots and another casting the molten iron into designated shapes.

Data from the new WBAATI survey provide an opportunity to assess the extent of these practices; see tables 6.8 and 6.9. With respect to vertical integration, African firms tend to engage significantly more in "downstream" integration (intracorporate sales of outputs) than "upstream" integration (intracorporate purchases of inputs). This is a different practice than that of both Chinese and Indian (as well as European) firms, where upstream integration dominates downstream integration. Across firms of different nationalities, there are also significant differences: whether in terms of downstream or upstream integration, Chinese businesses in Africa engage in substantially more vertical integration than do all other firms surveyed.

Generally speaking, it is not uncommon to find firms—regardless of locale—relying more on the open market than on internal channels for

sales of outputs or purchases of inputs, though of course there are variations across sectors due to differences in industries' underlying technologies. In the case of the surveyed firms in Africa, the data do indeed suggest
that these businesses generally transact more with independent, private
firms via the open market than through vertical integration. Where arms-
length interbusiness transactions are being conducted in Africa, the firms
engage in this practice more for output sales than for input purchases.
Across nationalities, however, the differences are striking. Businesses from
China transact with private firms in the open market—both for purchases
of inputs and sales of outputs—to a much smaller degree than other
nationality firms operating in Africa.

Taken together, the findings suggest that Chinese businesses, which
tend to rely both more heavily on vertical integration and less heavily on
arms-length transactions with independent private firms, perceive the
risks associated with commercial activity in Africa differently than do
Indian (or European) firms. This conclusion is consistent with the findings
above on differences across firm nationality in investment patterns.

TABLE 6.10
Geographic Distribution of Output Sales to Private Firms
(percent)

Location of purchasing firms	Firm nationality			
	African	Chinese	Indian	European
Domestic firms	83.0	79.0	84.0	73.0
Other African firms	8.5	10.5	8.0	17.0
Firms outside Africa	8.5	10.5	8.0	10.0

Source: World Bank staff.

Note: Data pertain to 2005 median values.

TABLE 6.11
Geographic Distribution of Input Purchases from Private Firms
(percent)

Location of selling firms	Firm nationality			
	African	Chinese	Indian	European
Domestic firms	62	49	30	50
Other African firms	9	7	9	6
Firms outside Africa	29	44	61	44

Source: World Bank staff.

Note: Data pertain to 2005 median values.

The *extent* to which firms operating in Africa engage in open market transactions with independent firms rather than vertical integration is one element depicting the pattern of these businesses' intraindustry and network trade. Another is the nature of the *geographic distribution* of such transactions. The WBAATI survey data provide information on this score; see tables 6.10 and 6.11. For arms-length sales of output to private firms, Chinese businesses transact less with local (African) firms than do African- or Indian-owned businesses. At the same time, however, Chinese firms engage in more interfirm output sales in the private sector in Africa's *regional* markets than do African or Indian firms. This finding is consistent with earlier ones pointing to the fact that Chinese firms tend to engage in more extensive regional integration than do domestic counterparts.

Regarding purchases of inputs from independent private entities, the variation among firms of differing nationality is far more notable. African firms rely much more heavily on procuring privately produced inputs in the local, domestic market than do either Chinese or Indian firms, especially the latter: Indian firms' arms-length input purchases from private local firms is half the magnitude of their African counterparts. On the other hand, while there is limited variation across different nationality businesses regarding interfirm input purchases in Africa's regional markets, Chinese and Indian firms operating on the continent procure significantly greater portions of inputs from private firms located outside Africa than do domestic firms, especially Indian businesses, which do so at twice the rate as their African counterparts.

Worldwide, firms that have been most effective in taking advantage of the new opportunities afforded by the growth in network trade and the accompanying increase in trade in parts and components are those who have been able to climb the value chain. This means moving from exporting raw materials to exporting goods that have been further processed. In doing so, a greater portion of the product's value is retained by the firm producing the raw material initially.

It has been widely documented that, at the national level, African countries rely heavily on exports of raw materials. As a result, value-added is being forgone. At the firm level, the WBAATI survey data suggest a similar story; see table 6.12. Indeed, in comparison with both Chinese and Indian (as well as European) firms operating in Africa, domestic firms tend to sell a larger portion of raw material products. Moreover, this pattern is evident not only in global trade outside the African continent, but also with regard to interregional trade *within* Africa.

TABLE 6.12
Extent of Value-Added in Output Sales and Exports, by Destination Market and Firm Nationality

(percent)

	Product	Firm nationality			
		African	Chinese	Indian	European
Domestic sales	Finished assembled	88	90	90	89
	Partially finished	5	9	4	4
	Raw material	6	0	5	6
Sales to other African countries	Finished assembled	83	89	100	78
	Partially finished	8	11	0	15
	Raw material	9	0	0	7
Export sales outside Africa	Finished assembled	77	75	100	90
	Partially finished	10	25	0	10
	Raw material	13	0	0	0

Source: World Bank staff.

Note: Data pertain to 2005 median values of sales to private firms.

Externalities from Chinese and Indian FDI in Africa: Technology Transfer

Worldwide, the presence of foreign firms usually has a profound effect on a host country's participation in international trade, because FDI is often associated with an increase in both exports and imports. Empirical evidence on a global basis suggests that firms with foreign capital tend to be more export-oriented than domestic firms, and are responsible for a large share of exports in many developing, as well as transition, economies.[32] The data presented in this chapter generally confirm these findings in the case of Chinese and Indian firms operating in Africa. In most regions of the world, the contribution of foreign firms to host-country exports may not be immediate. A surge in FDI inflows frequently results in a spike of imports as multinationals bring capital equipment for their newly established production plants. Because it takes several years to establish links with local suppliers, in the initial period of operation they may also rely on imported intermediate inputs before switching to local sourcing.

An important potential by-product of this process is that domestic firms become exposed to transfers of advances in technology or enhanced skills. Such exposure can engender positive spillover effects on the efficiency and competitiveness of host country firms; see box 6.5. [33] The possibility of positive spillovers to host markets in Africa by Chinese and Indian investors in the form of new skills was explored in detail in chapter 5. How these

BOX 6.5

International Evidence on Spillovers from Foreign Direct Investment

Spillovers from FDI take place when the entry or presence of multinational corporations increases the productivity of domestic firms in a host country and the multinationals do not fully internalize the value of these benefits. Spillovers may take place when local firms improve their efficiency by adopting the new technologies of foreign affiliates operating in the local market, either based on observation or by hiring workers trained by the affiliates. Spillovers also occur when multinational entry leads to greater competition in the host country market and forces local firms to use their existing resources more efficiently or to search for new technologies (Blomström and Kokko 1998).

To the extent that domestic firms are effective competitors with multinationals, the latter have an incentive to prevent technology leakage and "horizontal" spillovers from taking place. This can be achieved through formal protection of their intellectual property, trade secrecy, paying higher wages, or locating in countries or industries where domestic firms have limited imitative capacities to begin with. While foreign affiliates may want to prevent knowledge leakage to local firms against whom they compete, they may have an incentive to transfer knowledge to their local suppliers in upstream sectors. These "vertical" spillovers can take place through several channels. Multinationals may transfer knowledge about production processes, quality control techniques, or inventory management systems to their suppliers. By imposing higher requirements with respect to product quality and on-time delivery they may provide incentives to domestic suppliers to upgrade their production facilities or management. Indeed, the pressure from multinationals is often the driving force behind obtaining ISO quality certifications. Finally, increased demand for intermediate products due to multinational entry may allow local suppliers to reap the benefits of scale economies.

Source: Broadman 2005.

investors utilize new machinery is another avenue for spillovers. Indeed, a key sector in Africa where the importation of inputs is critical in affecting the export competitiveness of the continent's manufactured products is new machinery, since this is one input in the production process where the impacts of technological advances and innovation will likely be felt most.

Interestingly, there is significant variation in the source markets for new machinery purchases among different nationality firms covered in the WBAATI survey; see table 6.13. African firms buy the majority of their new machinery in their local, home markets. Chinese businesses also purchase a substantial portion of new machinery in Africa, indeed twice as much as do Indian firms. But it is the share of new machinery that Chinese firms buy in their home market that is striking in comparison with other firms: whereas machinery made in India constitutes 22 percent of Indian firms' new machinery purchases, for Chinese firms operating in Africa, 60 percent of their new machinery purchases are made at home. Indian firms in Africa also procure a substantial portion of new machinery in the Chinese market.

The findings from the business case studies provide additional insights to these survey data about the sources and disposition of machinery and equipment by Chinese and Indian firms operating in Africa, as well as those of their African counterparts. First, whereas these firms' raw materials are most often procured locally, much of their capital goods are imported, and not just from their home markets, but from Europe, the United States, and Japan. For instance, a Chinese construction firm in Tanzania recently purchased new Mack and Caterpillar trucks and other vehicles from the United States, and new Komatsu equipment from Japan.

TABLE 6.13

Purchases of New Machinery by Import Origin and Firm Nationality
(percent)

Import origin	Firm nationality			
	African	Chinese	Indian	European
Domestic	55	32	15	28
Other Africa	3	1	7	12
China	6	60	13	1
India	5	0	22	2
Other	31	8	44	56

Source: World Bank staff.

Note: Data pertain to 2005 median values.

Still, a key finding from the business case studies is that China and India are rapidly becoming important source markets for imports of sophisticated capital goods for firms producing on the African continent, and regardless of firm nationality. Price advantage appears to be a major factor. To take but a few examples, new Chinese-manufactured tower cranes and aviation control pumps newly built to custom specifications were recently purchased by firms in South Africa; and India has been a key source market for new road-paving equipment in Ghana, new water-purification systems in Senegal, and new automated nut-processing machines in Tanzania. A particularly interesting finding is that the transfers of technology are not unidirectional from China and India to Africa: in some cases, Africa has been a source market for capital goods exports to China and India, resulting in "reverse technology transfers"; see box 6.6

Second, the firms in Africa under study clearly make their capital goods purchase decisions based on price-quality tradeoffs. In particular, although machinery and other equipment available from China and India often embody a price advantage, firms covered in the business case studies indicated that in some instances due to lower quality, they purchased these capital goods elsewhere. Conversely, other firms are willing to accept lower-quality machinery in return for having to pay a lower price. For example, an African construction company looked into procuring Chinese

---

BOX 6.6

"Reverse Technology Transfers": Africa as a Capital Goods Source Market for China and India

Perhaps the most surprising finding from the business cases studies on the issue of technology spillovers involving Chinese and Indian firms in Africa is the phenomenon of "reverse transfers of technology." In several instances, *used* African-made capital goods are being purchased by Chinese and Indian firms to be used in *their* home countries. For example, a Chinese firm bought, dismantled, and then reconstructed in China a synthetic polymer plant that was operating in South Africa. An Indian firm did the same with an electric power station, also in South Africa.

Source: World Bank staff.

equipment, but did not do so due to inferior quality; instead it purchased more expensive equipment from Germany and United States. A foam mattress producer in Senegal tried to source covers from China, but ultimately cancelled the order due to poor craftsmanship. On the other hand, a bottled water manufacturer in Ghana recently purchased new filling machines and a new pasteurizer from China. Although the firm considers the Chinese equipment to be of a lower quality than European versions, the 25 percent cost advantage proved sufficiently offsetting.

Finally, there is a clear recognition among all nationality firms covered in the business case studies that export competitiveness in Africa hinges greatly on the use of new, as opposed to used, machinery, especially in global market–targeted investments—where exports are destined for advanced country markets. This business strategy is consistent with findings in the empirical literature showing a positive correlation between superior export performance and new vintage equipment.[34] Several examples illustrate the point. One Chinese affiliate in Tanzania indicated that headquarters management forbids it to utilize used machinery in Africa; at the same time, the firm is prohibited from selling any of its used machinery in Africa once a project is completed: rather, headquarters deploys such machinery to other African affiliates of the enterprise group. A long-established Indian textile firm in South Africa recently purchased new weaving machines from Germany and Italy to produce high-quality blankets it sells not only locally in South Africa and in neighboring countries, but also in the United Kingdom. And, a struggling African textile firm in Ghana still using 1960s-vintage machines just placed an order in China for state-of-the-art equipment so that it can export—for the first time in its history—to other African markets as well as to markets outside the continent, based on its recognition that only by competing in terms of quality, price, and time will it be able to expand its reach.

Meeting the Challenge of Network Trade: What Are Africa's Export Opportunities Presented by Chinese and Indian Foreign Investment?

The dynamics of recent economic development trends in other regions of the world suggest that for most African countries, buyer-driven networks offer several opportunities to export labor-intensive products in an increasingly globalized marketplace. While there are possibilities for the continent's participation in exporting through producer-driven value chains, they are far more limited at present. [35] In large part this is due to the largely rudimentary nature of the bulk of FDI inflows to Africa; it also is due to the limited volume of such flows: in 2005, Sub-Saharan Africa accounted for less than 2 percent of global FDI inflows.[36] One sector, however, where Africa's supply chain exports can be enhanced in the short- to medium-run is in the service sector—especially tourism. This is a labor-intensive industry that could yield significant benefits in terms of spillovers, growth, and employment generation. The dramatic recent increase in South-South FDI flows to Africa by China and India, especially in light of the nature and effects of these flows evidenced above, holds the promise for countries on the continent to exploit opportunities for network trade. There are brighter prospects for buyer-driven trade in the short run, with more producer-driven trade in the longer run. Even in buyer-driven networks, however, as well as in the tourism sector, African countries today face many challenges in both maintaining their foothold and in upgrading their current roles. In what follows, we assess several cases for such network trade opportunities.

African Buyer-Driven Network Trade Opportunities

Participation in the Global Food Network
For African farmers, there are inherently new risks and new opportunities associated with the globalization of the agricultural sector. Increasing quality, production, and employment standards are complemented by lower overall prices and heightened competition. Accessing global commodity chains can mean higher economic rents and more stability, but it is not an immunization against changing market conditions. For those firms that remain outside the value chain, the risks are even greater because they are subject to even more volatile markets.

Agriculture is one of the sectors with the greatest potential for integration of African producers into global buyer-driven networks. However, in the short run this development will be inhibited by poor transport and communications infrastructure, which are detrimental to perishable agricultural products. Africa's network trade in agriculture—and in all other sectors as well—will also be negatively affected by the deficiencies in the business climate and the lack of human capital. If these difficulties are overcome, the increased network participation will translate into higher agro-exports and higher employment in the sector, but its benefits are likely to accrue to larger producers.

Global food markets have undergone a rapid transformation in recent years, driven by changes in consumer demand, increased concerns about food safety, and the rise of modern retail systems. Growing incomes and changing lifestyles have increased consumer demand for variety, quality, food safety, year-round supply of fresh produce, "healthy" foods, and convenience. Concerns about the social and environmental conditions of food production have also become more prominent.[37]

The growing concerns about food safety have shifted the emphasis from product to process standards and have made product traceability and controlling the supply chain "from farm to shelf" a vital requirement in higher segments of the market. Sourcing in open markets with anonymous suppliers has been increasingly replaced with integrated supply chains that usually involve reliance on preferred suppliers and independent certification of good agricultural and manufacturing practices. In response to these changes, international food companies have become more reliant on standards that are often more stringent than the public sector requirements for food safety and quality. Most companies have begun to view food safety not only as an important commercial risk but also as an opportunity to distinguish themselves from competitors. This effort has also manifested itself through growing product differentiation, innovation, and branding.

At the same time, three important trends have been taking place in the structure of the global food industry during the past two decades.[38] First, there has been consolidation of food retailing. In 2001, just 30 grocery retail chains reached jointly more than $1 trillion in revenue, thus accounting for about 10 percent of global food sales. Within this group, the top 10 retailers constituted 57 percent of the combined total. The highest concentration ratios were observed in Europe. For example, the top five supermarket companies in France had a 90 percent market share and the corresponding figures for the Netherlands and Germany were 64 and 60 percent, respectively. While an acceleration in consolidation was also observed in the United States in the late 1990s, the top five supermarket chains commanded only about 35 percent of the overall market in 2004.

Second, there is an increasing reliance by major retail chains on their own agents for sourcing and thus declining importance of wholesale markets. While in the past, wholesale and terminal markets were responsible for 20 percent or more of food sales, their share in sales in industrialized countries has dropped to about 10 percent. Despite their declining importance, some wholesale markets still continue to play their traditional roles, serving as a buffer for overages and outages, an outlet for second-quality products, and a source for small shops and restaurants. Others have moved to more specialized roles in servicing ethnic food segments of the market.

Third is the rapid growth of the food service industry. For instance, in 2002, 46 percent of all food expenditures in the United States were spent in hotels, restaurants, and institutions. In the EU, consumer expenditures on food away from home were equal to about one-third of the value of retail food sales. In Japan, the food service sector accounted for 26 percent of total spending on food. The growing importance of food services has been associated with an increasing demand for a wide range of processed and semiprepared foods, large-volume contracts, extreme aversion to food safety risks and other product risks, and almost no direct foreign sourcing.

Overall, the consolidation of food retailing has given the market leaders extraordinary market and purchasing power and has resulted in a strong tendency toward global sourcing, the introduction of preferred-supplier arrangements, supply-chain integration and rationalization, and lower average prices but also lower variability in prices for contract or program suppliers.

That supermarkets are replacing wholesalers as the leading buyers in the global food sector has important implications for African producers. Compliance with the standards imposed by supermarkets is costly. It requires investment in machinery and facilities (for instance, cold storage and stainless steel tables), improvements in sanitation levels, worker hygiene, and skills, as well as investment in obtaining a formal certification. For instance, fruit producers in South Africa supplying supermarkets have had to comply with the HACCP (Hazard and Critical Control Point) program as well as the private standards of a particular buyer. Growers selling to U.K. supermarkets are also expected to comply with the Ethical Trading Initiative Baseline Code, which covers labor standards and includes requirements related to health, safety, and wages.[39] Such investments may be beyond the reach of smaller producers, who are often credit constrained. Supplying supermarkets may additionally involve an increase in variable costs, such as expenditure on microbiological testing. Timeliness is also an important aspect of serving supermarket chains. If a shipment gets delayed along the way and misses its vessel in the port, taking the next vessel might not be an option because the delay may result in deterioration of the product quality and thus the shipment may no longer meet the required standard.

However, there are several advantages of being a supplier servicing a supermarket chain. They include: higher margins than in wholesale transactions, more consistent and more predictable demand, the ability to obtain detailed information on changing developments and requirements within the market, the chance to receive very detailed guidelines for operations and good practice, and finally the ability to enhance one's reputation by being a supplier to a major retail chain.[40] In South Africa, for example, producers selling fruit to U.K. and European supermarkets have been able to obtain more stable outlets for their produce. For instance, most supermarkets negotiate purchases six months in advance. Moreover, producers servicing supermarkets on average receive better prices than those selling on the open market.[41] These benefits of the emergence of supermarkets as direct buyers extend outside the food sector, including for example, to the cut-flower industry; see box 6.7.

Increased safety and traceability requirements suggest two potential business strategies for African exporters. The first one is to remain small and to compete on price in wholesale markets or in Asian countries where high standards are not required. This strategy relies heavily on the ability to minimize overhead costs, but is not very demanding in terms of investment and skills required. It corresponds to the "SME generic exporter" category in the agro-exporter typology presented in table 6.14. The other strategy is to invest in facilities and systems to service the most discriminating buyers and benefit from the higher prices received for such products and thus become a "premium supplier," as in the case of Kenyan Kale Farmers; see box 6.8. From there, a company can move up the value-added ladder to supply premium, prepacked produce and thus become a "value-added prepared-food operator." The leap from the "SME generic exporter" category to the "premium exporter" status is huge, as is the jump to the highest category. At the same time, the road for small firms to grow into large generic exporters is closing. Thus, in the future, firms will most likely self-select into small operators with low profits or high value-added operators supplying premium products.

While many African growers may continue exporting their products to wholesale buyers or Asian markets, the coming years will most likely bring an increase in foreign sales of premium suppliers that in turn will lead to a higher concentration of exports. Such a trend has been observed in Kenya,

BOX 6.7

Benefits of Supermarkets as Direct Buyers in the Supply Chain: African Cut Flowers

The cut-flower industry offers one promising example for future Africa-Asia trade and investment. Traditionally, the majority of Kenyan cut flowers are exported to the Netherlands, where they are sold in auction houses and are then re-exported to large markets in the United States or Japan. This rather convoluted process contributes to a much shorter vase life of Kenyan flowers. An emergent trend in the industry is *direct sales* to supermarkets, which seem keen to cut out the auction houses and buy directly from flower farms abroad. African producers really are the main beneficiary of this new trend. For supermarkets, African flowers are attractive because they are inexpensive and their growers are willing to accept a fixed price. To the African growers, the arrangement is beneficial as well because supermarkets buy large quantities at fixed prices.[a] The commercial challenge for Kenya is to "cut out the Dutch middleman" and sell directly in the United States or in Japan's more than $10 billion flower market. This Kenyan example could perhaps even be expanded to the whole horticultural sector in Africa.

Source: Based on Jaffee (2003).

a. ILO 2000.

where in recent years only 13 companies account for about 90 percent of the country's fresh vegetable exports.[42] The small producers incapable of accumulating human and physical capital will be excluded from the global commodity chain and will capture lower returns.

However, thanks to their lower production costs in labor-intensive products, smallholder farmers will remain competitive suppliers to wholesalers and Asian markets where neither high process standards nor traceability are required. The cost advantage of smallholder farmers over large-scale commercial firms is about 20–40 percent, as the latter have high overhead and supervision costs and paid labor is in general less motivated than self-employed farmers.

Alternatively, smallholders may find opportunities in production under contract for private export firms. However, smallholder growers could be

TABLE 6.14
Typology of African Agro-Exporters

Type	Type name	Main characteristics	Major facilities	Main skills
1	"Briefcase" trader	Very small scale; intermittent and opportunistic sales	Pickup truck, fax machine	Some trading skills
2	SME generic exporter	Regular sales to regular clientele of one or two shipments per week; mostly sales of loose-packed produce; virtually all sales to wholesaler-based distribution channels	Small packing shed with some cold storage capacity and basic equipment (sorting tables) 3–4 pickup trucks	Trading and management skills. At least one quality control person. One or a few persons to interact with farmers. Several produce grades.
3	Large generic exporter	Regular sales to regular clientele virtually every day. Mix of loose and prepacked produce. Most sales to wholesaler-based distribution channels, some to smaller supermarkets.	Larger packing house facilities with some automation and significant cold store facilities. Larger fleet of trucks including several insulated trucks.	Supply chain management skills. More quality control staff. Several agronomists and larger number of field staff.
4	"Premium" supplier	Regular supplier to super-markets and other upmarket distributors. Most sales are of prepacked produce with improved packaging and product combinations.	Potentially requires develop-ment and operation of one or more farms (to ensure supply control and trace-ability) with investments in farm equipment. Upgraded central pack house facilities (stainless steel tables, improved lighting, blast cooling system, good sanitation, and worker hygiene systems) plus precooling centers in major product sourcing areas.	Supply chain and food hygiene and HACCP management skills. Multiple layers of quality assurance personnel. Advanced production plan-ning skills, including pro-fessional farm management. Needs to be an "accredited" supplier.
5	Value-added prepared food operator	Same as "premium" supplier with the addition of a "high-care" line of prepared ready foods	The above, plus separation of high- and low-risk areas and distinct "high-care" rooms with the necessary temperature control and air venting systems, metal detectors, heat sealing equipment.	The above, plus additional food science personnel.

Source: Jaffee 2003.

BOX 6.8

Kenyan Kale Farmers Upgrade Physical and Human Capital to Supply Supermarkets

The example of kale farmers in Kenya illustrates the implications of supplying supermarkets as opposed to distributing the product through traditional channels. Although the supermarket buyers in Kenya are mostly domestic, the transition required by farmers to qualify as suppliers involves upgrading human and physical capital. Kale is a useful example because it is the most widely grown and consumed vegetable in Kenya, and because it is a relatively labor-intensive crop with reliable yield and low market price, making it common among smallholder farmers.

Farms supplying kale to supermarkets achieve higher land and labor productivity rates than farms supplying brokers, wholesalers, or retailers. For land productivity, the difference between the two groups is 59 percent, while the corresponding figure for labor productivity is 73 percent. These differences are due to the fact that farms selling to supermarkets are larger, use an average of twice the amount of inputs per unit of land, and incur higher variable costs in the form of tractor rentals and irrigation operating expenses. Their share of irrigated land in total land under cultivation is almost four times higher than in the case of other farms. For instance, while only 5 percent of traditional farms have electricity, this is true of all farms supplying supermarkets. Similar differences can be found with respect to having a phone line or a transportation vehicle. Producers selling to supermarkets have higher profits, pay 25 percent higher wages, and enjoy greater revenue stability than traditional-channel farms.

Meeting the higher standards for food safety, quality, and other delivery conditions requires additional human capital. The average education of workers on farms supplying supermarkets is 13 years of schooling, which is almost twice the 7 years obtained by workers on traditional-channel farms. The vast majority of workers in the latter scenario are family members, whereas the opposite is true for supermarket chain suppliers.

Source: Neven 2004.

marginalized by higher standards imposed by food importers on premium suppliers: suppliers would need to bear the costs to provide the necessary training and oversight to a large number of small growers. Indeed, working with smallholder farmers is difficult for trading and processing companies. Quantities of products are small and heterogeneous in quality, supply can be haphazard, and bulking-up of volume into a steady stream of product of constant quality is difficult to achieve. Other weaknesses of smallholder farmers are the lack of knowledge of modern markets, technologies, and inputs, and poor access to capital, which prevents them from upgrading their production. These factors constitute a serious constraint to supplying high-end modern supply chains. In fact, the share of smallholder farmers (and medium-scale growers) in Kenya has decreased over the past decade, although the absolute volume of smallholder-produced vegetables for export is approximately the same.[43]

Participation in the Global Apparel Network
The apparel industry is another sector in which production is increasingly distributed across low-income countries by buyers searching for cheaper labor. The global trend is one of continuous differentiation and externalization of traditional functions by buyers. It began with a shift in production of standard, low-value garments to suppliers and was followed by a shift in production of higher-value apparel.

The experience of countries that have made this transition, such as Korea, Taiwan (China), and Hong Kong (China), suggests the importance of organizational learning.[44] As these countries upgraded and outsourced production to suppliers with cheaper labor, they themselves moved from being original equipment manufacturers (OEM) to serving as original brand name manufacturers of garments. Acquiring the capabilities needed for transition was achieved by firms that integrated into the buyer-driven networks of developed countries, not by those for which participation did not extend beyond simple assembly.[45]

As a result of Africa's preferential access to foreign markets, a significant amount of such production was moved from newly industrialized countries in Asia to Africa. FDI from Asia, induced by the quota system of the Multifibre Arrangement (MFA) and the U.S. Africa Growth and Opportunity Act (AGOA), enabled rapid growth of the African apparel sector. One of the beneficiaries was Lesotho, which, thanks to its cheap labor costs, was an ideal host for Asian capital seeking to avoid the textile quotas constraining exports from their home country. Investors from Taiwan (China) and China helped to make the textiles industry in Lesotho the single largest employer, accounting for 90 percent of export earnings.[46] Other African producers also benefited from AGOA. In 2004, Sub-Saharan African exports of apparel to the United States exceeded $1.5 billion.[47]

The expiration of the MFA on January 1, 2005, ushered in a new apparel trade environment, however. On the one hand it unleashed a new wave of Chinese sales on the world market. The ILO, in its analysis of the post-MFA environment, reported that textiles and apparel exports under the AGOA fell to $270 million in the first quarter of 2005 versus $361 million a year earlier. The 25 percent reduction contrasts with a 19 percent increase in China's exports for the same period.[48] On the other hand, following the expiration of the MFA, many companies that had invested in Africa to take advantage of the quota began moving back to China in search of cheaper labor.[49] Between January and March 2005, Kenya exported $60 million of textile and clothing products to the United States, which was 13 percent or $9 million less than the exports during the same period in 2004.[50] But, important to note, the stepped-up competition African apparel makers face today is not just an Asian phenomenon: indeed, just as fierce competition comes from other Southern markets, such as Central and Latin America; figure 6.8 shows a value-chain comparison between Kenya's and Honduras' apparel sectors.

FIGURE 6.8
Apparel Value Chain Comparison Between Kenya and Honduras

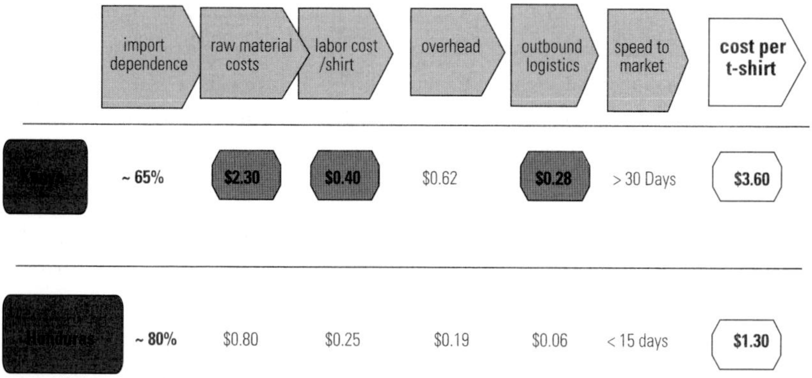

	import dependence	raw material costs	labor cost /shirt	overhead	outbound logistics	speed to market	cost per t-shirt
Kenya	~ 65%	$2.30	$0.40	$0.62	$0.28	> 30 Days	$3.60
Honduras	~ 80%	$0.80	$0.25	$0.19	$0.06	< 15 days	$1.30

Source: Subramanian 2006.

Today, the increased competitive pressures in the global apparel market call for significant upgrading of Africa's apparel industry. Much as in Africa's agricultural sector, suppliers striving to get preferred status in global apparel-production chains must be capable of meeting ever-rising quality, production, and employment standards while at the same time lowering costs, inventory, and lead times on delivery. In the United States, textile and garment buyers demand quick and accurate response systems of their suppliers. Quick response entails technological integration within the supply chain to shorten lead times. Accurate response comprises integration of forecasting, planning, and production activities to allow manufacturers to postpone production until forecasts can be validated at the point-of-sale.

Reducing inventory and delivery lead times can be challenging for small firms because it involves integrating within the supply chain and investing in process improvement, infrastructure, technology, and training. To be successful, suppliers have to coordinate with customers in various process areas, including customer relationship management, demand management, enterprise resource planning, product development, order fulfillment, and procurement, among other items. It also includes adoption of new systems ranging from electronic data interchange to bar coding, often to customer specifications.

Despite the complexity of commodity chain integration, an opportunity for medium-sized African firms lies in the fact that global buyers seek nimble suppliers with low inventory. A good organizational structure with well-trained staff and close integration within the network should enable even small producers to avoid a make-to-stock production configuration that poses an expensive risk of obsolete inventories. However, it is also clear in light of the scale and competitive advantage that Chinese and Indian textile and apparel firms have in the mass-market portion of the sector that African firms should focus on niche markets.

There is little question that recent developments in the international trading system mean that without substantial improvements in Africa's behind-the-border business climate, the opportunities for apparel exporters on the continent may be rapidly diminishing, notwithstanding the fact that preferential access to the U.S. market under AGOA still presents a window of opportunity for African-based suppliers. Many global buyers seek not only low-cost labor and production flexibility, but also value geographic diversity of supply to reduce exposure to risks. This is yet another opportunity for African suppliers to enter the global apparel supply chain. However, all these opportunities will not be realized without substantial investments in transportation and communications infrastructure and in trade facilitation, as discussed earlier in chapters 4 and 5.

Producer-Driven Network Trade Opportunities for Africa

Because producer-driven global networks are characterized by high levels of vertical ownership within the supply chain, a significant amount of FDI is usually required in producing countries. Producer-driven networks also prevail in industries with greater capital intensity and greater reliance on skilled labor. As new research on the recent experience of the transition countries in Eastern Europe and the former Soviet Union illustrates, there indeed exists a positive correlation between the amount of FDI received and country participation in producer-driven production networks; see figure 6.9.[51] The same research found a positive correlation between the stock of FDI and the share of skilled-labor- and capital-intensive exports.[52] Given the limited amount of FDI attracted by most African economies— apart from the oil-dominated countries—(see table 6.15), with a few exceptions aside, the prospects for entry by African producers into these

FIGURE 6.9

Producer-Driven Network Trade Positively Correlates with FDI: International Evidence

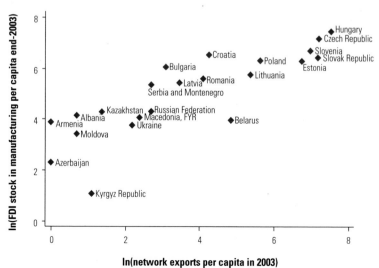

Source: Broadman 2005.

TABLE 6.15

Africa Net FDI Inflows Per Capita

(dollars)

Country name	Average 2003–05
Equatorial Guinea	1,404
Seychelles	633
Angola	248
Congo, Rep.	166
Gabon	136
Botswana	108
Namibia	97
Mauritania	75
Sudan	48
Lesotho	44
Chad	40
Cape Verde	38
Nigeria	32
South Africa	30
Mauritius	30
Gambia, The	24
Cameroon	22
São Tomé and Principe	22
Swaziland	19
Zambia	16
Mozambique	13
Ghana	12
Guinea	12
Côte d'Ivoire	10
Tanzania	10
Togo	8
Senegal	8
Uganda	8
Congo, Dem. Rep.	7
Mali	7
Benin	6
Eritrea	5
Zimbabwe	4
Sierra Leone	4
Malawi	3
Madagascar	3
Guinea-Bissau	3
Central African Republic	2
Kenya	1
Burkina Faso	1
Niger	1
Ethiopia	1
Comoros	1
Rwanda	1
Burundi	*
Liberia	n.a.
Somalia	n.a.

Source: IMF WEO database, except Burkina Faso, Côte d'Ivoire, Kenya, Niger, Tanzania, Togo, and Zambia, where the World Bank WDI data were used. For WDI data, the most recent three-year average was used.

Note: * indicates negligible amount FDI; n.a. indicates no data available.

networks seem limited in the near future. One sector where such opportunities do exist is the automotive assembly and parts industry in South
Africa.

Producer-Driven Network Trade for South Africa's Automotive Industry
Since the early 1960s, South Africa's government has pursued a proactive
policy of support for developing the nation's automotive sector; see box 6.9.
Just like many formerly inward-oriented economies, South Africa's industry
started to face a radically new competitive environment as its trade barriers
began to fall starting in the late 1980s.[53] The initial result was a sharp increase
in the trade deficit in the automobile and components sector. In 1995, the

---

BOX 6.9

South Africa's Automotive Industry Policy

South Africa's policy of support for developing the nation's automotive sector has evolved through several phases over the last 40 years. Its overarch-
ing objectives have been to develop a globally integrated and competitive
local motor vehicle and component industry; stabilize long-term employment levels in the industry; improve the affordability and quality of vehicles;
promote the expansion of automotive exports and improve the sector's
trade balance; and contribute to the country's economic development.

The initial strategy emphasized import substitution strongly influenced by
protectionism, including local content policy. In the late 1980s, in line with
the country's progress toward trade liberalization, a structural adjustment
program for the motor industry that primarily focused on the objective of
saving foreign currency and enhancing automotive exports was introduced.
In the mid-1990s, to make the framework consistent with the then-new
WTO, the Motor Industry Development Program (MIDP) was initiated; it
continues to this day. In general, the MIDP has entailed a phase-down of
tariffs; removal of local content requirements; duty-free imports of components up to 27 percent of the wholesale value of a vehicle; and duty rebate
credits to be earned on exports. The provisions of the current phase of the
MIDP extend to 2007. Recently, it was publicized that a third phase of the
MIDP is anticipated to run from 2008 to 2012.

Sources: Kaplan 2005; and Barnes, Kaplinsky, and Morris 2004.

South African government's Motor Industry Development Program (MIDP) heralded a much-lauded shift in vision and aims. Its main objective was to improve the international competitiveness of firms in the industry, enhance growth through exports, and stabilize employment levels. To achieve these objectives, a series of export-oriented incentives were introduced, coupled with a reduction in import tariffs between 1995 and 2002.[54]

Since the implementation of the MIDP, South Africa has seen rapid growth in the auto sector, based on a speedy rise in global exports of completely-built-up units (CBUs), especially after 1998. In addition to these exports of CBUs, there was also a marked increase in global exports of direct car components.

With respect to CBU global exports, several of the leading international automotive companies have been sourcing large numbers of cars from South Africa for sale *outside* the continent.[55] (This is in contrast to the Chinese and Indian entrants to the South African CBU market—noted above—where all of their sales are *within* Africa, and mostly in South Africa itself.) BMW has been largely specializing in the 3-series car to obtain scale economies. Its exports of CBUs increased steadily from 4,346 units in 1998 to 43,583 units in 2002; its exports have been sold in North American, Australian, European, and Asian markets. Volkswagen has sourced an increasing number of Golf 4 cars for the U.K. and European markets, with exports growing from 10,485 units in 1998 to 30,533 units in 2002. Daimler-Chrysler exported 36,324 C-Series Mercedes Benzs to the United Kingdom, Australia, and Asia in 2002, a 20-fold increase on exports of only 1,752 vehicles in 1998. Toyota began exporting its Corolla to Australia and New Zealand in April 2003.

Global exports of South African–produced automotive components have also grown, particularly catalytic converters. A major conduit for these exports were the non-German OEMs who satisfied their need for duty credits by purchasing these from component suppliers. Catalytic converters are an especially interesting case, because initially the level of value-added was low. However, as scale has been built up, investment of more than 2 billion rand (more than $200 million) has been made into a deepening of the production process. In 2002, South Africa supplied 12 percent of the global catalytic converter market and was the most important supplier of catalytic converters to the EU.

South Africa's success in tapping into global production sharing in the automotive sector is driven in large part by the economy's well-developed infrastructure, high labor productivity, speed to market, product quality, and flexibility. Its accommodative foreign trade and investment policy regime has also been a key factor. At present, very few other countries on the continent can match these attributes or possess the resources that South Africa has devoted to developing this industry. With the implementation of certain policy reforms, other countries may well be able to achieve a modicum of success in this regard.

As the case of South Africa's development of its automotive sector shows, however, not only can entry barriers to global production networks be appreciable, but the role of government in supporting certain policies has had to evolve. This evolution has been driven in part by fiscal considerations at home. Moreover, changes in international trade rules regarding interventionist export promotion policies have also played a role. Indeed, in general there are important lessons in this regard for the African continent, not only from South Africa's experience but from that of other regions—most notably East Asia—as well; see box 6.10.

Services Network Trade Opportunities in Africa: The Case of Tourism

As fast growth rates and rising disposable incomes in the Chinese and Indian economies foster the creation of a growing Asian middle class, the opportunity for Africa to attract more tourists from that part of the world becomes greater. Indeed, China's government formally encourages tourism in Africa. The government has approved 16 African countries as outbound destinations for Chinese tourists, including Ethiopia, Kenya, and Zimbabwe. This pushed the number of Africa's Chinese tourists to 110,000 in 2005, a 100 percent increase over 2004, according to Chinese government figures.[56]

The tourism sector covers hotels and restaurants, travel agencies, tour operator services, and tourist guide services, and its development could have a myriad of positive spillover effects for Sub-Saharan African countries: improved transportation, enhanced communications infrastructure, and transfers of technology, knowledge, and managerial skills. It also can make significant contributions to foreign exchange earnings. And, perhaps most important from the standpoint of increasing growth and reducing poverty, tourism is a labor-intensive industry, and its development therefore can be a major source of employment.

BOX 6.10

Lessons for Africa from the "East Asian Miracle"

Africa's economies (as well as those of developing countries elsewhere) face significant challenges in trying to duplicate the interventionist "export-push" strategies of the earlier high-performing Asian economies that gave rise to the so-called "East Asian Miracle." In part, these challenges arise from the fact that the international trading system today, under WTO rules, embodies constraints on the use of certain national policies that were absent 15 years ago. At the same time, in light of the economic crises many of the East Asian countries experienced in the 1990s, governments rightfully face tougher questions now about which parts of the earlier approaches should be implemented. At a very minimum, off-the-shelf applications of these approaches seem unwise: policies need to be shaped to local conditions. There are valuable lessons from the earlier experiences to be shared, if none other than that the most successful approaches build on a government's ability to adapt to a constantly changing global economic environment.

Exports can be promoted by a variety of means that are consistent with obligations for market access and limited subsidies under the WTO. Improving the efficiency of institutions such as customs services, implementing duty drawbacks and related measures in a transparent manner, and minimizing trade diversion under free trade regimes are all WTO-consistent and can be effective mechanisms for export promotion—all other things equal. In addition, aggressively courting export-oriented FDI and focusing infrastructure development in areas that facilitate exports are unlikely to provoke opposition from trading partners. Export credits, while more controversial, remain feasible instruments under certain conditions; however, these measures must be of limited duration. Fiscal discipline, moreover, will require that the costs of any such programs be kept in check.

Tourism already dominates African services exports, both for the region overall and for several countries; it also exhibits the fastest growth rate of services exports for the region; see figures 6.10a and 6.10b. South Africa is the most important tourist destination on the continent, followed by Mauritius, Tanzania, and Botswana. For the whole of Sub-Saharan Africa,

Regardless of whether such initiatives are in compliance with international commitments, a prerequisite for their effectiveness is the establishment of basic market institutions—those that stimulate interenterprise competition, protect private property rights, ensure the free flow of labor and capital, and foster effective disciplines for sound governance, among other characteristics. Without such market institutions in place, any presumed national benefits from interventionist export policies can be eroded by distortions and the misallocation of resources. Clearly, the role of government is to ensure the establishment of such institutions insofar as they are public "goods," the provision of which can compensate for basic market failures.

For firms attempting to enter export markets, it cannot be assumed that simply achieving low production costs is sufficient to realize foreign sales. Today, firms increasingly need to be embedded in international production networks. Four decades since the East Asian Miracle, the emergence of international production networks has transformed the world marketplace into one where there is very fast innovation with dramatic declines in product prices, rapidly changing product characteristics, new products that quickly lead to the obsolescence of older ones, and a premium on the ability to rapidly communicate electronically. In such a setting, government's role in foreseeing and successfully dealing with market changes more effectively than businesses themselves is likely to be more limited. The experience of a number of countries in the last two decades suggests that private firms often have been successful at certain strategies previously advocated to be provided by government. For example, the growth of the Indian software sector was primarily driven by private sector agents, often from abroad. In this regard, governments can play an effective supporting role in providing an inviting environment for firms to encourage the return of nationals working abroad, which can provide a large reservoir of new knowledge and effect the transfer of best practice methods.

Sources: World Bank staff, based on World Bank (1993) and Pack and Saggi (2006).

South Africa accounts for about 57 percent of the market share of total travel services exports.

But there is great potential for further development of the industry. Mozambique provides an interesting case for unexploited tourism development that could have quite positive value-chain effects (see box 6.11).

FIGURE 6.10a
Tourism: Africa's Largest Service Export

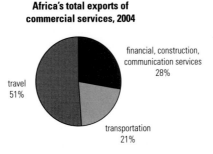

Africa's total exports of
commercial services, 2004

FIGURE 6.10b
Where Tourism is the Main Service Export

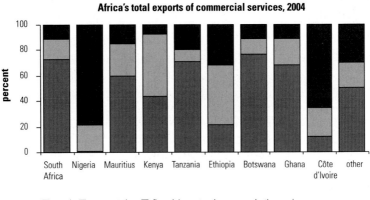

Africa's total exports of commercial services, 2004

Source: IMF Balance of Payments.

African countries are engaged in a concerted effort to explore tourism potential at the subregional level. For example, Southern African Development Community (SADC) countries have established an SADC Tourism Sector Coordination Unit, based in Mauritius, which has been coordinating initiatives at the regional level. Along the same lines, East African Community countries, as part of the regional strategy for 2006–10, have developed a concerted action plan to increase exports of tourism services. Still, further efforts are needed to enhance tourism exports. For example, the sector is constrained by the limited presence of African tourist suppliers in the travel-originating distribution centers, and by poor access to the Global Distribution System and the Computer Reservation System.

BOX 6.11

Developing Services Supply Chains: Tourism in Mozambique

Mozambique has underdeveloped tourism potential. Since the 1980s, the government of Mozambique (GOM) has implemented many "first-generation" structural reforms such as adopting sound fiscal and monetary policies, privatizing public enterprises, and liberalizing trade. The reforms have helped stabilize macroeconomic balances and supported the remarkable growth performance since 1992. In 2000, the GOM adopted the Action Plan for Reduction of Absolute Poverty (PARPA) as a medium-term rolling instrument incorporated into the public planning system. Tourism is seen as a priority area in which additional investment may create the jobs that are necessary to meet the PARPA objectives. This expectation is sensible and reasonable, because most developing countries have increased market shares in international tourism. Sub-Saharan Africa, in particular, has experienced very strong growth in tourism within the last two decades—increasing its market share of global arrivals from 1.5 percent in 1970 to 4.5 percent by 2003.

Despite a strong tourism asset base and its geographic proximity to South Africa, one of the world's top destinations, Mozambique still trails behind all its neighbors except Malawi. Despite quite an impressive annual growth rate of 13 percent (1999–2003), the average number of tourists per 100 inhabitants, at 2 for Mozambique, is half of that of Africa's average, and well below the world average of 11 per 100 inhabitants. Mozambique's poor performance reflects problems with the country's overall image, product variety, and quality of tourists' experiences. Realizing this potential depends substantially on the ability of all players in the Mozambique tourism value chain—from providers of final goods and services, to other suppliers and government officials—to create and deliver high-quality tourism experiences that can transform the country into a "must-see" destination in Africa.

However, the requirements for turning Mozambique into a regional tourism star are extremely high. First, the country needs to address its cumbersome visa regulations. Many countries in the area do not require visas at all from EU citizens (Mauritius, Seychelles, Maldives). Second, there are also limited intercontinental flights from Europe, and significant delays and hassles for tourists in airports. Third, there is a weak presence of Mozambican tour operators in regional and global markets and limited collaboration between foreign and Mozambican tour operators. Finally, there are no clear or concerted mechanisms to ensure the development and restoration of historic monuments and sites (for example, elephant reserves, Ilha da Mocambique, ruins of the Bazaruto Fishing Pearls Company).

Source: FIAS 2006.

To facilitate African countries' realization of the benefits that tourism development can offer, there are several areas for proactive government actions. First, incentives for private investment—both by domestic entrepreneurs and foreign businesses—in the sector are low in light of the inherent public-good nature of many national (and cross-national) tourism assets. Public investment in tourism development and marketing is relatively small by world standards, except in countries like Kenya and South Africa. Second, there is limited coordination among the industry's stakeholders. Airlines, hotels, tour operators, retailers, restaurants, and a whole range of public sector agencies are not effectively working intersectorally to develop, promote, and manage tourism destinations and, more broadly, Africa's tourism image and positioning in world markets. Last, the roles and responsibilities among tourism-related agencies lack clarity and reforms are needed to avoid overlapping and inefficiently allocated limited funds.

What Lessons Emerge from Africa's Experience in Exploiting Opportunities for Network Trade?

Several factors appear to be critical in fostering successful engagement in network trade by African producers, as illustrated by the following examples. Exploiting price sensitivity is one. Pineapples sold in Europe have become a major export for Ghana in the last few years. Ghana's pineapples are of a lower quality than those of its main competitors in the European market, Costa Rica and Côte d'Ivoire, but even so, Ghana's prices were relatively high due to an inefficient national transport system. Largely as a result of the country's enhanced sea-freighting capacity in the mid-1990s, Ghana's pineapple shipping costs to Europe were reduced significantly compared to former airfreight means. This in turn allowed Ghana's pineapple exporters to reduce the export price and compete more effectively in Europe. While this has been a sound market-entry strategy, Ghana faces a significant risk in this low-price and low-margin market unless it can ramp up quality as well as increase scale.[57]

Speed-to-market, a second factor, has been crucial in the success of highly perishable commodities, such as Kenyan cut flowers, as discussed above. The fact that there are several planes leaving Nairobi every day for its main markets in the EU makes for fast delivery—an obvious competitive advantage. Kenya was one of the first African countries to privatize its airline industry in 1996. This infrastructure asset also allows African producers tapping into distant export markets to be highly responsive and flexible to market changes. Recently, an Air Services Agreement between China and Kenya was signed; Kenya Airways has been granted landing rights in several cities in China and is now operating direct flights to Hong Kong (China) and Guangzhou in southern China from Nairobi. Since Kenya was granted Preferred Tourist Destination Status in 2004, arrivals from China have more than doubled and are expected to grow even more. Similar to the policies with China, Kenya could seek enhanced access to other Asian markets, such as India, Japan, and Korea.

High labor productivity is clearly a critical factor. It explains in part why, as discussed above, South Africa is essentially the only country in Sub-Saharan Africa to participate in producer-driven network trade. At the same time, low labor productivity is a major weakness for the Kenyan apparel industry: even though Kenyan wages are lower than those in Honduras, for example, the labor cost for producing one t-shirt in Kenya is 1.6 times that of Honduras. In addition to shop-floor productivity-enhancement programs, implementation of specific policies to improve labor productivity is required in education, skills training, and health policies.

Finally, the importance of product quality cannot be overstated. Nigeria's shrimp industry has been transformed and is now increasingly profitabe thanks to the high quality of its exports to a growing European market. However, if Ghana wants to increase the profitability of its pineapple industry, it will have to start focusing on ways to produce higher-quality produce through the implementation of standards and quality certification.[58]

To be sure, as the foregoing analysis makes clear, these attributes are not easy to develop. They are complex to implement, require significant investment in resources, and they take time. The experience of many of the developing countries in the world that have been successful in entering network trade—even more so those that were not successful—testifies to this. The barriers to entry to global production sharing should not be underestimated.

Conclusions and Policy Implications

Firms in Africa—both domestic and foreign owned—have had international operations and trading relationships for decades. But in recent years the world's marketplace has witnessed the formation of new global-scale economic systems that are tightly integrated, and the rise of trade in intermediate goods constitutes a fundamental shift in the structure of the global trading system. These transformations pose a major challenge for African policy makers in their understanding of how their countries fit into today's international division of labor. Under traditional notions of international trade, the direction of trade (that is, which countries produce what goods for export) was determined by the principle of "comparative advantage" and a country specialized in the production and export of the good (or goods) for which its relative productivity advantage exceeded that of foreign countries. It is clear, however, that a radically different notion of comparative advantage has now emerged due to the significant role that intermediate goods play in overall international trade, giving rise to *intraindustry* trade. This is true whether the trade is done *within* firms as a result of FDI or through more arms-length transactions, such as through subcontracting.[59] In this environment, it is hard to imagine that the future of Africa's economic development can be isolated from these systems.

Summary of Main Findings

It is in this context that a key issue facing the countries of Sub-Saharan Africa is how they can successfully leverage the newfound investment and trade interest of China and India so that the continent can become a more proactive player in modern global network trade. Over the last 15 years, Asia has already been Africa's fastest-growing export market and is much more open to trade than are Europe and America. And there is no evidence to suggest that this trend will not continue. Yet, in spite of the many opportunities offered by trade in global supply chains, few African countries have been able to make the leap and exploit these opportunities. As the preceding analysis suggests, investment and trade activities by China and India with Africa can facilitate the continent's ability to avail itself of such opportunities.

Evidence presented in this chapter from new firm-level survey data and original business case studies developed in the field provides strong support for the notion that, as is happening elsewhere in the world, in Africa, trade flows and FDI are complementary activities, rather than substitutes. (This finding at the firm level parallels that presented at the country level in chapter 2). The data clearly point to the fact that Chinese and Indian firms operating in Africa have been playing a significant role in facilitating this complementarity. For one thing, Chinese and Indian businesses tend to achieve larger-sized operations than do their African counterparts within the same sectors, and this appears to allow them to realize economies of scale. It is not surprising, then, that the evidence shows that, all other things equal, Chinese and Indian firms have significantly greater export intensity than do African firms. Moreover, the exports from Africa produced by Chinese and Indian businesses are considerably more diversified and higher up the value chain than exports sold by domestic firms.

The corporate structures of Chinese and Indian firms also differ from those of African businesses: the former tend to have more extensive participation in group enterprises or holding companies (with headquarters in their home countries). At the same time, relative to their African counterparts, Chinese and Indian firms engage more extensively in regional integration on the continent. They also exhibit more extensive integration into a greater variety of third countries outside of Africa than do African businesses. And Chinese and Indian firms tend to be vehicles for the transmission of advances in technology and new equipment to the African continent.

But the data also suggest that there are significant differences between Chinese and Indian firms operating in Africa. Chinese businesses in Africa tend to have a different risk-aversion profile than Indian firms, as reflected in their foreign investment entry decisions, their degree of vertical integration, the origin of source markets for their inputs, and the strength of affiliation with state (as opposed to private) entities in conducting transactions, among other attributes. Chinese businesses in Africa pursue business strategies that yield them greater control up and down the production line, resulting in enclave types of corporate profiles, with somewhat limited spillover effects. Indian firms, conversely, pursue African investment strategies that result in greater integration into domestic markets and operate extensively through informal channels, indeed even into facets of the local political economy, surely a result of the fact that there is a longer tradition of Indian ethnic ties to Africa.

That global value chains offer real opportunities for African countries to use Chinese and Indian investment and trade activities to increase the volume, diversity, and value-added of exports from the continent is corroborated by the evidence presented. Indeed, as has happened elsewhere in the world, even landlocked countries in Africa—with the right mix of policies—may well be able to engage in network trade. Value-chain analysis of particular industry cases in Africa shows that certain factors are likely to be especially critical in successful network trade. These include implementing a pricing scheme that fully takes into account market conditions, such as production and distribution costs, the strength of competition, and so forth; enhancing product quality; organizing the business to be flexible and responsive to changes in market conditions; enhancing labor productivity; and developing the capacity to maximize speed to market. As the analysis shows, there are several industries in Africa that have either already engaged in or have strong prospects to engage in buyer-driven network trade, including food, fresh-cut flowers, apparel, and fisheries, among others. These are all products where African exports face far tougher competition in international markets than the continent's traditional raw commodities, and they must meet world-class standards. However, there are also examples where Africa can exploit its endowment of natural resources and climb the value chain.

The prospects for African industries to engage in producer-driven network trade in the short- to medium-run, apart from some sectors in South Africa, such as automotive assembly and parts and components, are far more limited—without attracting substantial FDI by firms plugged into such networks. Increasingly, as the chapter suggests, Chinese and Indian firms have these attributes. Still, the barriers to entry to global production sharing are significant.

Finally, there is evidence that African services exports can engender significant supply-chain spillover effects domestically. Some countries already are doing so, such as Ghana, Senegal, and Tanzania in back-office services. A second concrete opportunity for growth in services exports is tourism. With rising middle classes in China and India looking to spend a significant part of their increased disposable incomes on holidays, there is clear potential for Africa to reap the benefits. Through positioning itself as a relatively close and attractive holiday destination, the gain for Sub-Saharan Africa would not just be *direct* (in tourism services, hotels, restaurants, and the like) but also *indirect*: the fact that more and more flights arrive in African airports makes transport cheaper and Asian markets more readily accessible for African goods and services.

Policy Implications

As is the case in other regions of the world, African countries' participation in international production networks will be an important path for exporting to foreign markets and more generally integrating into the global economy. FDI has been the driver behind involvement in international production chains. Indeed, the evidence suggests that countries that have been most heavily involved—or have the strongest prospects for involvement—in network trade are the countries that have received large FDI inflows.[60] Thus, examining the reasons why some countries have been more successful in attracting FDI can help explain why they have been more involved in international production networks, particularly because many determinants of FDI inflows also determine the country's ability to participate in international trade. This analysis readily yields insights as to what policies African governments should pursue.

Cross-country differences in the amount of FDI received over the past decade in Africa have been striking, whether considering oil-producing countries or not.[61] What explains success or failure in attracting FDI inflows? At the macro level, one obvious factor is political stability. In Africa, as is the case worldwide, the presence of political instability generally always discourages FDI inflows, all other things equal. Consider the experience of Sierra Leone: it has attracted just $4 per capita of FDI annually between 2003 and 2005. Of course, political stability is not a sufficient condition, as the example of some African countries shows. Burkina Faso enjoyed relative stability but no significant FDI inflows over the same period.

Also at the macro level, empirical studies of capital flows seem to agree on two observations: official flows lead or stimulate countries' reform efforts, whereas private capital flows, with FDI as their most important component, follow or respond to certain reform measures.[62] On a global basis, research shows that a sound and stable economic policy regime provides a potent explanation of variation in FDI flows. To this end, maintenance of macroeconomic fundamentals as measured by GDP growth or low inflation is important.

But there are FDI-specific policy measures that also are key in this regard.[63] The most effective reforms of FDI policy regimes have included steps to (i) grant nondiscriminatory, "national treatment" to foreign investors for both right-of-establishment and post-establishment operations; (ii) prohibit the imposition of new and the phase-out of existing trade-related investment measures (TRIMs), for example, local content measures, export performance requirements, restrictions on the use of foreign exchange, and trade balance measures, including those prohibited by the WTO, among others, on FDI; (iii) provide freedom to FDI projects regarding all investment-related transfers, for example, profits, royalties, the right of compensation for confiscation, requisition, and other guarantees; (iv) provide for binding international arbitration for investor-state disputes; and (v) abide by international law standards for expropriation, that is, expropriation only for a public purpose and with prompt, adequate, and effective compensation.

Sound and stable economic and FDI-specific policies alone, however, are not sufficient to attract FDI. The overwhelming bulk of empirical research in many regions around the world points to progress in establishing behind-the-border market-supporting institutions, especially those assuring a competitive business environment, legal protection and enforcement of property rights, sound governance,[64] and market-reinforcing regulatory regimes governing the provision of basic infrastructure services, as critical.[65] This suggests that the FDI inflow differentials observed across African countries are likely to be significantly determined by the quality of the underlying domestic business climate and related institutional conditions, both within individual countries and on a regional basis. If this is the case, the focus of reforms should be on the factors that shape a country's microeconomic fabric at a deeper level beyond that touched by reform of so-called administrative barriers—such as speeding up the pace of business registration or of obtaining a business license—which has become conventional wisdom as the way in which improvement in the investment climate comes about.

Proximity to markets, which is strongly related to geography, also explains a relatively larger FDI stock in some countries. To some extent, however, geographical disadvantage can be overcome. To some extent, sound governance can compensate for distance to major markets. More important, engaging in regional trade agreements that effectively increase the size of the market and foster regional integration can be a strong counterweight to poor proximity to markets. Thus, an effective way for land-locked remotely located countries to attract larger FDI inflows is to improve the quality of governance and cooperate on arrangements that would reduce transactions costs associated with moving shipments through their respective territories.

Moreover, trade transactions costs associated with FDI depend crucially on a country's trade-facilitating infrastructure, such as the performance of the customs administration and the quality of transportation and communication networks. Long delays at the border and high variance in clearing times make it difficult for potential foreign investors to commit to a particular delivery time. Corruption at border crossings increases the costs of doing business, thus lowering the competitiveness in world markets of locally produced goods. The poor condition of transport networks increases the cost and time needed for shipping goods. High costs of communications, whether through fixed-line telephony, cellular network, or Internet, increase the costs of doing business. In light of the public-goods aspects of developing adequate infrastructure, a legitimate role for government action—including potential investment outlays—probably exists.

The quality of infrastructure services is another crucial component of a business-friendly climate that facilitates both FDI inflows and participation in international production networks. Well-designed liberalization of services sectors can lead to higher competition, greater range of services available, and more efficient services provision, which in turn decrease the costs of doing business and attract new entry by both domestic and foreign entrepreneurs.

Of course, many other factors may influence attractiveness to FDI. For instance, investors operating in high technology and services sectors will be looking for availability of skilled labor and protection of intellectual property rights. To enhance Africa's attraction for investment in back-office services, enlarging the pool of skilled workers is key. Those interested in simple labor-intensive assembly operations will be more sensitive to labor costs and labor market flexibility.

Beyond the investment-related policies enunciated above, what trade-related policies might be considered by African policy makers to facilitate participation in international production networks? One option concerns export processing zones (EPZs). Experience from other parts of the world suggests caution in pursuing this route. The bulk of international evidence shows that, while many countries have established these special-incentive regimes, relatively few have succeeded in encouraging exports on a sustainable and economywide basis. Indeed, most such regimes are not readily amenable to generating horizontal and vertical spillovers. In addition, in certain cases, these incentives create opportunities for discretionary behavior and corruption. Finally, resorting to these incentives appears to signal to international investors fundamental weaknesses in the underlying business climate for which such measures are meant to compensate.

A second option would be introducing duty drawbacks or other systems offsetting import tariffs. Although such measures may offset the bias in favor of production for domestic market, experience around the world indicates that they require sophisticated administrative capacities for effective implementation. In most of Sub-Saharan Africa, these are lacking.

Trade policy reforms that would likely be the most effective in engendering Africa's participation in global network trade are those that would provide for economywide trade liberalization, in line with these countries' WTO obligations. These reforms should be combined with proactive trade facilitation measures and WTO-consistent actions that would encourage regional integration, especially those that can create needed economies of scale, including through regional cooperation in customs administration and conditions for transit. In essence, then, countries should rely on a two-pronged trade policy strategy encompassing improvements in both domestic and external conditions, and use of WTO rules as a tool to leverage both domestic and regional reforms.

Overall, the shift in the views of many governments—not only on the African continent, but worldwide—toward a more positive stance vis-à-vis FDI has increased competition for such investment. Having more potential host countries to choose from, FDI inflows have become more sensitive to differences in investment climates. As a result of the fragmentation of international trade, multinational corporations have become more foot-loose, being better able to shift their own production (or their subcontracting) activities relatively easily from one geographic location to another in response to changes in the cost of production, competition, and market access; regulatory and governance conditions; and perceived political risks. All of the factors that would make Sub-Saharan African exports competitive in Europe or the United States—especially price, speed-to-market, labor productivity, flexibility, and product quality—are equally *if not more* important in the fiercely competitive Asian markets. Of course this presumes an Asian playing field where market access to African exports is not distorted through trade policy measures, such as the case of escalating tariffs in certain South-South trade arrangements.[66]

The experience of countries that have successfully taken advantage of opportunities offered by global markets suggests that two elements have to be in place—successful implementation of first-generation reforms (liberalization of prices, foreign trade, and exchange regimes) and consistent movement toward a rules-based institutional regime with the capacity of enforcement. This means it is a priority for Sub-Saharan Africa to accelerate efforts at getting its own house in order and to implement the policies, institutions, and trade-enabling physical infrastructure that will be the critical foundations to allow African countries to successfully integrate into today's international economy.

Endnotes

1. Broadman 2005.
2. For a discussion of these trade preference arrangements see chapter 3.
3. See chapter 2.
4. See annex 1A for a description of the survey and business case study databases.
5. In fact, as discussed below, because of weak implementation of regional free trade agreements in Africa, companies have been induced to engage in cross-border investment rather than serving regional markets through trade.
6. See Blonigen (2001) for a literature review. At the product level, many empirical studies also find that trade and FDI tend to be complements, although there are a few exceptions, such as Blonigen's (2001) study of Japanese trade and FDI in the U.S. automobile market, where the evidence suggests both substitution and complementarity effects.
7. UNCTAD 1996.
8. UNCTAD 2005d.
9. For an extensive discussion of issues involved, see Jones and Kierzkowski (2004).
10. Gereffi 1999a.
11. For analysis of the Armenia case, see Broadman (2005).
12. Feenstra 1998.
13. World Bank 2004b.
14. Brenton and Hoppe 2006.
15. This categorization builds on that developed in World Bank (2004b).
16. See below for further discussion of services in this context.
17. For the Japanese case see World Bank (2004b).
18. Eisenman and Kurlantzick 2006.
19. See Broadman (2001).
20. Yao and He 2005.
21. Yao and He 2005.
22. See Goldstein et al. 2006.
23. See, for example, Legget 2005; O'Hara 2005; White 2006; Timber 2006; Economist Intelligence Unit 2006.
24. For example, Chinese textile investments in Côte d'Ivoire, Mauritius, Rwanda, and Swaziland are commonly thought of as AGOA-related investments.
25. As table 1A.3 in the annex to chapter 1 shows, for the specific sectors that table 6.3 indicates there are significant differences in the form of entry; in the

case of construction, surveyed Chinese and Indian firms have essentially the same representation; in the case of non-oil minerals and metals, the surveyed Chinese firms have about half the representation as the Indian firms. The latter may account for the Indians' greater reliance on entry through acquisition.

26. See below.
27. This finding is consistent with various World Bank Investment Climate Assessments (ICAs) of African countries.
28. On China, see Broadman (2001); on India, see Saez and Yang (2001).
29. Yao and He 2005.
30. Micro firms have 10 or fewer employees; small firms have more than 10 but fewer than 51 employees; medium firms have between 51 and 100 employees; large firms have more than 100 but fewer than 201 employees; and very large firms have 200+ employees.
31. See chapter 1.
32. UNCTAD 2002a.
33. Clerides, Lach, and Tybout 1998; Bernard and Jensen 1999.
34. Bernard and Jensen 1999.
35. See the discussion in the second section of this chapter.
36. UNCTAD 2006a.
37. van der Meer 2005.
38. These points drawn from Jaffee (2003).
39. Barrientos and Kritzinger 2004.
40. Jaffee 2003.
41. Barrientos and Kritzinger 2004.
42. Jaffee 2003.
43. Jaffee 2003.
44. Gereffi 1999b.
45. Gibbon 2001.
46. Peta 2005.
47. ILO 2005.
48. ILO 2005.
49. Between October 2004 and May 2005, a loss of 6,000 out of 39,000 jobs was also reported. In Lesotho, where the garment sector accounted for more than 90 percent of the country's exports and was by far the largest single employer, 6,650 out of 56,000 workers were terminated at the end of 2004 and 10,000 more were moved to short-term contracts (ILO 2005).
50. ILO 2005.
51. Broadman 2005.
52. Broadman 2005.
53. Barnes and Kaplinsky 2000.
54. For the specifics on those export incentives, see Barnes, Kaplinsky, and Morris (2004).
55. Barnes, Kaplinsky, and Morris 2003.

56. Eisenman and Kurlantzick 2006.
57. Subramanian and Matthijs 2006.
58. Subramanian and Matthijs 2006.
59. Feenstra 1998.
60. Jones, Kierzkowski, and Lurang 2005.
61. Recall table 6.15.
62. The literature is large; among others, see UNCTAD (2005).
63. See Broadman and Recanatini (2002).
64. Although the quality of governance tends to matter less for attracting FDI to countries that happen to be amply endowed in natural resources, especially oil and natural gas, the exclusion of FDI in extractive industries does not significantly change the findings in the literature.
65. For one such examination in the case of South Eastern Europe, see Broadman et al. (2003).
66. Recall the case of the Tanzanian cashews produced by an Indian firm that faces escalating import tariffs on processed cashews in India (see chapter 3).

Bibliography

Acquaah, Moses. 2005. "Enterprise Ownership, Market Competition and Manufacturing Priorities in Sub-Saharan African Emerging Economy: Evidence from Ghana." *Journal of Management and Governance* 9 (3-4): 205–35.

Aitken, Brian J., and Ann E. Harrison. 1999. "Do Domestic Firms Benefit from Direct Foreign Investment? Evidence from Venezuela." *American Economic Review* 89(3): 605–18.

Amjadi, A., and A.Yeats. 1985. "Have Transport Costs Contributed to the Relative Decline of Sub-Saharan African Exports?" World Bank Working Paper 1559, Washington, DC.

Anderson, James E., and Douglas Marcouiller. 2002. "Insecurity and the Pattern of Trade: An Empirical Investigation." *Review of Economics and Statistics* 84(2): 342–52.

Arora, Ashish, Andrea Fosfuri, and Alfonso Gambardella. 2001. *Markets for Technology: The Economics of Innovation and Corporate Strategy.* Cambridge, MA: MIT Press.

Arora, Ashish, and Alfonso Gambardella. 2004. "The Globalization of the Software Industry: Perspectives and Opportunities for Developed and Developing Countries." National Bureau of Economic Research Working Paper 10538, Cambridge, MA.

Asia Pacific Foundation of Canada. 2006. "Can India Revitalize its Special Economic Zones to Rival Those in China?" Asia Pacific Bulletin, February 1. http://www.asiapacificbusiness.ca/apbn/pdfs/bulletin244.pdf.

Asia Pacific Foundation of Canada, China Council for the Promotion of International Trade. 2005. "China Goes Global, A Survey of Chinese Companies' Outward Direct Investment Intentions." September. http://www.asiapacific.ca/analysis/pubs/pdfs/surveys/china_goes_global.pdf.

A.T. Kearney Global Business Policy Council. 2005. *FDI Confidence Index 2005,* Volume 8. http://www.atkearney.com/shared_res/pdf/FDICI_2005.pdf.

Aw, Bee Yan, Sukkyun Chung, and Mark J. Roberts. 2000. "Productivity and Turnover in the Export Market: Micro-level Evidence from the Republic of Korea and Taiwan (China)." *World Bank Economic Review* 14(1): 65–90.

Azam, Jean-Paul, Marie-Françoise Calmette, Catherine Loustalan, and Christine Maurel. 2001. "Domestic Competition and Export Performance of Manufacturing Firms in Côte d'Ivoire." Toulouse, France: University of Toulouse.

Barnes, J., and R. Kaplinsky. 2000. "Globalization and Trade Policy Reform: Whither the Automobile Components Sector in South Africa?" *Competition and Change* 4(2).

Barnes, J., R. Kaplinsky, and M. Morris. 2004. "Industrial Policy in Developing Economies: Developing Dynamic Comparative Advantage in the South African Automobile Sector." *Competition and Change* 8(2).

Barr, A. 2000. "Social Capital and Technological Information Flows in the Ghanian Manufacturing Sector." *Oxford Economic Papers* 52(3): 539–59.

Barrett, H., B. W. Ilbery, A. Brown, and T. Binns. 1997. "Prospects for Horticultural Exports under Trade Liberalization in Adjusting African Economies." Working paper. Report submitted to DFID (ESCOR).

Barrientos, Stephanie, and Andrienetta Kritzinger. 2004. "Squaring the Circle: Global Production and the Informalization of Work in the Food Sector." *Journal of International Development* 16: 81–92.

Battat, Joseph, and Dilek Aykut. 2005. "Southern Multinationals: A Growing Phenomenon." Note prepared for the conference, "South Multinationals: A Rising Force in the World Economy," 9–10 November, Mumbai, India.

Bauer, Thomas K., Magnus Lofstrom, and Klaus Zimmermann. 2000. "Immigration Policy, Assimilation of Immigrants and Natives' Sentiments towards Immigrants. Evidence from 12 OECD Countries." Discussion Paper No. 187, IZA, Germany.

Beine, Michel, Frederic Docquier, and Hillel Rapoport. 2001. "Brain Drain and Economic Growth: Theory and Evidence." *Journal of Development Economics* (64)1: 275–89.

Bernard, Andrew, Jonathan Eaton, J. Bradford Jensen, and Samuel Kortum. 2003. "Plants and Productivity in International Trade." *American Economic Review* 93: 1268–90.

Bernard, Andrew, and J. Bradford Jensen. 1999. "Exceptional Exporter Performance: Cause, Effects, or Both?" *Journal of International Economics* 47(1): 1–26.

Bester, Hennie, Louis de Koker, and Ryan Hawthorne. 2004. "Access to Financial Services in South Africa: A brief case study of the effect of the implementation of the Financial Action Task Force Recommendations." Genesis Analytics, Johannesberg, South Africa.

Biggs, Tyler, and Manju Kedia Shah. 2006. "African Small and Medium Enterprises, Networks, and Manufacturing Performance." World Bank Policy Research Working Paper 3855, Washington, DC.

Biggs, Tyler, Manju Kedia Shah, and Pradeep Srivastava. 1995. "Technological Capabilities and Learning in African Enterprises." World Bank Africa Technical Department Paper Series 288, Washington, DC.

Bigsten, Arne, Paul Collier, Stefan Dercon, Marcel Fafchamps, Bernard Gauthier, Jan Willem Gunning, Abena Oduro, Remco Oostedorp, Catherine Pattillo, Mans Soderbom, Francis Teal, and Albert Zeufeck. 2004. "Do African Manufacturing Firms Learn from Exporting?" *Journal of Development Studies* 40(3): 115–41.

Black, Richard, R. King, and R. Tiemoko. 2003. "Migration, Return and Small Enterprise Development in Ghana: A Route Out of Poverty?" Sussex Migration Working Paper No. 9, Sussex Centre for Migration Research, University of Sussex.

Black, Richard, K. Koseer, and N. Al-Ali. 2000. "Transnational Communities." Economic and Social Research Council (ESRC), Swindon, United Kingdom.

Blomström, Magnus, and Ari Kokko. 1998. "Multinational Corporations and Spillovers." *Journal of Economic Surveys* 12(2): 1–31.

Blonigen, Bruce A. 2001. "In Search of Substitution between Foreign Production and Exports." *Journal of International Economics* 53: 81–104.

Blonigen, Bruce A., and R. Davis. 2000. "The Effects of Bilateral Tax Treaties on U.S. FDI Activity." NBER Working Paper 7929, Cambridge, MA.

Boyenge, Jean-Pierre Singa. 2003. *ILO Database on Export Processing Zones, 2003.* ILO Office, Geneva.

Brenton, Paul, and Takako Ikezuki. 2004. "The Initial and Potential Impact of Preferential Access to the U. S. Market under the African Growth and Opportunity Act." World Bank Policy Research Working Paper 3262. Washington, DC.

Brenton, Paul, and Mombert Hoppe. 2006. "AGOA, Exports, and Development in Sub-Saharan Africa." World Bank Policy Research Working Paper 3996. Washington, DC.

British Broadcasting Corporation (BBC). 2006. *Africa's Economy.* Online, available at http://news.bbc.co.uk/2/shared/spl/hi/africa/05/africa_economy/html/trade.stm.

Broadman, Harry G. 1994. "The Uruguay Round Accord on Trade in Services." *The World Economy* 17(3).

———. 2001. "The Business(es) of the Chinese State." *The World Economy* 24(7).

———. 2005. *From Disintegration to Reintegration: Eastern Europe and the Former Soviet Union in International Trade.* Washington, DC: World Bank.

Broadman, Harry G., J. Anderson, S. Claessens, R. Ryterman, S. Slavova, M. Vaglasindi, and G. Vincelette. 2004. *Building Market Institutions in South Eastern Europe.* Washington, DC: World Bank.

Broadman, Harry G., and Francesca Recanatini. 2002. "Corruption and Policy: Back to the Roots." *Journal of Policy Reform* 5: 37–49.

Cadot, Olivier, and John Nasir. 2001. "Incentives and Obstacles to Growth: Lessons from Manufacturing Case Studies in Madagascar." Regional Program on Enterprise Development Paper 117, World Bank, Washington, DC.

CARANA. 2003. "The Role of Transportation and Logistics in International Trade: The Developing Country Context." Available at http://www.tessproject .com/product/special_studies/trans&log_phase_1_report.pdf.

Chanda, R. 2001. "Trade in health services." Paper WG4:5, Commission on Macroeconomics and Health. Available at http://www.cmhealth.org/docs/wg4_ paper5.pdf.

Chen, Tsunehiro Otsuki, and John Wilson. 2006. "Do Standards Matter for Export Success?" World Bank Policy Research Paper, Washington, DC.

Claessens, S., D. Oks, and R. Polastri. 1998. "Capital Flows to Central and Eastern Europe and Former Soviet Union." Working paper. World Bank, Washington, DC.

Clarke, George. 2005. "Beyond Tariff and Quotas: Why Don't African Manufacturing Enterprises Export More?" World Bank Policy Research Working Paper WPS3617, Washington, DC.

Clarke, George, and Scott Wallsten. 2006. "Has the Internet Increased Trade? Developed and Developing Country Evidence." *Economic Inquiry* 44(3): 465–84.

Clerides, Sofronis K., Saul Lach, and James R. Tybout. 1998. "Is Learning by Exporting Important? Micro-Dynamic Evidence from Colombia, Mexico, and Morocco." Finance and Economic Discussion Series No. 96-30, Board of Governors of the Federal Reserve System.

Collier, Paul. 2006. "Africa: Geography and Growth." Draft. Center for the Study of African Economies, Oxford University.

Cudmore, Edgar, and John Whalley. 2004. "Border Delays and Trade Liberalization." University of Western Ontario and NBER Peking University CESIfo (June).

DFID (Department for International Development). 2000. "Viewing the World: A Study of British Television Coverage of Deveeloping Countries." U.K.

Djankov, Simeon, Caroline Freund, and Cong Pham. 2006. "Trading on Time." World Bank Policy Research Working Paper 3909, Washington, DC.

Dollar, David, Mary Hallward-Driemeier, and Taye Mengistae. 2004. "Investment Climate and International Integration." World Bank Policy Research Working Paper WPS3323, Washington, DC.

Dreyhaupt, Stephan J. 2006. *Locational Tournaments in the Context of the EU Competitive Environment.* Wiesbaden: Deutscher Universitätsverlag.

Easterly, William, and Ross Levine. 1997. "Africa's Growth Tragedy: Policies and Ethnic Divisions." *Quarterly Journal of Economics* 112(4): 1203–1205.

Eaton, J., and Samuel Kortum. 2001. "Trade in Capital Goods." *European Economic Review* 45(7): 1195–1235.

ECA (Economic Commission for Africa). 2005. *Economic Report on Africa: Meeting the Challenges of Unemployment and Poverty in Africa.*

Economist Intelligence Unit. 2006. "Africa Economy: China Syndrome." Country Briefing. Viewswire Africa.

Eifert, Benn, Alan Gelb, and Vijaya Ramachandran. 2005. "Business Environment and Comparative Advantage in Africa: Evidence from the Investment Climate Data." World Bank Africa Region, Regional Program of Enterprise Development Working Paper 56, Washington, DC.

Eisenman, Joshua, and Joshua Kurlantzick. 2006. "China's Africa Strategy." *Current History* (May): 219–24.

Ernst, D., J. Faberberg, and J. Hildrum. 2002. "Do Global Production Networks and Digital Information Systems Make Knowledge Spatially Fluid?" TIK Working Paper 13, University of Oslo, Norway.

Evans, Peter. 1979. *Dependent Development: The Alliance of Multinational, State, and Local Capital in Brazil.* Princeton, NJ: Princeton University Press.

Fafchamps, Marcel. 1999. "Networks, Communities, and Markets in Sub-Saharan Africa: Implications for Firm Growth and Investment." Centre for Study of African Economics Working Paper Series 1999–24, Oxford University.

———. 2002. "Returns to Social Network Capital among Traders." *Oxford Economic Papers* 54(2): 173–206.

Faini, Riccardo. 2002. "Development, Trade, and Migration." *Revue d'Économie et du Développement*, proceedings from the ABCDE Europe Conference (1–2): 85–116.

Feenstra, Robert. 1998. "Integration of Trade and Disintegration of Production." *Journal of Economic Perspectives* 12(4): 31–50.

FIAS (Foreign Investment Advisory Service). 2005. "Value Chain Analysis of Selected Sectors in Kenya." World Bank Group, prepared by Global Development Solutions, Washington, DC.

———. 2006. "The Tourism Sector in Mozambique: A Value Chain Analysis." World Bank Group, Washington, DC.

———. Forthcoming. *Free Zones: Performance, Lessons Learned and Implications for Zone Development.* Washington, DC: World Bank.

Financial Times. 2006. "China Winning Resources and Royalties of Africa. February 28.

Frankel, Jeffrey. 1997. *Regional Trading Blocs in the World Economic System.* Washington, DC: Institute for International Economics.

Frankel, Jeffrey, and Andrew Rose. 2002. "An Estimate of the Effects of Common Currencies on Trade and Income." *Quarterly Journal of Economics* 117(2): 437–66.

Frazer, Garth. 2005. "Which Firm Dies? A Look at Manufacturing Firm Exit in Ghana." *Economic Development and Cultural Change* 53(3): 585–617.

Freund, Caroline, and Diana Weinhold. 2004. "The Effect of the Internet on International Trade." *Journal of International Economics* 62(1): 171–89.

Garibaldi, Pietro, Nada Mora, Ratna Sahay, and Jeromin Zettelmeyer. 2002. "What Moves Capital to Transition Economies?" IMF Working Paper WP/02/64, Washington, DC.

Gelb, Stephen. 2005. "South-South Investment: The Case of Africa." In *Africa in the World Economy—The National, Regional and International Challenges*. The Hague: Fondad. Online, available at http://www.fondad.org.

Gereffi, G. 1999a. "International Trade and Industrial Upgrading in the Apparel Commodity Chain." *Journal of International Economics* (48): 37–70.

————. 1999b. "The Organization of Buyer-Driven Global Commodity Chains: How US Retailers Shape Overseas Production Networks." In *Commodity Chains and Global Capitalism*, ed. G. Gereffi and M. Korzeniewicz, 95–122. Westport, CT: Praeger.

Ghai, Dharam. 2004. "Diasporas and Development: The Case of Kenya." *Global Migration Perspectives* 10 (October), Global Commission on International Migration.

Gibbon, Peter. 2001. "Upgrading Primary Production: A Global Commodity Chain Approach." *World Development* 29(2): 345–63.

Goldstein, Andrea, Nicolas Pinaud, Helmut Reisen, and Xiaobao Chen. 2006. *The Rise of China and India: What's in It for Africa?* Paris: OECD.

Gould, David. 1990. "Immigrant Links to the Home Country: Implications for Trade, Welfare and Factor Returns?" Ph.D. dissertation, University of California, Los Angeles.

————. 1994. "Immigrants' Links to the Home Country: Empirical Implications for U.S.-Bilateral Trade Flows." *Review of Economics and Statistics* 76(2).

Groff, Alberto. 2005. "Migration Partnerships: New Tools in the International Migration Debate." *Global Migration Perspectives* 21 (January), Global Commission on International Migration.

Guarnizo, Luis, and Michael Smith. 1998. "The Locations of Transnationalism." In *Transnationalism from Below*, ed. Michael Smith and Luis Guarnizo. New Brunswick, NJ: Transaction Publishers.

Hajim, Semboja Haji Hatibu. 2001. "An Analysis on Increased Competitive Pressure in the Tanzanian Manufacturing." Tanzania Economic and Social Research Foundation.

Hale, David. 2006. "China's Economic Take Off: Implications for Africa." Brenthurst Discussion Paper.

Hallward-Driemeier, Mary. 2003. "Do Bilateral Investment Treaties Attract Foreign Direct Investment? Only a Bit...and They Could Bite." World Bank Policy Research Working Paper 3121, Washington, DC.

Hanson, Gordon, and Chong Xiang. 2004. "The Home-Market Effect and Bilateral Trade Patterns." *American Economic Review* 94(4): 1108–29.

Harding, Alan, Måns Soderböm, and Francis Teal. 2004. "Survival and Success in African Manufacturing Firms." Centre for Study of African Economics Working Paper Series 2004–05, Oxford University.

Haskel, Jonathan E., Sonia C. Pereira, and Matthew J. Slaughter. 2002. "Does Inward Foreign Direct Investment Boost the Productivity of Domestic Firms?" NBER Working Paper 8724, Cambridge, MA.

Hausman, Warren, Hau Lee, and Uma Subramanian. 2005. "Global Logistics Indicators, Supply Chain Metrics, and Bilateral Trade Patterns." World Bank Policy Research Working Paper 3773, Washington, DC.

Helpman, Elhanan. 2006. "Trade, FDI and the Organization of Firms." NBER Working Paper 12091, Cambridge, MA.

Helpman, Elhanan, Marc Melitz, and Stephan Yeaple. 2004. "Exports versus FDI with Heterogeneous Firms." *American Economic Review* 94(1): 300–16.

Henson, S., M. Bredahl, R. Loader, N. Lux, and A. Swinbank. 2000. "Impact of Sanitary and Phytosanitary Measures on Developing Countries." Center for Food Economics Research, University of Reading, UK.

Herander, Mark G., and Luz A. Saavedra. 2005. "Exports and the Structure of Immigrant-Based Networks: The Role of Geographic Proximity." *The Review of Economics and Statistics* (87): 323–35.

Hertel, Thomas W., William A. Masters, and Aziz Elbehri. 1998. "The Uruguay Round and Africa: A Global, General Equilibrium Analysis." *Journal of African Economies* 7(2): 208–34.

Hill, Robert C. 1989. "Comparing Transnational Production Systems: The Automobile Industry in the USA and Japan." *International Journal of Urban and Regional Research* 13(3): 462–80.

Hilsum, Lindsey. 2006. "We Love China." In *Granta 92: The View from Africa*. Online, available at http://www.granta.com/extracts/2616.

Hinkle, Larry, M. Hoppe, and R. Newfarmer. 2005. "Beyond Cotonou: Economic Partnership Agreements in Africa." Working paper, World Bank, Washington, DC.

Hodge, James. 2002. "Liberalization of Trade in Services in Developing Countries." In *Development, Trade, and the WTO, A Handbook,* ed. B. Hoekman, A. Mattoo, and P. H. English. Washington, DC: World Bank.

Horst, Cindy. 2004. "Money and Mobility: Transnational Livelihood Strategies of the Somali Diaspora." *Global Migration* 9 (October).

Ianchovichina, Elena, Aditya Mattoo, and Marcelo Olarreaga. 2001. "Unrestricted Market Access for Sub-Saharan Africa: How Much Is It Worth and Who Pays?" *Journal of African Economy* 10(4): 410–32.

ILO (International Labour Organization). 2000. "The World Cut Flower Industry: Trends and Prospects." Sector Publications. Online, available at http://www.ilo.org/public/english/dialogue/sector/papers/ctflower/139e3.htm.

————. 2005. "Promoting Fair Globalization in Textiles and Clothing in a Post-MFA Environment." Report for discussion at the Tripartite Meeting on Promoting Fair Globalization in Textiles and Clothing in a Post-MFA Environment, Geneva.

IMF (International Monetary Fund). 2005a. "Central African Economic and Monetary Community: Selected Issues." Country Report No. 05/390. International Monetary Fund, Washington, DC.

————. 2005b. *Direction of Trade Statistics Yearbook.* Washington, DC: International Monetary Fund.

————. 2006a. *Balance of Payments Statistics.* Washington, DC: International Monetary Fund.

————. 2006b. "Integrating Poor Countries into the World Trading System." *Economic Issues* 37. International Monetary Fund, Washington, DC.

————. 2006c. *International Financial Statistics.* Washington, DC: International Monetary Fund.

Jaffee, Steven. 1995. "The Many Faces of Success: The Development of Kenyan Horticultural Exports." In *Marketing Africa's High-Value Foods,* ed. Steven Jaffee and John Morton. Washington, DC: World Bank.

————. 2003. "From Challenge to Opportunity: Transforming Kenya's Fresh Vegetable Trade in the Context of Emerging Food Safety and Other Standards in Europe." Agriculture and Rural Development Discussion Paper 1. World Bank, Washington, DC.

Javorcik, Beata Smarzynska. 2004. "Does Foreign Direct Investment Increase the Productivity of Domestic Firms? In Search of Spillovers through Backward Linkages." *American Economic Review* 94(3): 605–27.

————. 2006. "Investment Promotion Agencies in Sub-Saharan Africa." World Bank Background Paper for *Africa's Silk Road*, Washington, DC.

Jones, Ronald W., and Henryk Kierzkowski. 2004. "International Fragmentation and the New Economic Geography." *North American Journal of Economics and Finance* 5(2).

Jones, Ronald, Henryk Kierzkowski, and Chen Lurong. 2005. "What Does Evidence Tell Us About Fragmentation and Outsourcing?" *International Review of Economics and Finance* 14(3).

Kahn, Matthew, and Yutaka Yoshino. 2004. "Testing for Pollution Havens Inside and Outside of Regional Trading Blocs." *Advances in Economic Analysis and Policy* 4(2): 1288. Article 4. Available at http://www.bepress.com/bejeap/advances/vol4/iss2/art4.

Kaplan, David. 2005. "The Effect of the MIDP on the Price of Cars in South Africa." Trade Law Centre for Southern Africa Working Paper, TRALAC, Stellenbosch, South Africa.

Kaplinsky, R., D. McCormick, and M. Morris. 2006. "The Impact of China on Sub-Saharan Africa." Institute of Development Studies, University of Sussex. Online, available at http://www.ids.ac.uk/ids/global/AsianDriverpdfs/DFIDAgenda Paper06.pdf.

Kee, Hiau Looi, Alessandro Nicita, and Marcelo Olarreaga. 2006. "Estimating Trade Restrictiveness Indices." World Bank Policy Research Working Paper WPS 3840, Washington, DC.

Keller, Wolfgang, and Stephen Yeaple. 2003. "Multinational Enterprises, International Trade and Productivity Growth: Firm Level Evidence from the United States." NBER Working Paper 9504, Cambridge, MA.

Kenya Flower Council. 2006. "Industry Information and Market Data." Online, available at http://www.kenyaflowers.co.ke/industryinfo/marketdata.php.

Konings, Jozef. 2001. "The Effects of Foreign Direct Investment on Domestic Firms." *Economics of Transition* 9(3): 619–33.

Krumm, K., and H. Kharas. 2004. *East Asia Integrates: A Trade Policy Agenda for Shared Growth.* Washington, DC: World Bank.

Lederman, Daniel, William F. Maloney, and Luis Serven. 2004. *Lessons from NAFTA for Latin American and Caribbean Countries: A Summary of Research Findings.* Washington, DC: World Bank.

Lederman, Daniel, Marcelo Olarreaga, and Lucy Payton. 2006. "Export Promotion Agencies: What Works, What Doesn't?" Draft. World Bank, Washington, DC.

Legget, K. 2005. "China Flexes Economic Muscle Throughout Burgeoning Africa," *Wall Street Journal,* March 29.

Levy Yeyati, E., E. Stein, and C. Daude. 2004. "The FTAA and the Location of FDI." Paper for Central Bank for Chile and World Bank Conference, "The Future of Trade Liberalization in the Americas," March 22–23, Santiago, Chile.

Liu, Dongkai. 2006. "China Africa Economic and Trade Collaborations Are Aiming at Win Win and Mutual Development." *Xinhua News,* January 10.

Madani, Dorsati. 1999. "A Review of the Role and Impact of Export Processing Zones." World Bank Policy Research Paper 2238, Washington, DC.

Mattoo, A., and Arvind Subramanian. 2004. "The WTO and the Poorest Countries: The Stark Reality, May 2004." IMF Working Paper WP/04/81, Washington, DC.

Mayer, Jorg, and Pilar Fajarnes. 2005. "Tripling Africa's Primary Exports: What? How? Where?" UN Discussion Paper No. 180, New York.

Mengistae, Taye, and Catherine Pattillo. 2004. "Export Orientation and Productivity in Sub-Saharan Africa." *IMF Staff Papers* 51(2): 327–53.

MIGA (Multilateral Investment Guarantee Agency). 2005a. *Competing for FDI.* MIGA-FIAS Investing in Development Series, Washington, DC.

———. 2005b. *The Impact of Intel in Costa Rica: Nine Years after the Decision to Invest.* Washington, DC: Multilateral Investment Guarantee Agency.

MIGA-FIAS (Multilateral Investment Guarantee Agency-Foreign Investment Advisory Service). Forthcoming. "China's Outward Foreign Direct Investment:

A Company Survey." A publication based on research conducted by the China Center for Economic Research, Beijing University.

Milberg, William. 2004. "The Changing Structure of International Trade Linked to Global Production Systems: What are the Policy Implications?" International Labour Organization Policy Integration Department Working Paper 33, Geneva.

Milner, Chris, and Verena Tandrayen. 2004. "The Impact of Exporting and Export Destination on Manufacturing Wages: Evidence for Sub-Saharan Africa." University of Nottingham CREDIT Research Paper 04/01, Nottingham, UK.

Ministry of Foreign Affairs of the People's Republic of China. 2006. "China's African Policy." January. Online, available at http://www.fmprc.gov.cn/eng/zxxx/ t230615.htm.

Moran, Theodore. 1998. *Foreign Direct Investment and Development: The New Policy Agenda for Developing Countries and Economies in Transition.* Washington, DC: Institute for International Economics.

Morisset, Jacques. 2003. "Using Tax Incentives to Attract Foreign Direct Investment." Private Sector and Infrastructure Network of the World Bank Note 253, Washington, DC.

Morisset, Jacques, and Kelly Andrews. 2004. "The Effectiveness of Promotion Agencies at Attracting Foreign Investment." FIAS Occasional Paper 16, Foreign Investment Advisory Service, Washington, DC.

Nanda, Ramana, and Tarun Khanna. 2005. "Firm Location and Reliance on Cross-Border Ethnic Networks: Evidence from India's Software Industry." Paper presented at the MIT Strategy Seminar, Cambridge, MA.

National Bureau of Statistics of China. 2005a. *The Bulletin of China FDI Outflow in 2004.*

————. 2005b. *China Economy and Social Development Report, 2004 and 2005.*

Naude, W., Bernard Michael Gilroy, and Thomas Gries, eds. 2005. *Multinational Enterprises, Foreign Direct Investment and Growth in Africa: South African Perspectives.* Heidelberg, New York: Physica-Verlag.

Navaretti, Giorgio Barba, and Isidro Soloaga. 2001. "Weightless Machines and Costless Knowledge: An Empirical Analysis of Trade and Technology Diffusion." World Bank Paper 2598, Washington, DC.

Neven, David. 2004. "Farm Level Perspectives on the Impact of Domestic Supermarkets on Kenya's Fresh Fruits and Vegetables Supply System." In *Three Essays on the Rise of Supermarkets and Their Impact on Fresh Fruits and Vegetables Supply Chains in Kenya.* Ph.D. dissertation, Michigan State University.

Ng, Francis, and Alexander Yeats. 2001. "Production Sharing in East Asia: Who Does What, For Whom, and Why?" In *Global Production and Trade in East Asia,* ed. Leonard K. Cheng and Henryk Kierzkowski. Norwell, Massachusetts: Kluwer Academic Publishers.

Nordas, H. K. 2004. *The Global Textile and Clothing Industry post the Agreement on Textile and Clothing.* Geneva: World Trade Organization.

OECD (Organisation for Economic Co-operation and Development). 1999. "China's Unfinished Open-Economy Reforms: Liberalizaation of Services." OECD Development Centre Working Paper No. 147, Paris.

———. 2002. *Foreign Direct Investment for Development: Maximising Benefits, Minimizing Costs.* Paris: OECD.

Office of the United States Trade Representative. 2005. *2005 National Trade Estimate Report on Foreign Trade Barriers.*

O'Hara, C. 2005. "Seeing Green in Africa." *Foreign Policy.*

Otsuki, Tsunehiro, John S. Wilson, and Mirvat Sewadeh. 2001. "Saving Two in a Billion: Quantifying the Trade Effect of European Food Safety Standards on African Exports." *Food Policy* 26(5): 495–514.

Pack, Howard, and K. Saggi. 2006. "The Case for Industrial Policy: A Critical Survey." *The World Bank Research Observer* 21(2): 267–97.

Pandey, Abhishek, Alok Aggarwal, Richard Devane, and Yevgeny Kusznetsov. 2004. "India's Transformation to Knowledge-based Economy—Evolving Role of the Indian Diaspora." Draft. World Bank, Washington, DC.

Pang, T., M.A. Lansang, and A. Haines. 2002. "Brain Drain and Health Professionals: A Global Problem Needs Global Solutions." *British Medical Journal* (324): 499–500.

Peta, Basildon. 2005. "The Chinese Tsunami that Threatens to Swamp Africa." *The Independent*, April 25, p. 64.

Puri, Lakshmi. 2004. *Silent Revolution in South-South Trade.* Geneva: WTO.

Rapoport, Hillel, and Frederic Docquier. 2005 "The Economics of Migrants' Remittances." IZA Discussion Paper 1531, Institute for the Study of Labor, Bonn, Germany.

Rauch, James. 1999. "Networks versus Markets in International Trade." *Journal of International Economics* 48 (June): 7–35.

———. 2001. "Business and Social Networks in International Trade." *Journal of Economic Literature* 39(4): 1177–1203.

———. 2003. "Diasporas and Development: Theory, Evidence, and Programmatic Implications." Department of Economics, University of California, San Diego.

Rauch, James, and Alessandra Casella. 1998. "Overcoming Informational Barriers to International Resource Allocation: Prices and Group Ties." NBER Working Paper 6628, Cambridge, MA.

Rauch, James, and Victor Trindade. 2002. "Ethnic Chinese Networks in International Trade." *Review of Economics and Statistics* 84(1): 116–30.

Reinikka, Ritva, and Jakob Svensson. 1999. "Confronting Competition: Investment Response and Constraints in Uganda." World Bank Policy Research Working Paper WPS 2242, Washington, DC.

Roberts, Mark J., and James R. Tybout. 1997. "The Decision to Export in Colombia: An Empirical Model of Entry with Sunk Costs." *American Economic Review* 87(4): 545–64.

Roy, Jayanta. 2004. "Trade Facilitation in India: Current Situation and the Road Ahead." Paper presented at the EU-World Bank/BOAO Forum for Asia Workshop on "Trade Facilitation in East Asia," November 3–5, China.

Roy, Jayanta, and Shweta Bagai. 2005. "Key Issues in Trade Facilitation: Summary of World Bank/EU Workshops in Dhaka and Shanghai in 2004." World Bank Policy Research Working Paper 3703, Washington, DC.

Saez, Lawrence, and Joy Yang. 2001. "The Deregulation of State Owned Enterprises in India and China." *Comparative Economic Studies* 43.

Saxenian, A.L. 2001. *The Silicon Valley Connection: Transnational Networks and Regional Development in Taiwan, China and India.* Philadelphia: University of Pennsylvania, Institute for the Advanced Study of India.

———. 2005. "The International Mobility of Entrepreneurs and Regional Upgrading in India and China." Draft UNU-WIDER Project on the International Mobility of Talent. Paper presented at Santiago, Chile, May 26–27, 2005.

Schiff, Maurice, and L. Alan Winters. 2003. *Regional Integration and Development.* Washington, DC: World Bank.

Schmitz, Hubert, and Peter Knorringa. 2001. "Learning from Global Buyers." Institute for Development Studies, University of Sussex.

Servant, Jean-Christophe. 2005. "China's Trade Safari in Africa." *Le Monde Diplomatique*, May. Online, available at http://mondediplo.com/2005/05/11chinafrica.

Soderböm, Måns, and Francis Teal. 2002. "Are Manufacturing Exports the Key to Economic Success in Africa?" Draft, Oxford University.

Soloaga, Isidro, John S. Wilson, and Alejandro Mejia. 2006. "Moving Forward Faster: Trade Facilitation Reform and Mexican Competitiveness." World Bank Policy Research Working Paper 3953, Washington, DC.

Sowinski, Lara L. 2006. "The African Emergence." *World Trade Magazine* (January): 74–5.

Stark, O., and Y. Wang. 2002. "Inducing Human Capital Formation: Migration as a Substitute for Subsidies." *Journal of Development Economics* 86(1): 29–46.

Sturgeon, T. 2001. "How Do We Define Value Chains and Production Networks?" *IDS Bulletin* 32(3).

Subramanian, Uma. 2006. "Being Competitive: Value Chain Analysis and Solution Design." FIAS (IFC–World Bank Group).

Subramanian, Uma, and Matthias Matthijs. 2006. "Can Sub-Saharan Africa Leap into Global Network Trade?" FIAS (IFC–World Bank Group).

Teal, Francis, James Habyarimana, Papa Demba Thiam, and Ginger Turner. 2006. "Ghana: An Analysis of Firm Productivity." World Bank Africa Region Regional Program on Enterprise Development, World Bank, Washington, DC.

Tong, Sarah Y. 2005. "Ethnic Networks in FDI and the Impact of Institutional Development." *Review of Development Economics* 9(4): 563–80.

Tucci, Alessandra. 2005. "Trade, Foreign Networks and Performance: A Firm-Level Analysis for India." Development Studies Working Paper 199 (March), Centro Studi Luca D'Agliano, Turin.

Tybout, James R. 2000. "Manufacturing Firms in Developing Countries: How Well Do They Do and Why?" *Journal of Economic Literature* 38: 11–44.

UN (United Nations). 2006. "COMTRADE Database." UN Statistics Division, New York.

UNCTAD (United Nations Conference on Trade and Development). 1993. *World Investment Report.* Geneva: United Nations.

———. 1996. *World Investment Report: Investment, Trade and International Policy Arrangements.* New York and Geneva: United Nations.

———. 1998. *Bilateral Investment Treaties in the Mid-1990s.* New York and Geneva: United Nations.

———. 2002a. *World Investment Report: Transnational Corporations and Export Competitiveness.* New York and Geneva: United Nations.

———. 2002b. *The World of Investment Promotion at a Glance: A Survey of Investment Promotion Practices.* New York: United Nations.

———. 2004a. "India's Outward FDI, A Giant Awakening?" New York and Geneva: United Nations.

———. 2004b. *The Least Developed Countries Report, 2004.* New York and Geneva: United Nations.

———. 2004c. *World Investment Report, 2004.* Geneva: United Nations.

———. 2005a. *Economic Development in Africa: Rethinking the Role of Foreign Direct Investment.* Geneva: United Nations.

———. 2005b. *Global Investment Prospects Assessment.* Geneva: United Nations.

———. 2005c. *Methodologies, Classifications, Quantification and Development Impacts of Non-Tariff Barriers.* Geneva: United Nations

———. 2005d. "The New Geography of International Economic Relations." Background Paper prepared for Doha High Level Conference on Trade and Investment. United Nations, New York.

———. 2005e. *Statistical Profiles of the Least Developed Countries, 2005.* New York and Geneva: United Nations.

———. 2005f. "Trade in Services and Development Implications." Trade Development Board document. Geneva, March 14–18.

———. 2005g. *World Investment Report: Transnational Corporations and the Internationalization of R&D.* New York and Geneva: United Nations.

———. 2006a. "Globalization of R&D and Developing Countries." Proceedings of the Expert Meeting, Geneva, January 24–26.

———. 2006b. "A Survey of Support by Investment Promotion Agencies to Linkages." United Nations Conference on Trade and Development. UNCTAD/ITE/IPC/2005/12.

UNIDO (United Nations Industrial Development Organization). 2002. "Foreign Direct Investor Perceptions in Sub-Saharan Africa. UNIDO Pilot Survey in Ethiopia, Nigeria, Uganda, and Tanzania." UNIDO, Vienna.

———. 2006. "Africa Foreign Investor Survey Report 2005: Understanding the Contributions of Different Investor Categories to Development Implications for Targeting Strategies." UNIDO, Vienna.

U.S. Agency for International Development. 2002. "Industry Action Plan for Nigerian Shrimp and Prawns." Online, available at http://www.usaid.gov/ng/downloads/markets/shrimp_and_prawns_industry_action_plan.pdf.

U.S. Department of Commerce. 2006. *Office of Textiles and Apparel.* Online, available at http://www.otexa.ita.gov.

Van der Meer, Cornelius L. J. 2005. "Exclusion of Small-Scale Farmers from Coordinated Supply Chains: Market Failure, Policy Failure or Just Economies of Scale." Draft, World Bank, Washington, DC.

Venables, Anthony, and Nuno Limao. 1999. "Infrastructure, Geographic Disadvantage, and Transport Cost." World Bank Policy Research Working Paper 2257, Washington, DC.

Walkenhorst, Peter, and Tadashi Yasui. 2003. "Quantitative Assessment of the Benefits of Trade Facilitation." OECD. Unclassified. TD/TC/WP(2003)31/FINAL.

Washington Post. 2006. "Trade Brings Growth, Unease." June 13.

Watson, Peter L. 2001. "Export Processing Zones: Has Africa Missed the Boat? Not Yet!" African Region Working Paper No. 17, World Bank, Washington, DC.

Wei, Djao. 2003. *Being Chinese: Voices from the Diaspora.* Tucson, AZ: University of Arizona Press.

Wells, Louis T., and Alvin G. Wint. 2000. "Marketing a Country." Foreign Investment Advisory Service Occasional Paper 13, World Bank, Washington, DC.

Wickramasekera, Piyasiri. 2002. "Asian Labour Migration: Issues and Challenges in an Era of Globalization." International Migration Program, International Labour Office, Geneva.

Wilson, John S., Xubei Luo, and Harry G. Broadman. 2006. "Entering the Union: European Accession and Capacity-Building Priorities." World Bank Research Working Paper 3832, Washington, DC.

Wilson, John S., and Tsunehiro Otsuki. 2003. "Standards and Technical Regulations and Firms' Ability to Export: New Evidence from World Bank Technical Barriers to Trade Survey." Working Paper, World Bank, Washington, DC.

Wood, Adrian, and Kersti Berge. 1997. "Exporting Manufactures: Human Resources, Natural Resources, and Trade Policy." *Journal of Development Studies* 34: 35–39.

Wood, Adrian, and Jorge Mayer. 2001. "Africa's Export Structure in a Comparative Perspective." *Cambridge Journal of Economics* 25: 369–394.

World Bank. 1993. *The East Asian Miracle*. Washington, DC: World Bank.

———. 2003. *Doing Business in 2004: Understanding Regulations*. Washington, DC: World Bank and Oxford University Press.

———. 2004a. *Investment Climate Assessment: Improving Enterprise Performance and Growth in Tanzania*. Washington, DC: World Bank.

———. 2004b. *Patterns of Africa-Asia Trade and Investment: Potentials and Ownership*. Washington, DC: World Bank.

———. 2004c. *World Development Report 2005: A Better Investment Climate for Everyone*. Washington, DC: World Bank and Oxford University Press.

———. 2005a. *Doing Business in 2006: Creating Jobs*. Washington, DC: World Bank and Oxford University Press.

———. 2005b. *Global Economic Prospects 2005: Trade, Regionalism, and Development*. Washington, DC: World Bank.

———. 2005c. *Presidential Investors' Advisory Councils in Africa: Impact Assessment Study*. Washington, DC: World Bank.

———. 2005d. *Senegal: Une évaluation du climate de investissements*. Washington, DC: World Bank.

———. 2005e. *South Africa: Assessment of Investment Climate*. Washington, DC: World Bank.

———. 2006a. *African Development Indicators*. Washington, DC: World Bank.

———. 2006b. "Mauritius: From Preferences to Global Competitiveness." Report of the Aid for Trade Mission. Washington, DC.

Wurcel, Gabriela. 2004. "Movement of Workers in the WTO Negotiations: A Development Perspective." *Global Migration Perspectives* (15). Global Commission on International Migration.

Xiaoyang Chen, Maggie, Tsunehiro Osuki, and John S. Wilson. 2006. "Do Standards Matter for Export Success?" World Bank Policy Research Working Paper 3809, Washington, DC.

Yao, Yang, and Yin He. 2005. *Chinese Outward Investing Firms, A Study for FIAS/IFC/MIGA*. Working paper, Foreign Investment Advisory Service.

Yap, Josef T. 2005. "The Boom in FTAs: Let Prudence Reign." The Philippine Institute for Development Studies, PIDS Discussion Paper Series No. 2005–32, Makati City, Philippines.

Yeats, A. J. 2001. "Just How Big Is Global Production Sharing?" In *Fragmentation: New Production Patterns*, ed. S. Arndt and H. Kierzkowski. Oxford: Oxford University Press.

Yoshino, Yutaka. 2006. "Trade Facilitation, Domestic Constraints and Export Performance in Regional and Global Markets: Firm-Level Evidence in African Manufacturing Sector." World Bank Africa Region, Regional Program on Enterprise Development, Washington, DC.

Index